ONI PRESS
PRESENTS

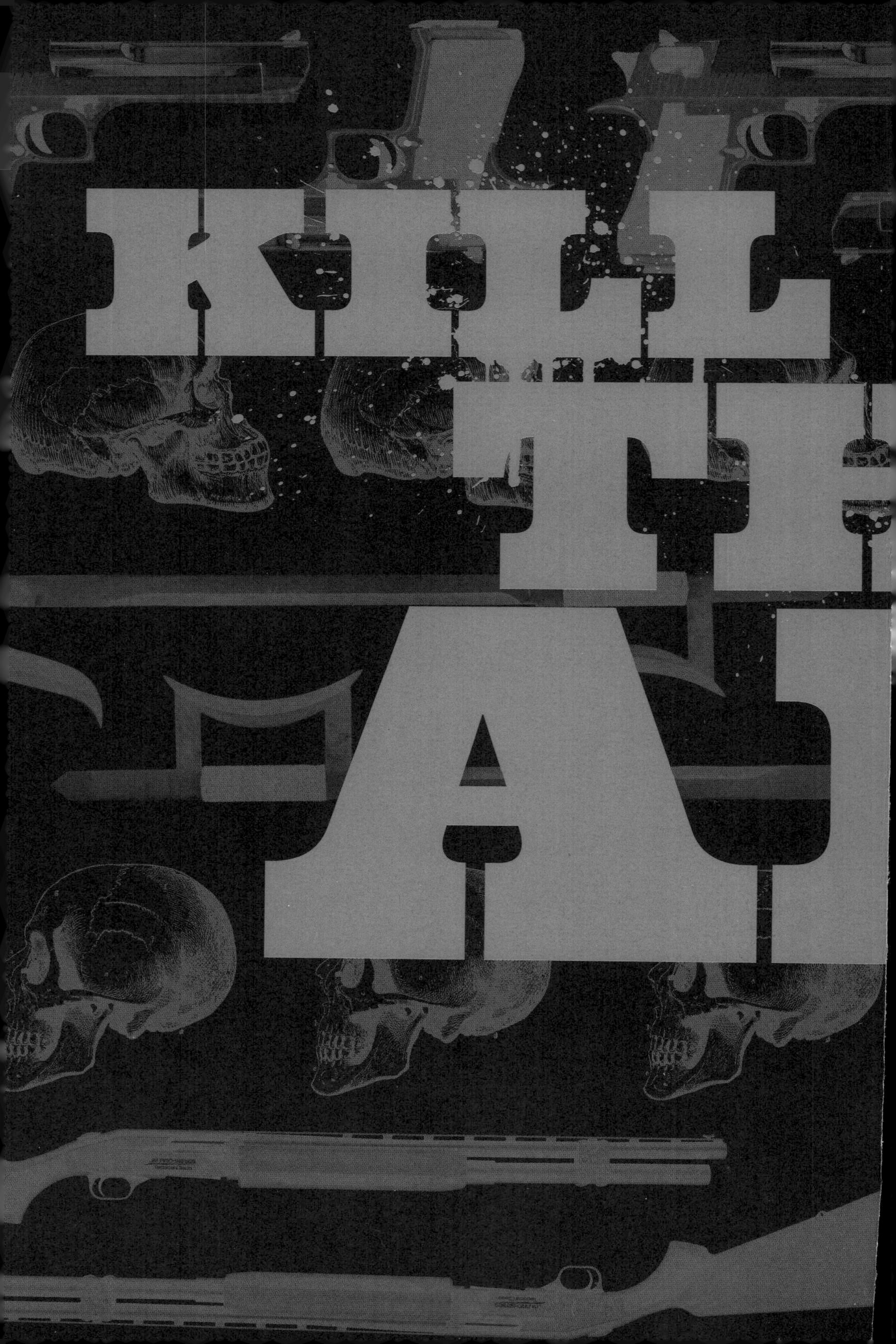
KILL

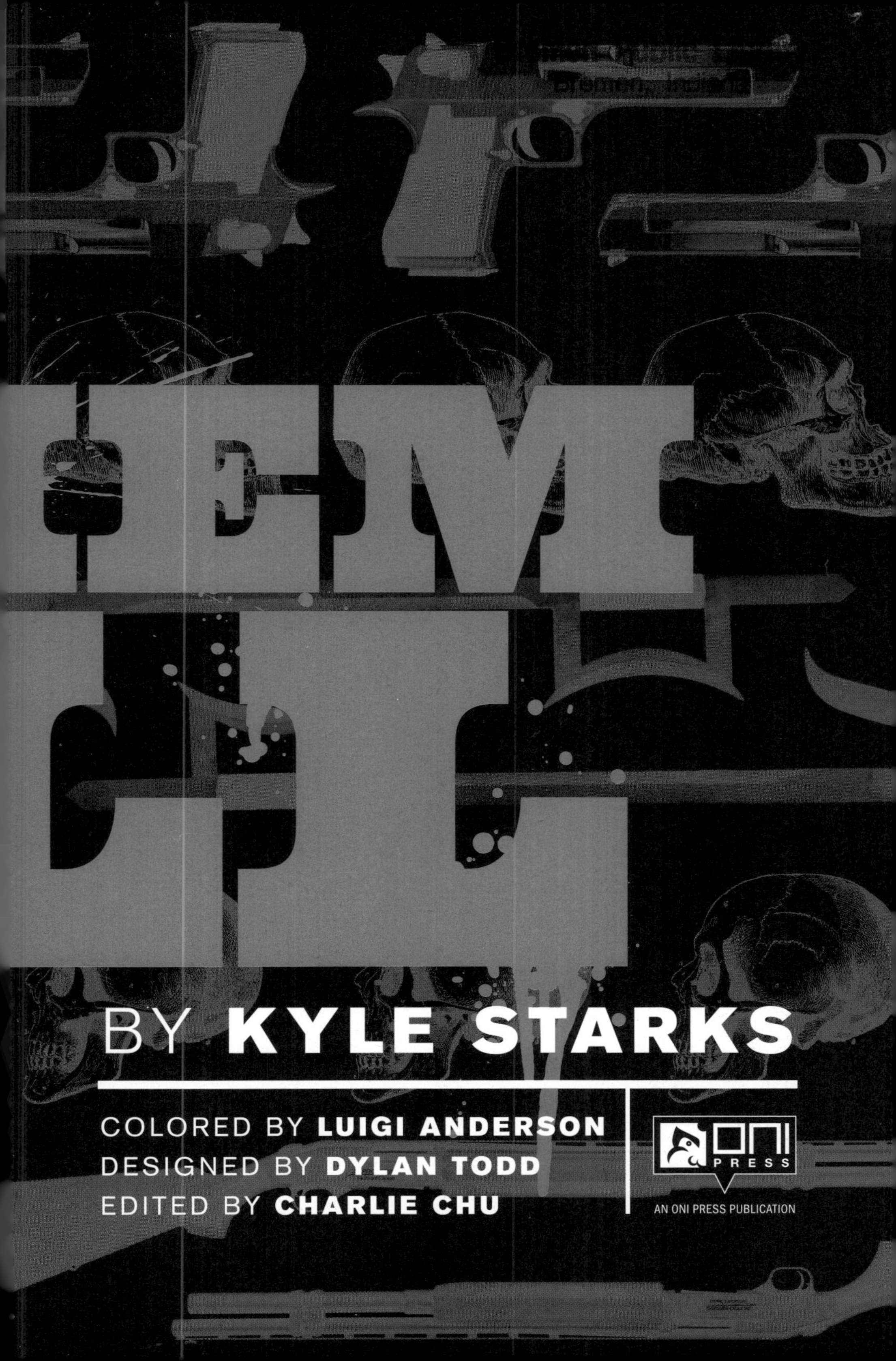

BY **KYLE STARKS**

COLORED BY **LUIGI ANDERSON**
DESIGNED BY **DYLAN TODD**
EDITED BY **CHARLIE CHU**

ONI PRESS
AN ONI PRESS PUBLICATION

KILL THEM ALL
BY KYLE STARKS | COLORED BY LUIGI ANDERSON

PUBLISHED BY ONI PRESS, INC.

Published by Oni Press, Inc.

Joe Nozemack **PUBLISHER**

James Lucas Jones **EDITOR IN CHIEF**

Brad Rooks **DIRECTOR OF OPERATIONS**

David Dissanayake **DIRECTOR OF SALES**

Rachel Reed **PUBLICITY MANAGER**

Troy Look **DIRECTOR OF DESIGN & PRODUCTION**

Hilary Thompson **GRAPHIC DESIGNER**

Kate Z. Stone **JUNIOR GRAPHIC DESIGNER**

Angie Dobson **DIGITAL PREPRESS TECHNICIAN**

Ari Yarwood **MANAGING EDITOR**

Charlie Chu **SENIOR EDITOR**

Robin Herrera **EDITOR**

Alissa Sallah **ADMINISTRATIVE ASSISTANT**

Jung Lee **LOGISTICS ASSOCIATE**

Oni Press, Inc
1319 SE Martin Luther King, Jr. Blvd
Suite 240
Portland, OR 97214

onipress.com
 facebook.com/onipress
 twitter.com/onipress
 onipress.tumblr.com
 instagram.com/onipress

kylestarks.com
 twitter.com/thekylestarks

FIRST EDITION: SEPTEMBER 2017

ISBN 978-1-62010-434-7
eISBN 978-1-62010-435-4

Library of Congress Control Number: 2017934228

1 2 3 4 5 6 7 8 9 10

Printed in China

FOR SHARA,
WHO MAKES ALL THINGS POSSIBLE.

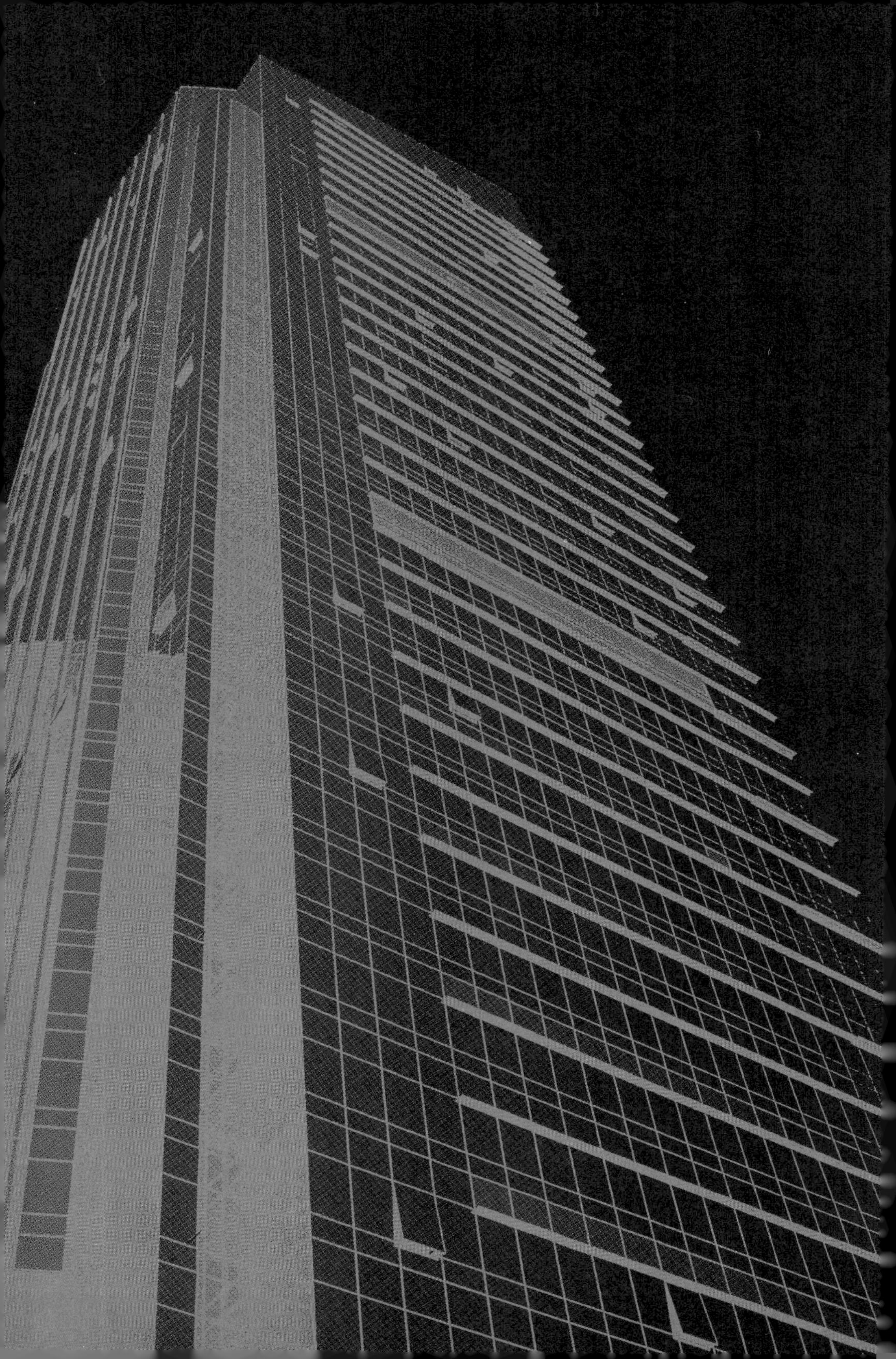

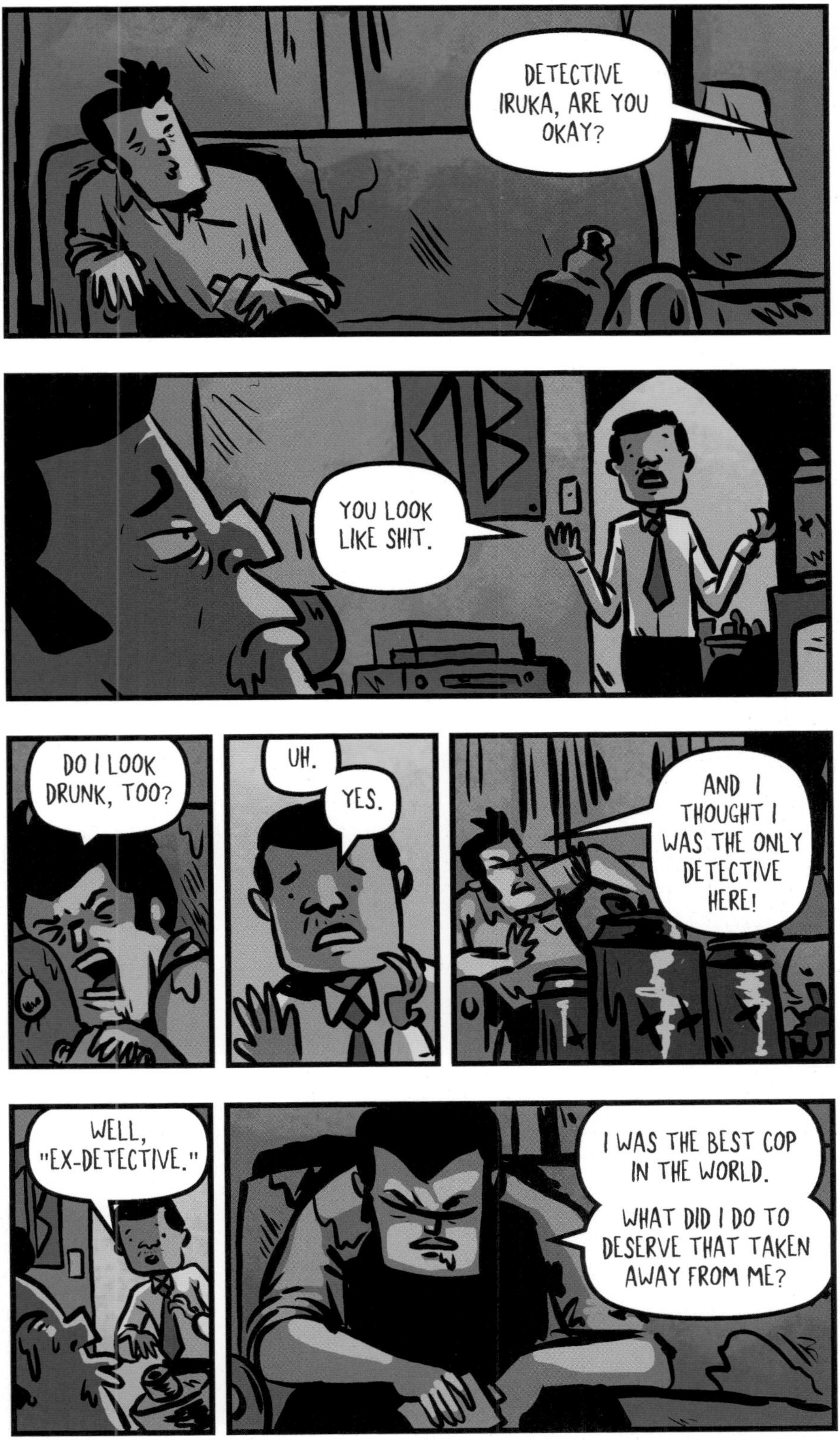
DETECTIVE IRUKA, ARE YOU OKAY?
YOU LOOK LIKE SHIT.
DO I LOOK DRUNK, TOO?
UH.
YES.
AND I THOUGHT I WAS THE ONLY DETECTIVE HERE!
WELL, "EX-DETECTIVE."
I WAS THE BEST COP IN THE WORLD.
WHAT DID I DO TO DESERVE THAT TAKEN AWAY FROM ME?

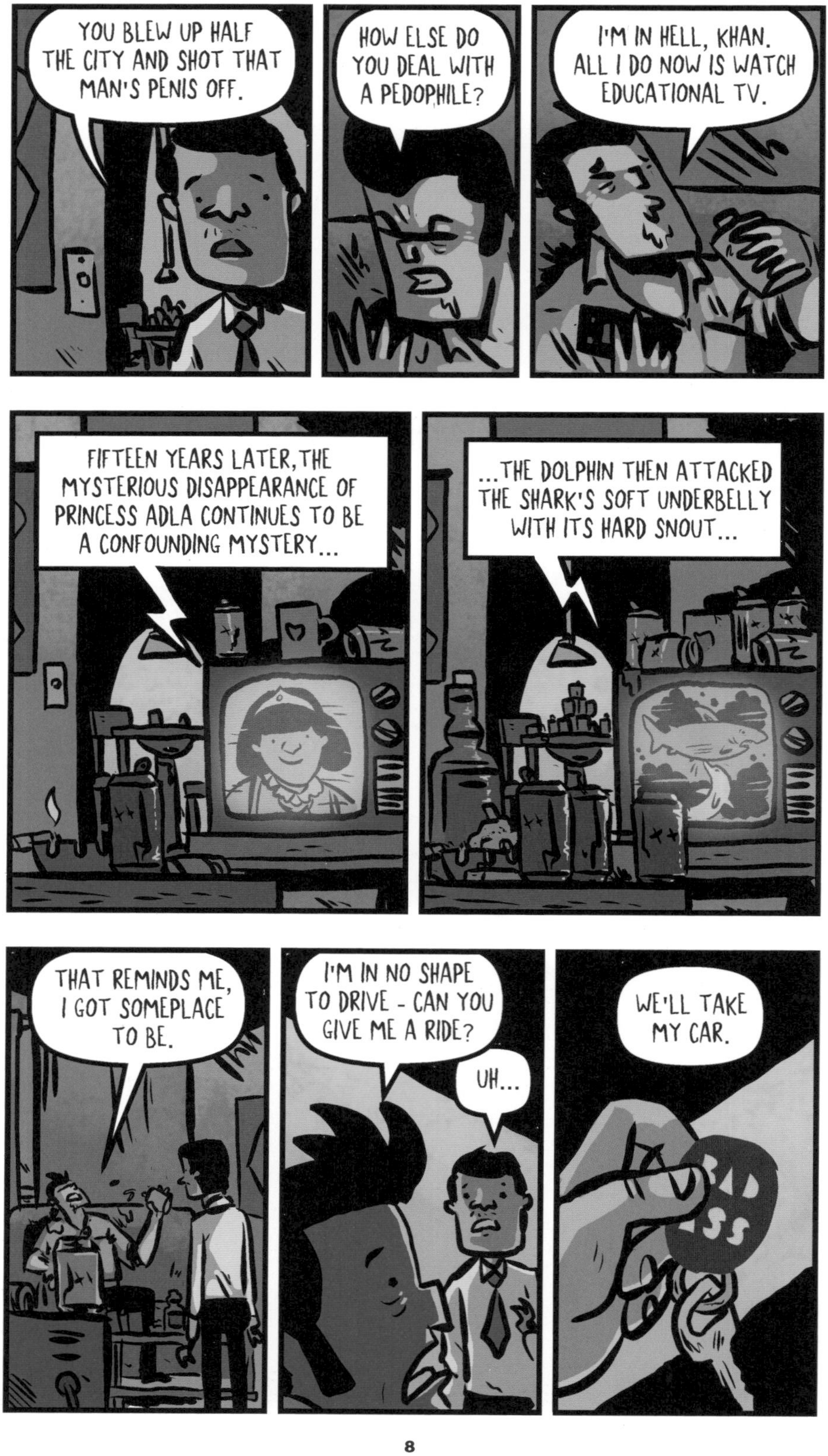
YOU BLEW UP HALF THE CITY AND SHOT THAT MAN'S PENIS OFF.
HOW ELSE DO YOU DEAL WITH A PEDOPHILE?
I'M IN HELL, KHAN. ALL I DO NOW IS WATCH EDUCATIONAL TV.
FIFTEEN YEARS LATER, THE MYSTERIOUS DISAPPEARANCE OF PRINCESS ADLA CONTINUES TO BE A CONFOUNDING MYSTERY...
...THE DOLPHIN THEN ATTACKED THE SHARK'S SOFT UNDERBELLY WITH ITS HARD SNOUT...
THAT REMINDS ME, I GOT SOMEPLACE TO BE.
I'M IN NO SHAPE TO DRIVE - CAN YOU GIVE ME A RIDE?
UH...
WE'LL TAKE MY CAR.

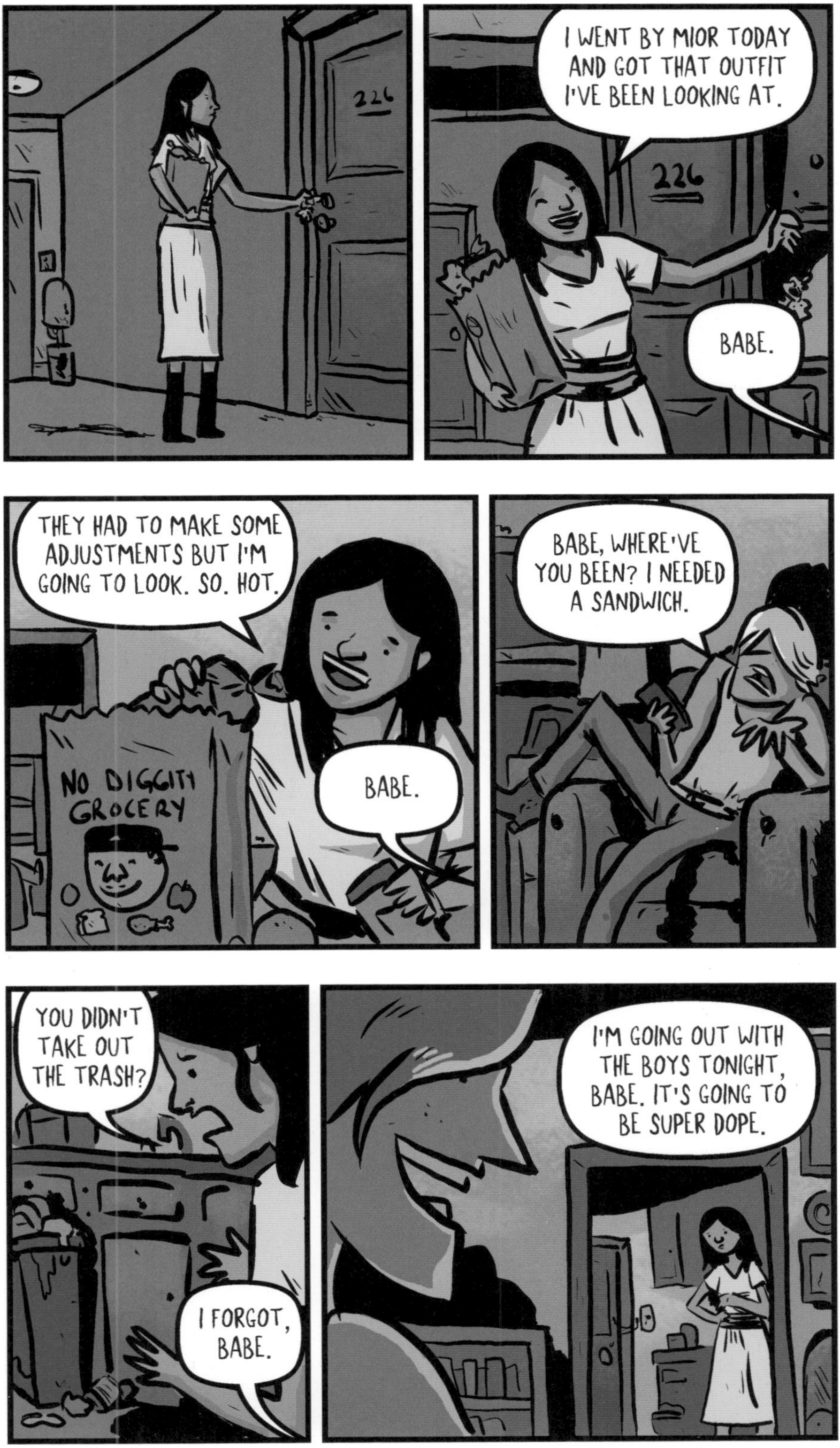
I WENT BY MIOR TODAY AND GOT THAT OUTFIT I'VE BEEN LOOKING AT.
BABE.
THEY HAD TO MAKE SOME ADJUSTMENTS BUT I'M GOING TO LOOK. SO. HOT.
NO DIGGITY GROCERY
BABE.
BABE, WHERE'VE YOU BEEN? I NEEDED A SANDWICH.
YOU DIDN'T TAKE OUT THE TRASH?
I FORGOT, BABE.
I'M GOING OUT WITH THE BOYS TONIGHT, BABE. IT'S GOING TO BE SUPER DOPE.

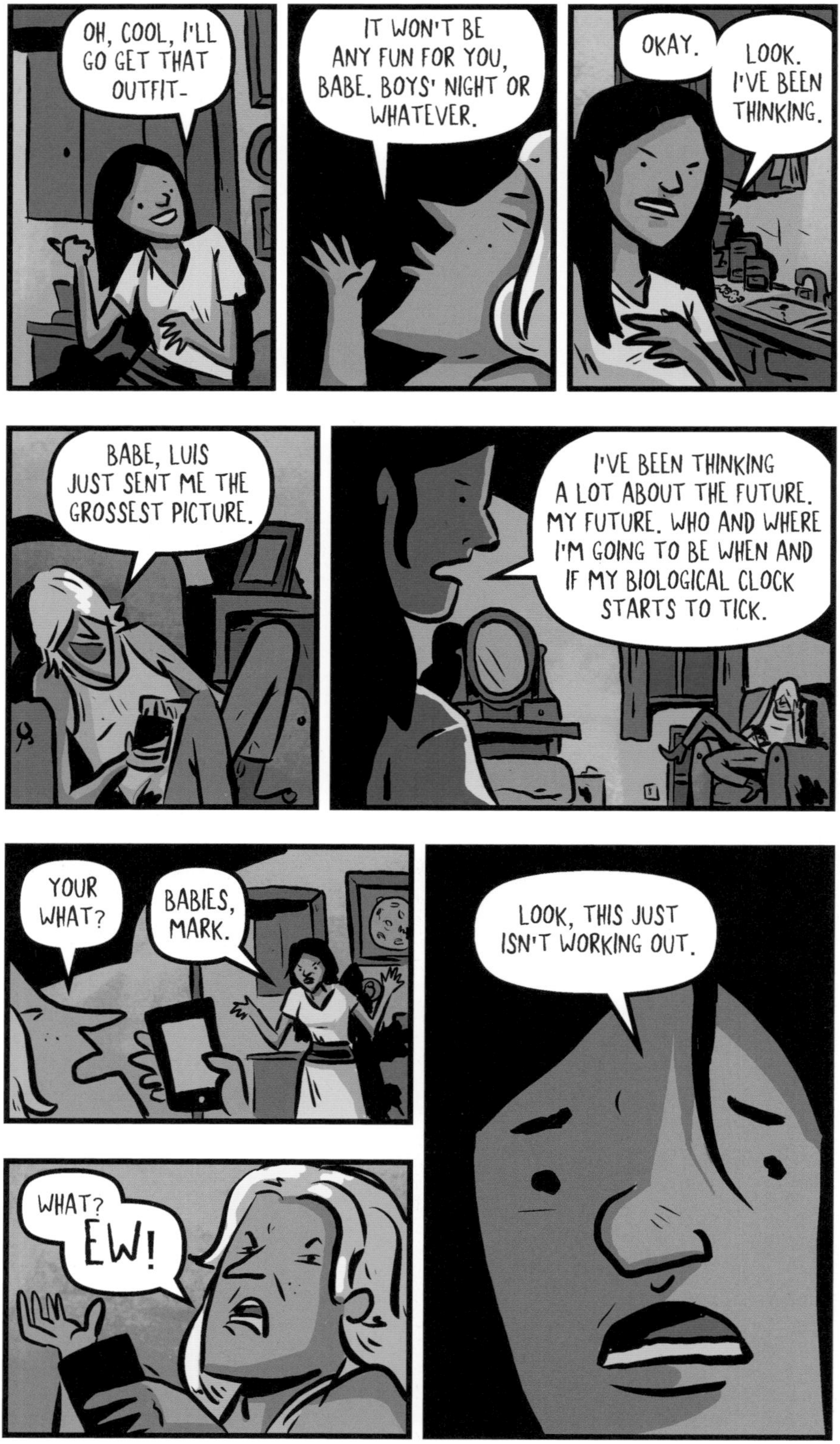
OH, COOL, I'LL GO GET THAT OUTFIT-
IT WON'T BE ANY FUN FOR YOU, BABE. BOYS' NIGHT OR WHATEVER.
OKAY.
LOOK. I'VE BEEN THINKING.
BABE, LUIS JUST SENT ME THE GROSSEST PICTURE.
I'VE BEEN THINKING A LOT ABOUT THE FUTURE. MY FUTURE. WHO AND WHERE I'M GOING TO BE WHEN AND IF MY BIOLOGICAL CLOCK STARTS TO TICK.
YOUR WHAT?
BABIES, MARK.
WHAT? EW!
LOOK, THIS JUST ISN'T WORKING OUT.

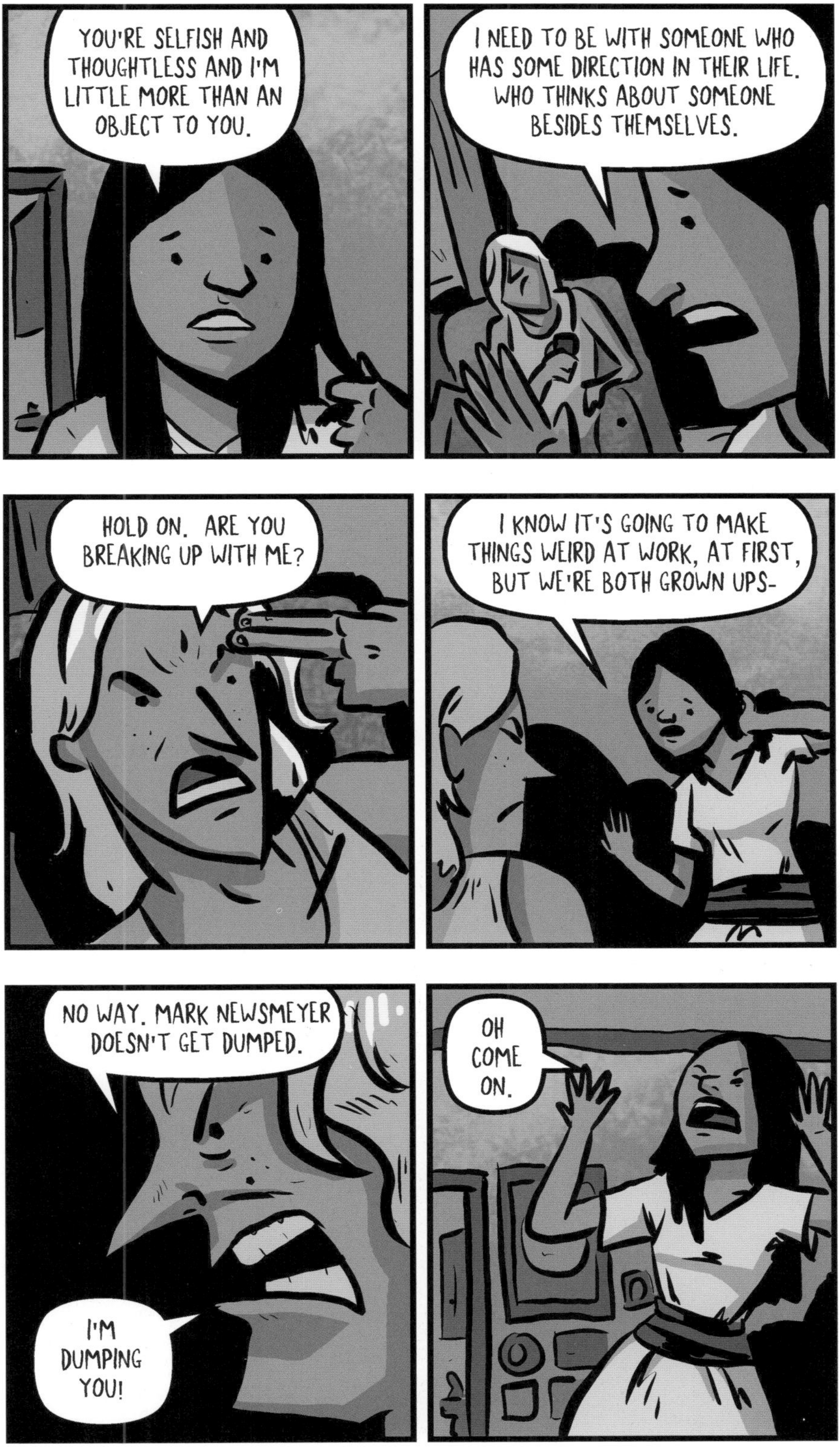
YOU'RE SELFISH AND THOUGHTLESS AND I'M LITTLE MORE THAN AN OBJECT TO YOU.
I NEED TO BE WITH SOMEONE WHO HAS SOME DIRECTION IN THEIR LIFE. WHO THINKS ABOUT SOMEONE BESIDES THEMSELVES.
HOLD ON. ARE YOU BREAKING UP WITH ME?
I KNOW IT'S GOING TO MAKE THINGS WEIRD AT WORK, AT FIRST, BUT WE'RE BOTH GROWN UPS-
NO WAY. MARK NEWSMEYER DOESN'T GET DUMPED.
I'M DUMPING YOU!
OH COME ON.

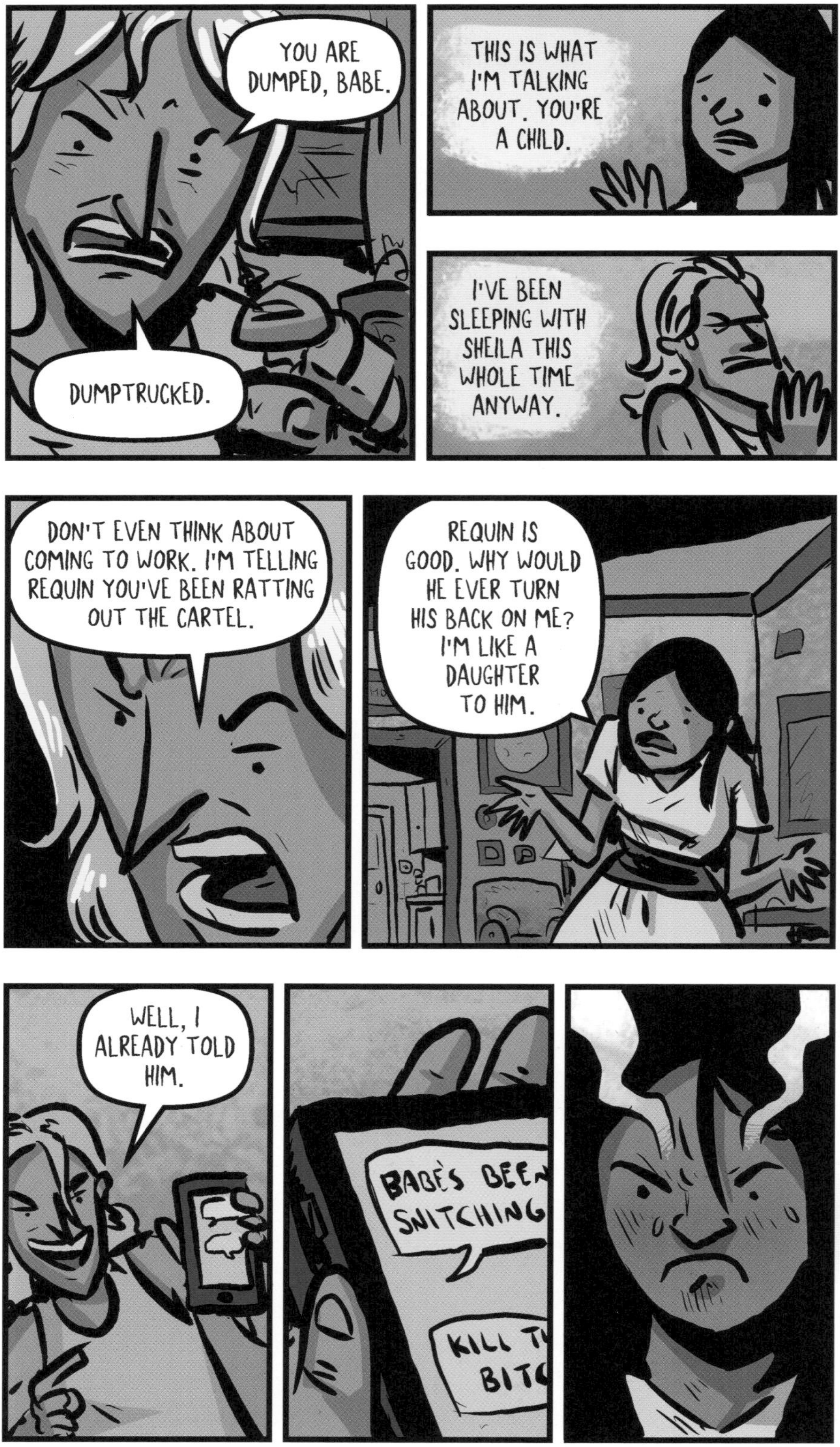
YOU ARE DUMPED, BABE.
DUMPTRUCKED.
THIS IS WHAT I'M TALKING ABOUT. YOU'RE A CHILD.
I'VE BEEN SLEEPING WITH SHEILA THIS WHOLE TIME ANYWAY.
DON'T EVEN THINK ABOUT COMING TO WORK. I'M TELLING REQUIN YOU'VE BEEN RATTING OUT THE CARTEL.
REQUIN IS GOOD. WHY WOULD HE EVER TURN HIS BACK ON ME? I'M LIKE A DAUGHTER TO HIM.
WELL, I ALREADY TOLD HIM.
BABE'S
SNITCHING
KILL

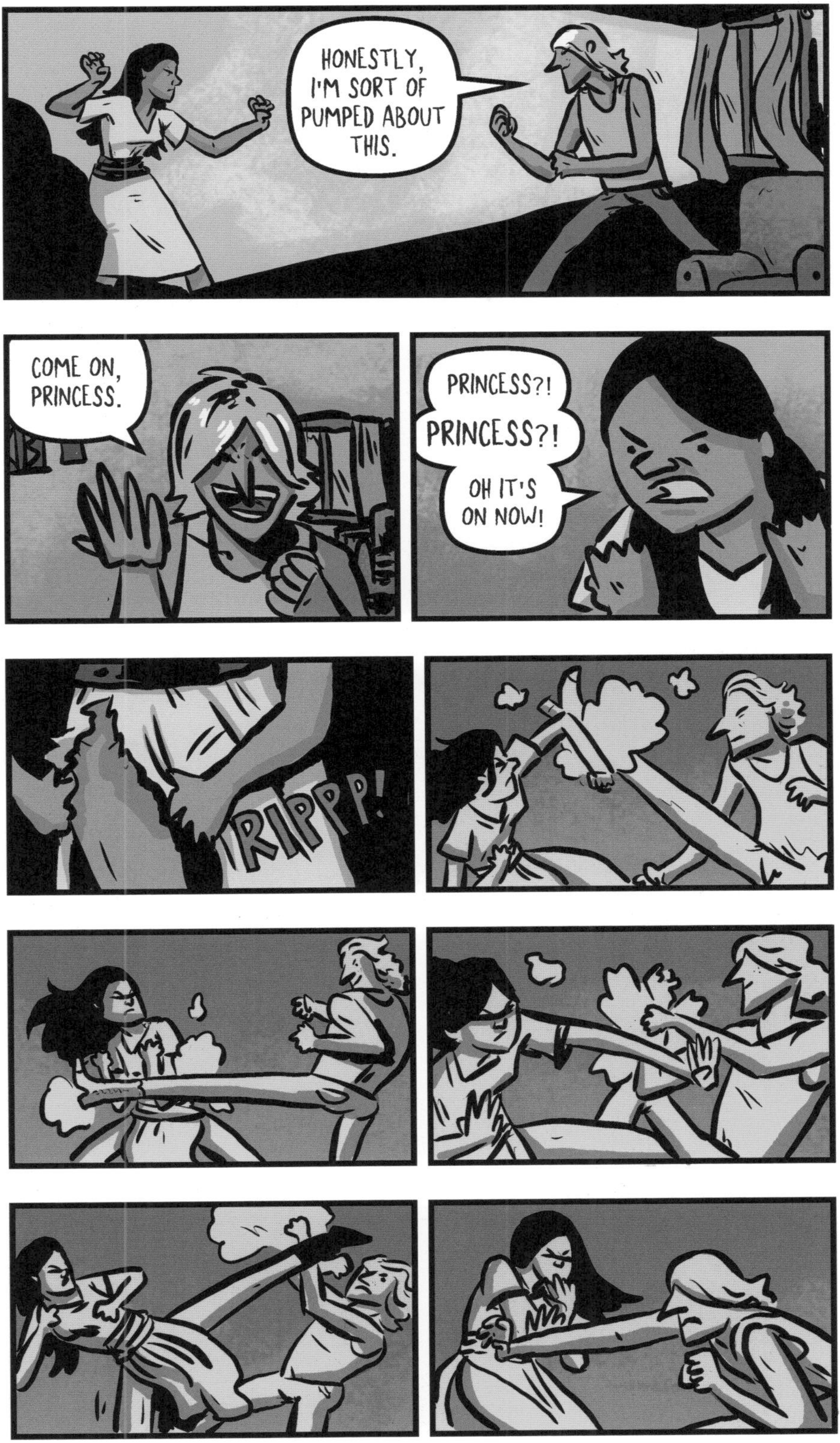
HONESTLY, I'M SORT OF PUMPED ABOUT THIS.
COME ON, PRINCESS.
PRINCESS?!
PRINCESS?!
OH IT'S ON NOW!
RIPPP!

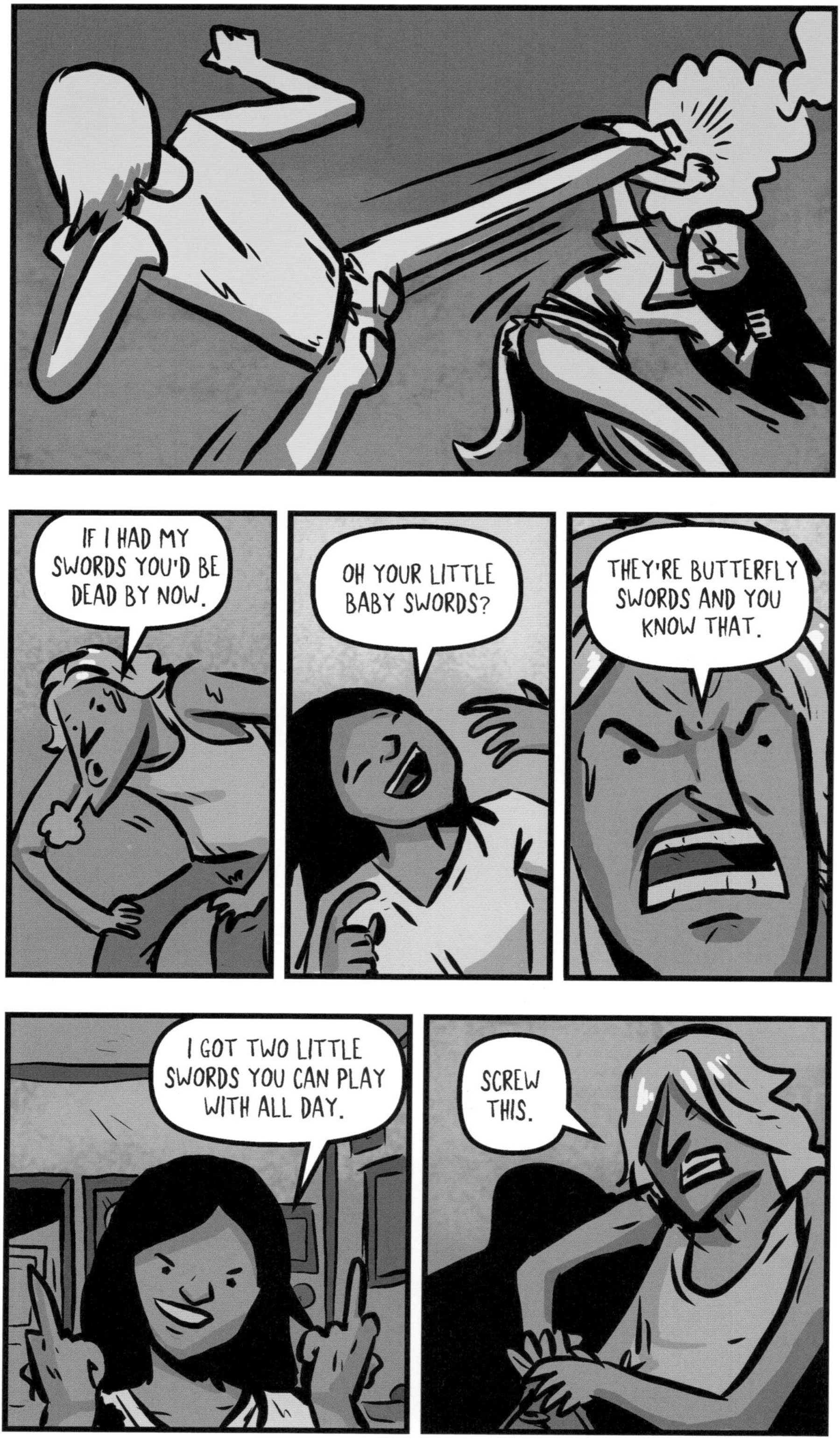
IF I HAD MY SWORDS YOU'D BE DEAD BY NOW.
OH YOUR LITTLE BABY SWORDS?
THEY'RE BUTTERFLY SWORDS AND YOU KNOW THAT.
I GOT TWO LITTLE SWORDS YOU CAN PLAY WITH ALL DAY.
SCREW THIS.

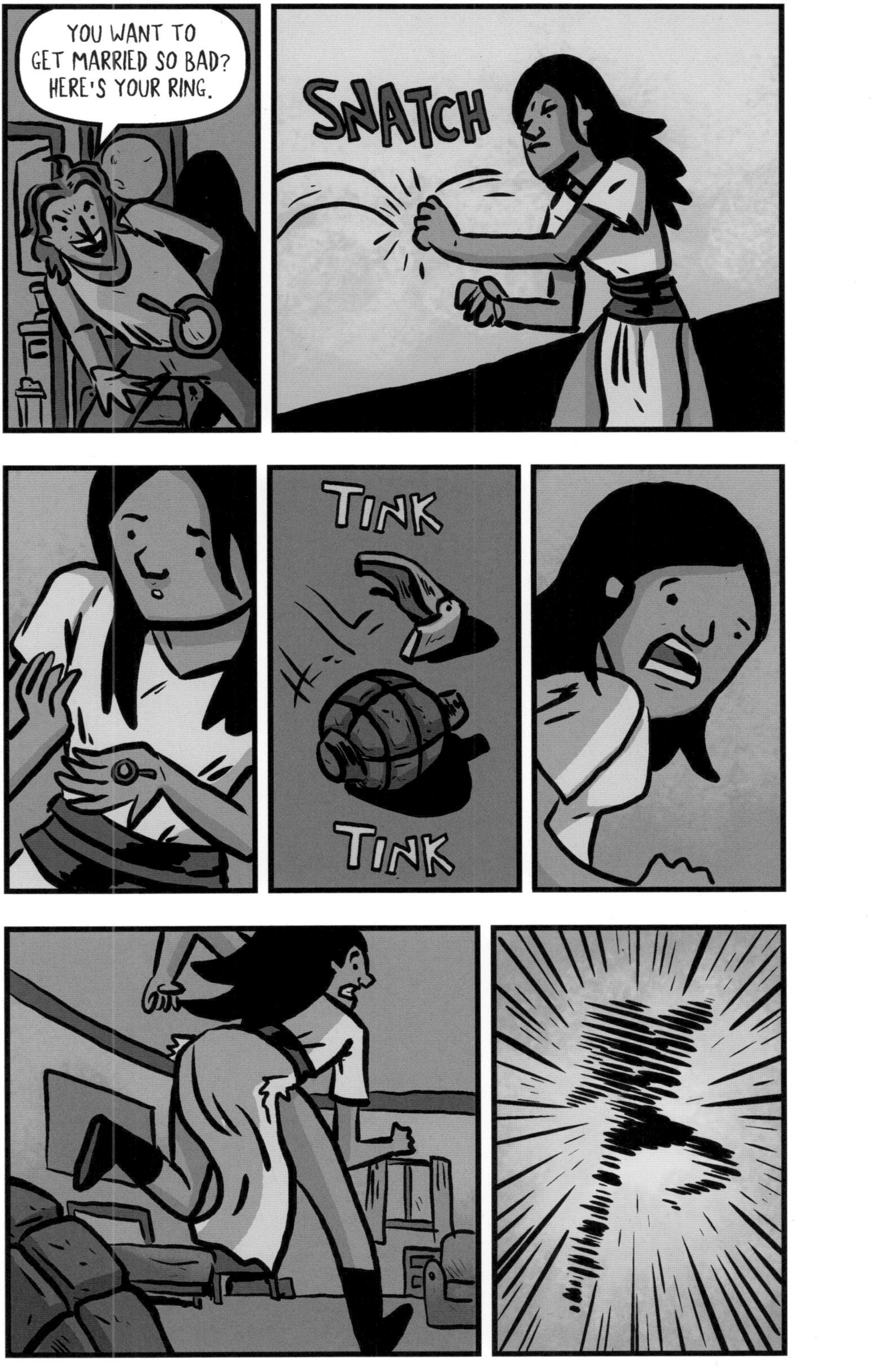
YOU WANT TO GET MARRIED SO BAD? HERE'S YOUR RING.
SNATCH
TINK
TINK

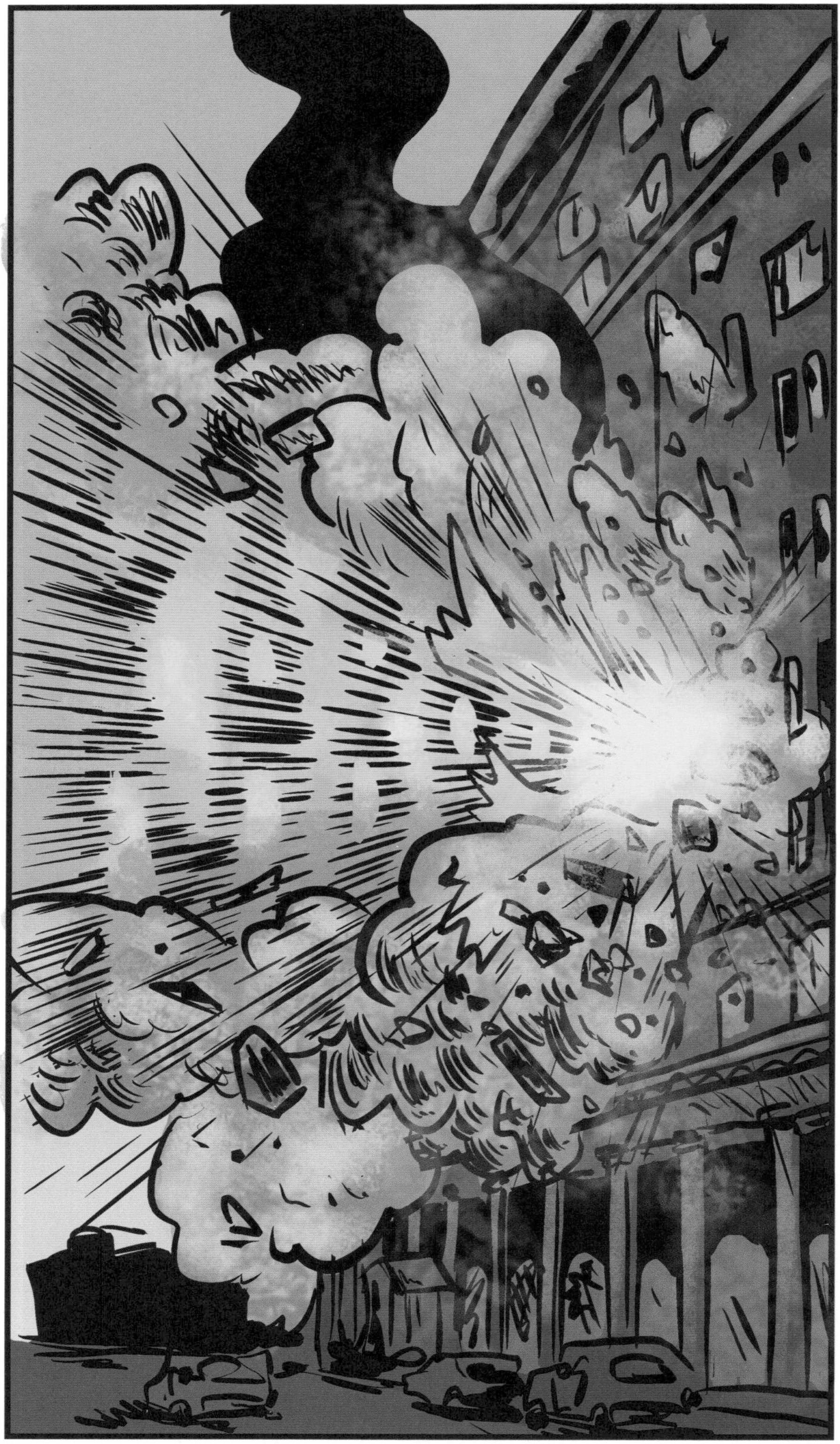

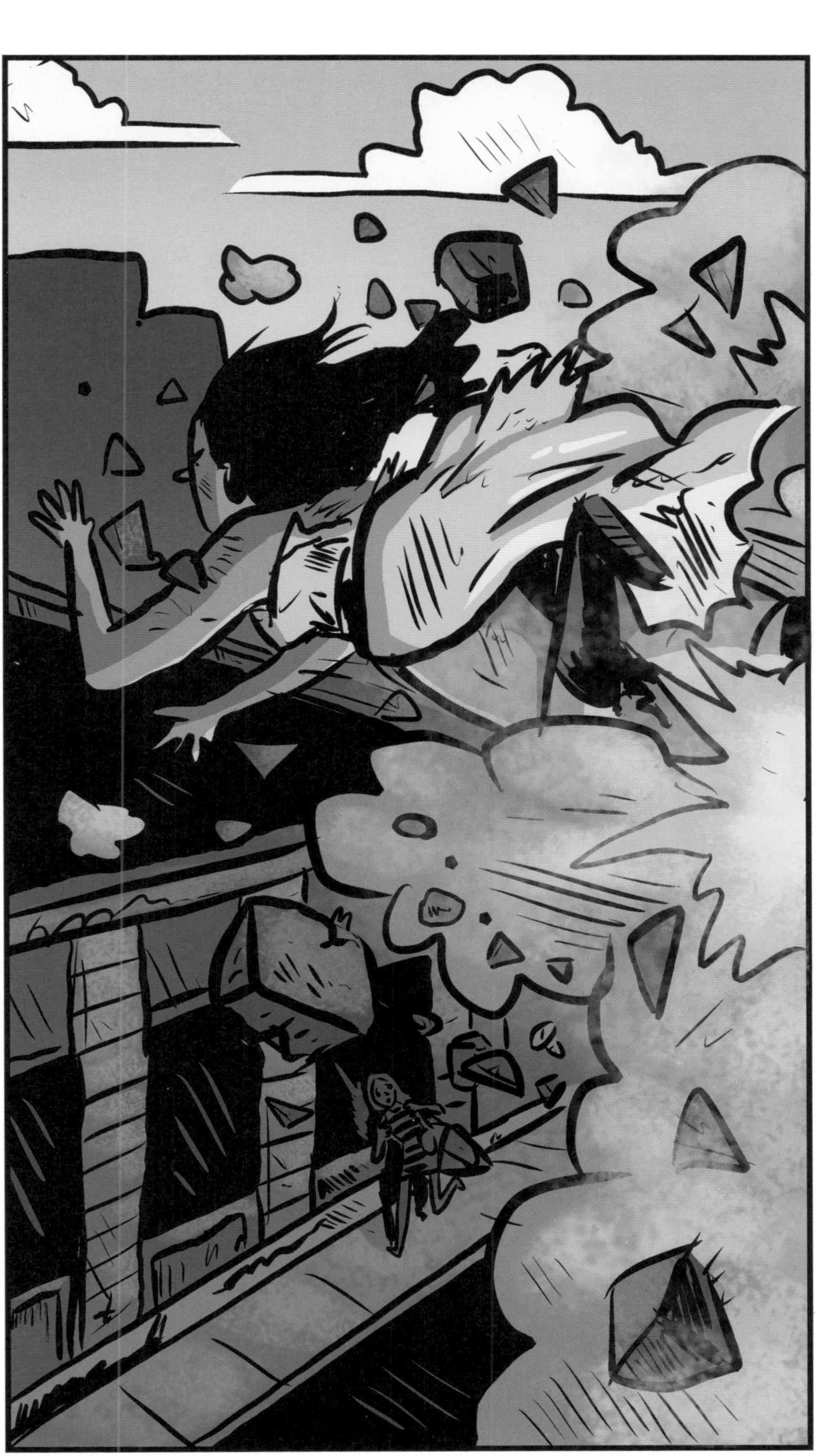

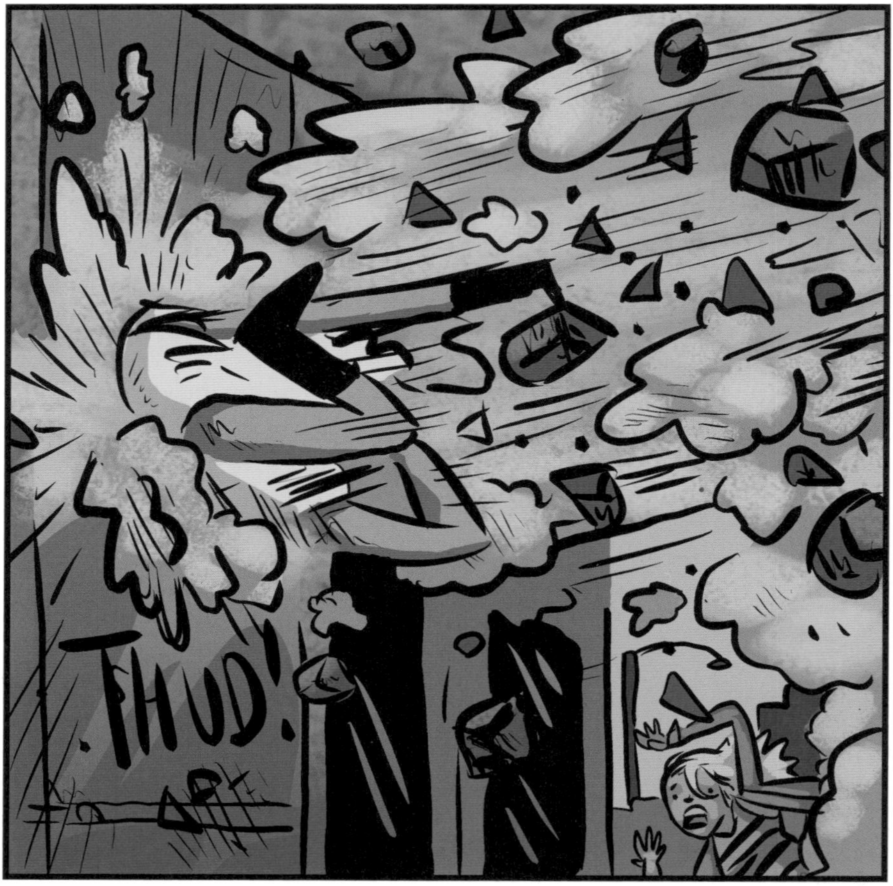
THUD!

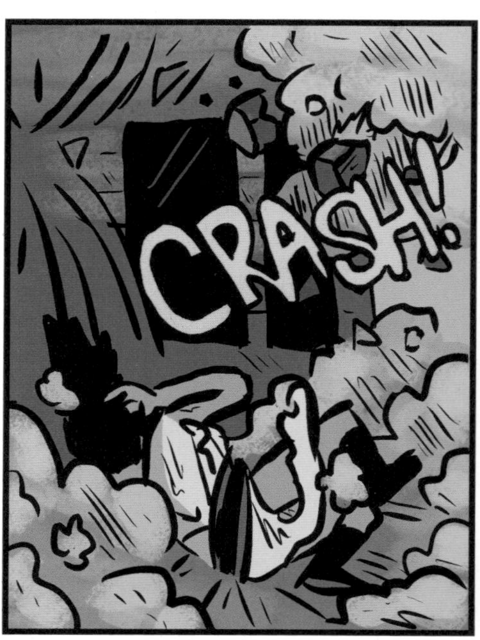
CRASH!

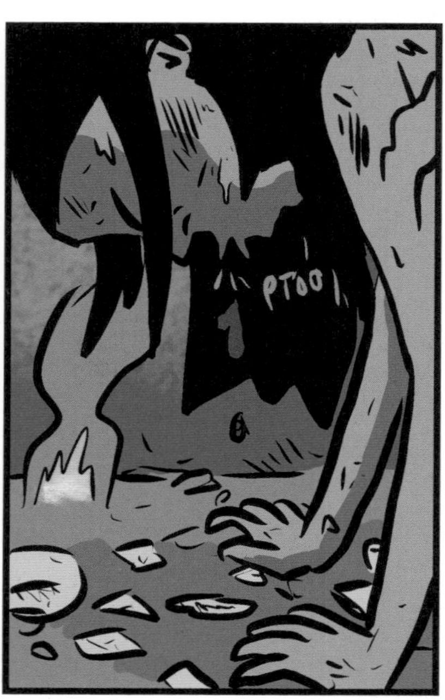
PTOO

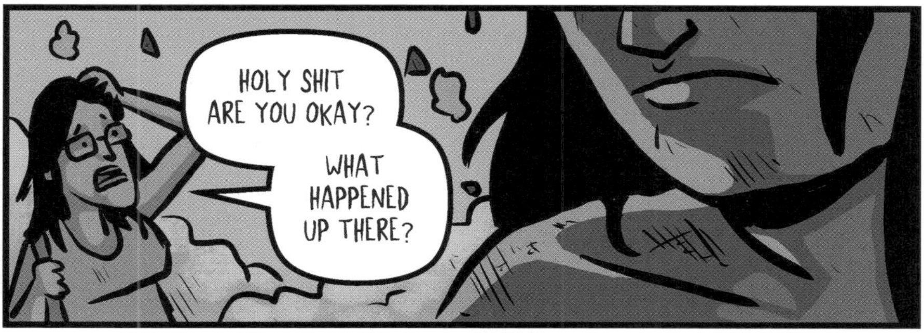
HOLY SHIT ARE YOU OKAY?
WHAT HAPPENED UP THERE?

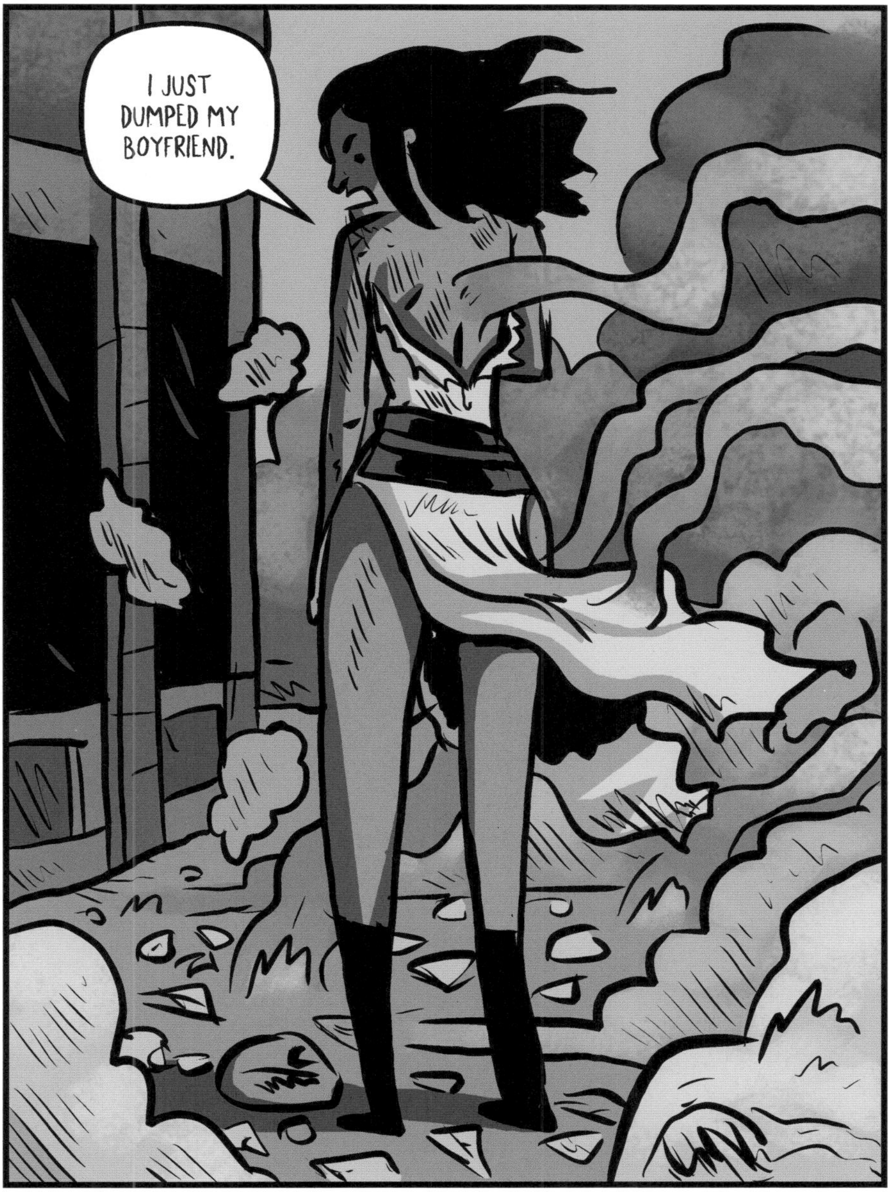
I JUST DUMPED MY BOYFRIEND.

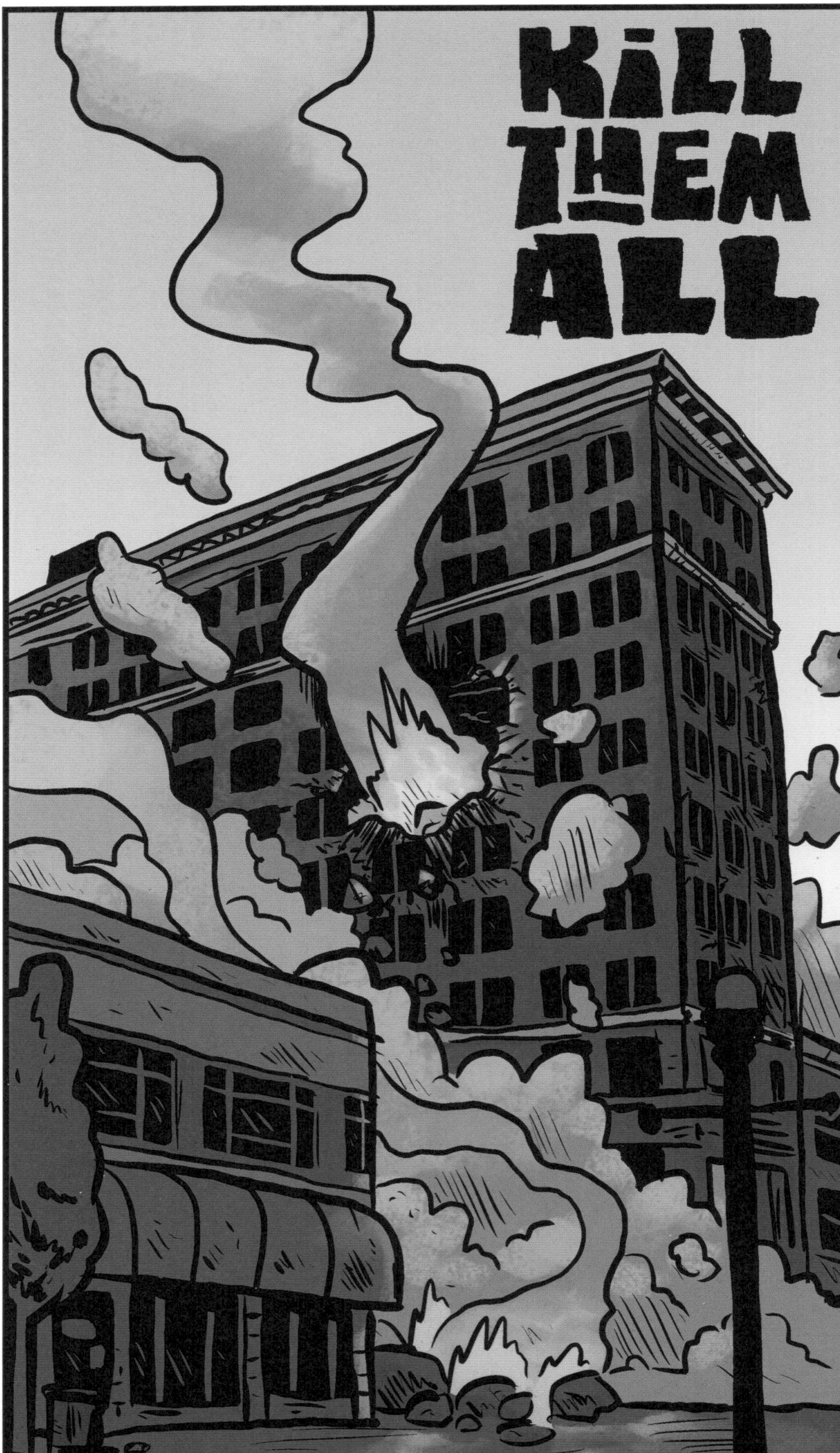
KILL THEM ALL

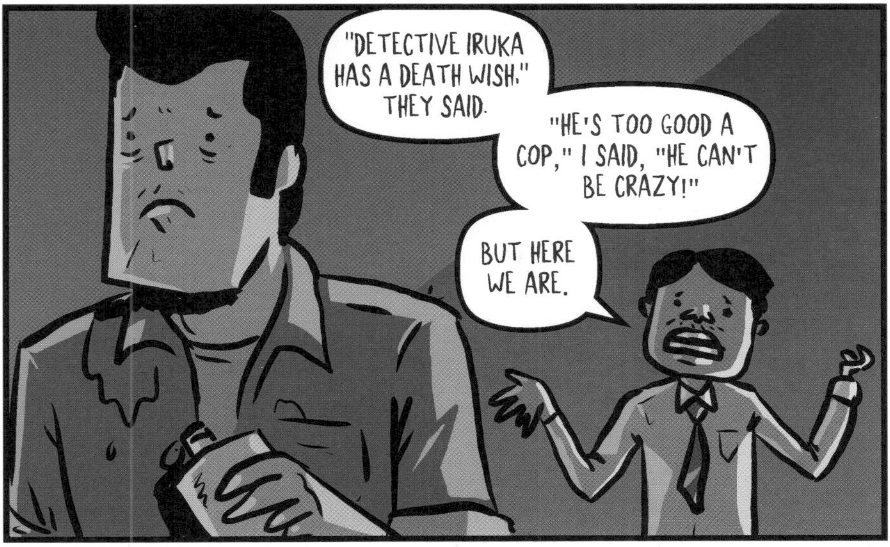
"DETECTIVE IRUKA HAS A DEATH WISH," THEY SAID.
"HE'S TOO GOOD A COP," I SAID, "HE CAN'T BE CRAZY!"
BUT HERE WE ARE.

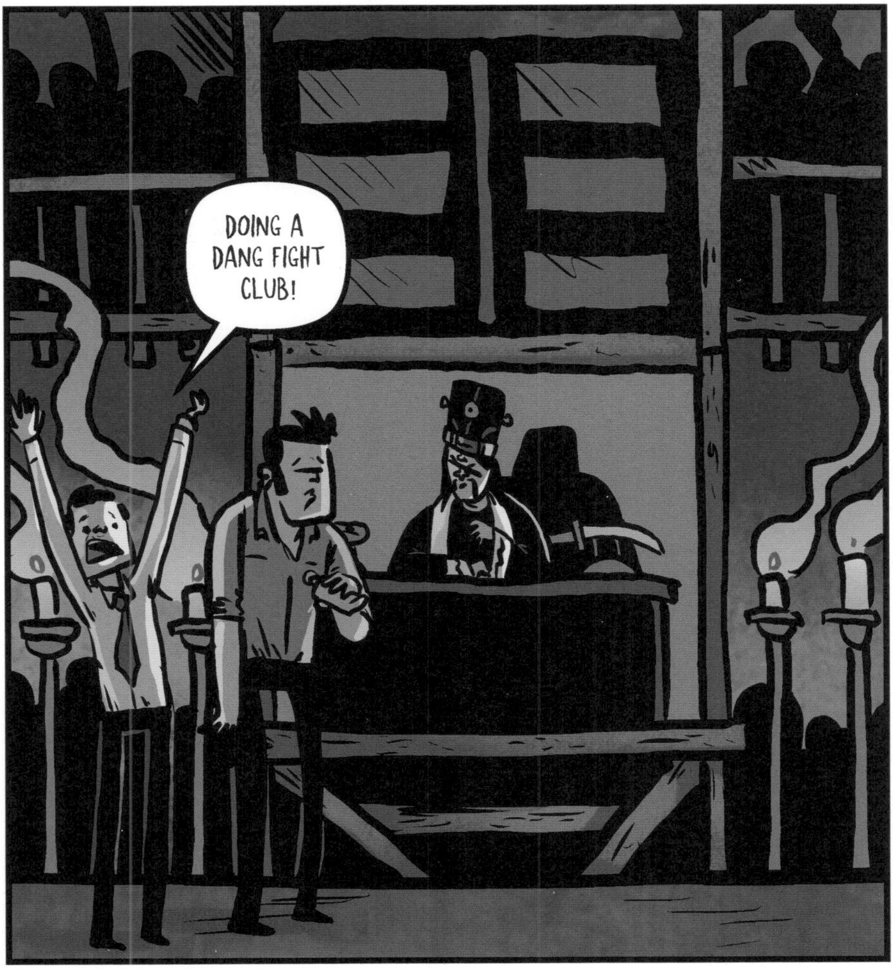
DOING A DANG FIGHT CLUB!

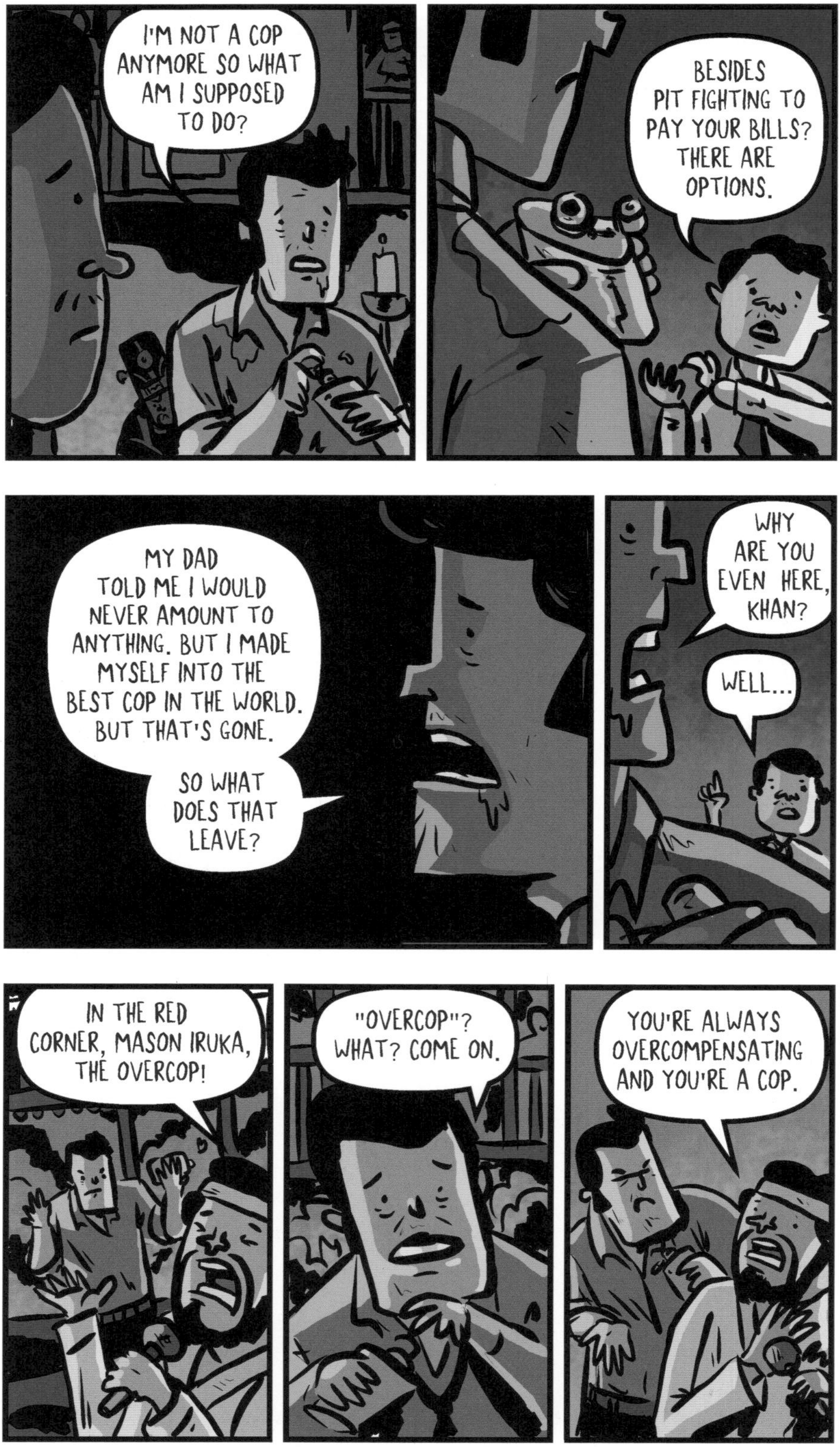
I'M NOT A COP ANYMORE SO WHAT AM I SUPPOSED TO DO?
BESIDES PIT FIGHTING TO PAY YOUR BILLS? THERE ARE OPTIONS.
MY DAD TOLD ME I WOULD NEVER AMOUNT TO ANYTHING. BUT I MADE MYSELF INTO THE BEST COP IN THE WORLD. BUT THAT'S GONE.
SO WHAT DOES THAT LEAVE?
WHY ARE YOU EVEN HERE, KHAN?
WELL...
IN THE RED CORNER, MASON IRUKA, THE OVERCOP!
"OVERCOP"? WHAT? COME ON.
YOU'RE ALWAYS OVERCOMPENSATING AND YOU'RE A COP.

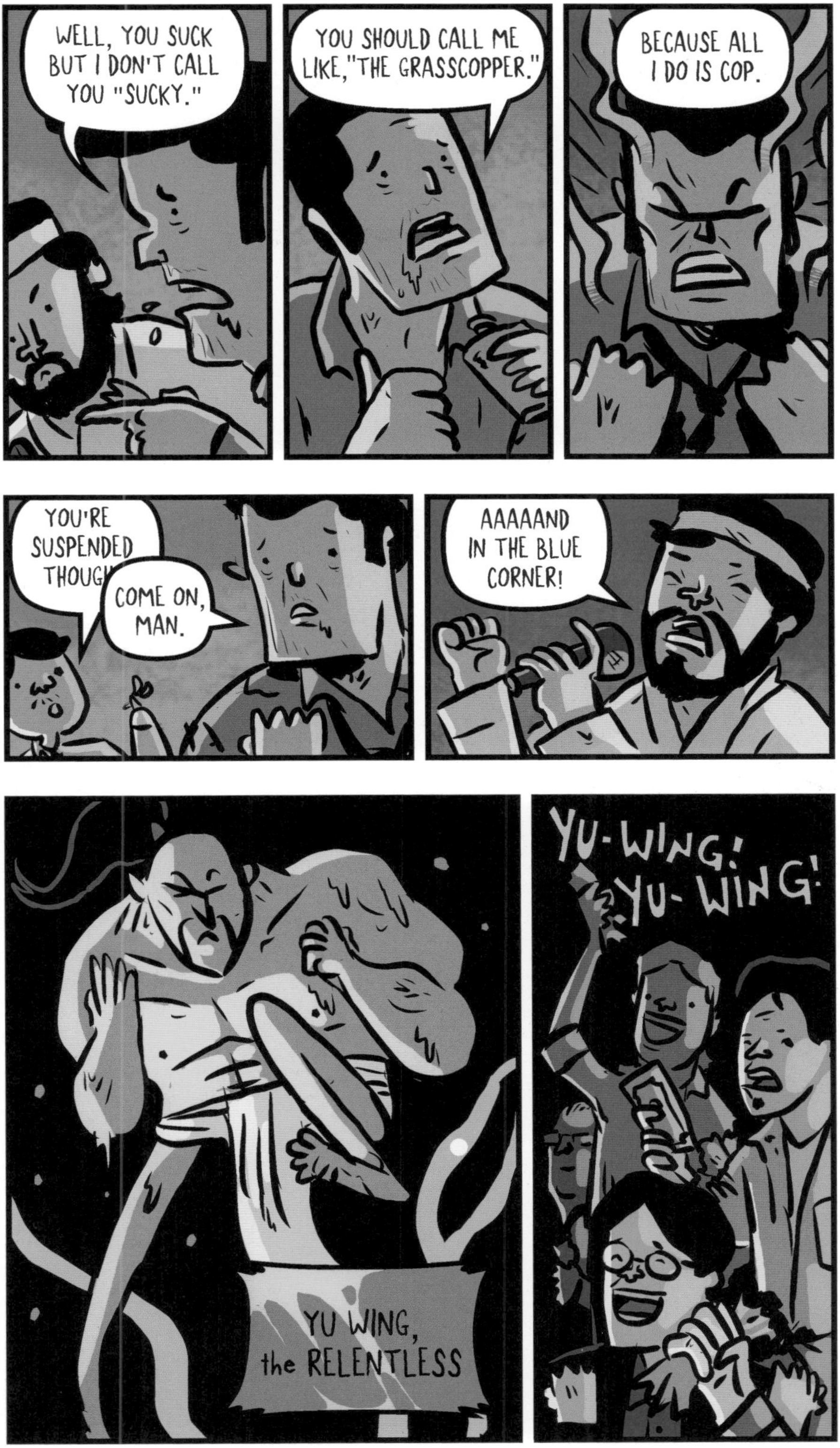
WELL, YOU SUCK BUT I DON'T CALL YOU "SUCKY."
YOU SHOULD CALL ME LIKE,"THE GRASSCOPPER."
BECAUSE ALL I DO IS COP.
YOU'RE SUSPENDED THOUGH
COME ON, MAN.
AAAAAND IN THE BLUE CORNER!
YU WING, the RELENTLESS
YU-WING! YU-WING!

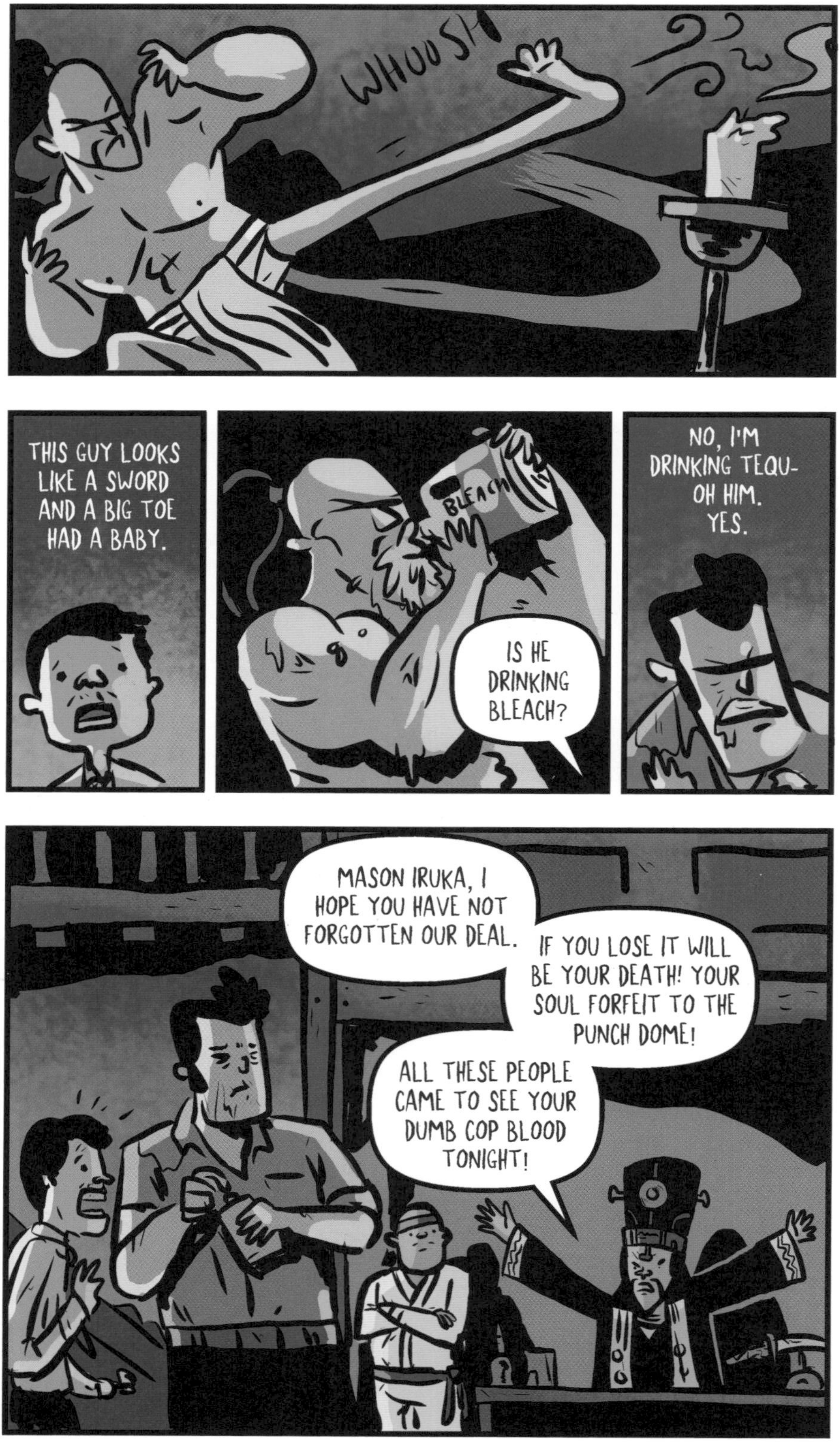
WHUOOSH
THIS GUY LOOKS LIKE A SWORD AND A BIG TOE HAD A BABY.
BLEACH
IS HE DRINKING BLEACH?
NO, I'M DRINKING TEQU- OH HIM. YES.
MASON IRUKA, I HOPE YOU HAVE NOT FORGOTTEN OUR DEAL.
IF YOU LOSE IT WILL BE YOUR DEATH! YOUR SOUL FORFEIT TO THE PUNCH DOME!
ALL THESE PEOPLE CAME TO SEE YOUR DUMB COP BLOOD TONIGHT!

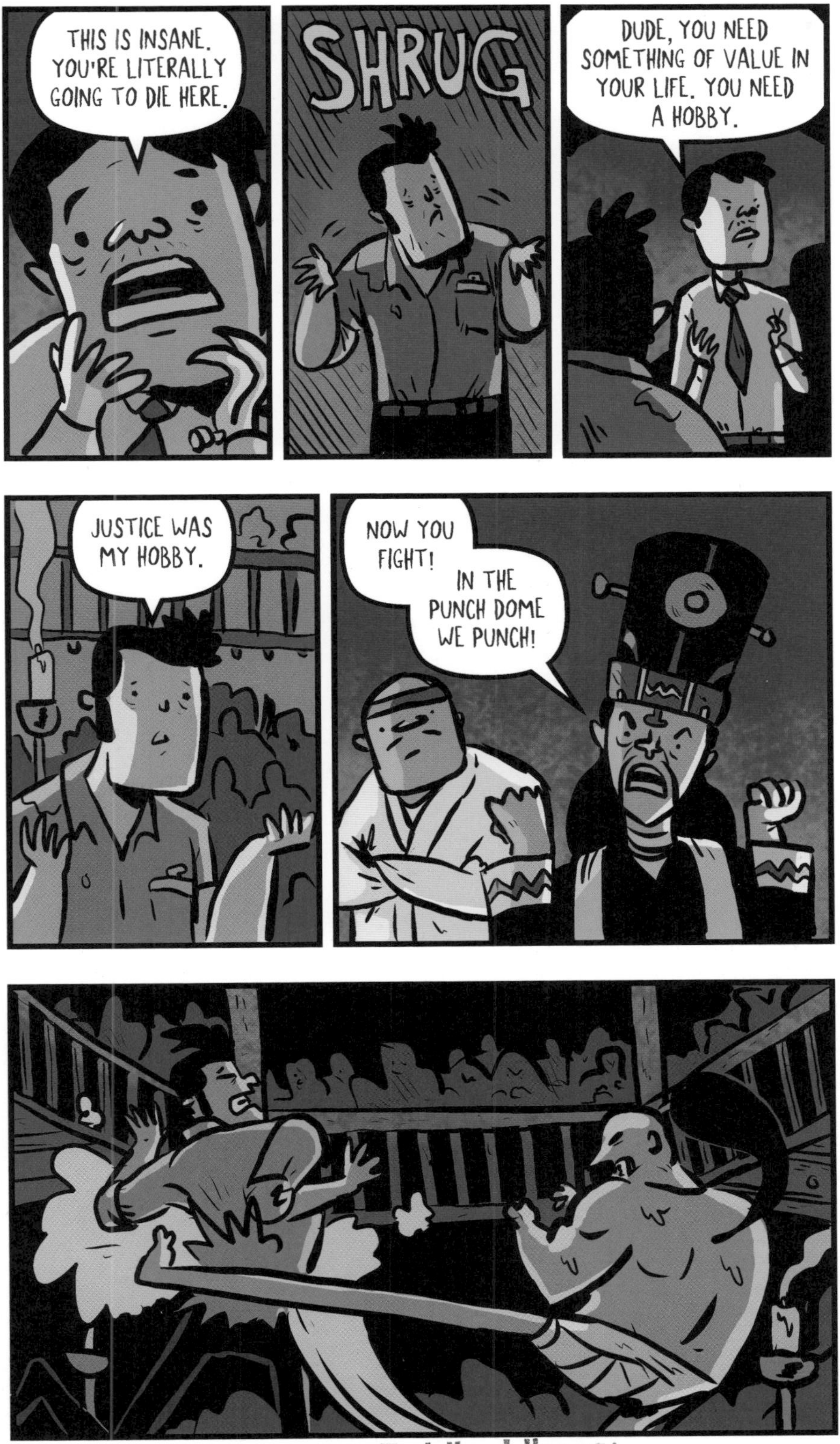
THIS IS INSANE. YOU'RE LITERALLY GOING TO DIE HERE.
SHRUG
DUDE, YOU NEED SOMETHING OF VALUE IN YOUR LIFE. YOU NEED A HOBBY.
JUSTICE WAS MY HOBBY.
NOW YOU FIGHT!
IN THE PUNCH DOME WE PUNCH!

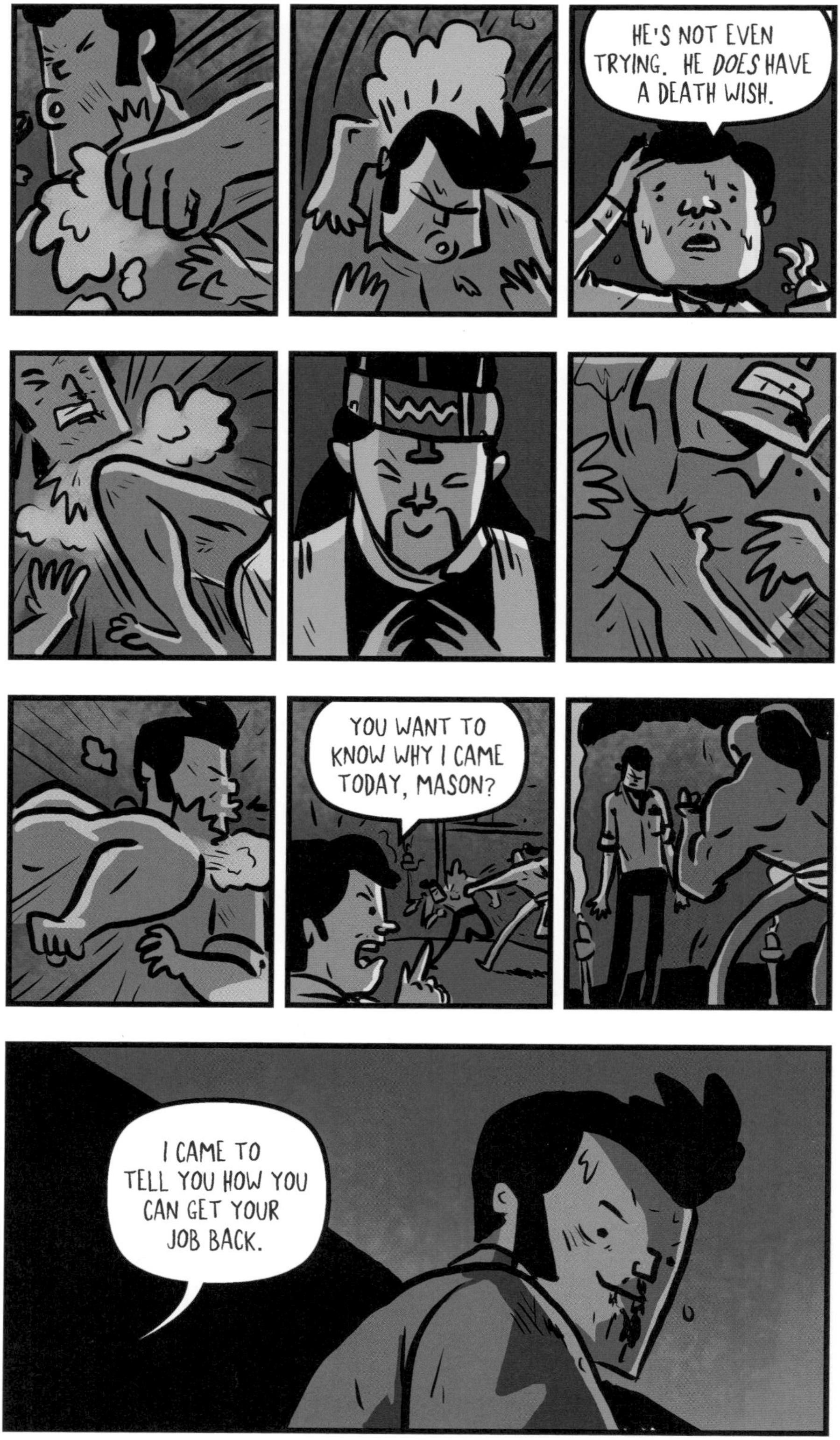
HE'S NOT EVEN TRYING. HE *DOES* HAVE A DEATH WISH.
YOU WANT TO KNOW WHY I CAME TODAY, MASON?
I CAME TO TELL YOU HOW YOU CAN GET YOUR JOB BACK.

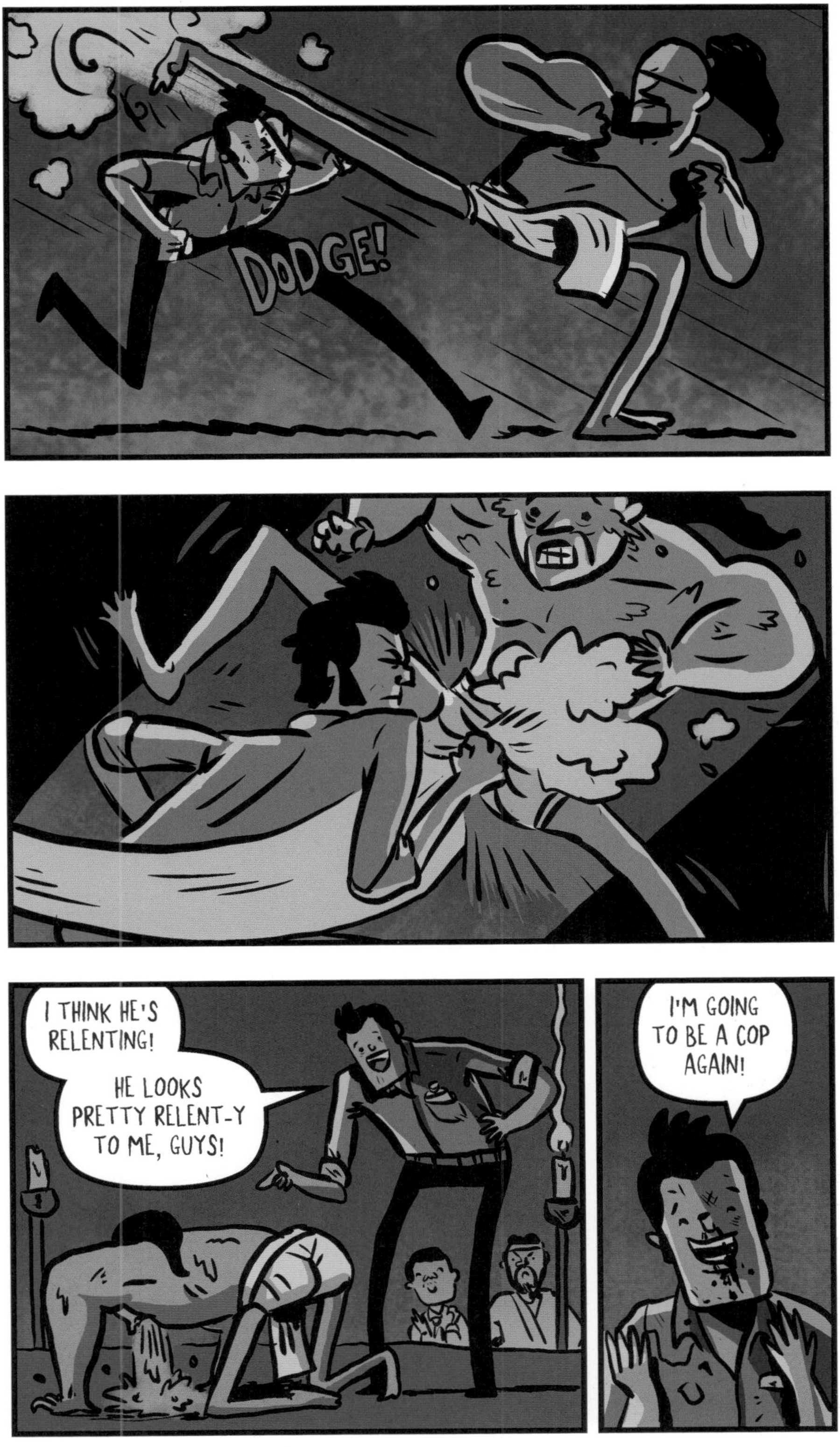
DODGE!
I THINK HE'S RELENTING!
HE LOOKS PRETTY RELENT-Y TO ME, GUYS!
I'M GOING TO BE A COP AGAIN!

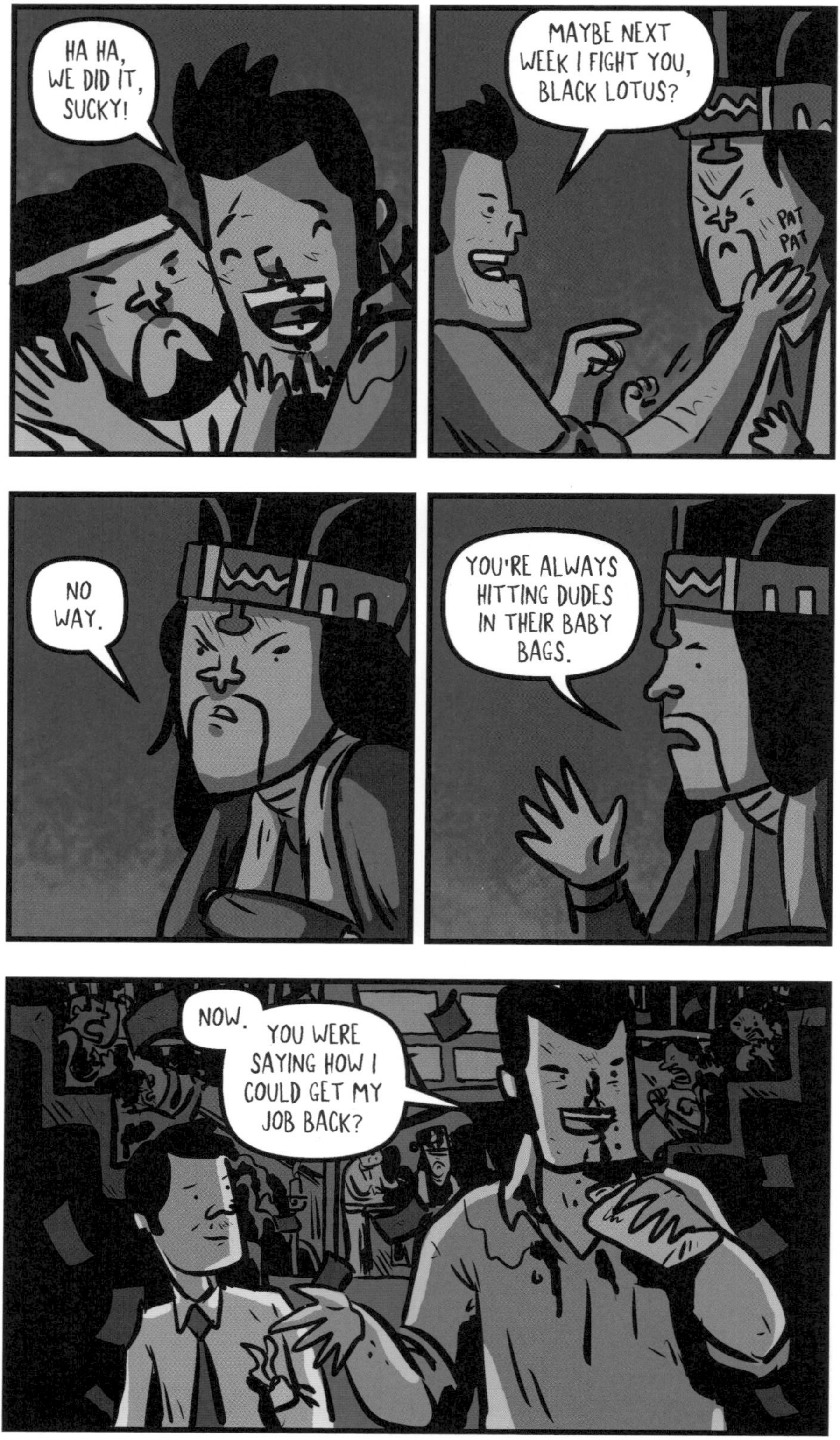
HA HA, WE DID IT, SUCKY!
MAYBE NEXT WEEK I FIGHT YOU, BLACK LOTUS?
PAT PAT
NO WAY.
YOU'RE ALWAYS HITTING DUDES IN THEIR BABY BAGS.
NOW.
YOU WERE SAYING HOW I COULD GET MY JOB BACK?

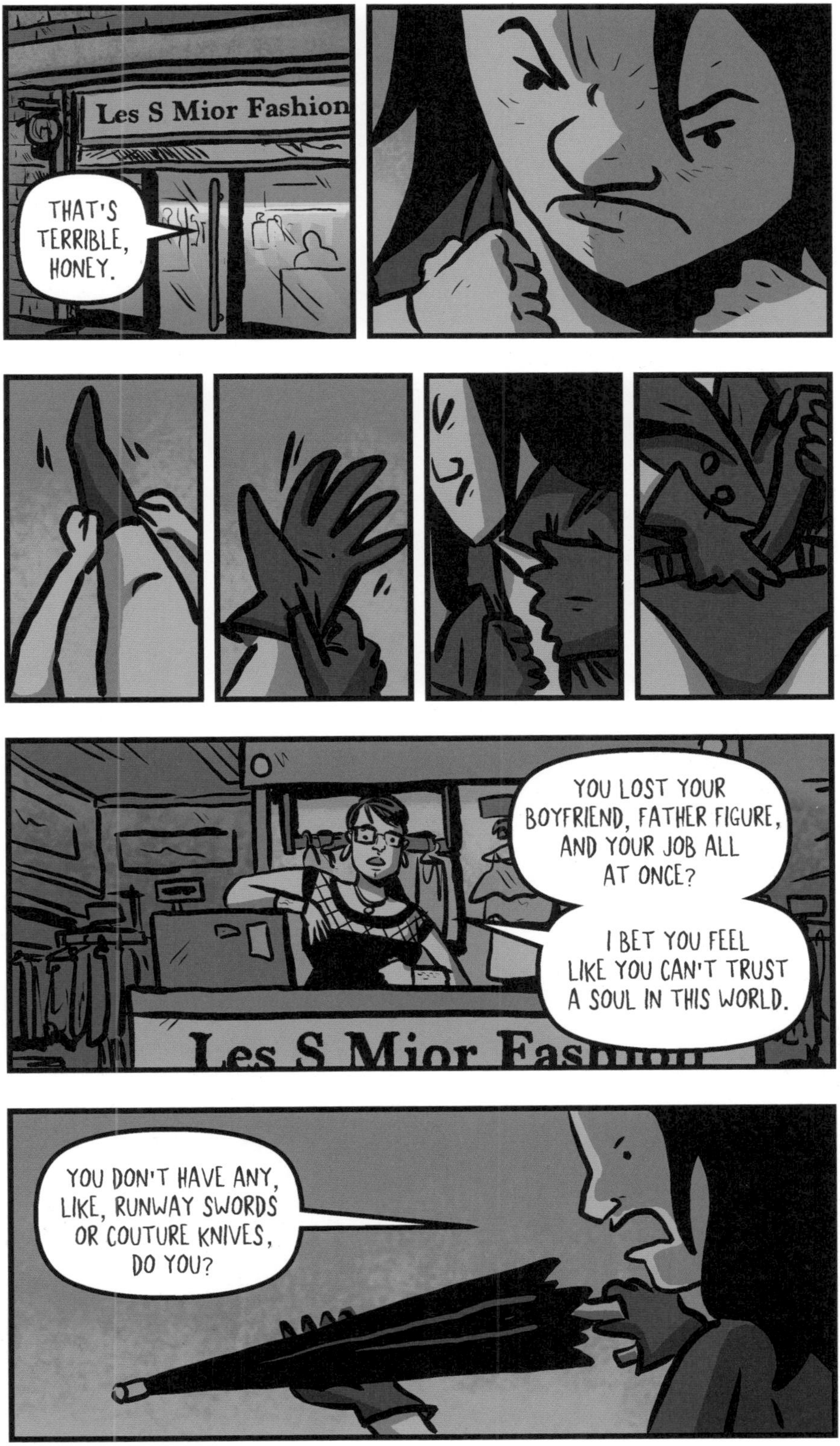
Les S Mior Fashion
THAT'S TERRIBLE, HONEY.
YOU LOST YOUR BOYFRIEND, FATHER FIGURE, AND YOUR JOB ALL AT ONCE?
I BET YOU FEEL LIKE YOU CAN'T TRUST A SOUL IN THIS WORLD.
Les S Mior Fashion
YOU DON'T HAVE ANY, LIKE, RUNWAY SWORDS OR COUTURE KNIVES, DO YOU?

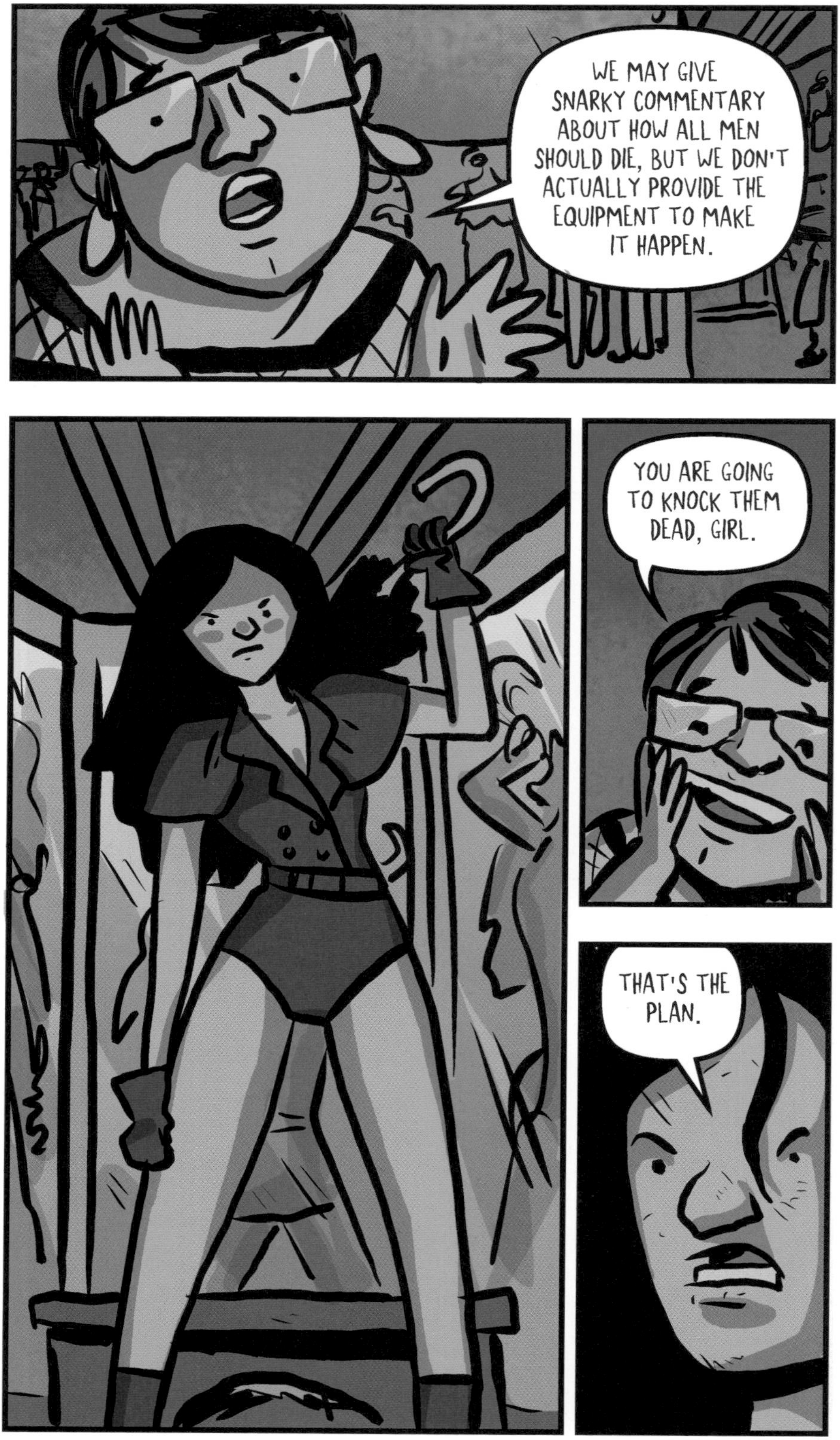
WE MAY GIVE SNARKY COMMENTARY ABOUT HOW ALL MEN SHOULD DIE, BUT WE DON'T ACTUALLY PROVIDE THE EQUIPMENT TO MAKE IT HAPPEN.
YOU ARE GOING TO KNOCK THEM DEAD, GIRL.
THAT'S THE PLAN.

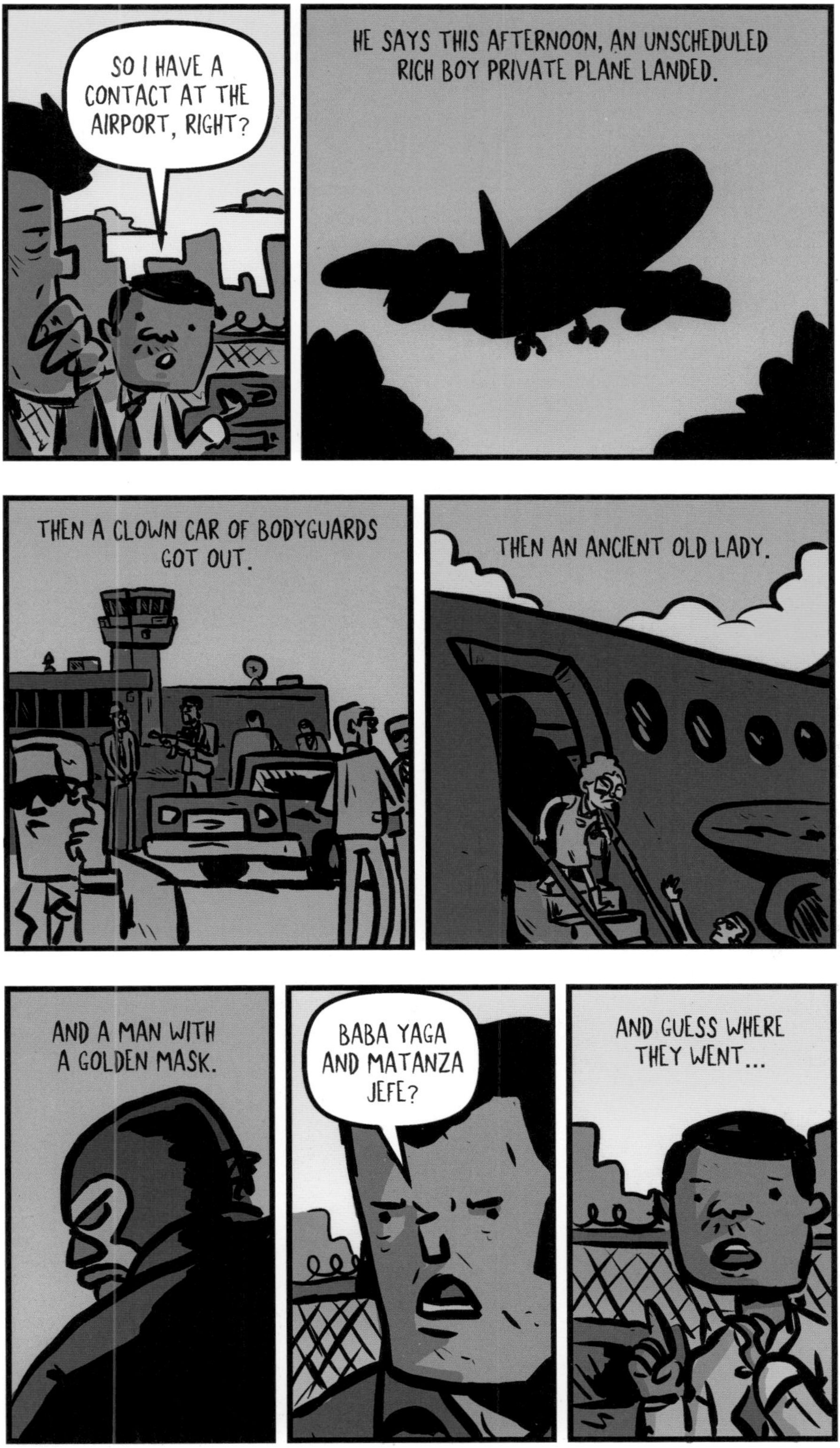
SO I HAVE A CONTACT AT THE AIRPORT, RIGHT?
HE SAYS THIS AFTERNOON, AN UNSCHEDULED RICH BOY PRIVATE PLANE LANDED.
THEN A CLOWN CAR OF BODYGUARDS GOT OUT.
THEN AN ANCIENT OLD LADY.
AND A MAN WITH A GOLDEN MASK.
BABA YAGA AND MATANZA JEFE?
AND GUESS WHERE THEY WENT...

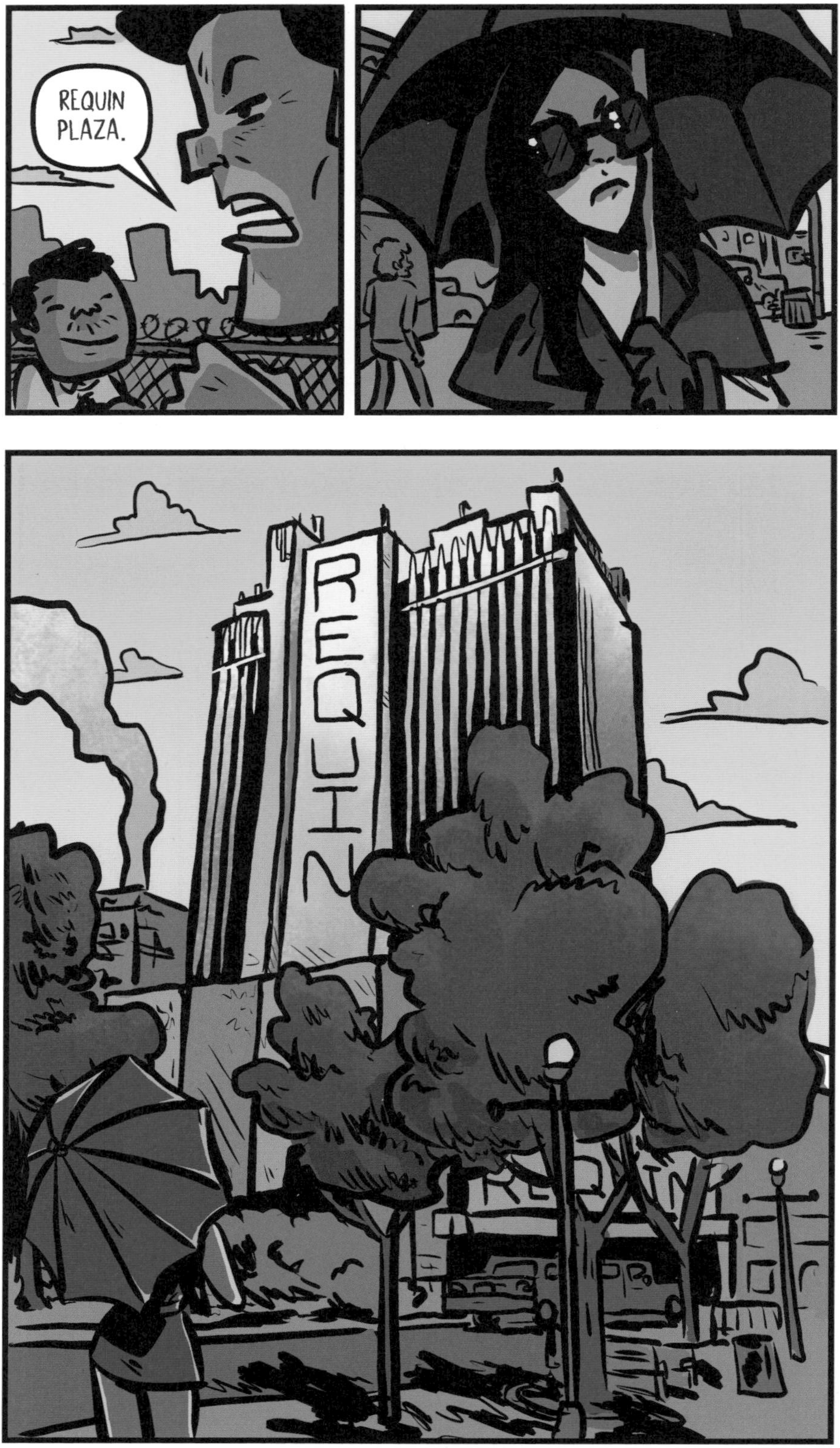
REQUIN PLAZA.
REQUIN

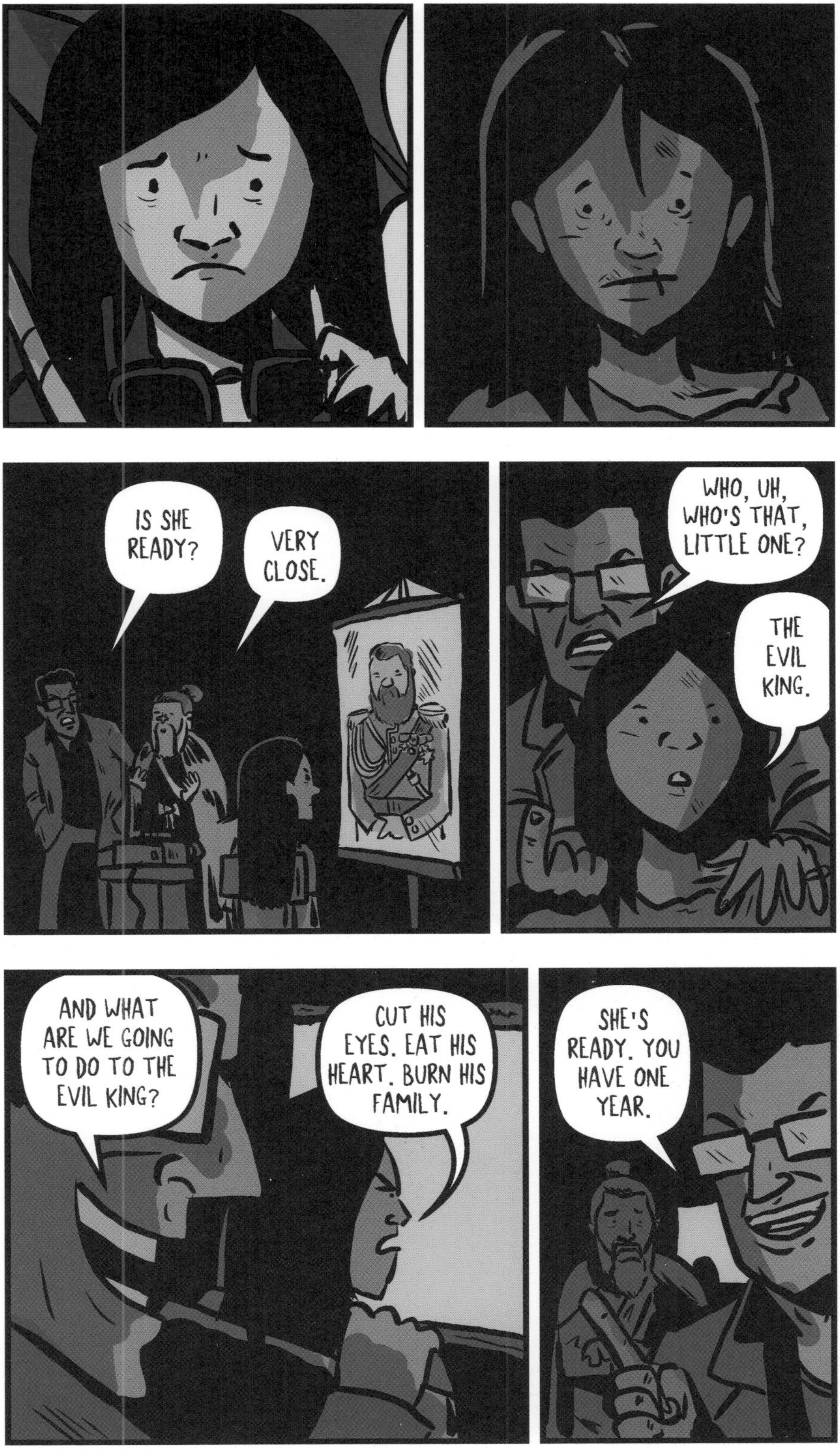
IS SHE READY?
VERY CLOSE.
WHO, UH, WHO'S THAT, LITTLE ONE?
THE EVIL KING.
AND WHAT ARE WE GOING TO DO TO THE EVIL KING?
CUT HIS EYES. EAT HIS HEART. BURN HIS FAMILY.
SHE'S READY. YOU HAVE ONE YEAR.

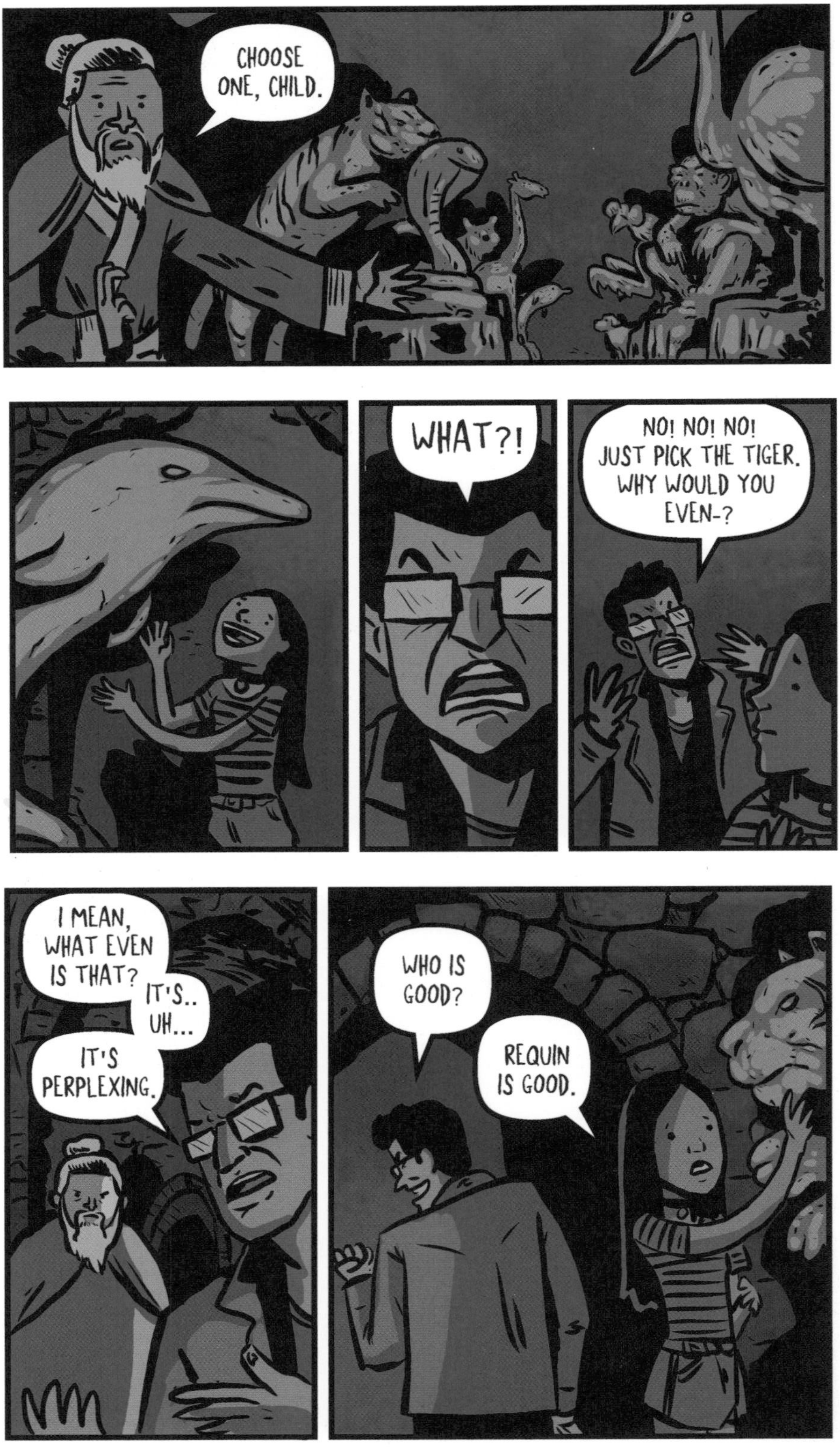
CHOOSE ONE, CHILD.
WHAT?!
NO! NO! NO! JUST PICK THE TIGER. WHY WOULD YOU EVEN-?
I MEAN, WHAT EVEN IS THAT?
IT'S.. UH...
IT'S PERPLEXING.
WHO IS GOOD?
REQUIN IS GOOD.

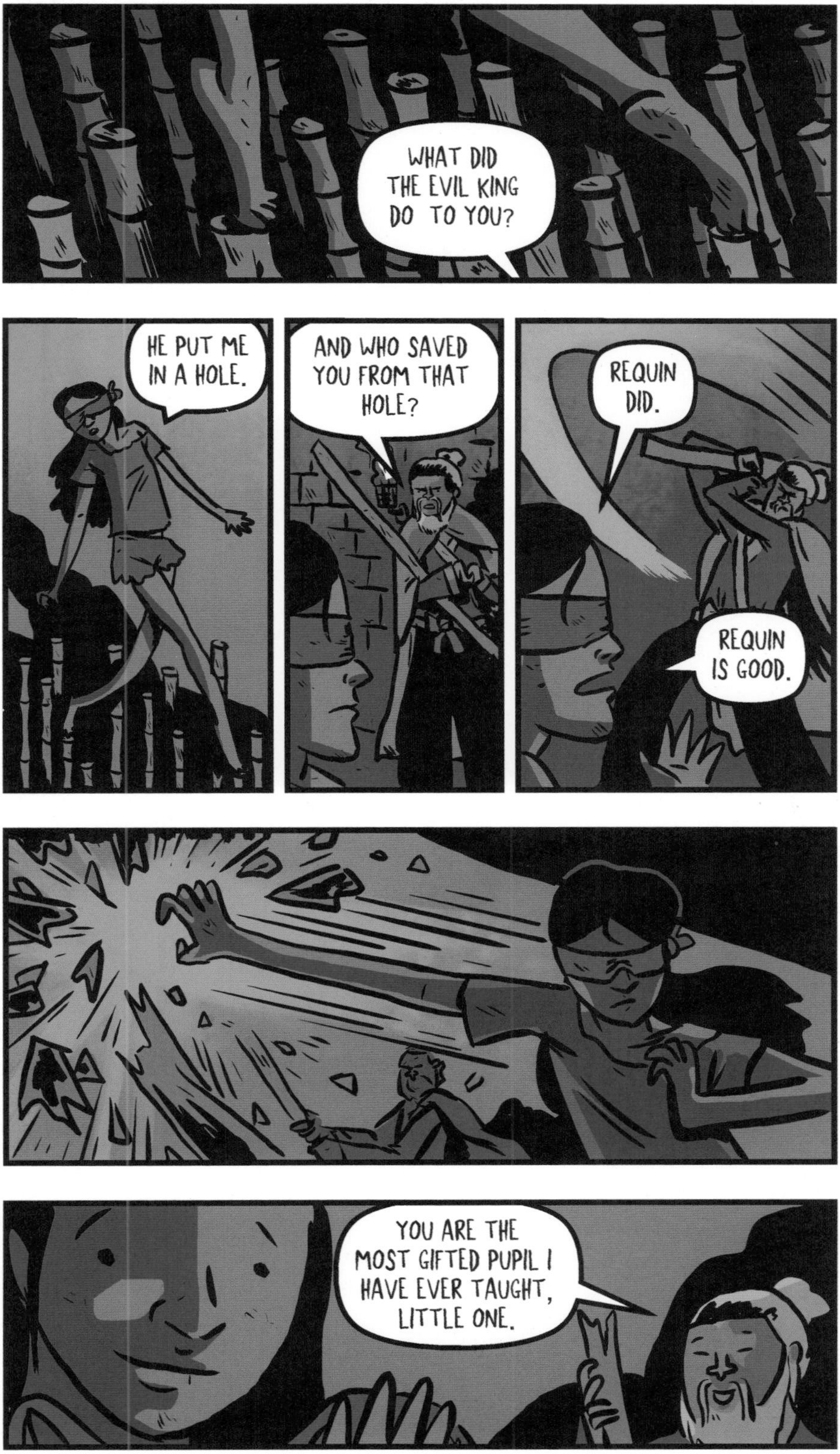
WHAT DID THE EVIL KING DO TO YOU?
HE PUT ME IN A HOLE.
AND WHO SAVED YOU FROM THAT HOLE?
REQUIN DID.
REQUIN IS GOOD.
YOU ARE THE MOST GIFTED PUPIL I HAVE EVER TAUGHT, LITTLE ONE.

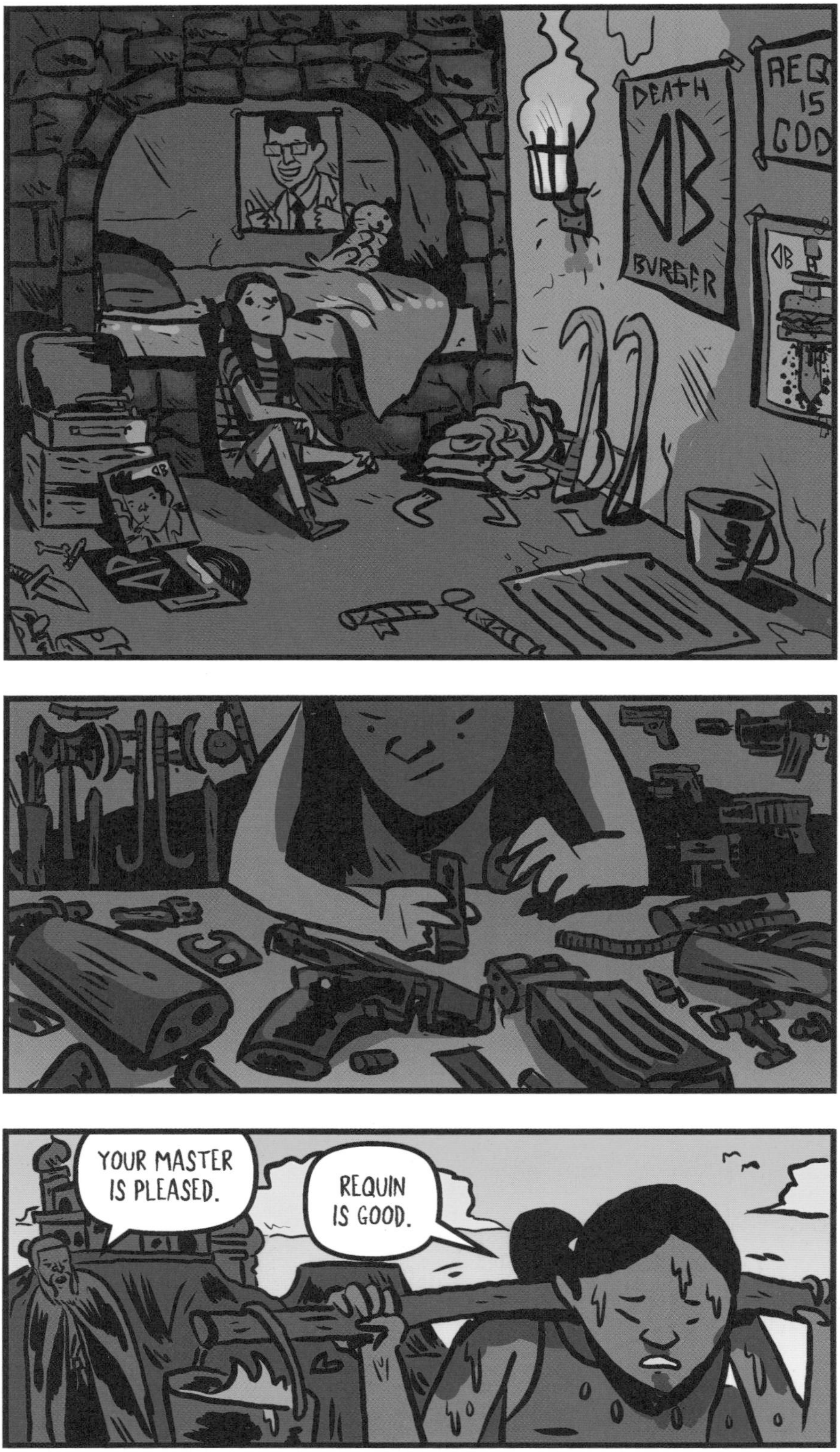
DEATH
BURGER
YOUR MASTER IS PLEASED.
REQUIN IS GOOD.

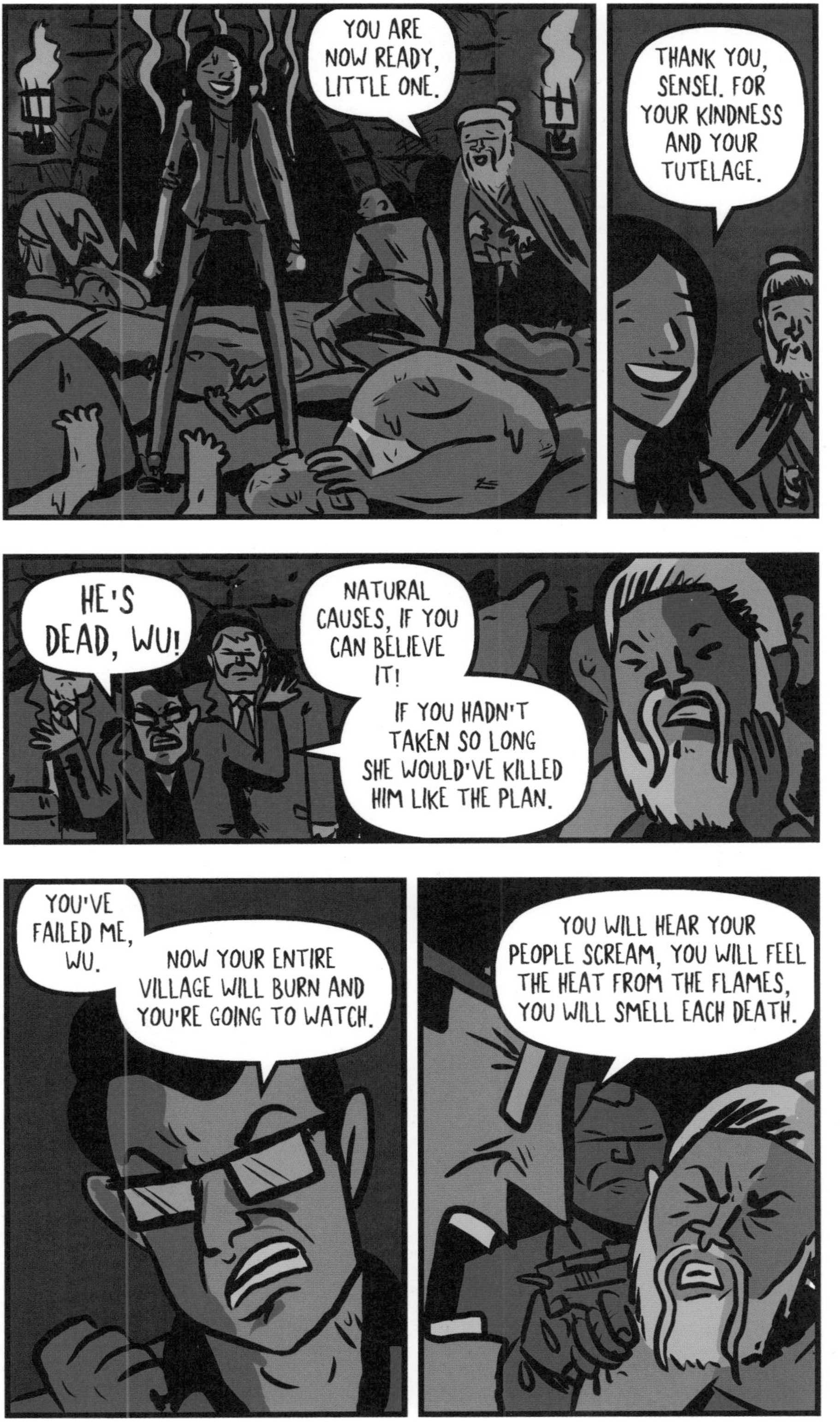
YOU ARE NOW READY, LITTLE ONE.
THANK YOU, SENSEI. FOR YOUR KINDNESS AND YOUR TUTELAGE.
HE'S DEAD, WU!
NATURAL CAUSES, IF YOU CAN BELIEVE IT!
IF YOU HADN'T TAKEN SO LONG SHE WOULD'VE KILLED HIM LIKE THE PLAN.
YOU'VE FAILED ME, WU.
NOW YOUR ENTIRE VILLAGE WILL BURN AND YOU'RE GOING TO WATCH.
YOU WILL HEAR YOUR PEOPLE SCREAM, YOU WILL FEEL THE HEAT FROM THE FLAMES, YOU WILL SMELL EACH DEATH.

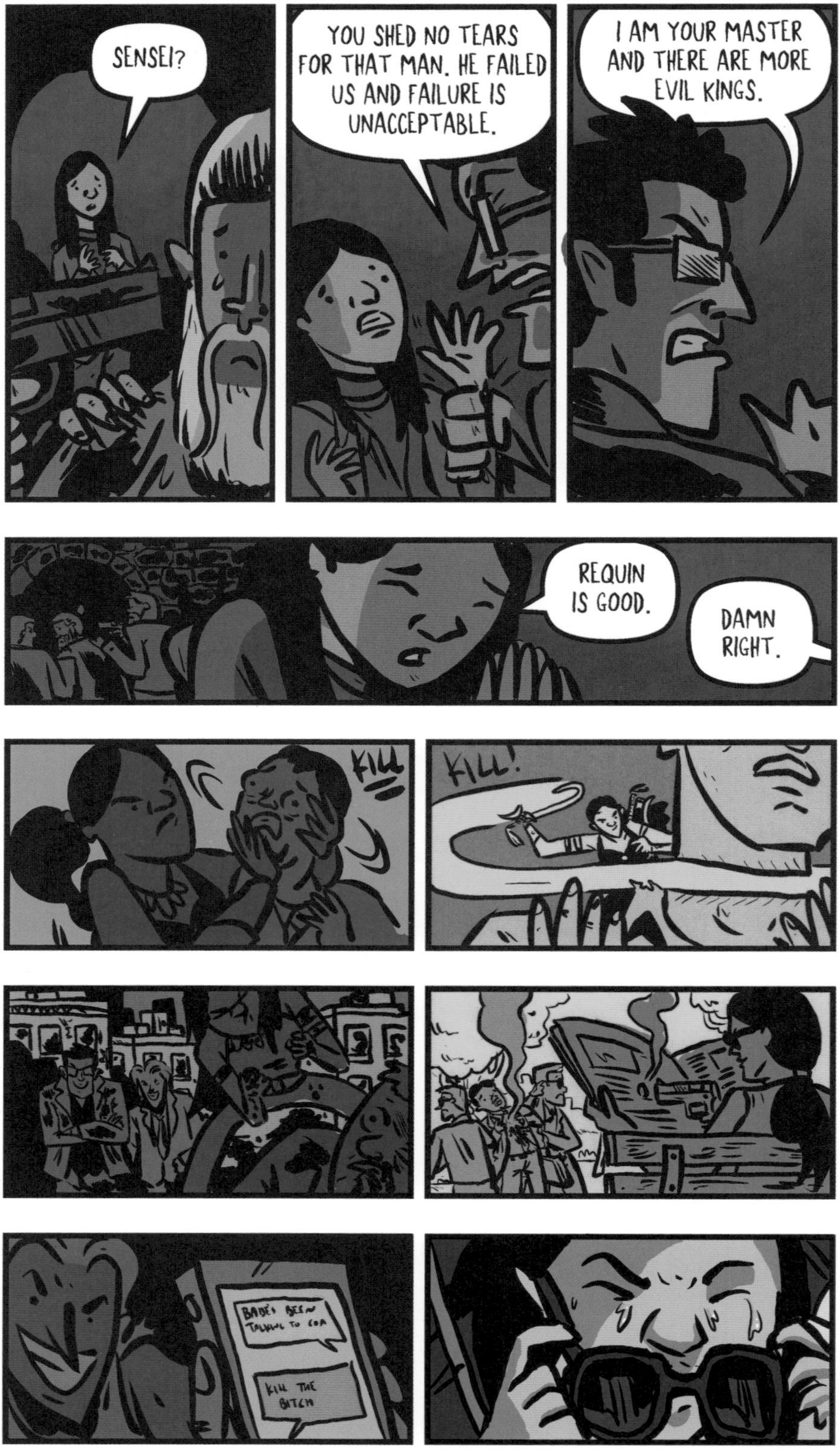
SENSEI?
YOU SHED NO TEARS FOR THAT MAN. HE FAILED US AND FAILURE IS UNACCEPTABLE.
I AM YOUR MASTER AND THERE ARE MORE EVIL KINGS.
REQUIN IS GOOD.
DAMN RIGHT.
KILL
KILL!
BABE'S BEEN TALKING TO CIA
KILL THE BITCH

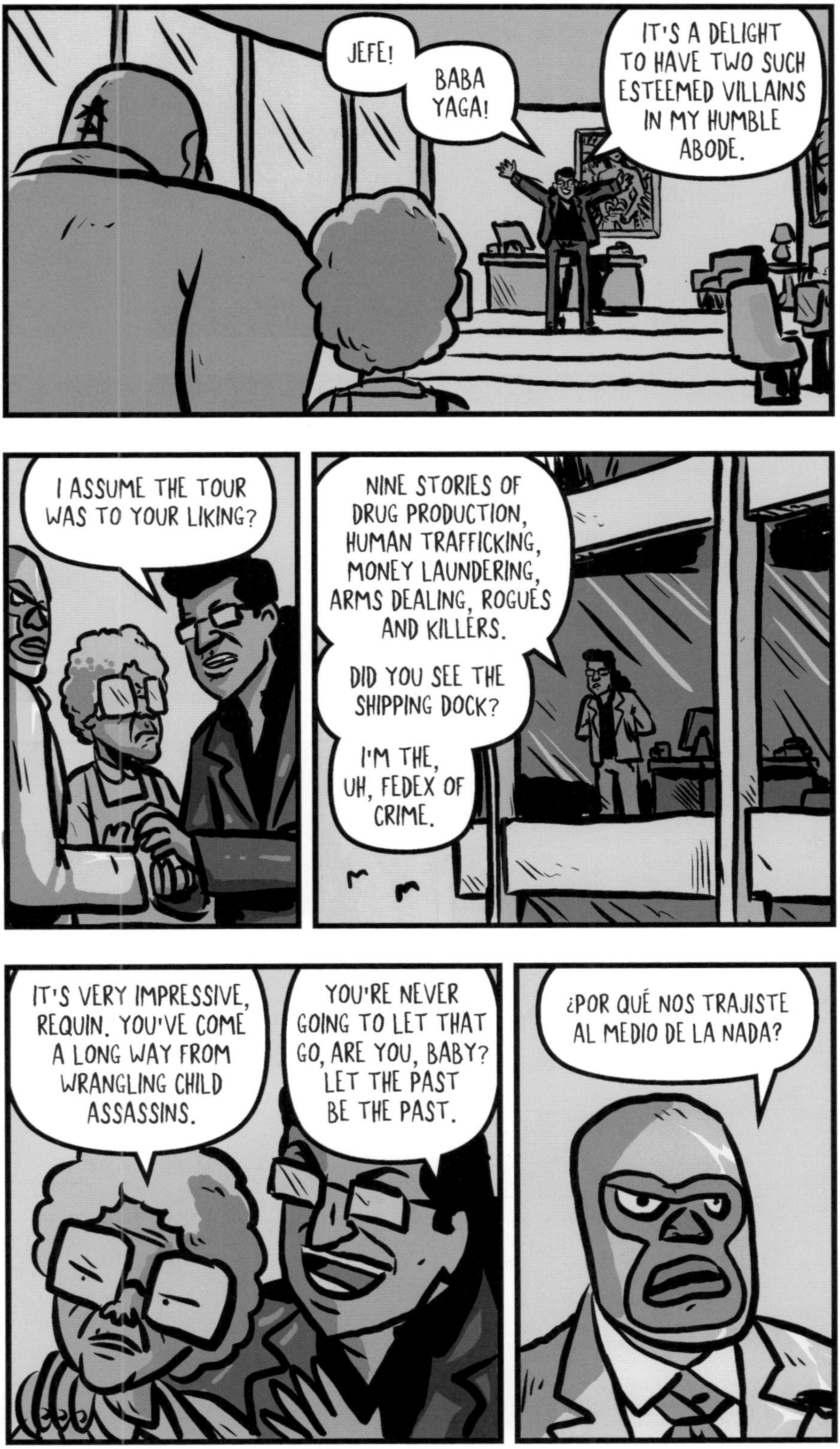
JEFE!
BABA YAGA!
IT'S A DELIGHT TO HAVE TWO SUCH ESTEEMED VILLAINS IN MY HUMBLE ABODE.
I ASSUME THE TOUR WAS TO YOUR LIKING?
NINE STORIES OF DRUG PRODUCTION, HUMAN TRAFFICKING, MONEY LAUNDERING, ARMS DEALING, ROGUES AND KILLERS.
DID YOU SEE THE SHIPPING DOCK?
I'M THE, UH, FEDEX OF CRIME.
IT'S VERY IMPRESSIVE, REQUIN. YOU'VE COME A LONG WAY FROM WRANGLING CHILD ASSASSINS.
YOU'RE NEVER GOING TO LET THAT GO, ARE YOU, BABY? LET THE PAST BE THE PAST.
¿POR QUÉ NOS TRAJISTE AL MEDIO DE LA NADA?

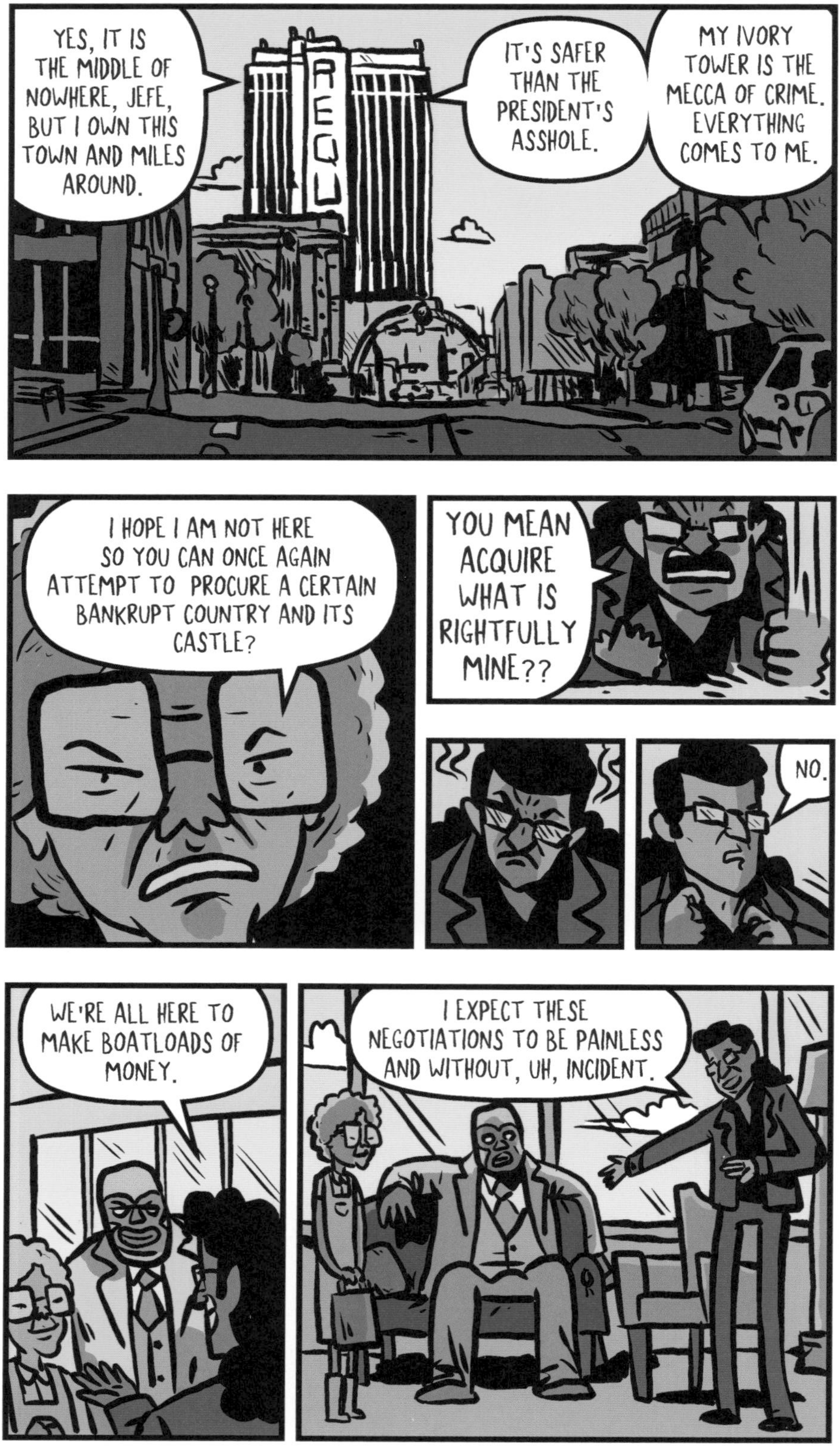
YES, IT IS THE MIDDLE OF NOWHERE, JEFE, BUT I OWN THIS TOWN AND MILES AROUND.
REQU
IT'S SAFER THAN THE PRESIDENT'S ASSHOLE.
MY IVORY TOWER IS THE MECCA OF CRIME. EVERYTHING COMES TO ME.
I HOPE I AM NOT HERE SO YOU CAN ONCE AGAIN ATTEMPT TO PROCURE A CERTAIN BANKRUPT COUNTRY AND ITS CASTLE?
YOU MEAN ACQUIRE WHAT IS RIGHTFULLY MINE??
NO.
WE'RE ALL HERE TO MAKE BOATLOADS OF MONEY.
I EXPECT THESE NEGOTIATIONS TO BE PAINLESS AND WITHOUT, UH, INCIDENT.

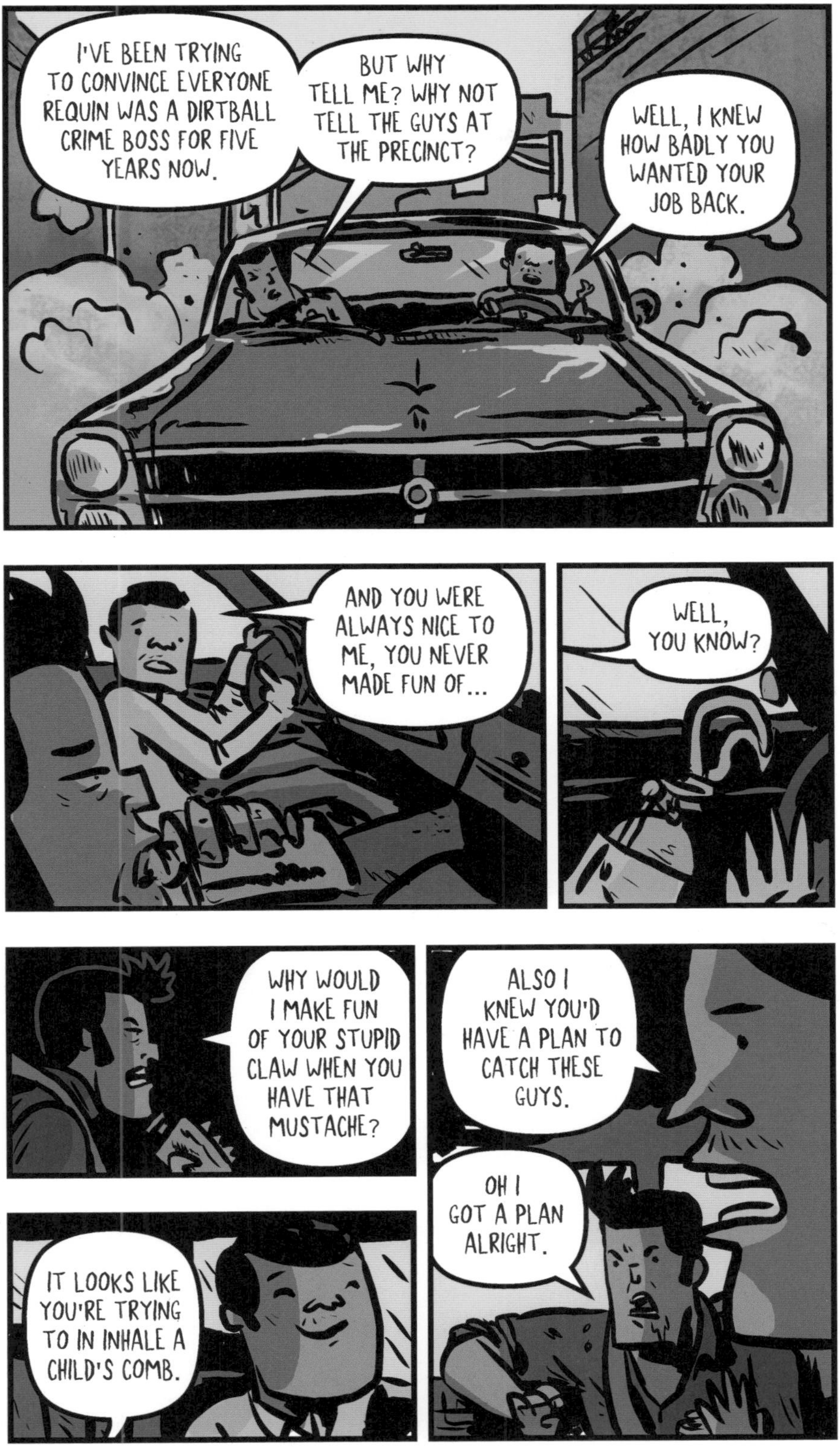
I'VE BEEN TRYING TO CONVINCE EVERYONE REQUIN WAS A DIRTBALL CRIME BOSS FOR FIVE YEARS NOW.
BUT WHY TELL ME? WHY NOT TELL THE GUYS AT THE PRECINCT?
WELL, I KNEW HOW BADLY YOU WANTED YOUR JOB BACK.
AND YOU WERE ALWAYS NICE TO ME, YOU NEVER MADE FUN OF...
WELL, YOU KNOW?
WHY WOULD I MAKE FUN OF YOUR STUPID CLAW WHEN YOU HAVE THAT MUSTACHE?
IT LOOKS LIKE YOU'RE TRYING TO IN INHALE A CHILD'S COMB.
ALSO I KNEW YOU'D HAVE A PLAN TO CATCH THESE GUYS.
OH I GOT A PLAN ALRIGHT.

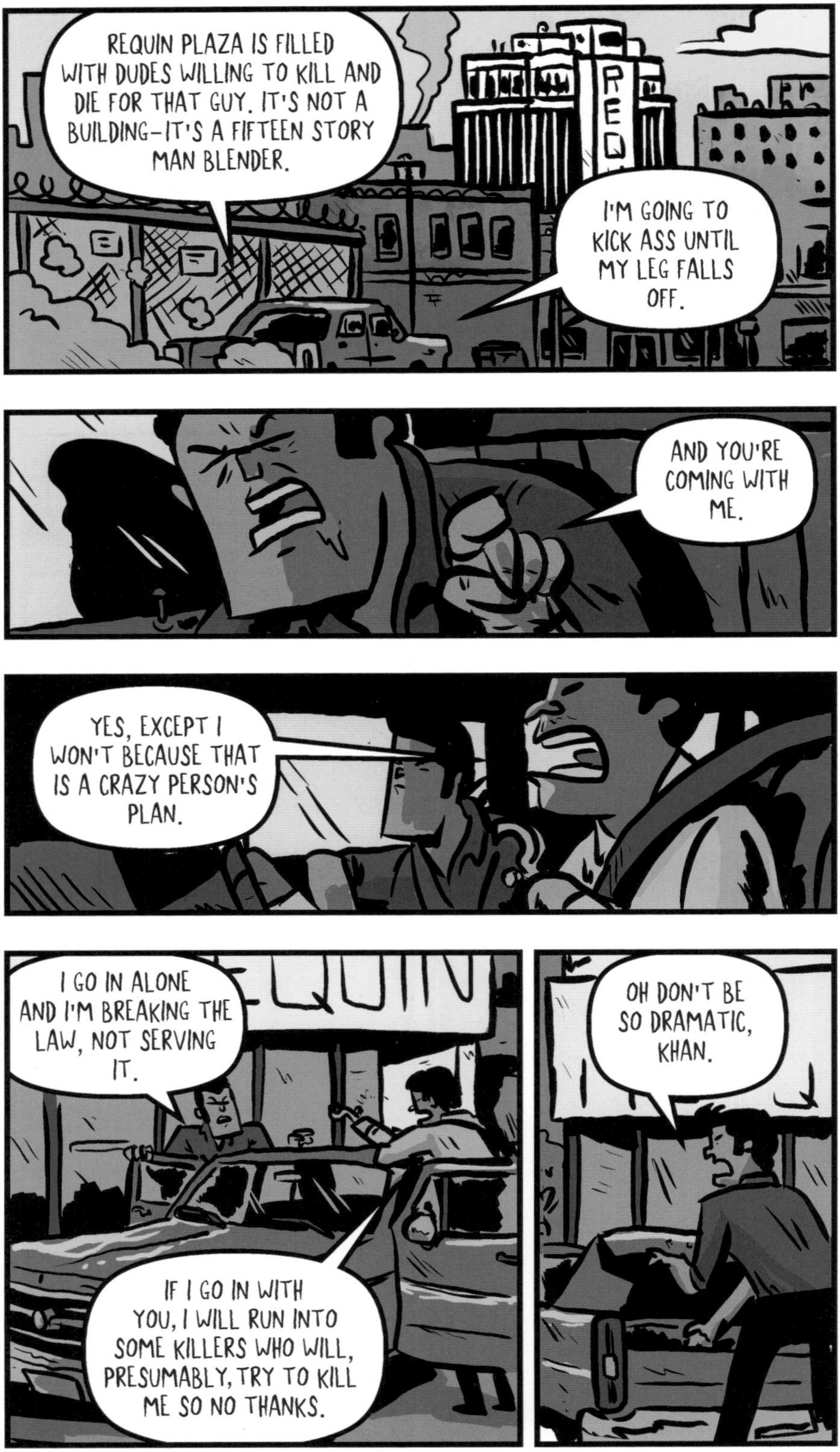
REQUIN PLAZA IS FILLED WITH DUDES WILLING TO KILL AND DIE FOR THAT GUY. IT'S NOT A BUILDING–IT'S A FIFTEEN STORY MAN BLENDER.
I'M GOING TO KICK ASS UNTIL MY LEG FALLS OFF.
AND YOU'RE COMING WITH ME.
YES, EXCEPT I WON'T BECAUSE THAT IS A CRAZY PERSON'S PLAN.
I GO IN ALONE AND I'M BREAKING THE LAW, NOT SERVING IT.
IF I GO IN WITH YOU, I WILL RUN INTO SOME KILLERS WHO WILL, PRESUMABLY, TRY TO KILL ME SO NO THANKS.
OH DON'T BE SO DRAMATIC, KHAN.

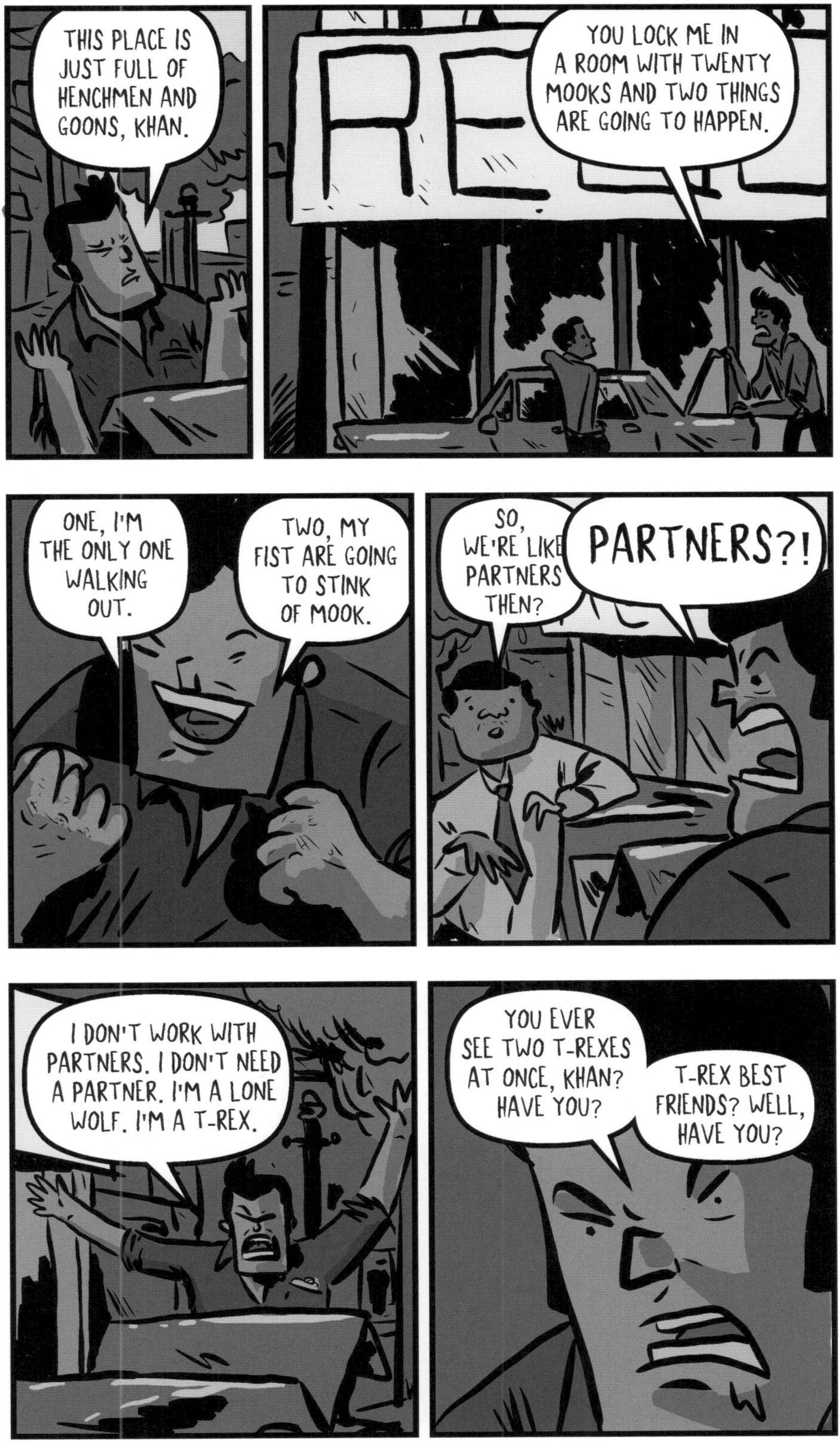
THIS PLACE IS JUST FULL OF HENCHMEN AND GOONS, KHAN.
YOU LOCK ME IN A ROOM WITH TWENTY MOOKS AND TWO THINGS ARE GOING TO HAPPEN.
ONE, I'M THE ONLY ONE WALKING OUT.
TWO, MY FIST ARE GOING TO STINK OF MOOK.
SO, WE'RE LIKE PARTNERS THEN?
PARTNERS?!
I DON'T WORK WITH PARTNERS. I DON'T NEED A PARTNER. I'M A LONE WOLF. I'M A T-REX.
YOU EVER SEE TWO T-REXES AT ONCE, KHAN? HAVE YOU?
T-REX BEST FRIENDS? WELL, HAVE YOU?

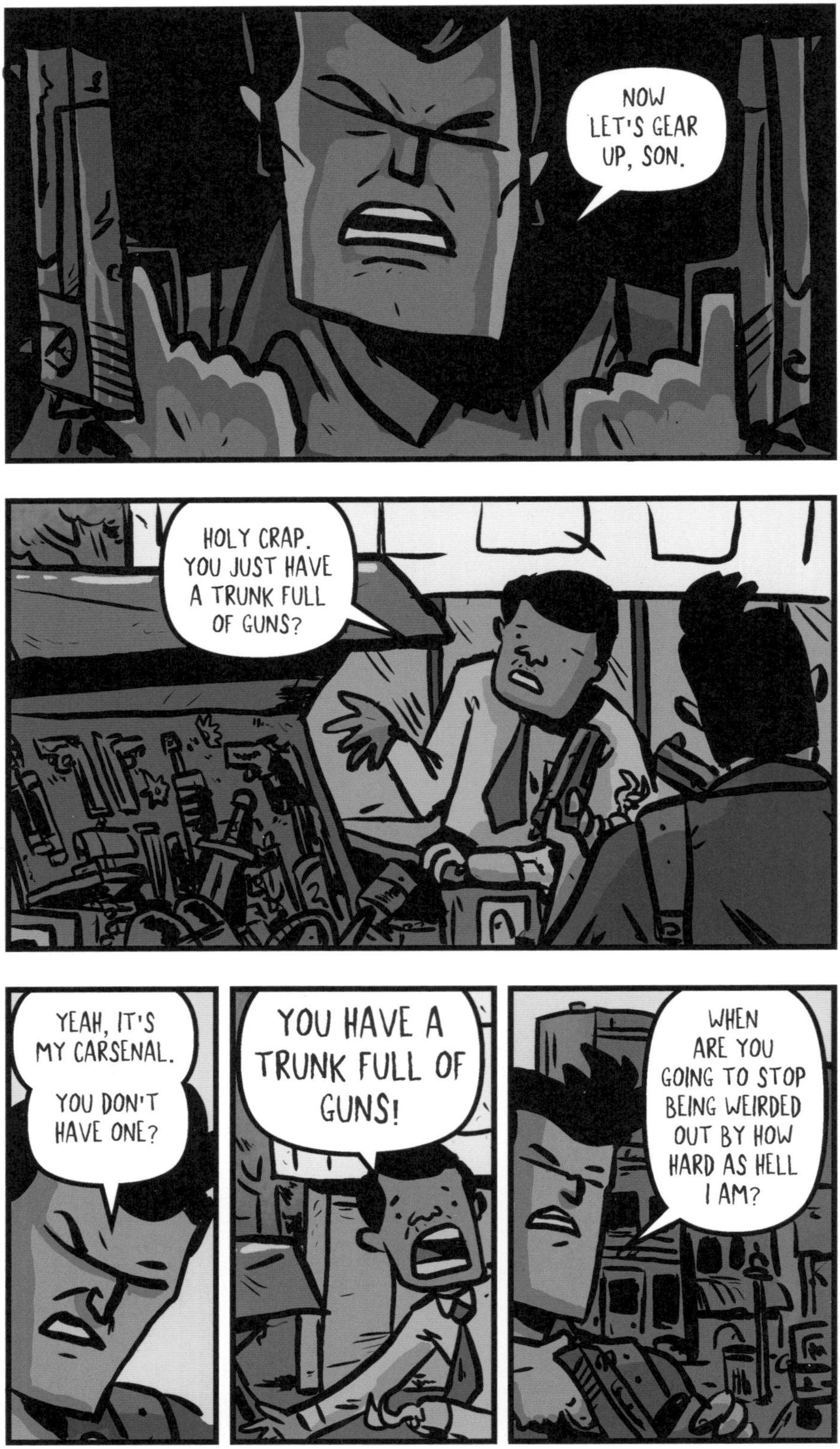
NOW LET'S GEAR UP, SON.
HOLY CRAP. YOU JUST HAVE A TRUNK FULL OF GUNS?
YEAH, IT'S MY CARSENAL.
YOU DON'T HAVE ONE?
YOU HAVE A TRUNK FULL OF GUNS!
WHEN ARE YOU GOING TO STOP BEING WEIRDED OUT BY HOW HARD AS HELL I AM?

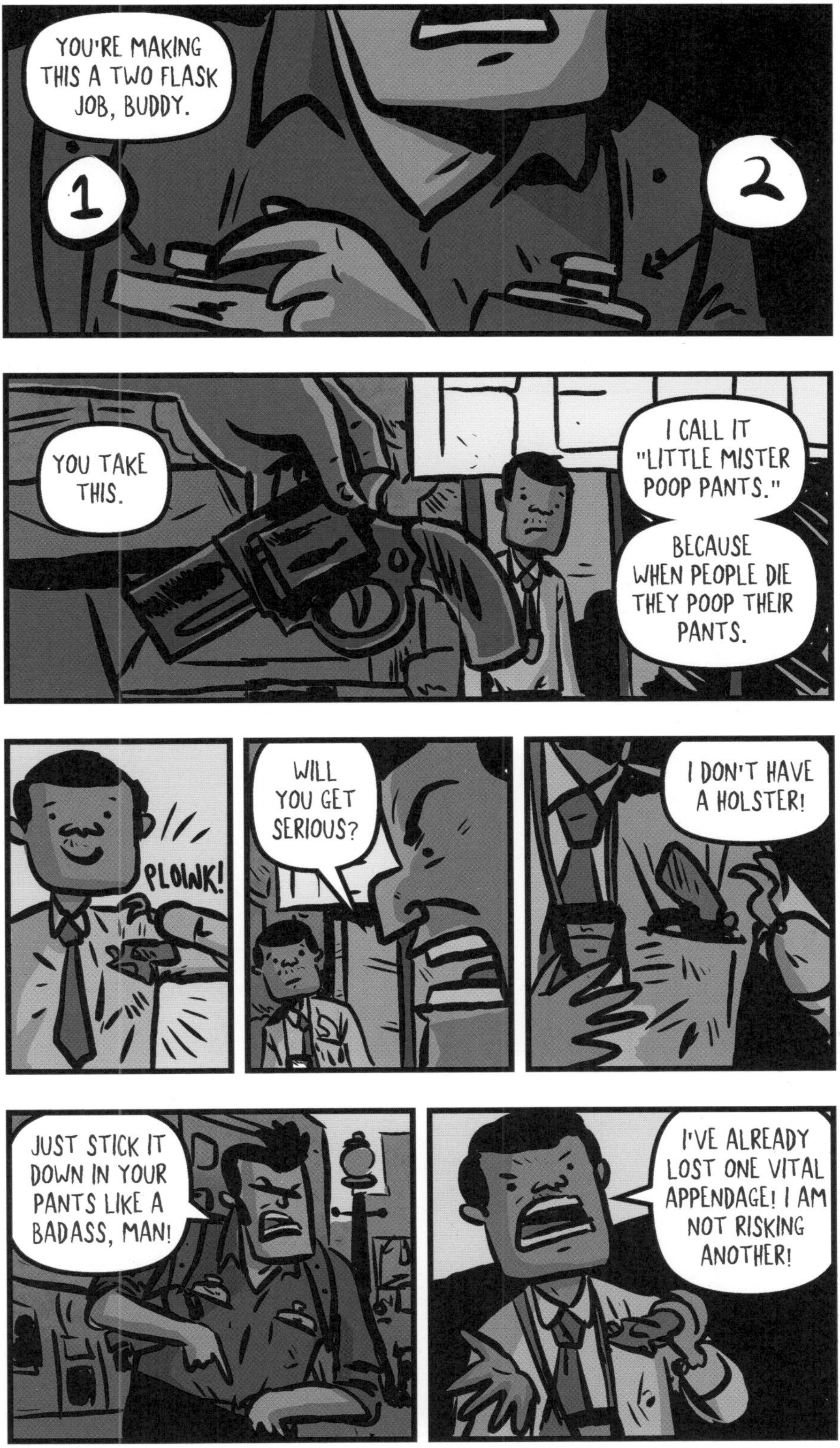
YOU'RE MAKING THIS A TWO FLASK JOB, BUDDY.
1
2
YOU TAKE THIS.
I CALL IT "LITTLE MISTER POOP PANTS."
BECAUSE WHEN PEOPLE DIE THEY POOP THEIR PANTS.
PLOINK!
WILL YOU GET SERIOUS?
I DON'T HAVE A HOLSTER!
JUST STICK IT DOWN IN YOUR PANTS LIKE A BADASS, MAN!
I'VE ALREADY LOST ONE VITAL APPENDAGE! I AM NOT RISKING ANOTHER!

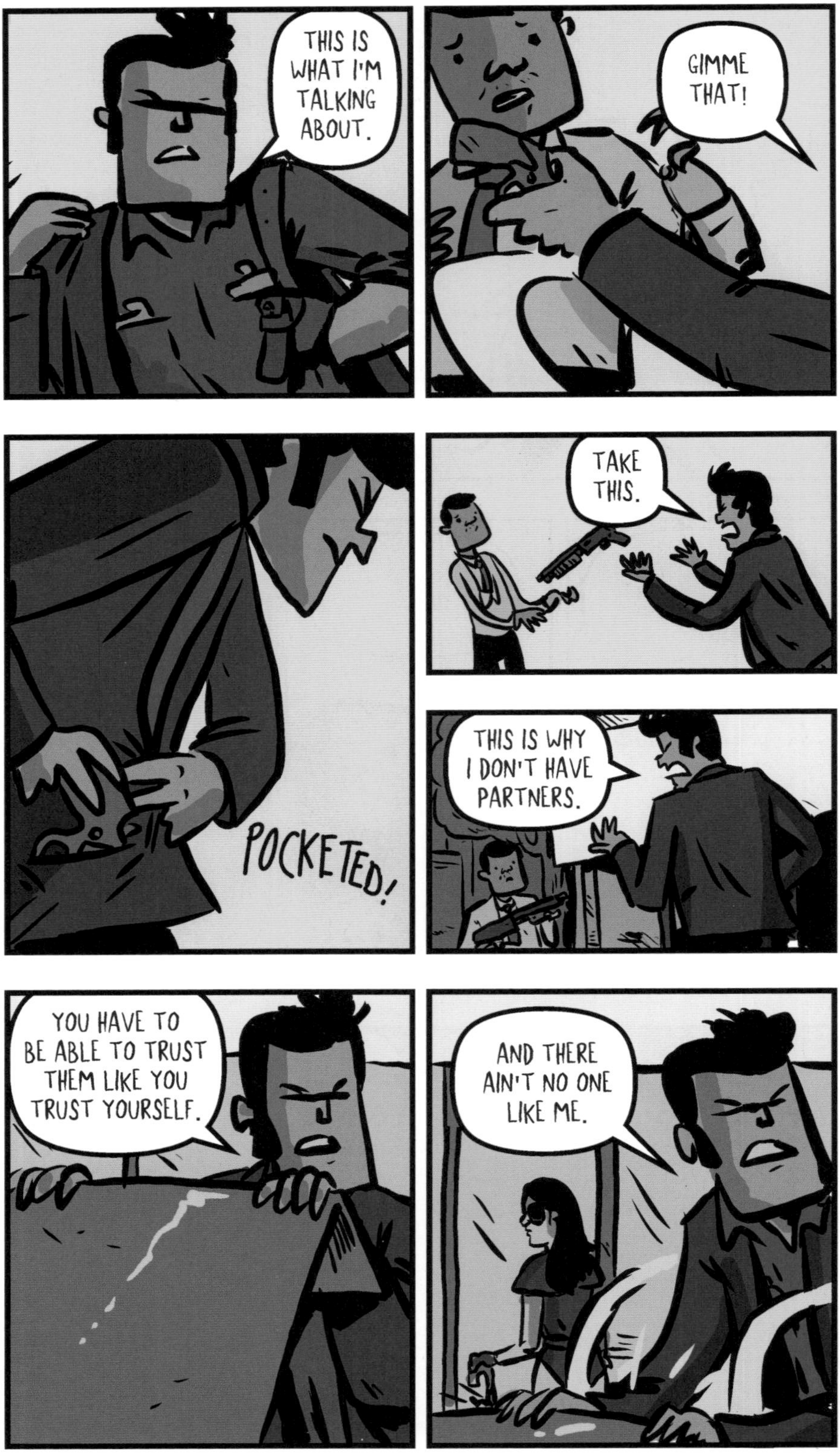
THIS IS WHAT I'M TALKING ABOUT.
GIMME THAT!
POCKETED!
TAKE THIS.
THIS IS WHY I DON'T HAVE PARTNERS.
YOU HAVE TO BE ABLE TO TRUST THEM LIKE YOU TRUST YOURSELF.
AND THERE AIN'T NO ONE LIKE ME.

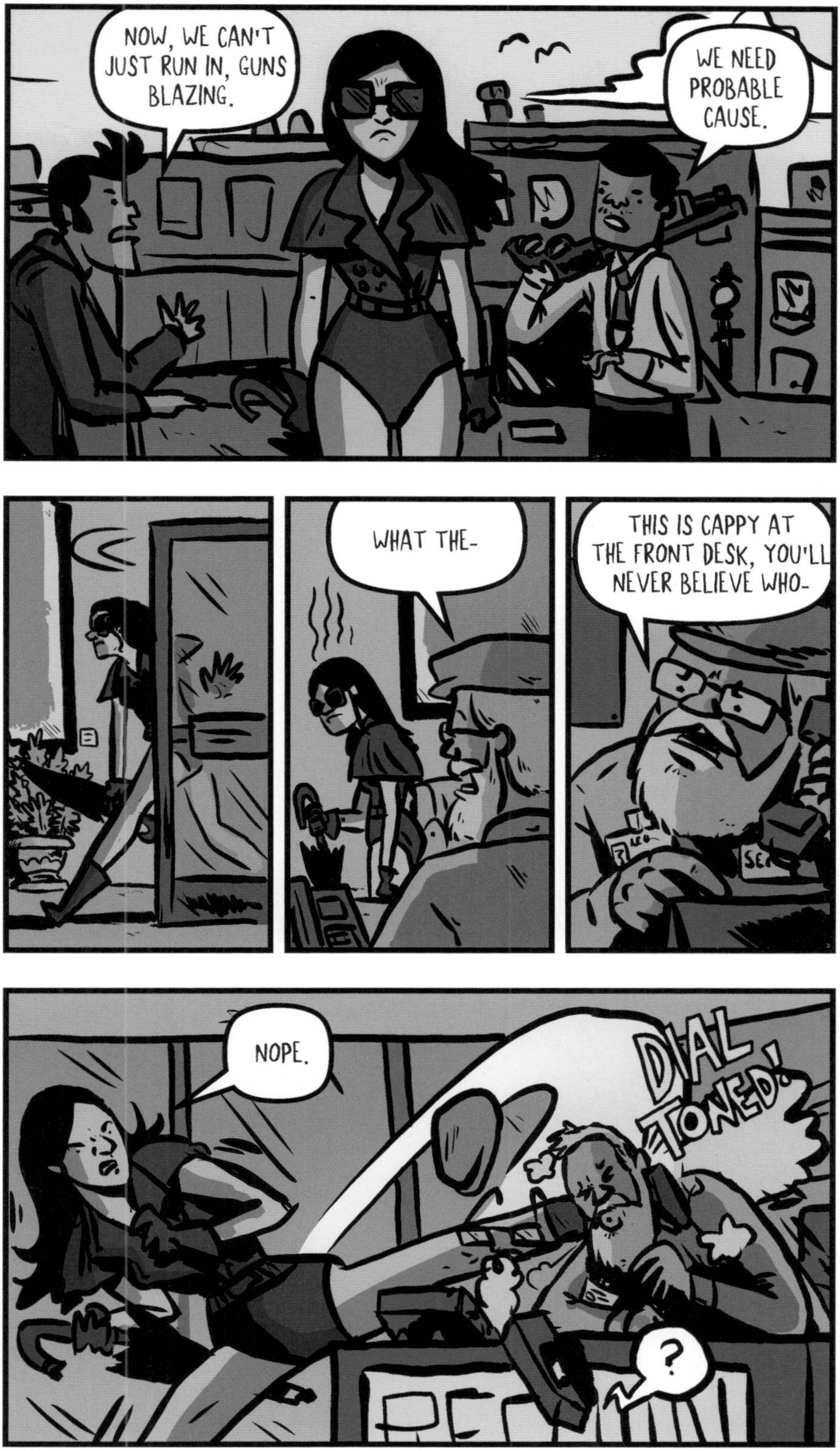
NOW, WE CAN'T JUST RUN IN, GUNS BLAZING.
WE NEED PROBABLE CAUSE.
WHAT THE-
THIS IS CAPPY AT THE FRONT DESK, YOU'LL NEVER BELIEVE WHO-
NOPE.
DIAL TONED!
?

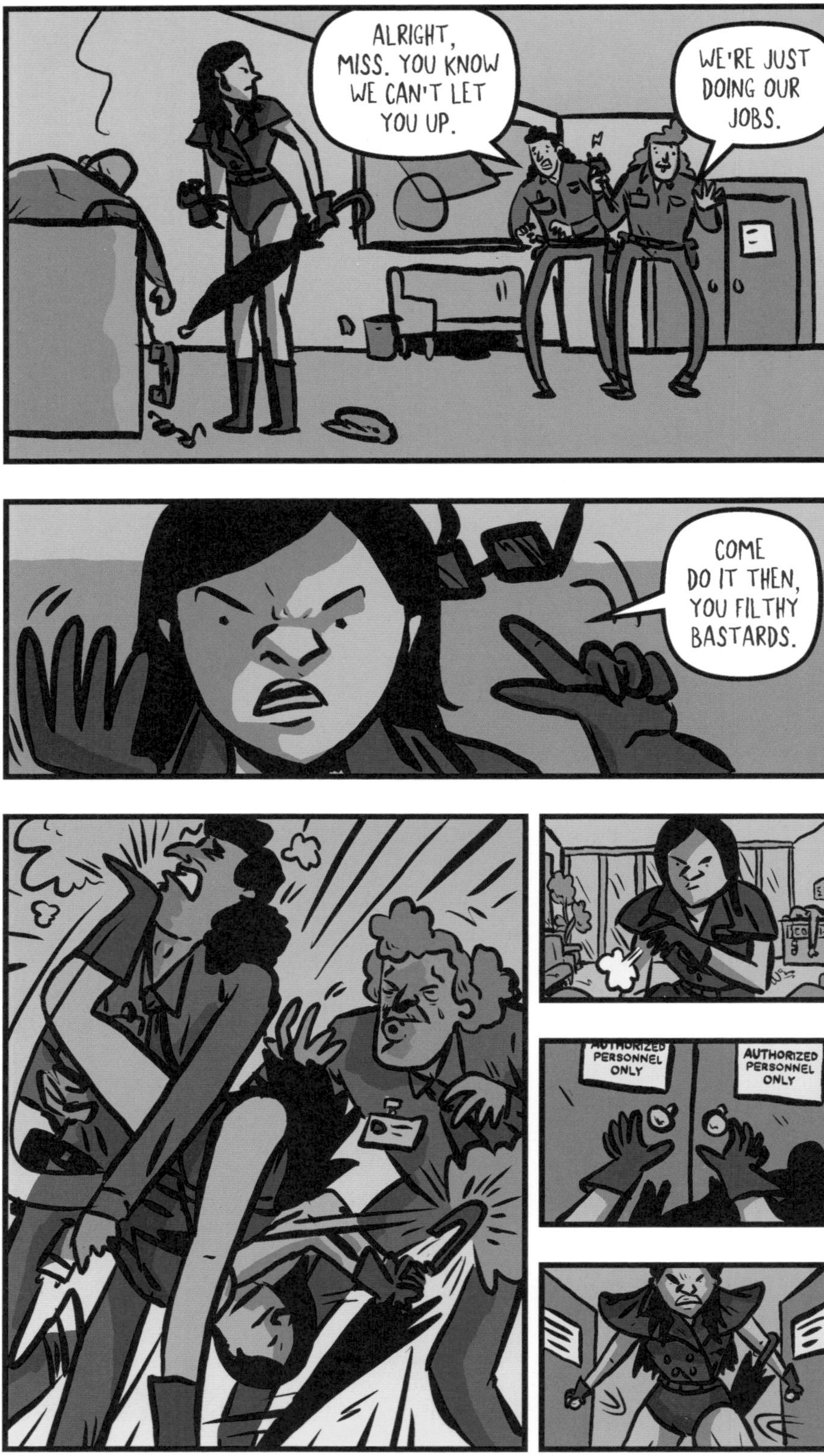
ALRIGHT, MISS. YOU KNOW WE CAN'T LET YOU UP.
WE'RE JUST DOING OUR JOBS.
COME DO IT THEN, YOU FILTHY BASTARDS.
AUTHORIZED PERSONNEL ONLY
AUTHORIZED PERSONNEL ONLY

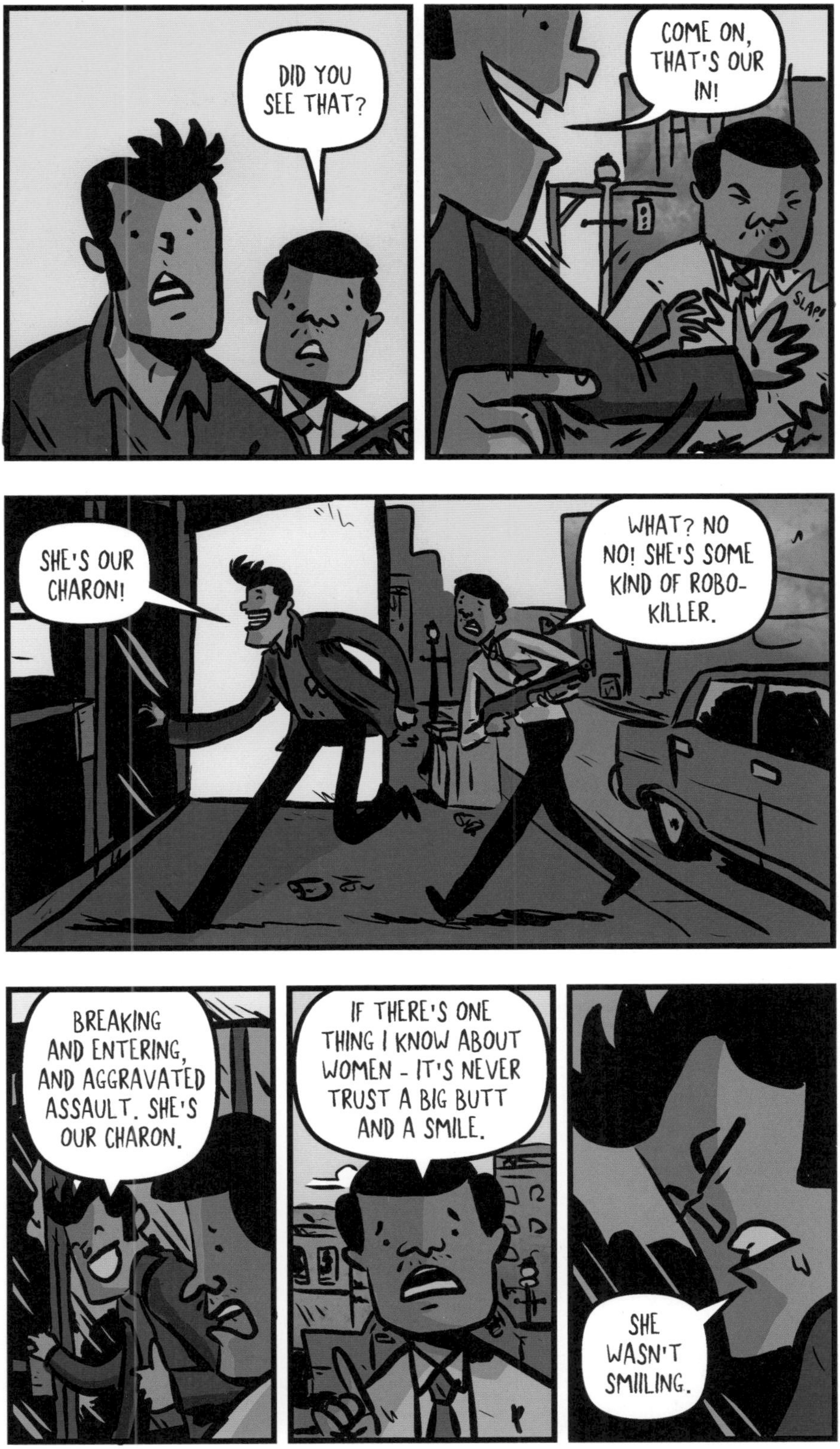
DID YOU SEE THAT?
COME ON, THAT'S OUR IN!
SLAP!
SHE'S OUR CHARON!
WHAT? NO NO! SHE'S SOME KIND OF ROBO-KILLER.
BREAKING AND ENTERING, AND AGGRAVATED ASSAULT. SHE'S OUR CHARON.
IF THERE'S ONE THING I KNOW ABOUT WOMEN - IT'S NEVER TRUST A BIG BUTT AND A SMILE.
SHE WASN'T SMIILING.

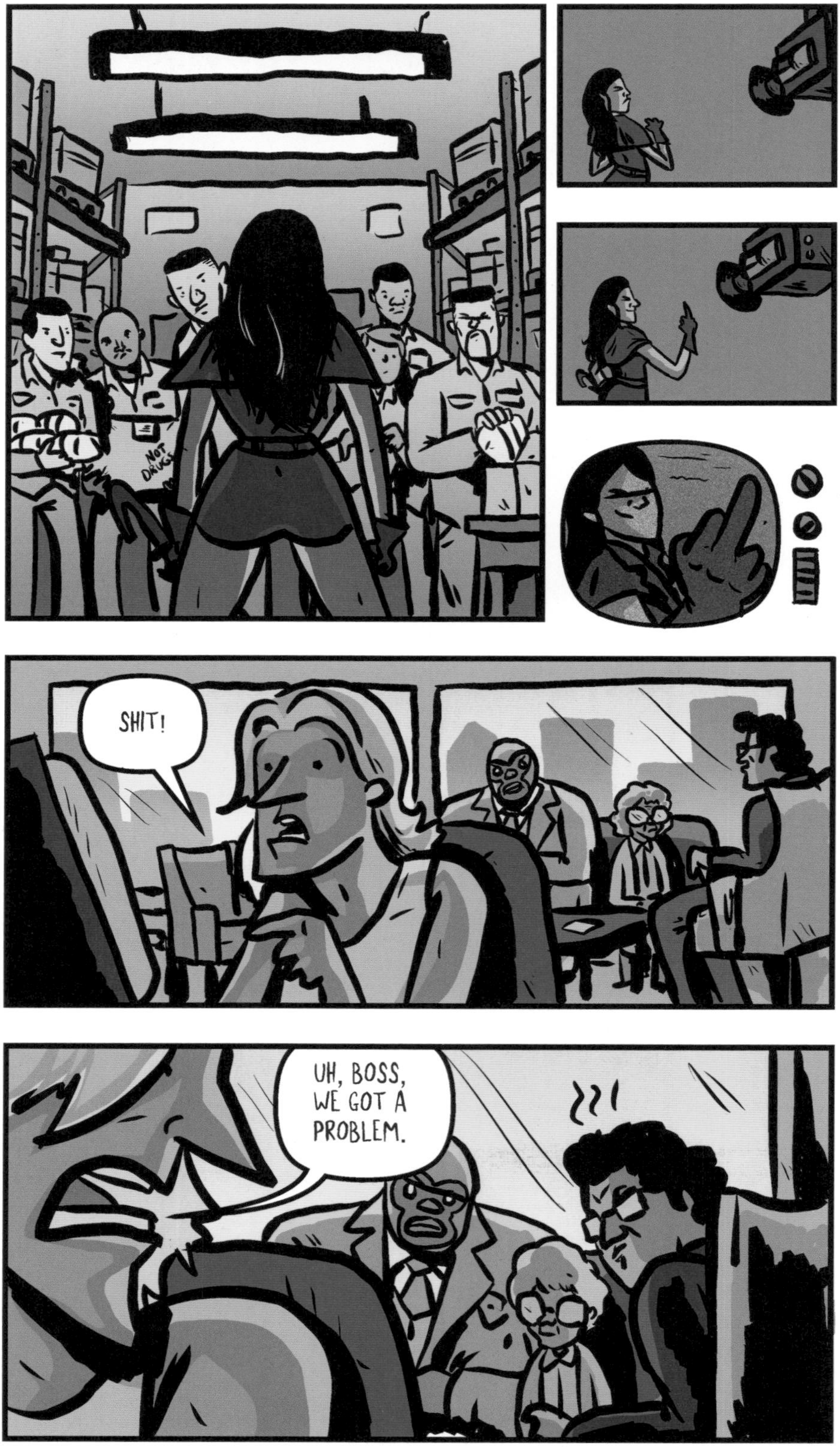
NOT DRUGS
SHIT!
UH, BOSS, WE GOT A PROBLEM.
???

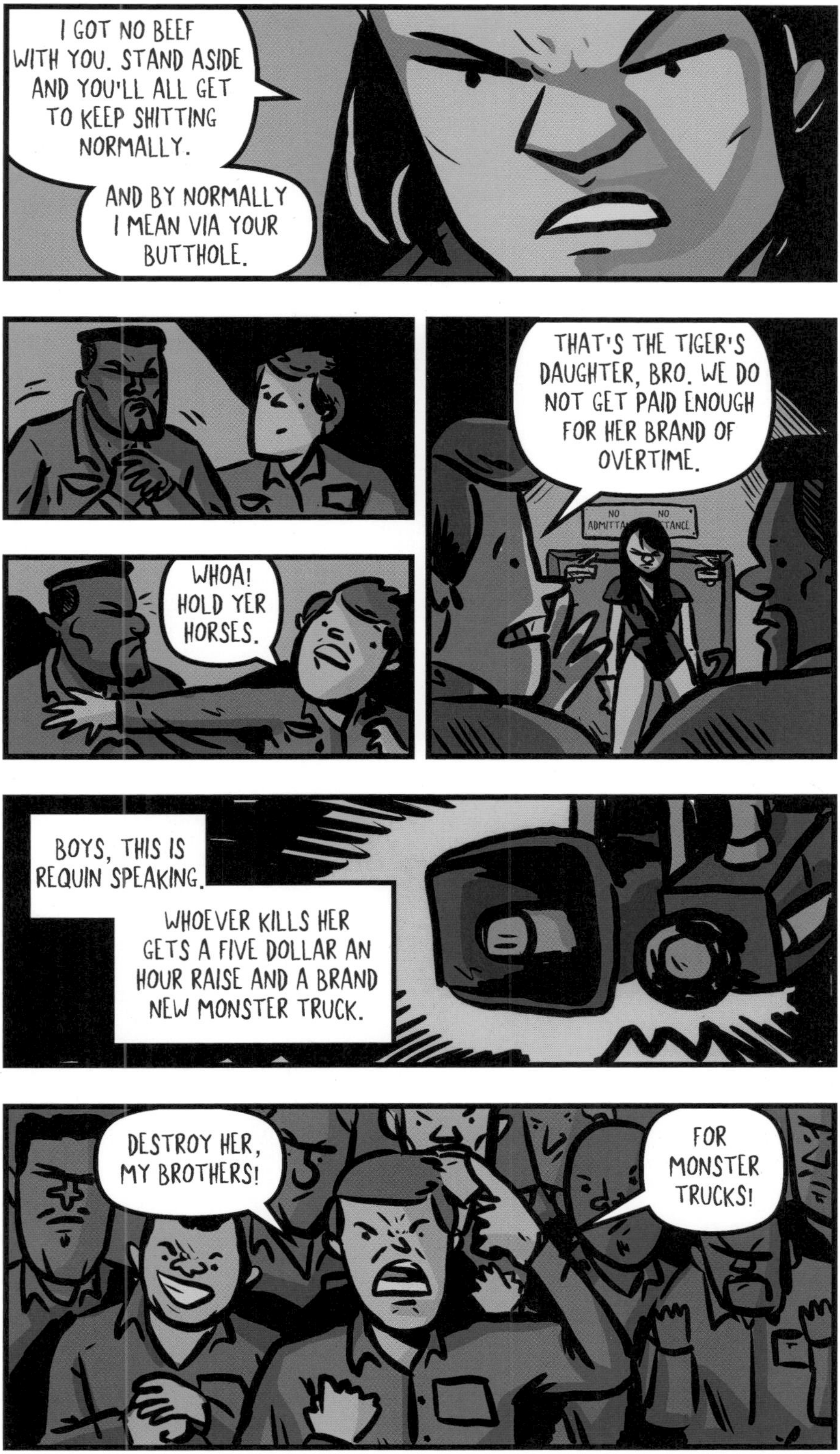
I GOT NO BEEF WITH YOU. STAND ASIDE AND YOU'LL ALL GET TO KEEP SHITTING NORMALLY.
AND BY NORMALLY I MEAN VIA YOUR BUTTHOLE.
WHOA! HOLD YER HORSES.
THAT'S THE TIGER'S DAUGHTER, BRO. WE DO NOT GET PAID ENOUGH FOR HER BRAND OF OVERTIME.
BOYS, THIS IS REQUIN SPEAKING.
WHOEVER KILLS HER GETS A FIVE DOLLAR AN HOUR RAISE AND A BRAND NEW MONSTER TRUCK.
DESTROY HER, MY BROTHERS!
FOR MONSTER TRUCKS!

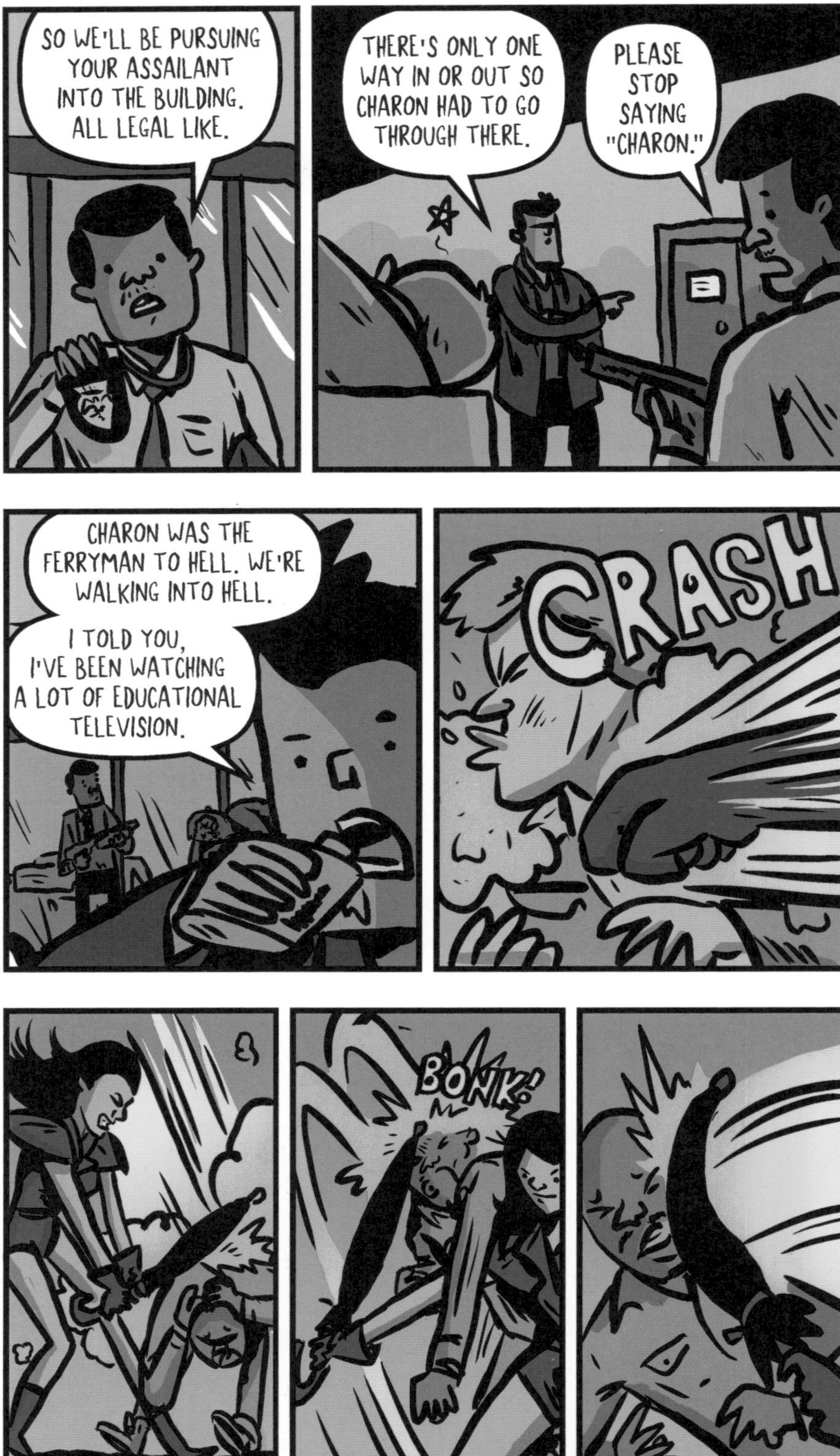
SO WE'LL BE PURSUING YOUR ASSAILANT INTO THE BUILDING. ALL LEGAL LIKE.
THERE'S ONLY ONE WAY IN OR OUT SO CHARON HAD TO GO THROUGH THERE.
PLEASE STOP SAYING "CHARON."
CHARON WAS THE FERRYMAN TO HELL. WE'RE WALKING INTO HELL.
I TOLD YOU, I'VE BEEN WATCHING A LOT OF EDUCATIONAL TELEVISION.
CRASH
BONK!

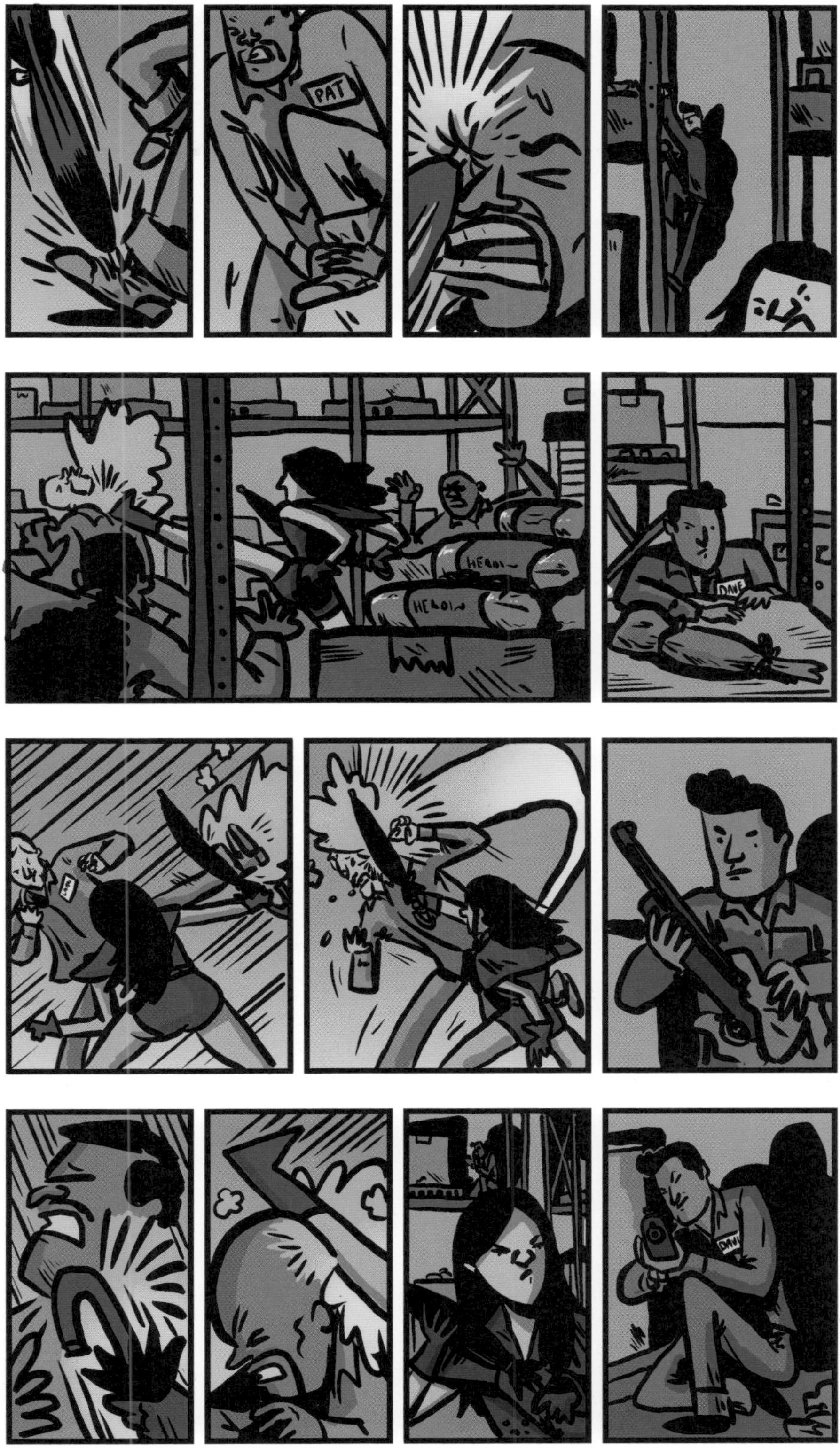
PAT
HEROIN
HEROIN
DAVE

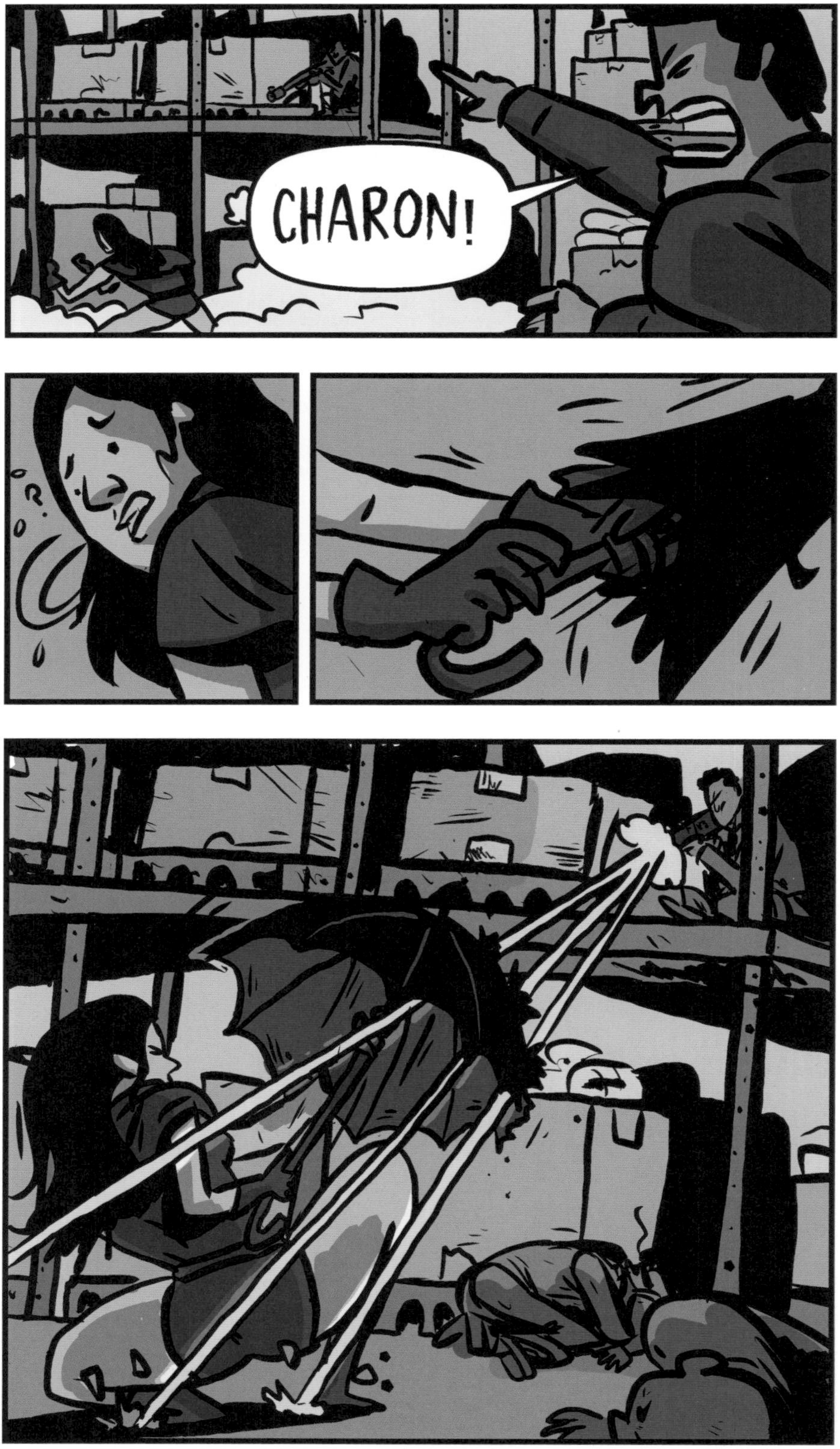
CHARON!

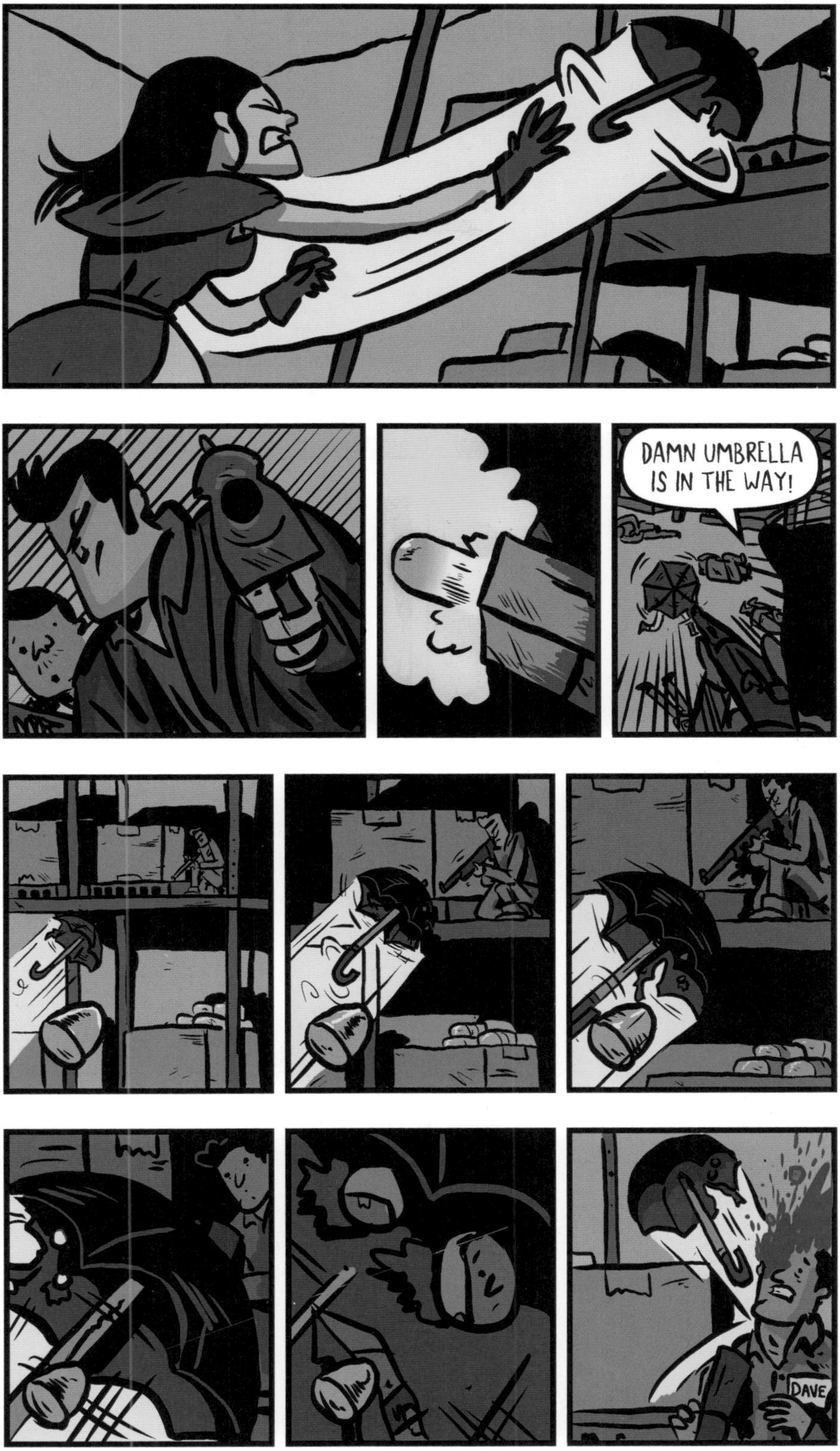
DAMN UMBRELLA IS IN THE WAY!
DAVE

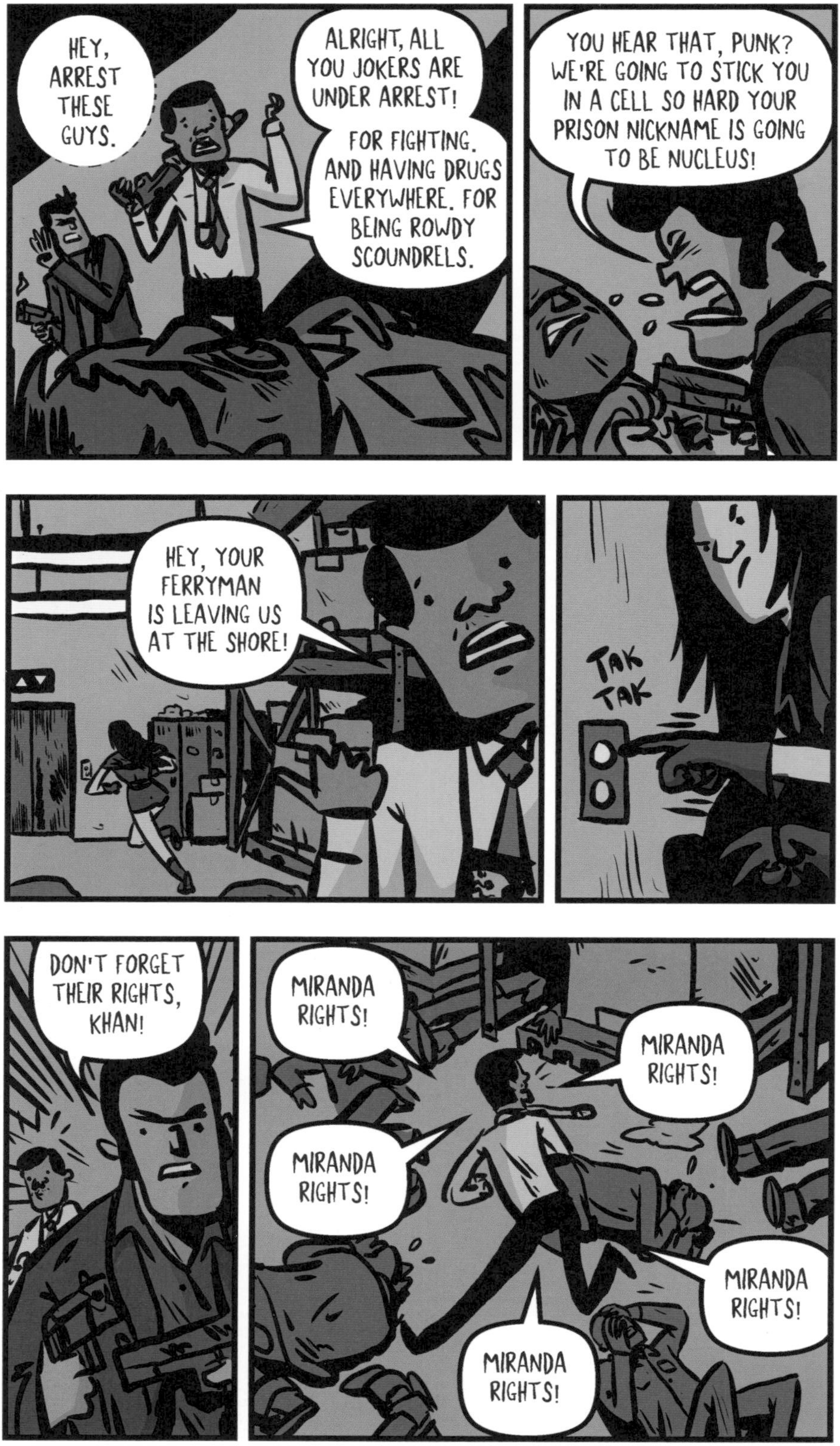
HEY, ARREST THESE GUYS.
ALRIGHT, ALL YOU JOKERS ARE UNDER ARREST!
FOR FIGHTING. AND HAVING DRUGS EVERYWHERE. FOR BEING ROWDY SCOUNDRELS.
YOU HEAR THAT, PUNK? WE'RE GOING TO STICK YOU IN A CELL SO HARD YOUR PRISON NICKNAME IS GOING TO BE NUCLEUS!
HEY, YOUR FERRYMAN IS LEAVING US AT THE SHORE!
TAK TAK
DON'T FORGET THEIR RIGHTS, KHAN!
MIRANDA RIGHTS!
MIRANDA RIGHTS!
MIRANDA RIGHTS!
MIRANDA RIGHTS!
MIRANDA RIGHTS!

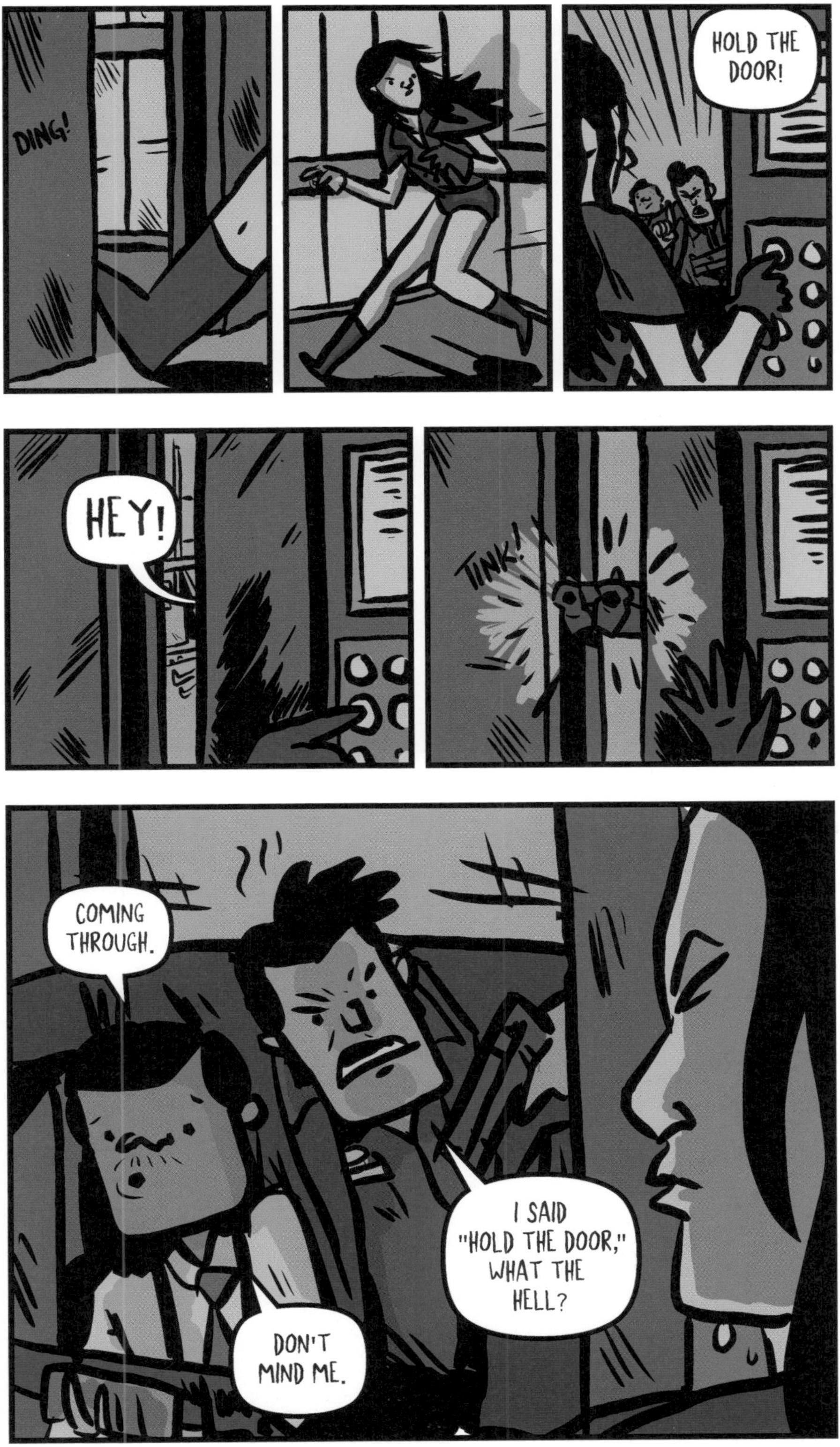
DING!
HOLD THE DOOR!
HEY!
TINK!
COMING THROUGH.
I SAID "HOLD THE DOOR," WHAT THE HELL?
DON'T MIND ME.

IT'S JUST COMMON COUR—

—TES—

PAT

SMACK

—Y!

SNATCH!

GRAB!

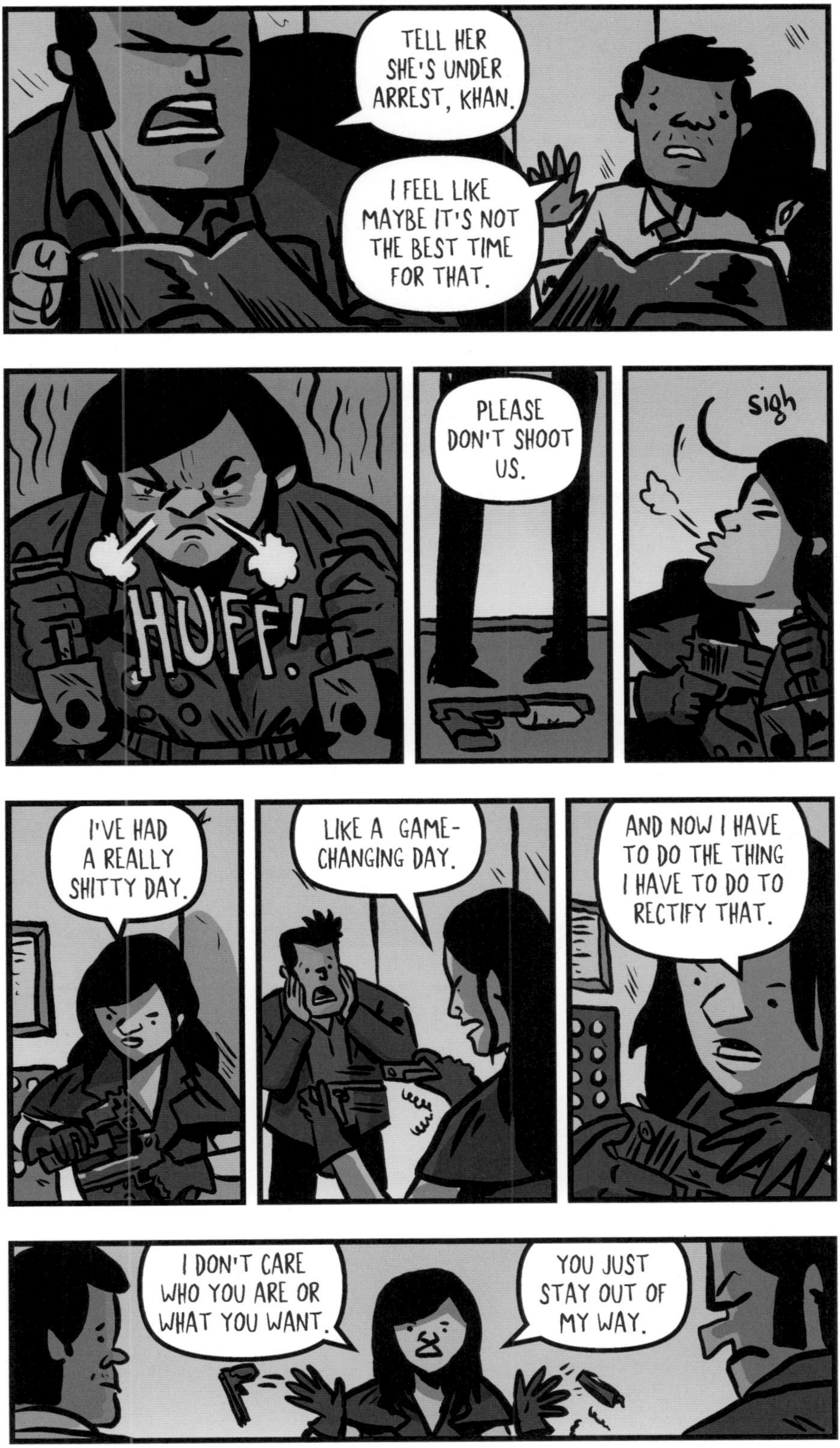
TELL HER SHE'S UNDER ARREST, KHAN.
I FEEL LIKE MAYBE IT'S NOT THE BEST TIME FOR THAT.
HUFF!
PLEASE DON'T SHOOT US.
sigh
I'VE HAD A REALLY SHITTY DAY.
LIKE A GAME-CHANGING DAY.
AND NOW I HAVE TO DO THE THING I HAVE TO DO TO RECTIFY THAT.
I DON'T CARE WHO YOU ARE OR WHAT YOU WANT.
YOU JUST STAY OUT OF MY WAY.

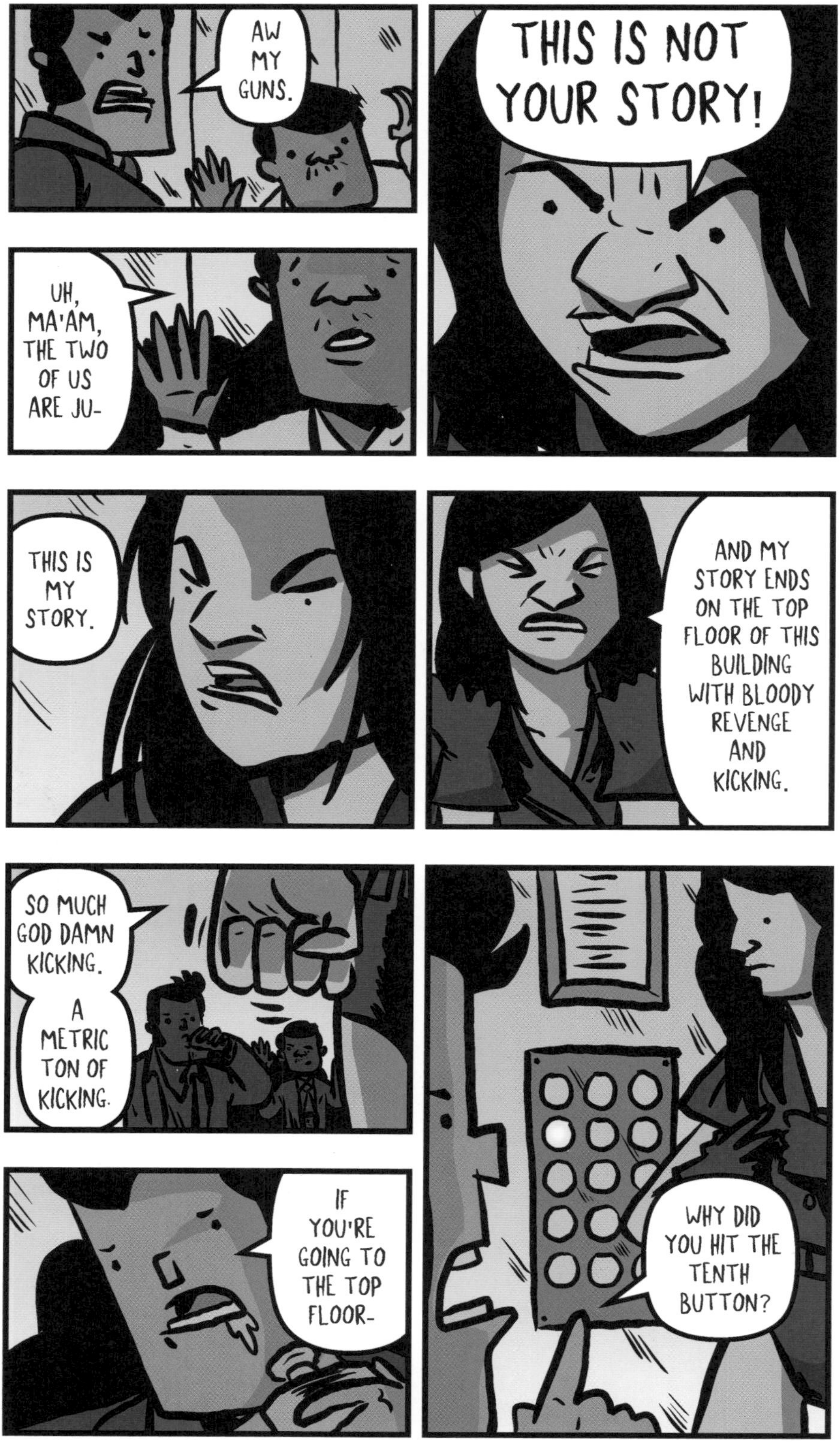
AW MY GUNS.
THIS IS NOT YOUR STORY!
UH, MA'AM, THE TWO OF US ARE JU-
THIS IS MY STORY.
AND MY STORY ENDS ON THE TOP FLOOR OF THIS BUILDING WITH BLOODY REVENGE AND KICKING.
SO MUCH GOD DAMN KICKING.
A METRIC TON OF KICKING.
IF YOU'RE GOING TO THE TOP FLOOR-
WHY DID YOU HIT THE TENTH BUTTON?

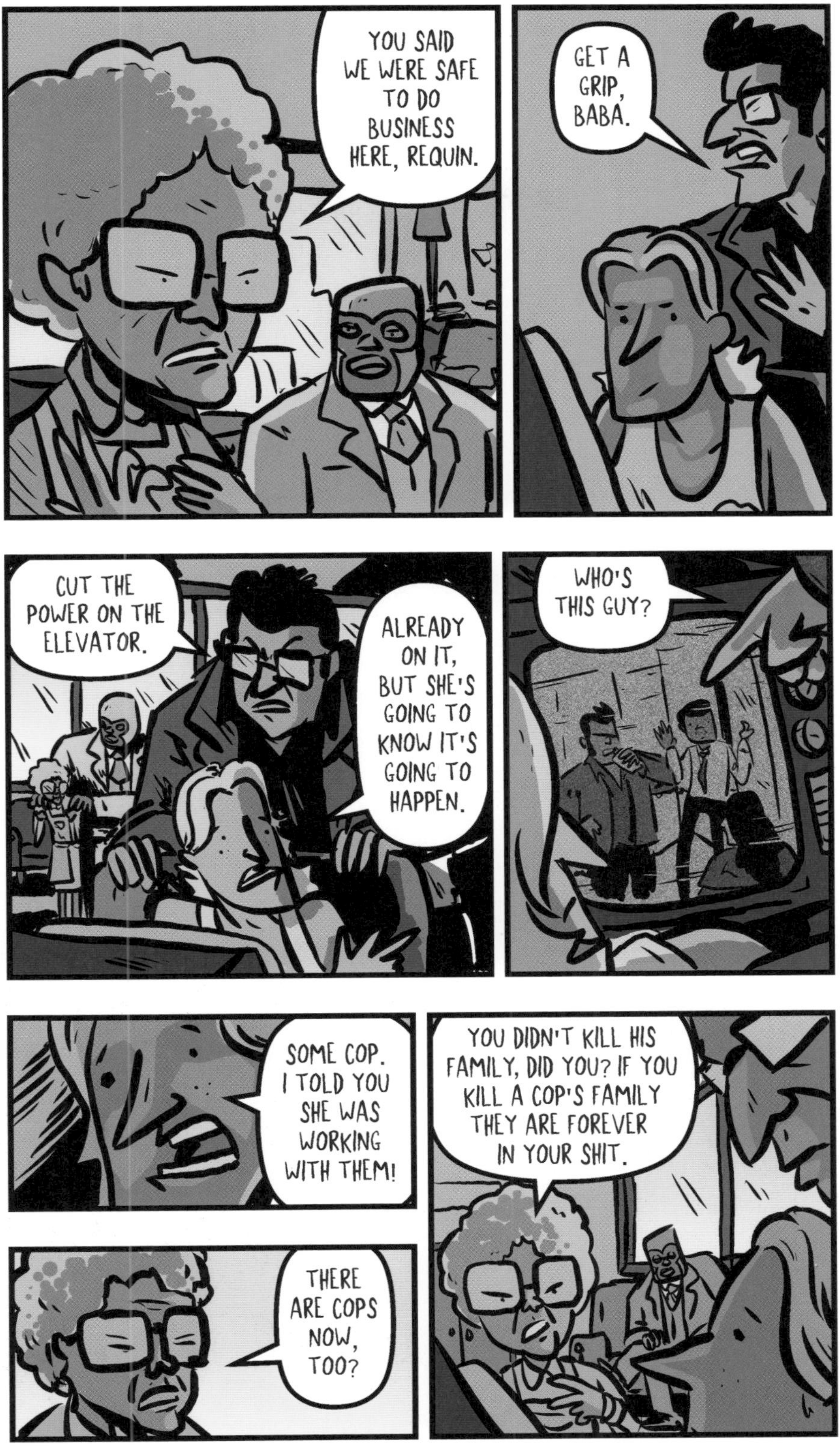

YOU SAID WE WERE SAFE TO DO BUSINESS HERE, REQUIN.
GET A GRIP, BABA.
CUT THE POWER ON THE ELEVATOR.
ALREADY ON IT, BUT SHE'S GOING TO KNOW IT'S GOING TO HAPPEN.
WHO'S THIS GUY?
SOME COP. I TOLD YOU SHE WAS WORKING WITH THEM!
THERE ARE COPS NOW, TOO?
YOU DIDN'T KILL HIS FAMILY, DID YOU? IF YOU KILL A COP'S FAMILY THEY ARE FOREVER IN YOUR SHIT.

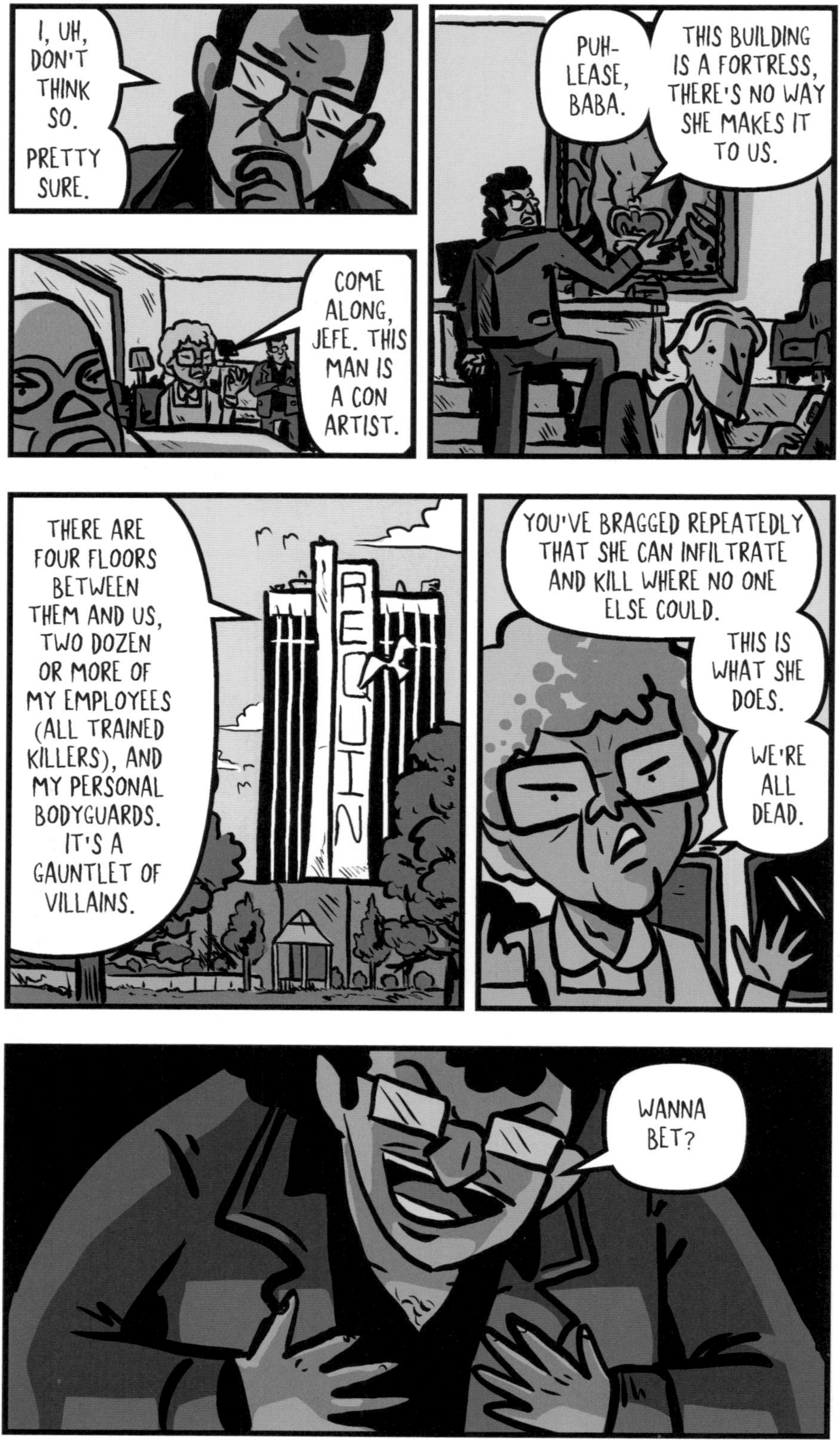
I, UH, DON'T THINK SO.
PRETTY SURE.
PUH-LEASE, BABA.
THIS BUILDING IS A FORTRESS, THERE'S NO WAY SHE MAKES IT TO US.
COME ALONG, JEFE. THIS MAN IS A CON ARTIST.
THERE ARE FOUR FLOORS BETWEEN THEM AND US, TWO DOZEN OR MORE OF MY EMPLOYEES (ALL TRAINED KILLERS), AND MY PERSONAL BODYGUARDS. IT'S A GAUNTLET OF VILLAINS.
REQUIN
YOU'VE BRAGGED REPEATEDLY THAT SHE CAN INFILTRATE AND KILL WHERE NO ONE ELSE COULD.
THIS IS WHAT SHE DOES.
WE'RE ALL DEAD.
WANNA BET?

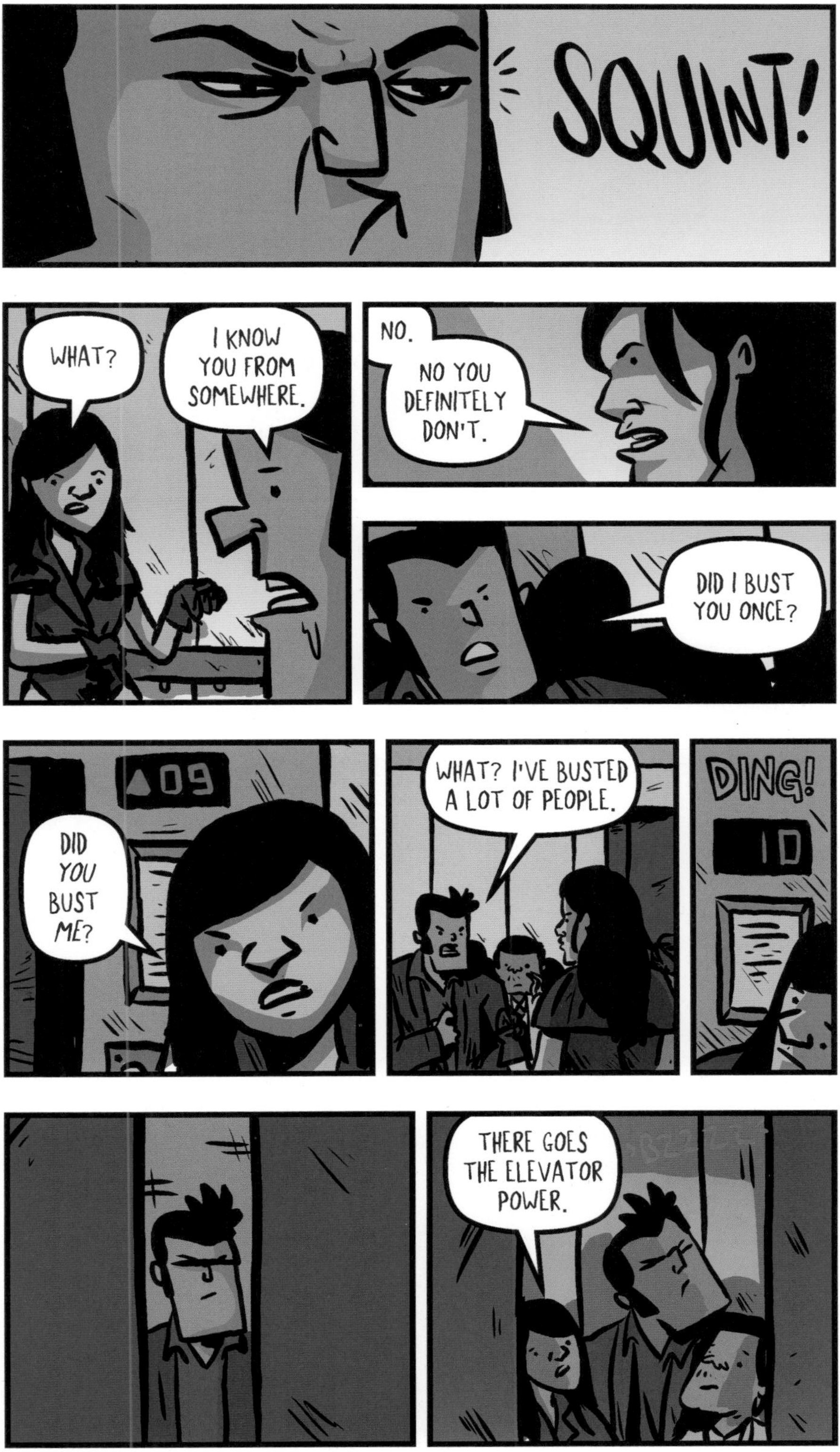
SQUINT!
WHAT?
I KNOW YOU FROM SOMEWHERE.
NO.
NO YOU DEFINITELY DON'T.
DID I BUST YOU ONCE?
09
DID YOU BUST ME?
WHAT? I'VE BUSTED A LOT OF PEOPLE.
DING!
10
THERE GOES THE ELEVATOR POWER.

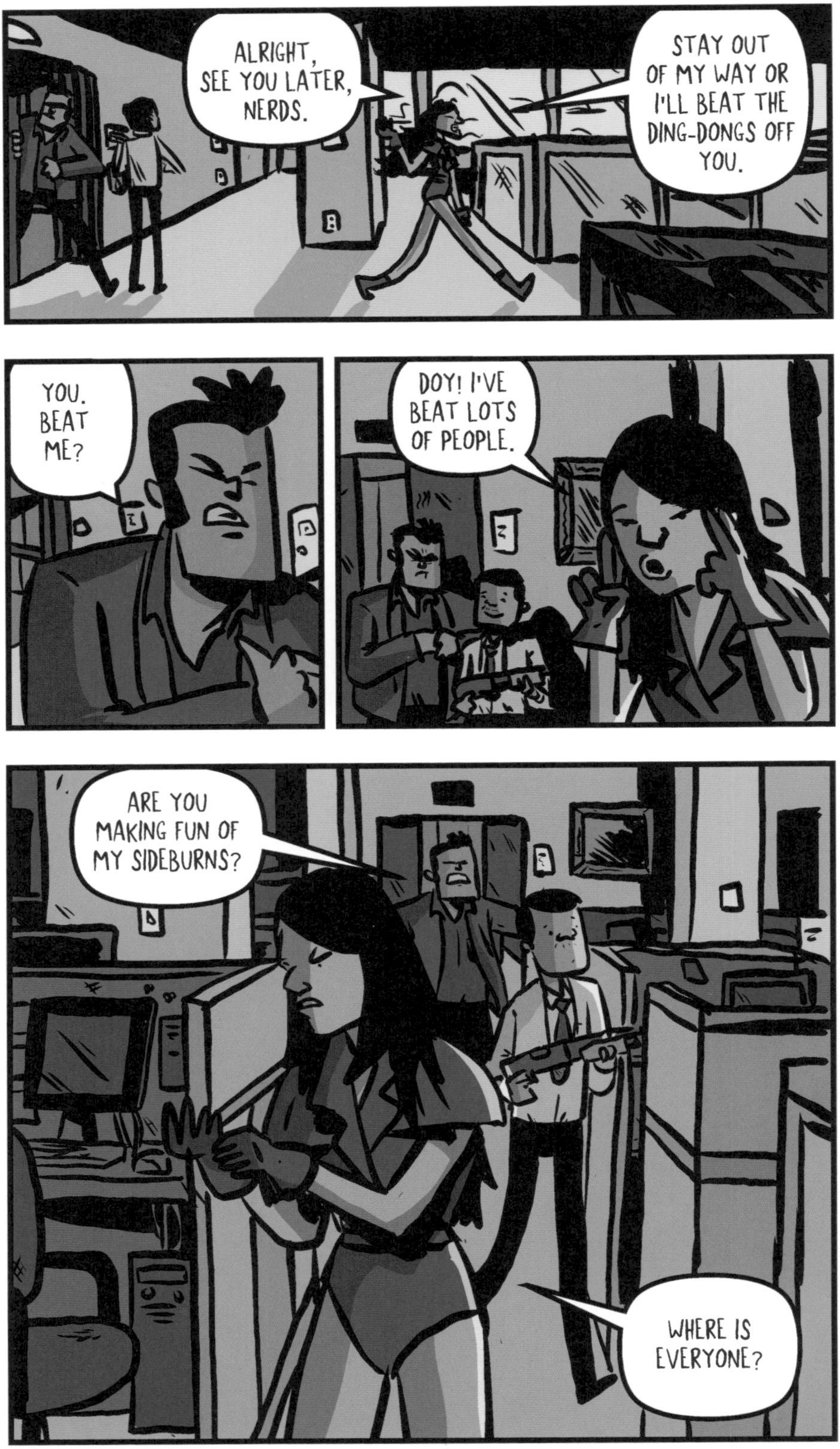
ALRIGHT, SEE YOU LATER, NERDS.
STAY OUT OF MY WAY OR I'LL BEAT THE DING-DONGS OFF YOU.
YOU. BEAT ME?
DOY! I'VE BEAT LOTS OF PEOPLE.
ARE YOU MAKING FUN OF MY SIDEBURNS?
WHERE IS EVERYONE?

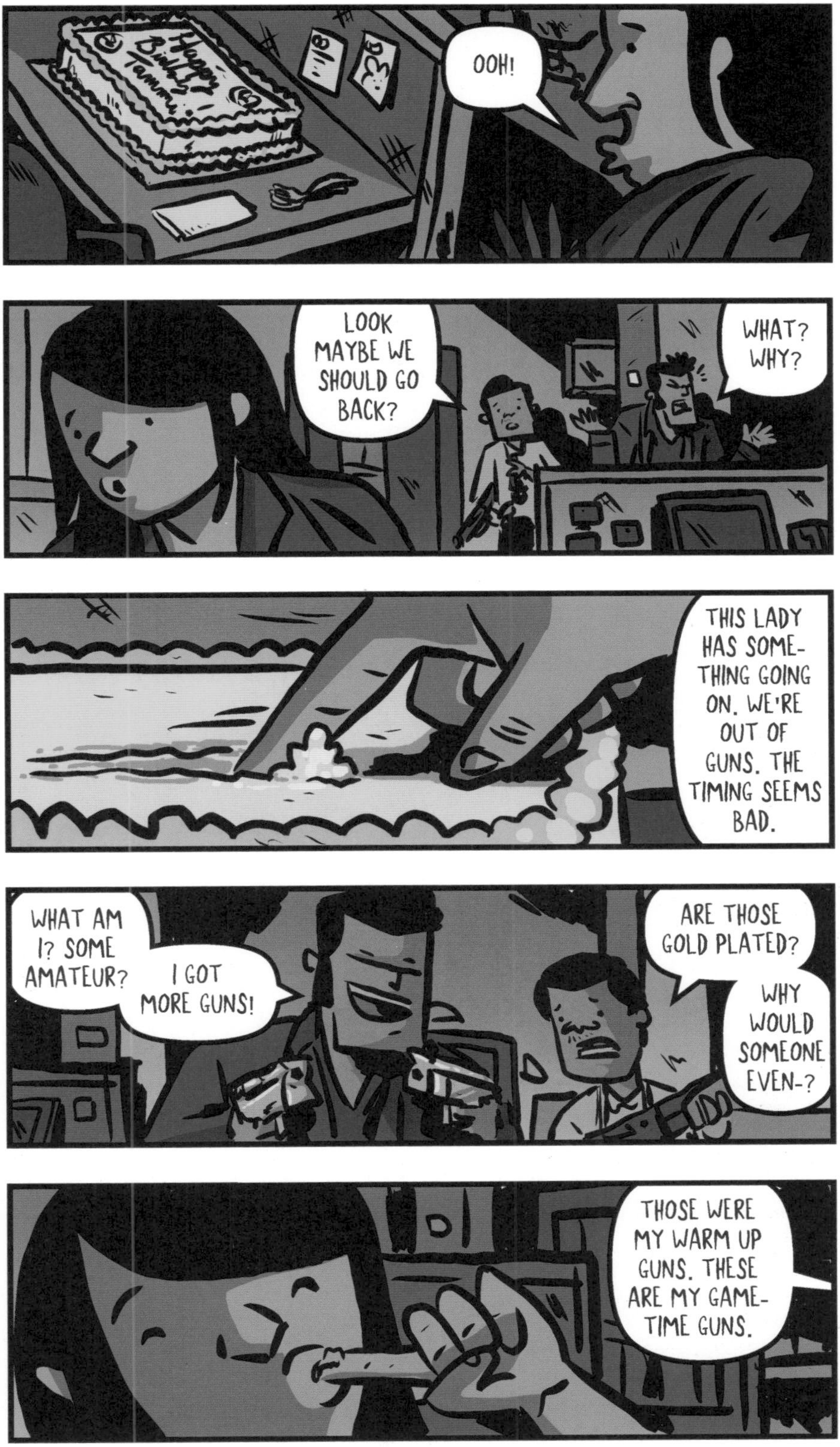
OOH!
LOOK MAYBE WE SHOULD GO BACK?
WHAT? WHY?
THIS LADY HAS SOME-THING GOING ON. WE'RE OUT OF GUNS. THE TIMING SEEMS BAD.
WHAT AM I? SOME AMATEUR?
I GOT MORE GUNS!
ARE THOSE GOLD PLATED?
WHY WOULD SOMEONE EVEN-?
THOSE WERE MY WARM UP GUNS. THESE ARE MY GAME-TIME GUNS.

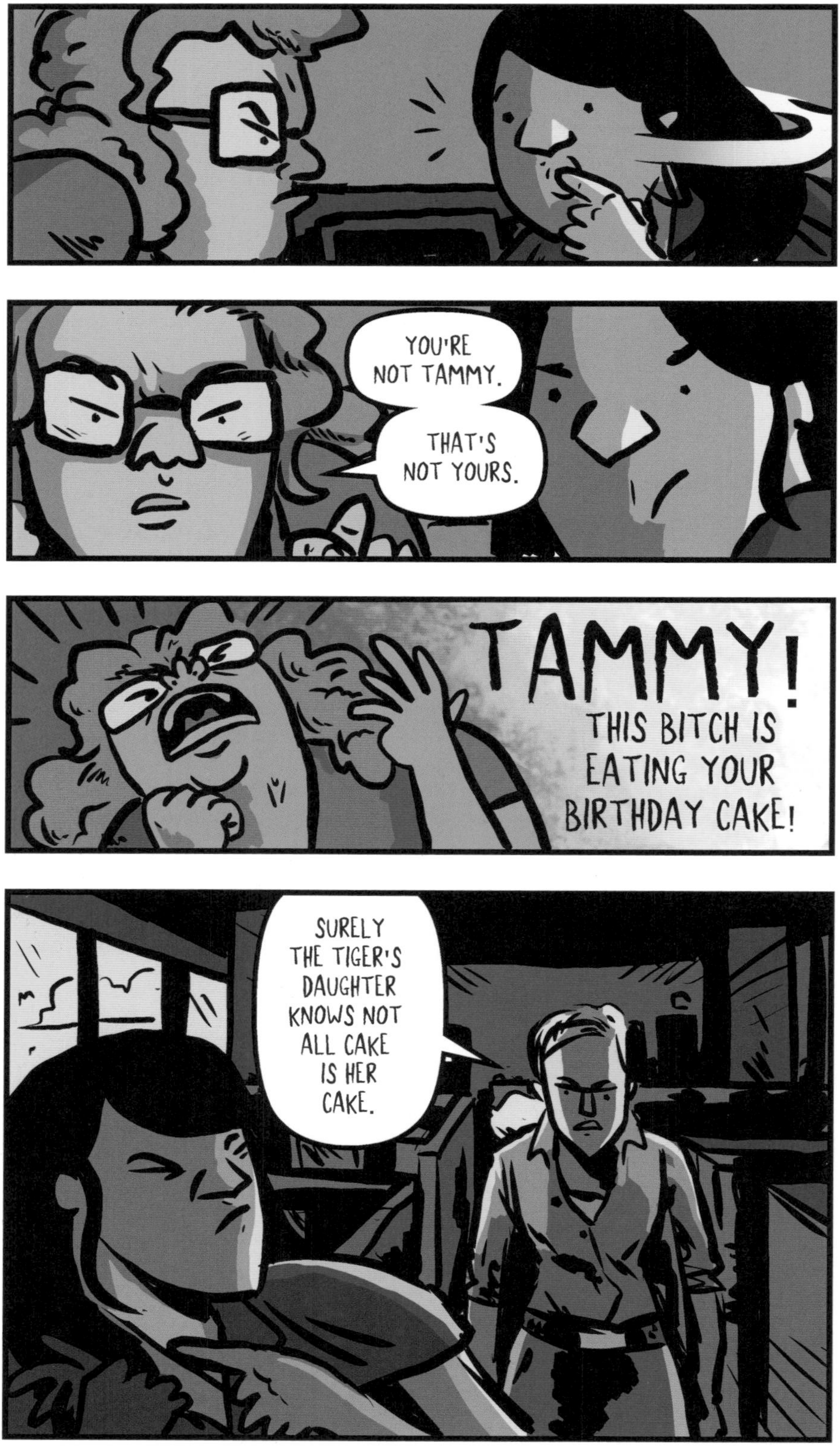
YOU'RE NOT TAMMY.
THAT'S NOT YOURS.
TAMMY!
THIS BITCH IS EATING YOUR BIRTHDAY CAKE!
SURELY THE TIGER'S DAUGHTER KNOWS NOT ALL CAKE IS HER CAKE.

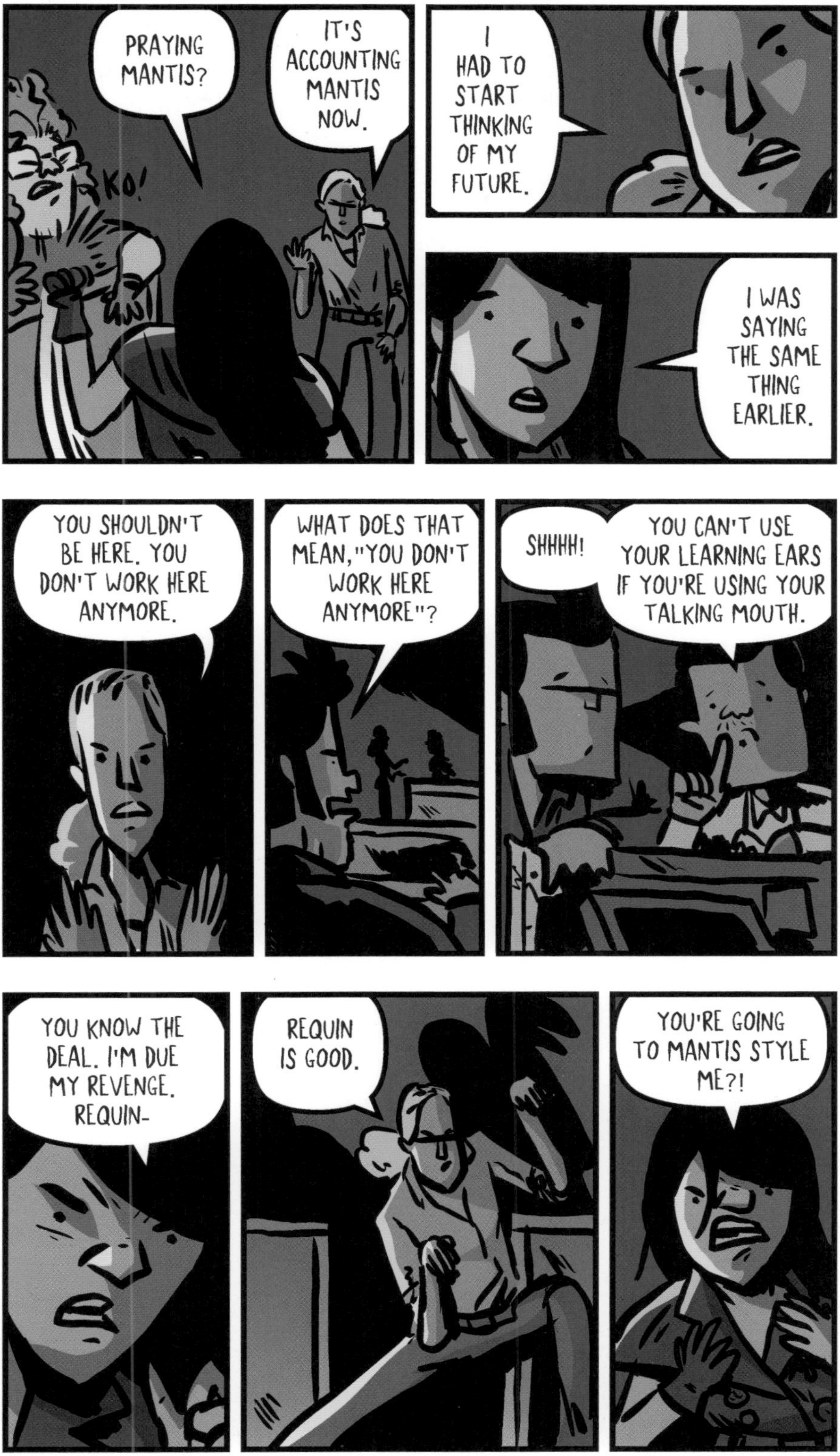
PRAYING MANTIS?
KO!
IT'S ACCOUNTING MANTIS NOW.
I HAD TO START THINKING OF MY FUTURE.
I WAS SAYING THE SAME THING EARLIER.
YOU SHOULDN'T BE HERE. YOU DON'T WORK HERE ANYMORE.
WHAT DOES THAT MEAN, "YOU DON'T WORK HERE ANYMORE"?
SHHHH!
YOU CAN'T USE YOUR LEARNING EARS IF YOU'RE USING YOUR TALKING MOUTH.
YOU KNOW THE DEAL. I'M DUE MY REVENGE. REQUIN-
REQUIN IS GOOD.
YOU'RE GOING TO MANTIS STYLE ME?!

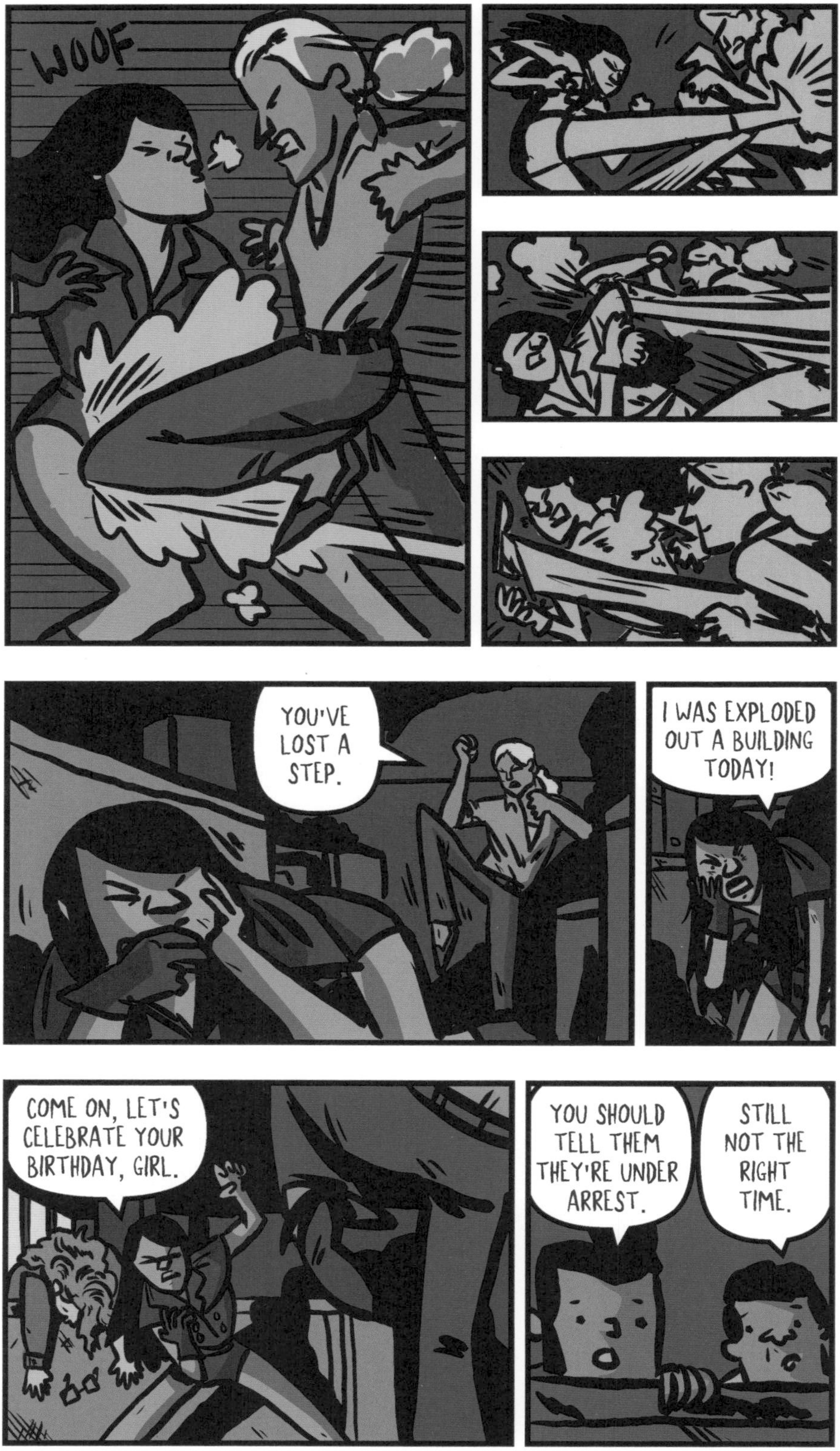
WOOF
YOU'VE LOST A STEP.
I WAS EXPLODED OUT A BUILDING TODAY!
COME ON, LET'S CELEBRATE YOUR BIRTHDAY, GIRL.
YOU SHOULD TELL THEM THEY'RE UNDER ARREST.
STILL NOT THE RIGHT TIME.

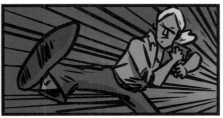

HEY CHARON, WHAT DID SHE MEAN YOU DON'T WORK HERE ANYMORE?

WHO'S KAREN? WHY DO YOU KEEP SAYING THAT?

THAT'S YOU! YOU'RE CHARON!

NO. I AM THE TIGER'S DAUGHTER.

WHAT DO YOUR FRIENDS CALL YOU?

THE TIGER'S DAUGHTER?

THERE'S NOT SOMETHING MORE CASUAL?

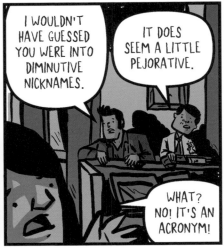

I WOULDN'T HAVE GUESSED YOU WERE INTO DIMINUTIVE NICKNAMES.

IT DOES SEEM A LITTLE PEJORATIVE.

WHAT? NO! IT'S AN ACRONYM!

MY EX CALLED ME "BABE"?

IT STANDS FOR BAD ASS BITCH EVERYDAY.

I THINK ITS AN ABBREVIATION FOR "BABY." LIKE YOU'RE A LITTLE BABY.

NOD NOD

GOD DAMN YOU, MARK NEWSMEYER.

RING RING

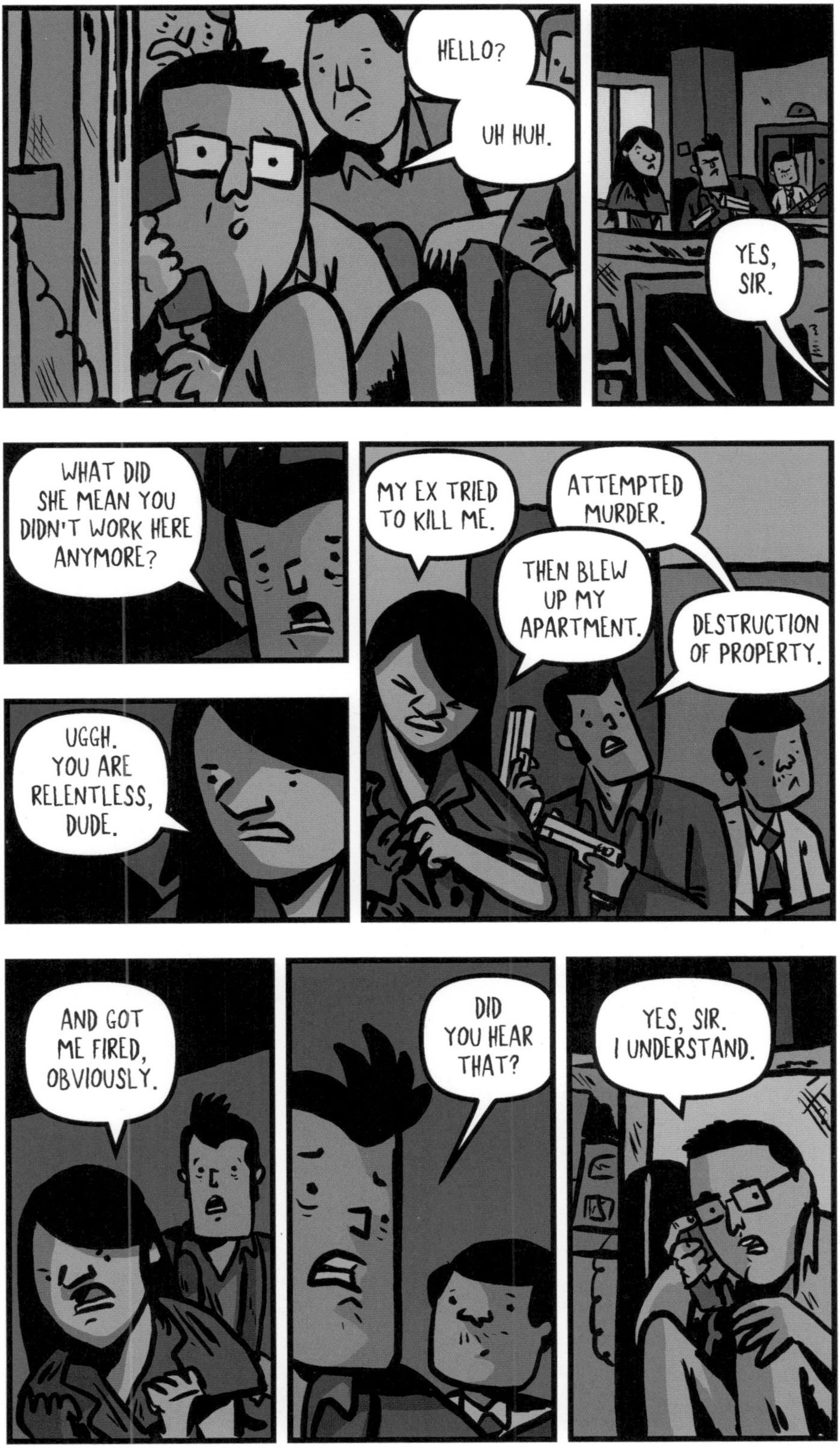
HELLO?
UH HUH.
YES, SIR.
WHAT DID SHE MEAN YOU DIDN'T WORK HERE ANYMORE?
UGGH. YOU ARE RELENTLESS, DUDE.
MY EX TRIED TO KILL ME.
ATTEMPTED MURDER.
THEN BLEW UP MY APARTMENT.
DESTRUCTION OF PROPERTY.
AND GOT ME FIRED, OBVIOUSLY.
DID YOU HEAR THAT?
YES, SIR. I UNDERSTAND.

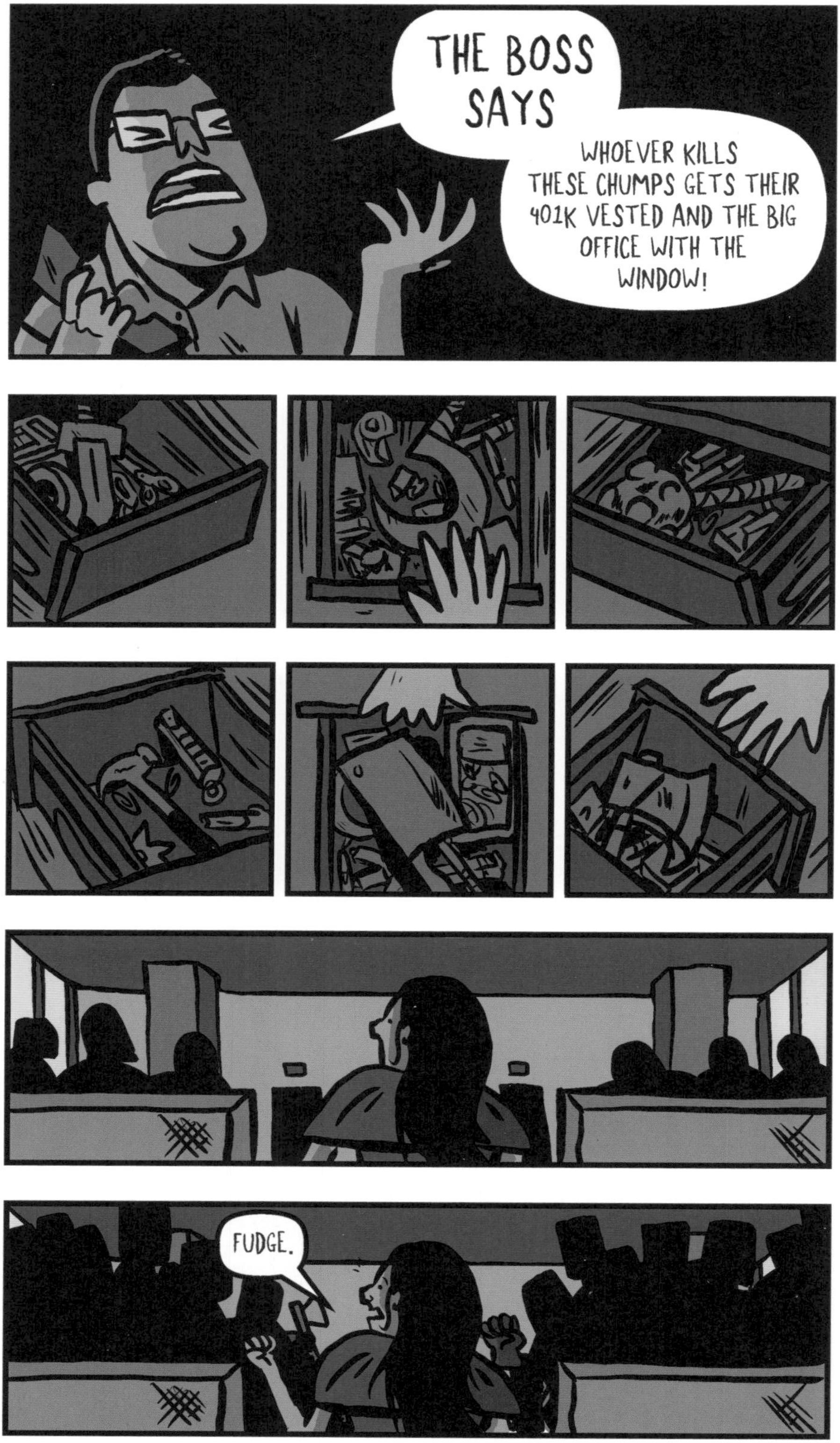
THE BOSS SAYS
WHOEVER KILLS THESE CHUMPS GETS THEIR 401K VESTED AND THE BIG OFFICE WITH THE WINDOW!
FUDGE.

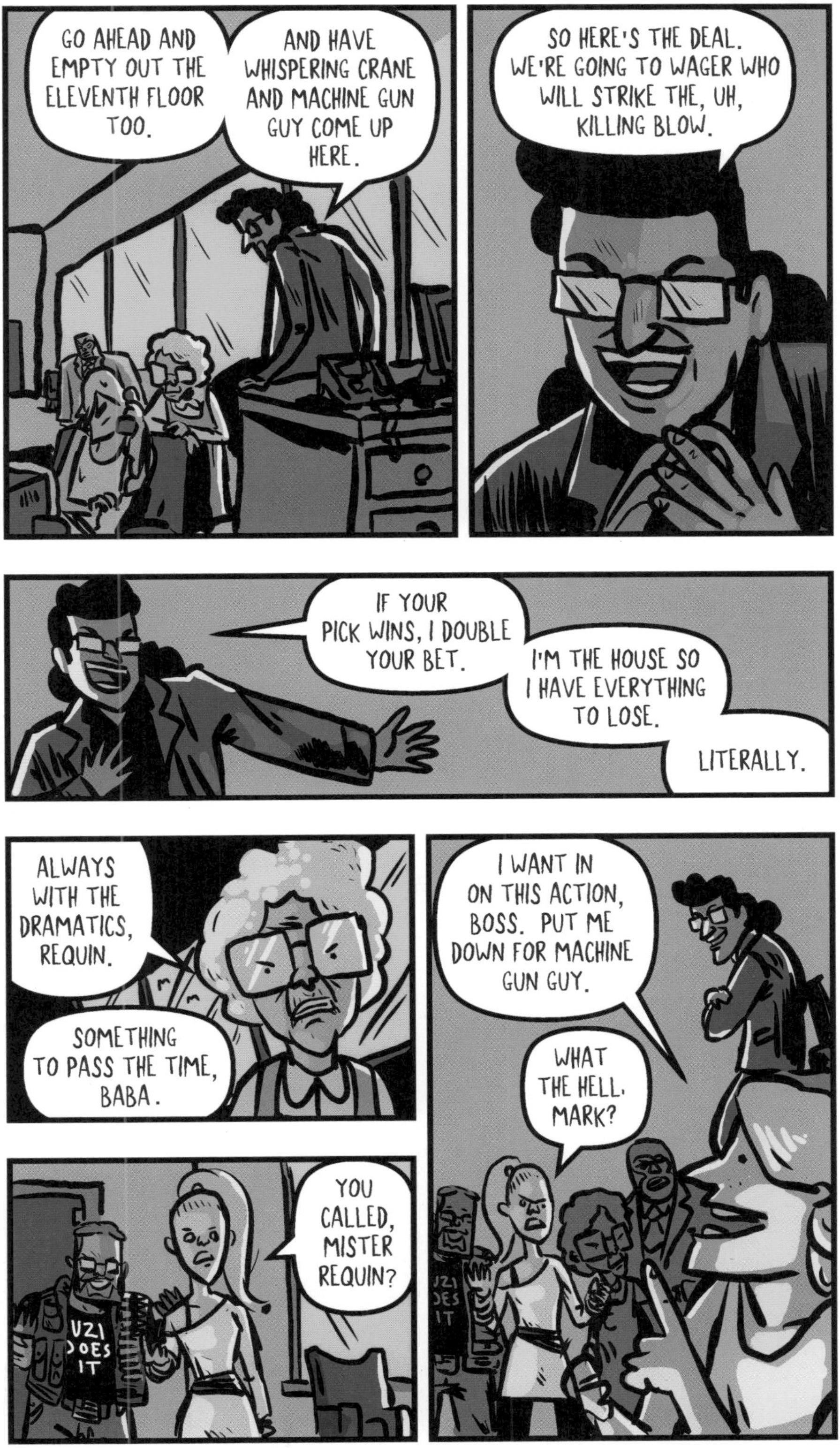
GO AHEAD AND EMPTY OUT THE ELEVENTH FLOOR TOO.
AND HAVE WHISPERING CRANE AND MACHINE GUN GUY COME UP HERE.
SO HERE'S THE DEAL. WE'RE GOING TO WAGER WHO WILL STRIKE THE, UH, KILLING BLOW.
IF YOUR PICK WINS, I DOUBLE YOUR BET.
I'M THE HOUSE SO I HAVE EVERYTHING TO LOSE.
LITERALLY.
ALWAYS WITH THE DRAMATICS, REQUIN.
SOMETHING TO PASS THE TIME, BABA.
YOU CALLED, MISTER REQUIN?
UZI DOES IT
I WANT IN ON THIS ACTION, BOSS. PUT ME DOWN FOR MACHINE GUN GUY.
WHAT THE HELL, MARK?

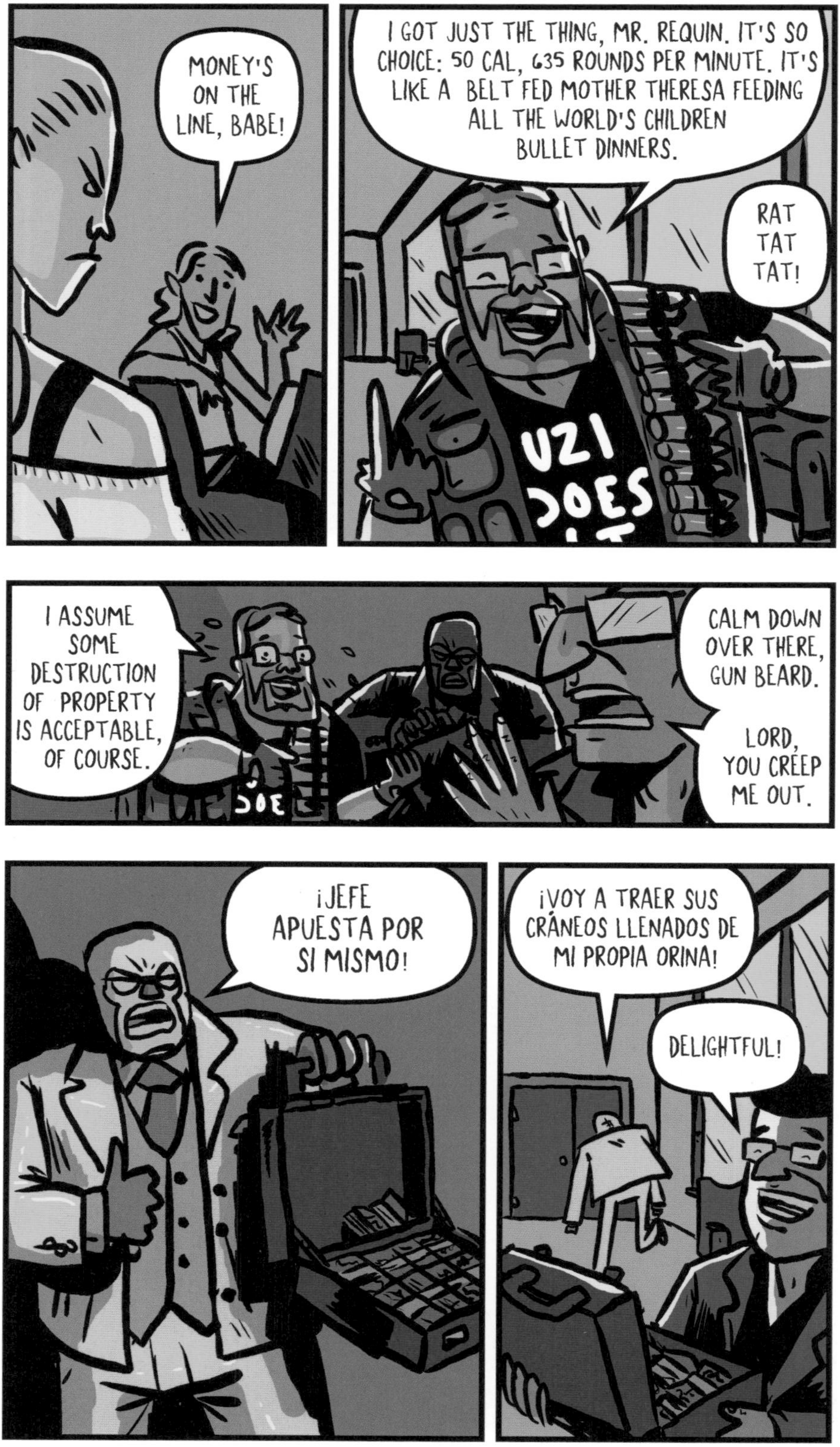
MONEY'S ON THE LINE, BABE!
I GOT JUST THE THING, MR. REQUIN. IT'S SO CHOICE: 50 CAL, 635 ROUNDS PER MINUTE. IT'S LIKE A BELT FED MOTHER THERESA FEEDING ALL THE WORLD'S CHILDREN BULLET DINNERS.
RAT TAT TAT!
UZI DOES
I ASSUME SOME DESTRUCTION OF PROPERTY IS ACCEPTABLE, OF COURSE.
CALM DOWN OVER THERE, GUN BEARD.
LORD, YOU CREEP ME OUT.
¡JEFE APUESTA POR SI MISMO!
¡VOY A TRAER SUS CRÁNEOS LLENADOS DE MI PROPIA ORINA!
DELIGHTFUL!

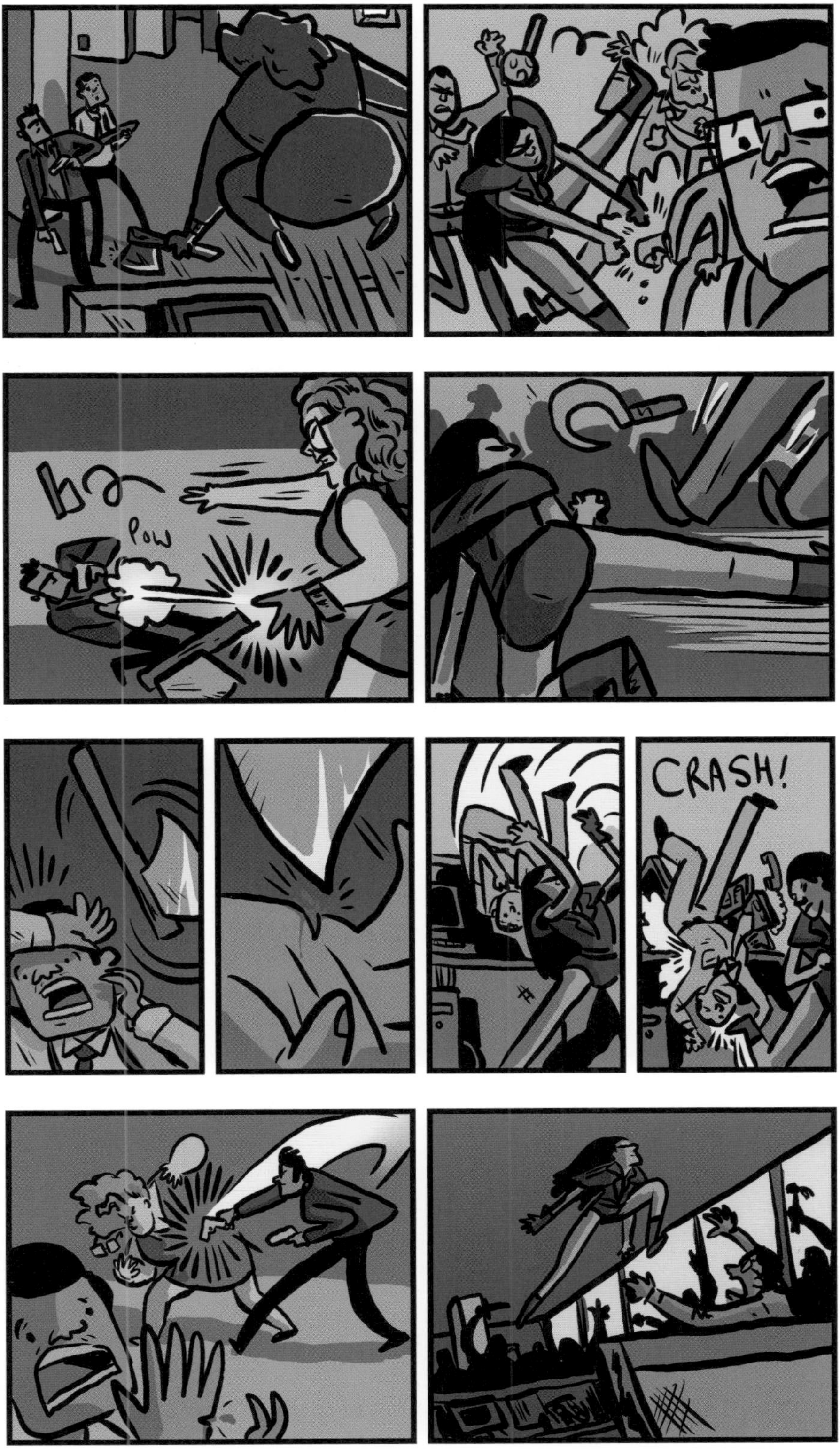
POW
CRASH!

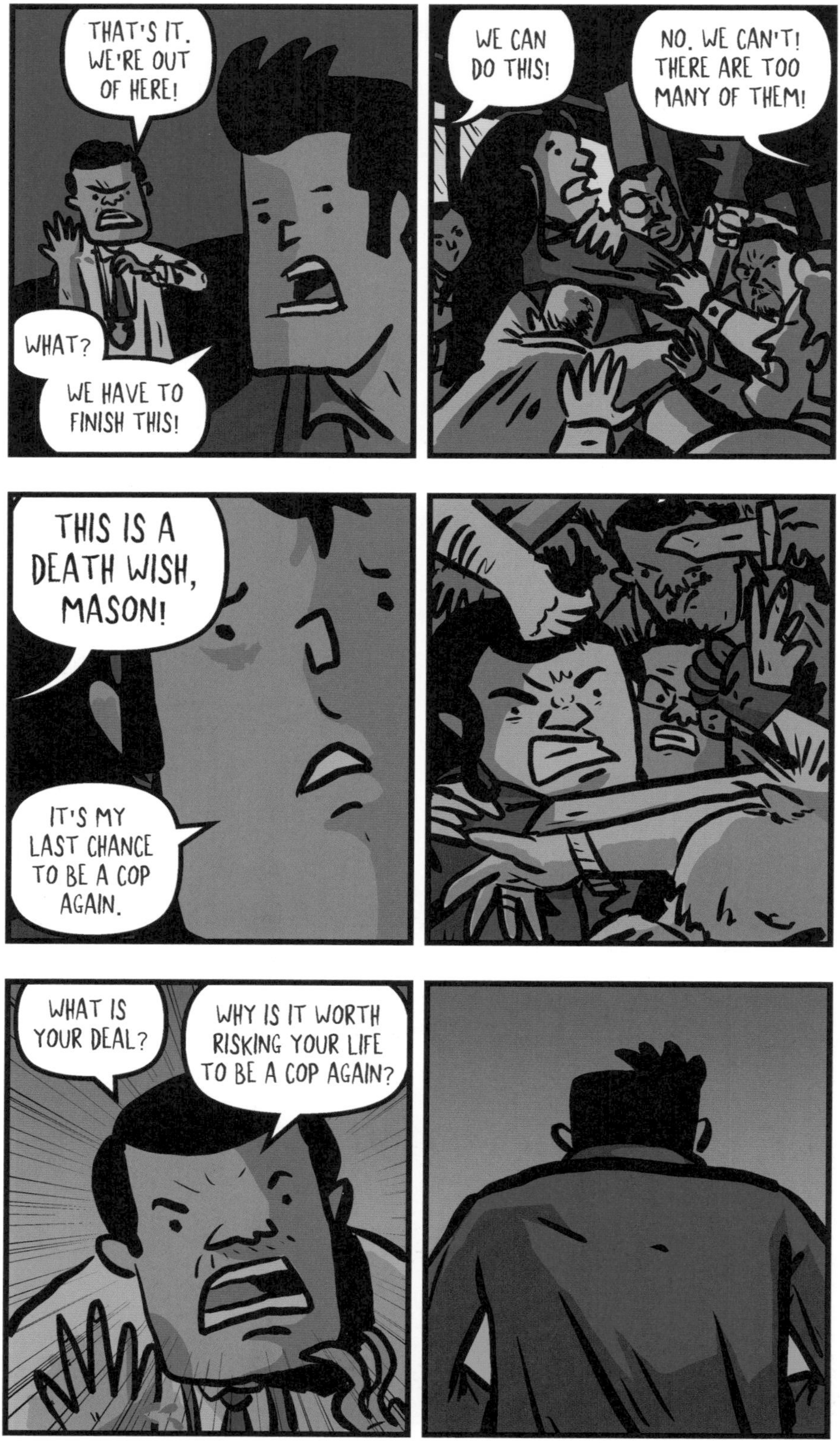
THAT'S IT. WE'RE OUT OF HERE!
WHAT?
WE HAVE TO FINISH THIS!
WE CAN DO THIS!
NO. WE CAN'T! THERE ARE TOO MANY OF THEM!
THIS IS A DEATH WISH, MASON!
IT'S MY LAST CHANCE TO BE A COP AGAIN.
WHAT IS YOUR DEAL?
WHY IS IT WORTH RISKING YOUR LIFE TO BE A COP AGAIN?

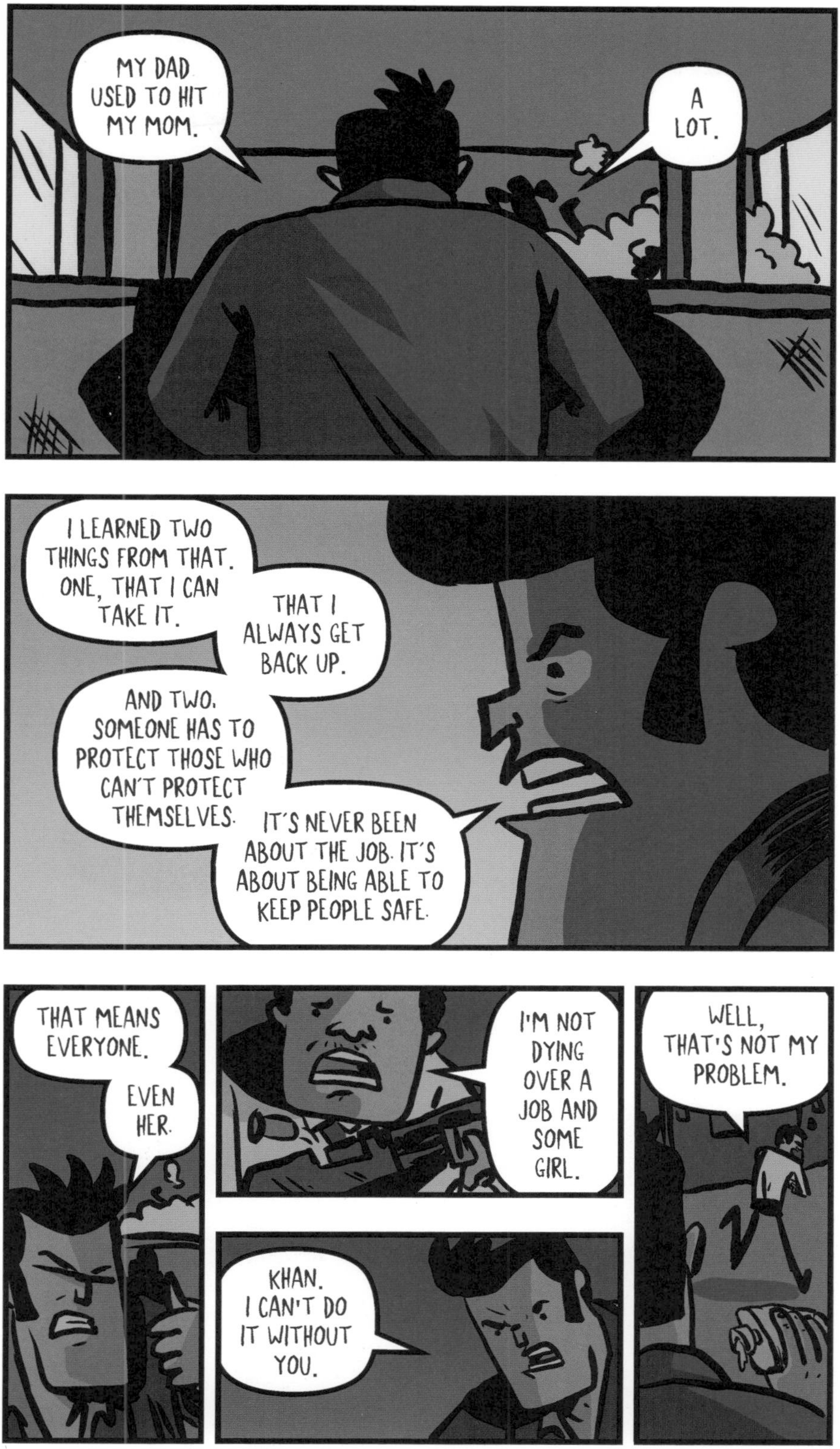
MY DAD USED TO HIT MY MOM.
A LOT.
I LEARNED TWO THINGS FROM THAT. ONE, THAT I CAN TAKE IT.
THAT I ALWAYS GET BACK UP.
AND TWO, SOMEONE HAS TO PROTECT THOSE WHO CAN'T PROTECT THEMSELVES.
IT'S NEVER BEEN ABOUT THE JOB. IT'S ABOUT BEING ABLE TO KEEP PEOPLE SAFE.
THAT MEANS EVERYONE.
EVEN HER.
I'M NOT DYING OVER A JOB AND SOME GIRL.
KHAN. I CAN'T DO IT WITHOUT YOU.
WELL, THAT'S NOT MY PROBLEM.

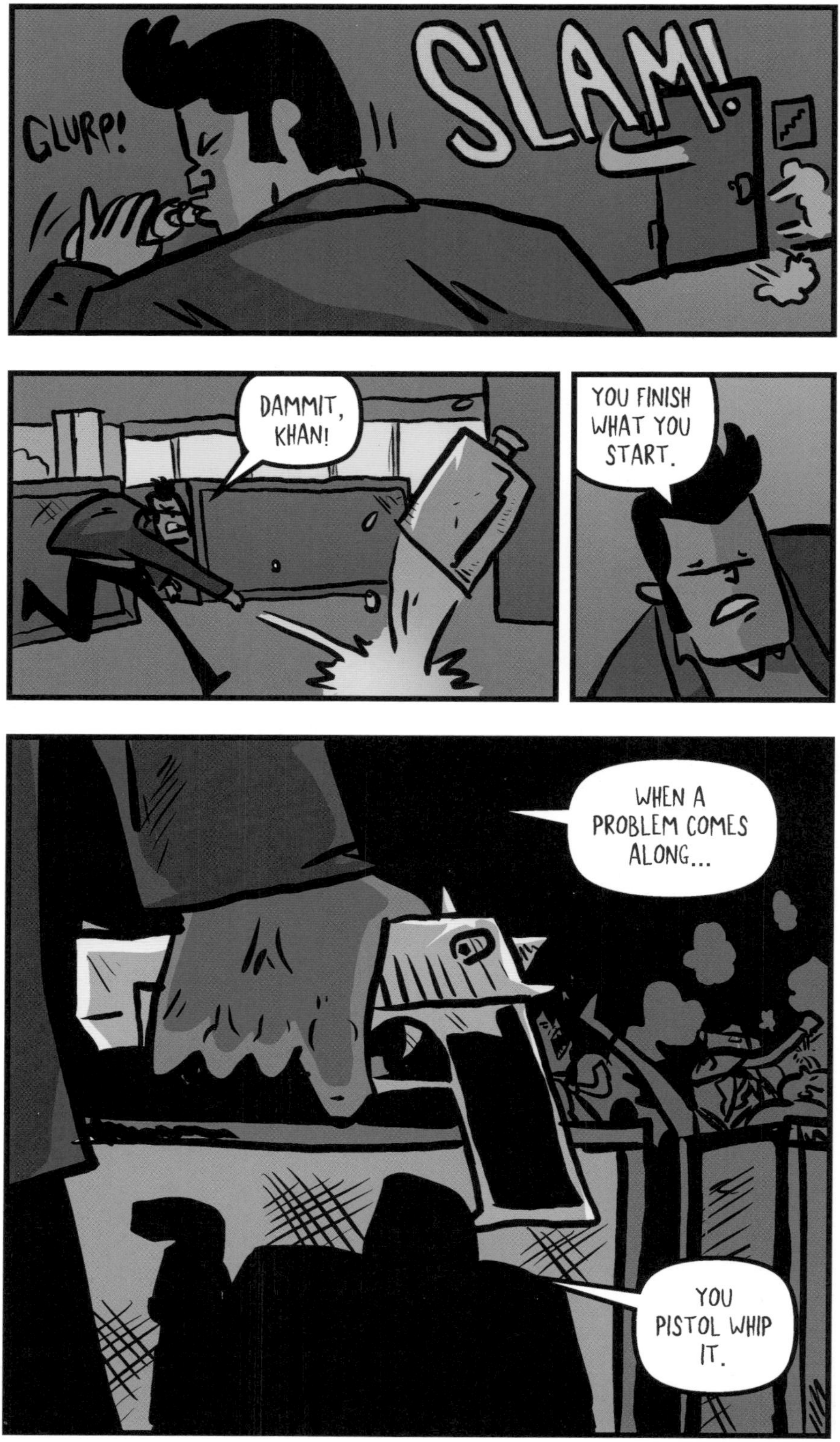
GLURP!
SLAM!
DAMMIT, KHAN!
YOU FINISH WHAT YOU START.
WHEN A PROBLEM COMES ALONG...
YOU PISTOL WHIP IT.

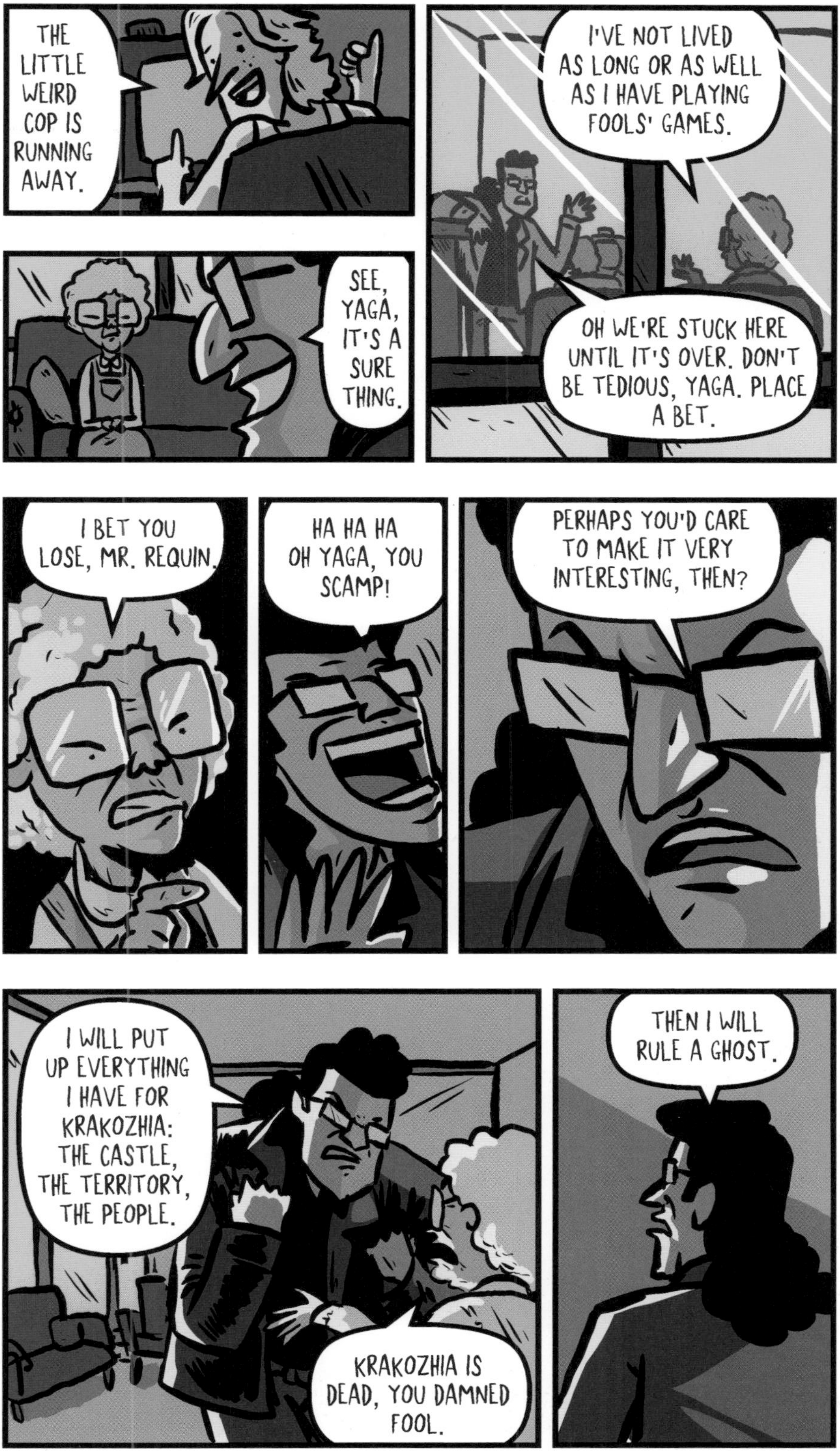
THE LITTLE WEIRD COP IS RUNNING AWAY.
I'VE NOT LIVED AS LONG OR AS WELL AS I HAVE PLAYING FOOLS' GAMES.
SEE, YAGA, IT'S A SURE THING.
OH WE'RE STUCK HERE UNTIL IT'S OVER. DON'T BE TEDIOUS, YAGA. PLACE A BET.
I BET YOU LOSE, MR. REQUIN.
HA HA HA OH YAGA, YOU SCAMP!
PERHAPS YOU'D CARE TO MAKE IT VERY INTERESTING, THEN?
I WILL PUT UP EVERYTHING I HAVE FOR KRAKOZHIA: THE CASTLE, THE TERRITORY, THE PEOPLE.
KRAKOZHIA IS DEAD, YOU DAMNED FOOL.
THEN I WILL RULE A GHOST.

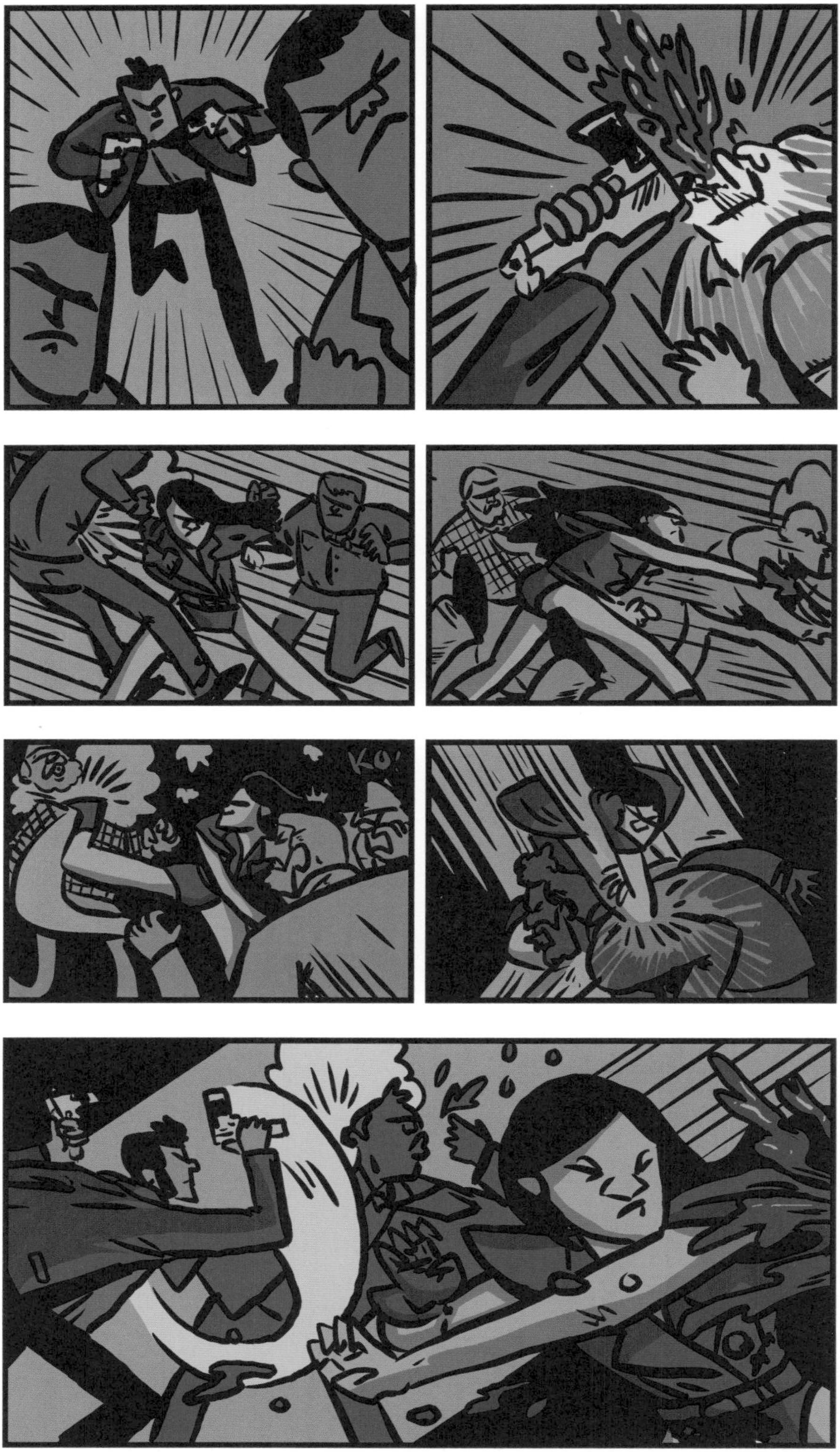
KO!

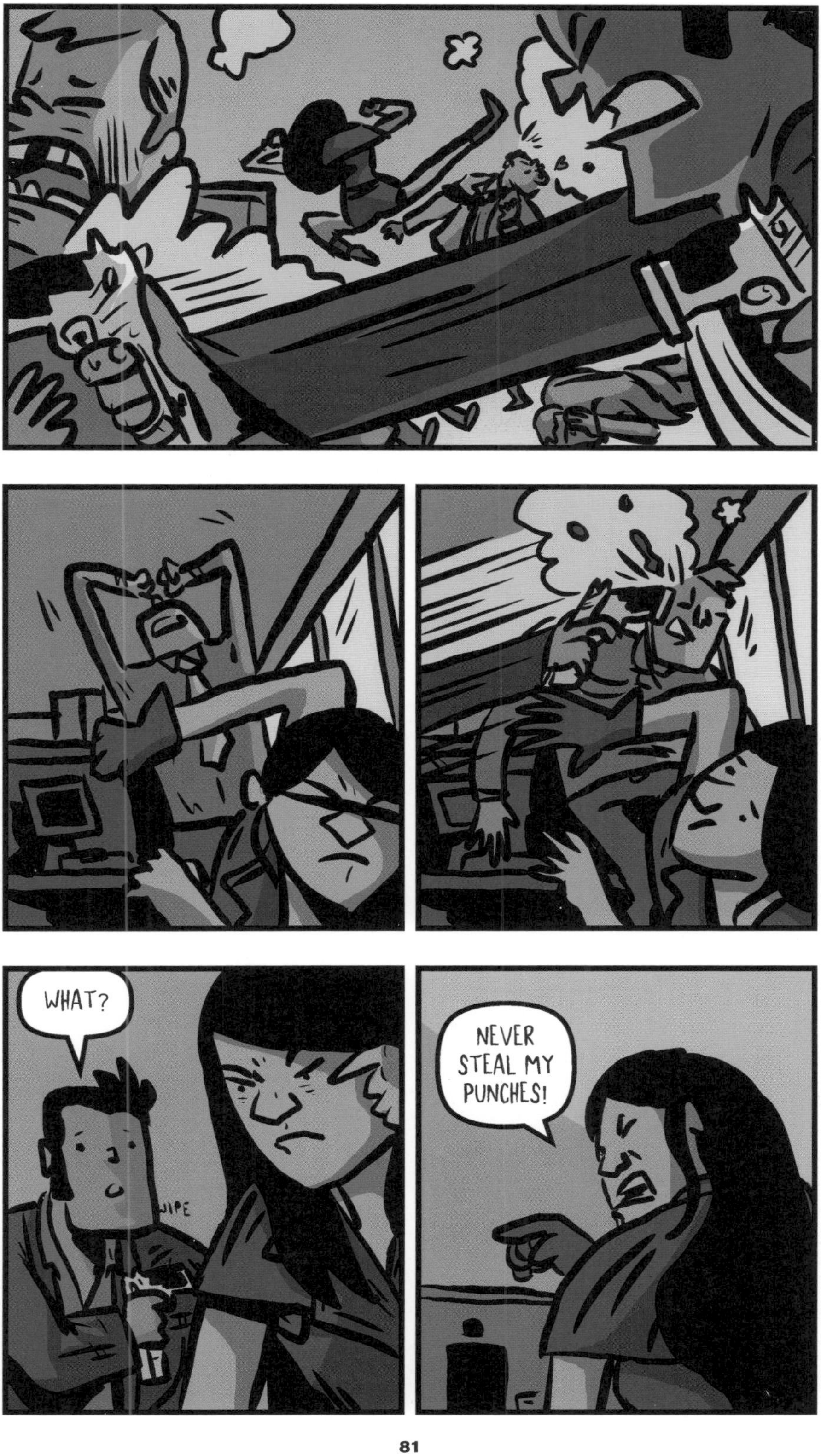
WHAT?
WIPE
NEVER STEAL MY PUNCHES!

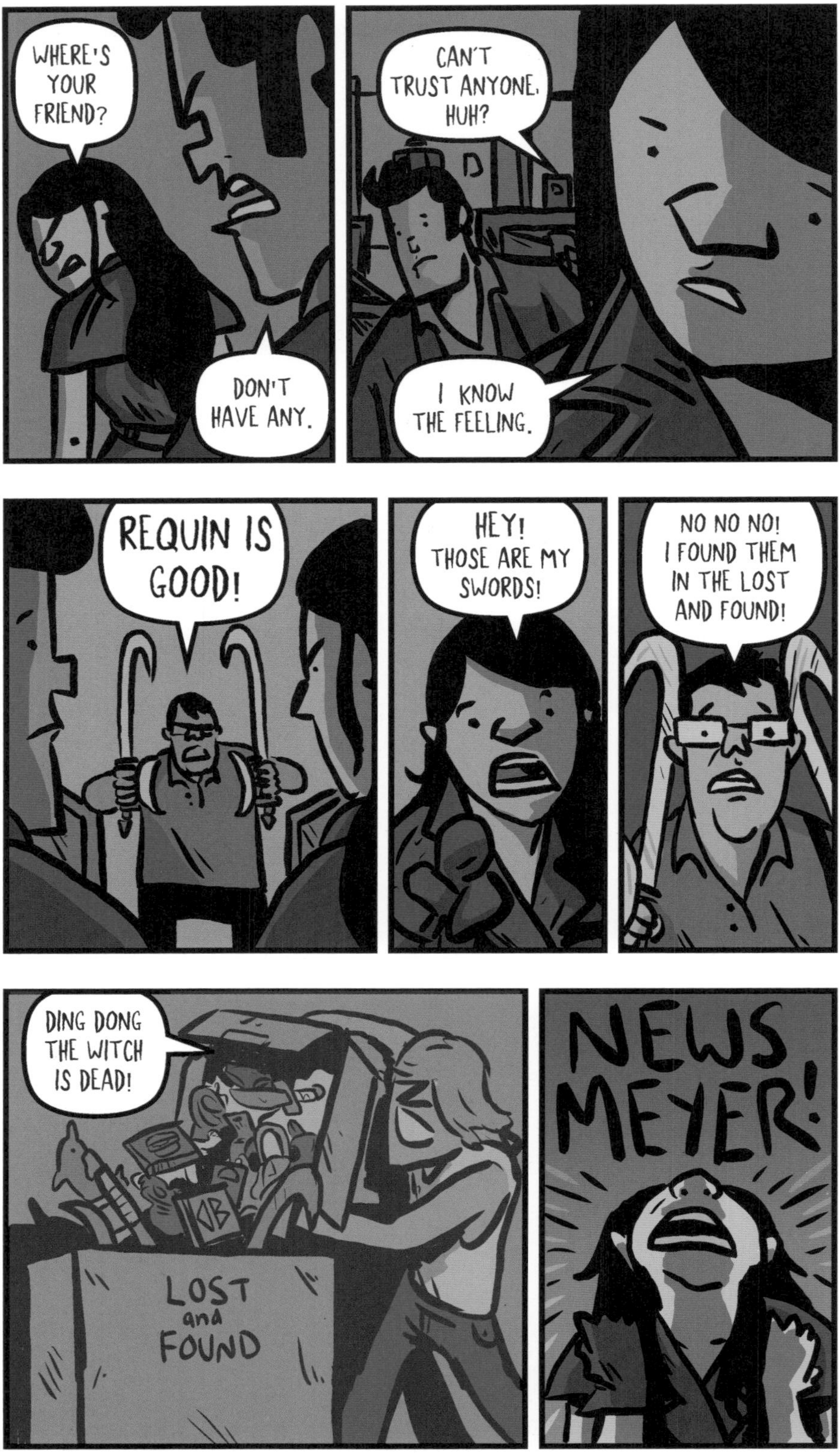
WHERE'S YOUR FRIEND?
DON'T HAVE ANY.
CAN'T TRUST ANYONE, HUH?
I KNOW THE FEELING.
REQUIN IS GOOD!
HEY! THOSE ARE MY SWORDS!
NO NO NO! I FOUND THEM IN THE LOST AND FOUND!
DING DONG THE WITCH IS DEAD!
LOST and FOUND
NEWS MEYER!

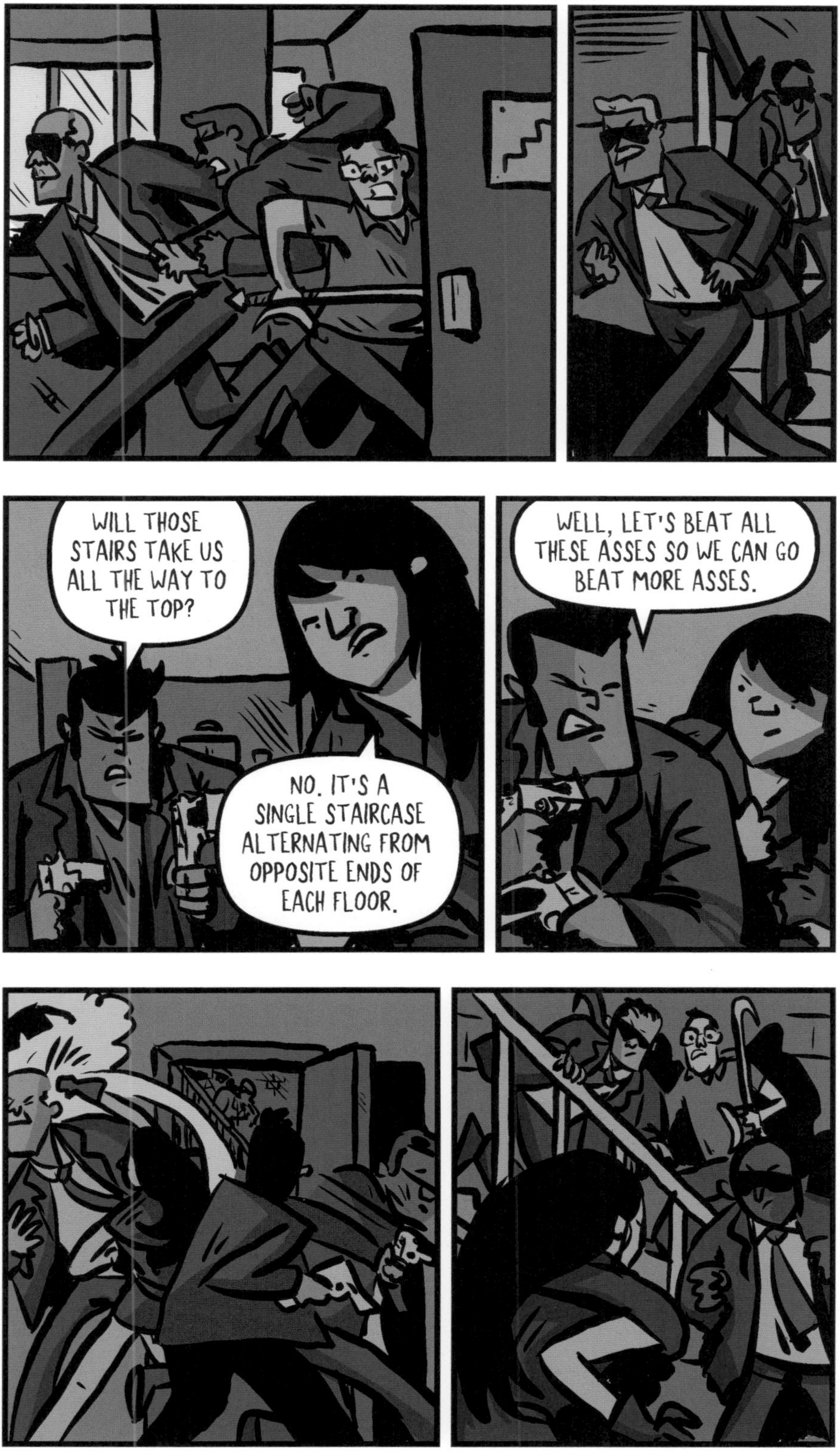
WILL THOSE STAIRS TAKE US ALL THE WAY TO THE TOP?
NO. IT'S A SINGLE STAIRCASE ALTERNATING FROM OPPOSITE ENDS OF EACH FLOOR.
WELL, LET'S BEAT ALL THESE ASSES SO WE CAN GO BEAT MORE ASSES.

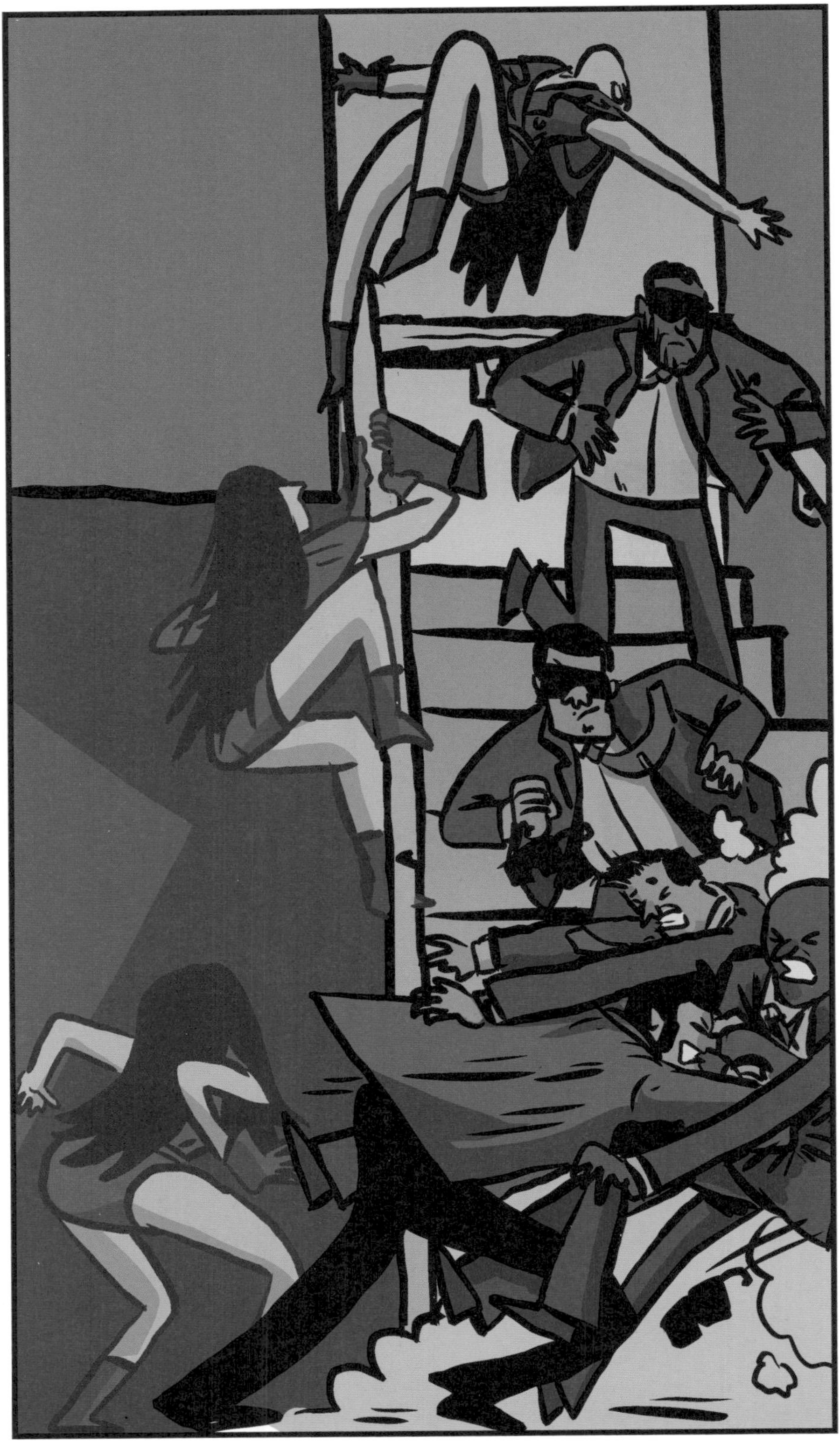

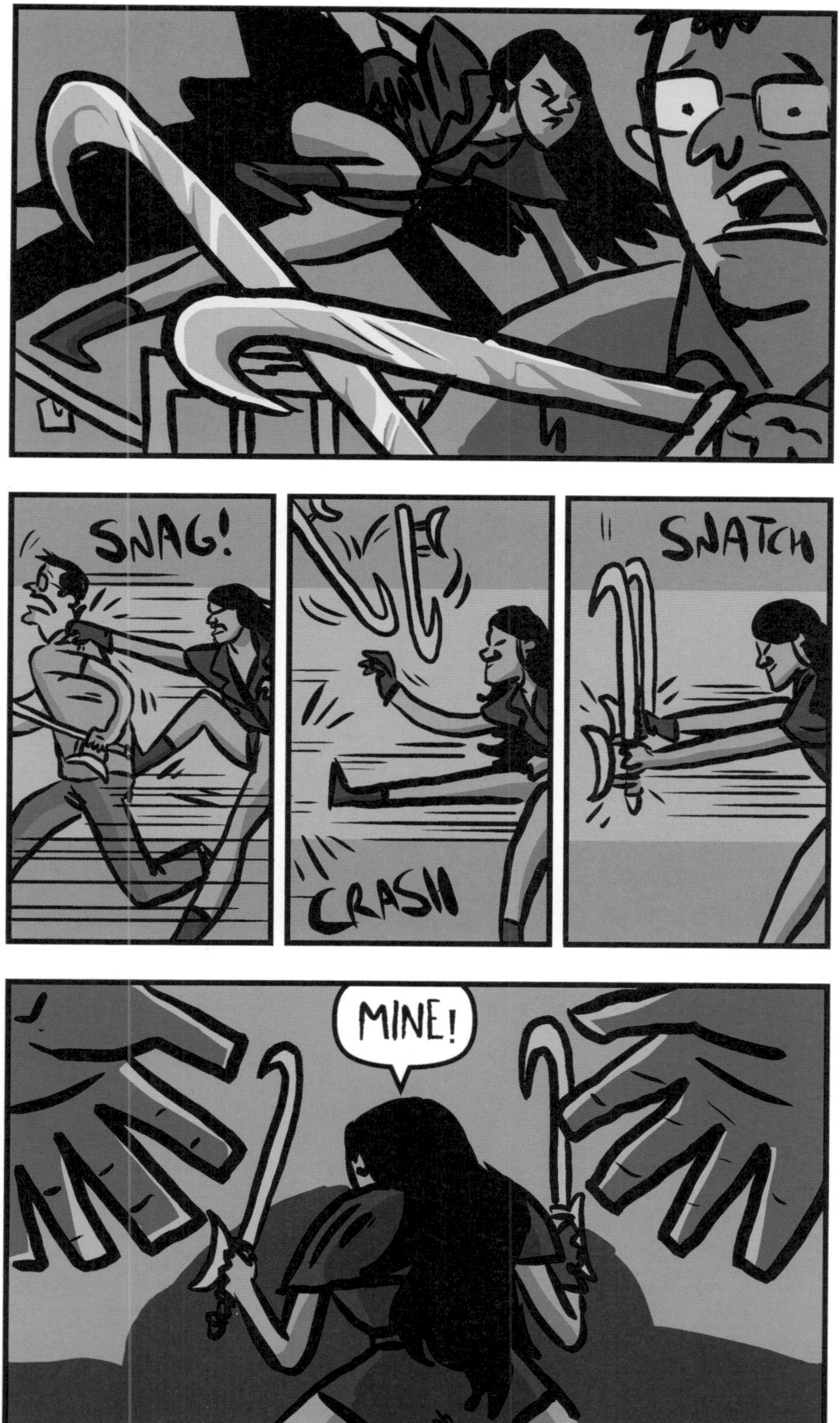
SNAG!
CRASH
SNATCH
MINE!

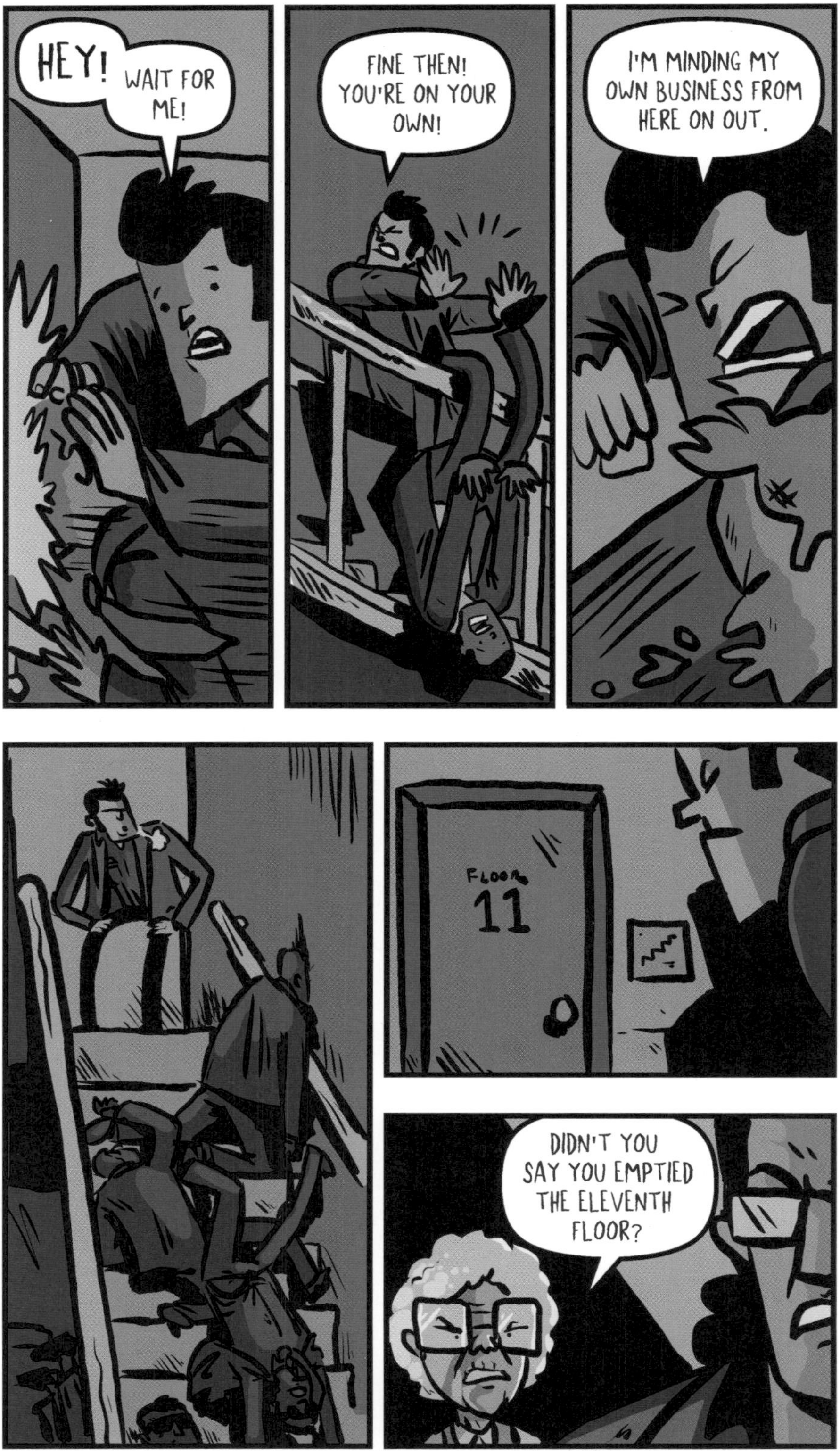
HEY!
WAIT FOR ME!
FINE THEN! YOU'RE ON YOUR OWN!
I'M MINDING MY OWN BUSINESS FROM HERE ON OUT.
FLOOR 11
DIDN'T YOU SAY YOU EMPTIED THE ELEVENTH FLOOR?

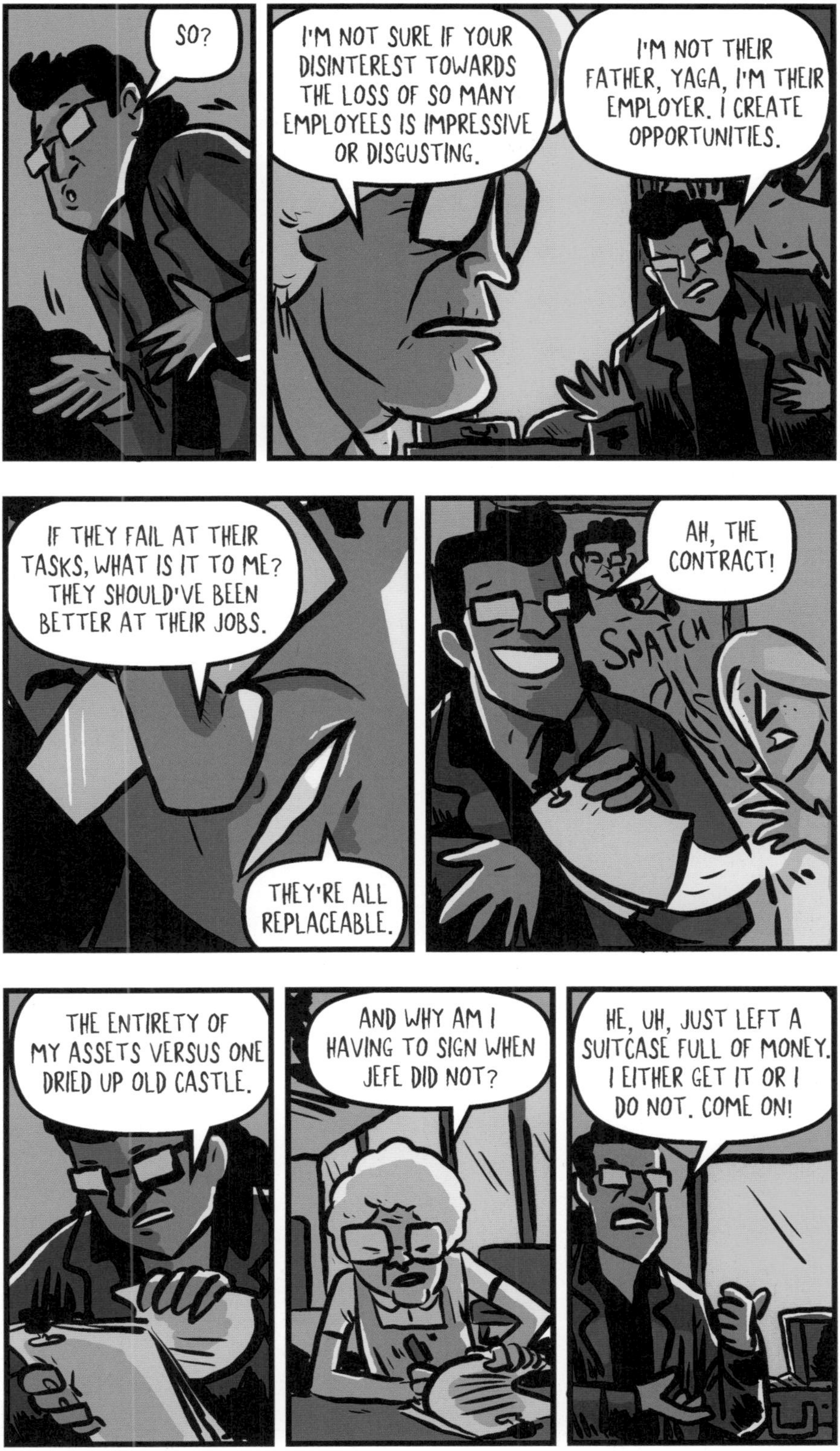
SO?
I'M NOT SURE IF YOUR DISINTEREST TOWARDS THE LOSS OF SO MANY EMPLOYEES IS IMPRESSIVE OR DISGUSTING.
I'M NOT THEIR FATHER, YAGA, I'M THEIR EMPLOYER. I CREATE OPPORTUNITIES.
IF THEY FAIL AT THEIR TASKS, WHAT IS IT TO ME? THEY SHOULD'VE BEEN BETTER AT THEIR JOBS.
THEY'RE ALL REPLACEABLE.
AH, THE CONTRACT!
SNATCH
THE ENTIRETY OF MY ASSETS VERSUS ONE DRIED UP OLD CASTLE.
AND WHY AM I HAVING TO SIGN WHEN JEFE DID NOT?
HE, UH, JUST LEFT A SUITCASE FULL OF MONEY. I EITHER GET IT OR I DO NOT. COME ON!

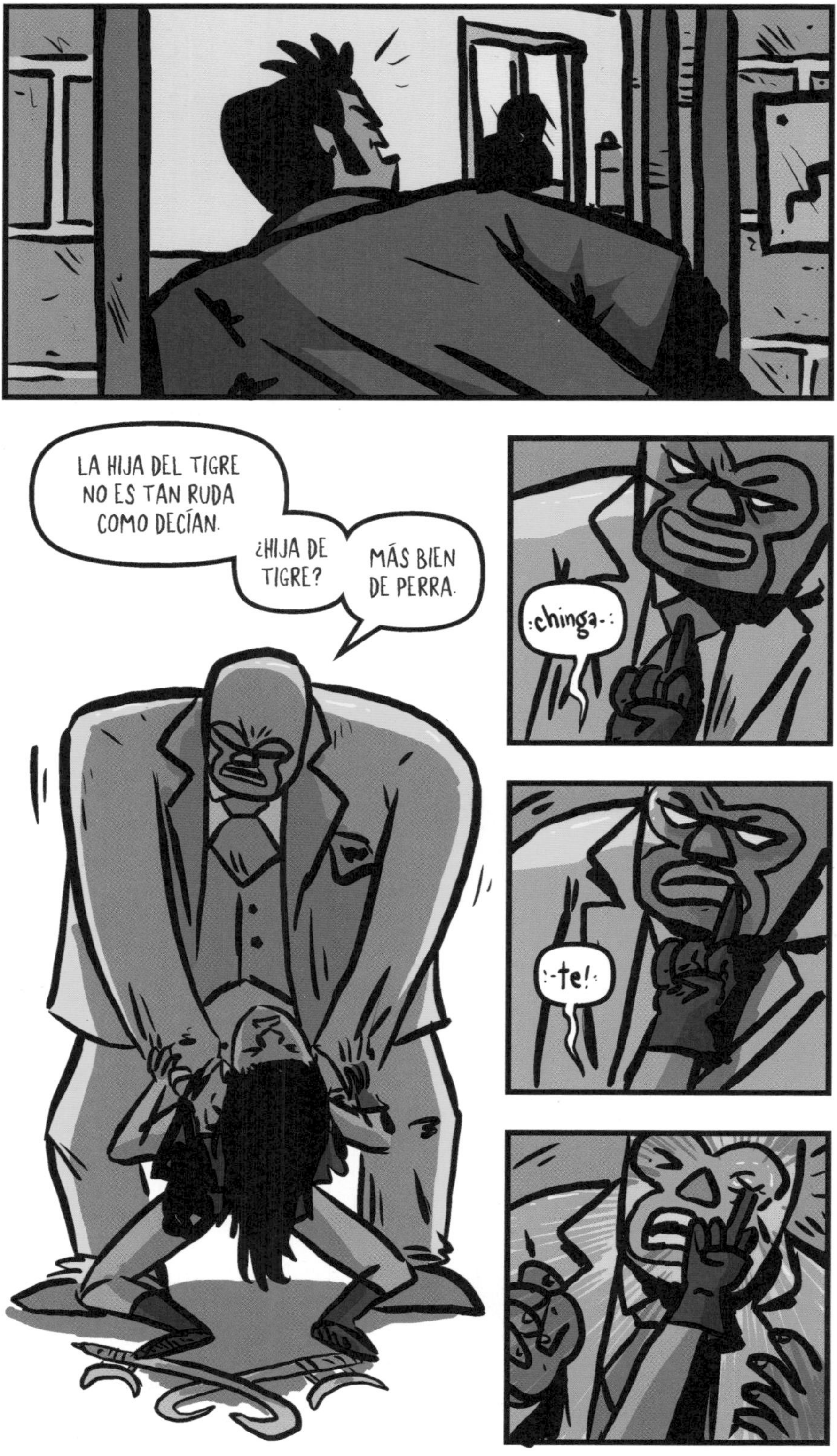
LA HIJA DEL TIGRE NO ES TAN RUDA COMO DECÍAN.
¿HIJA DE TIGRE?
MÁS BIEN DE PERRA.
¡chinga-!
¡-te!

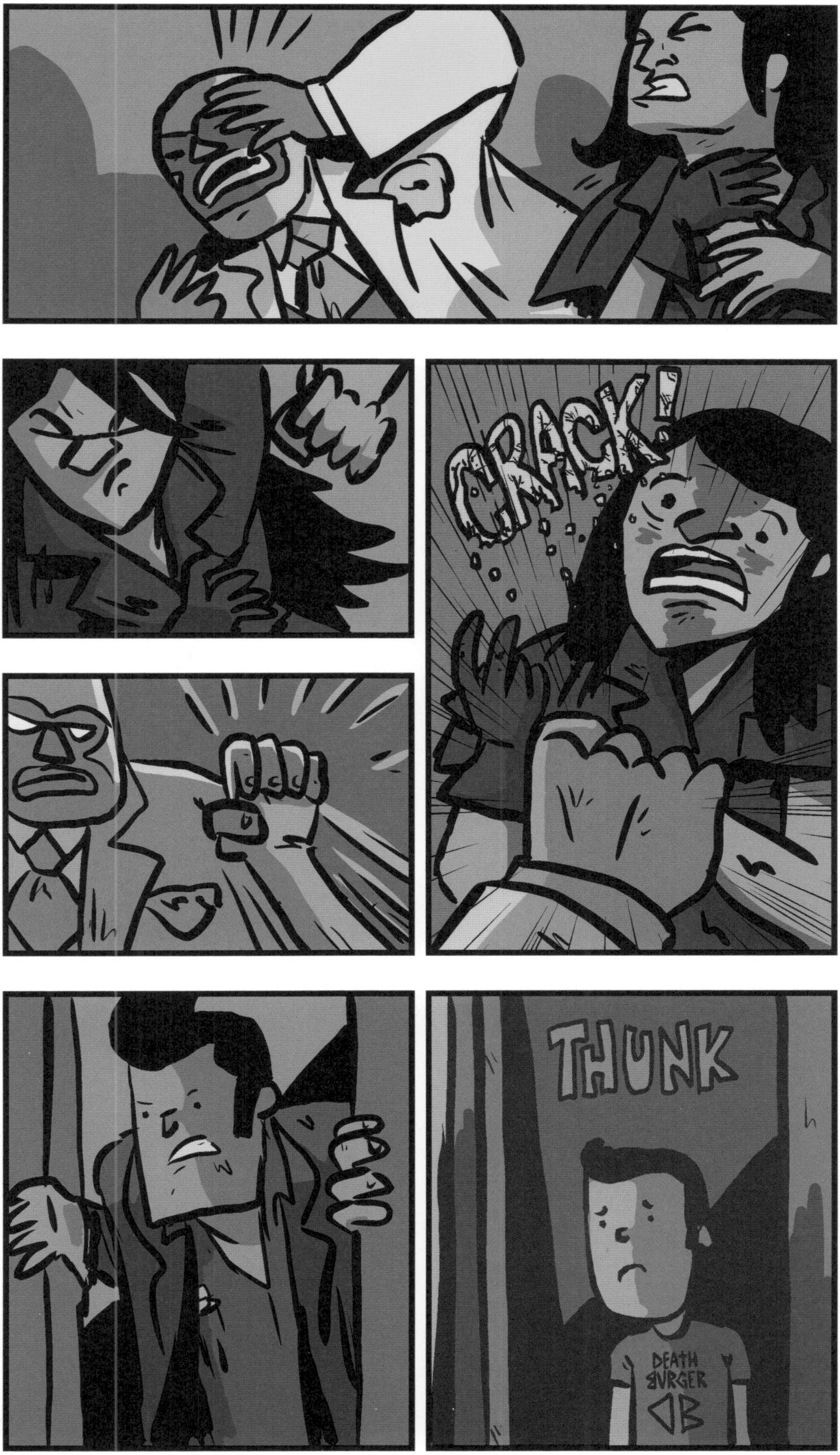
CRACK!
THUNK
DEATH
BURGER
DB

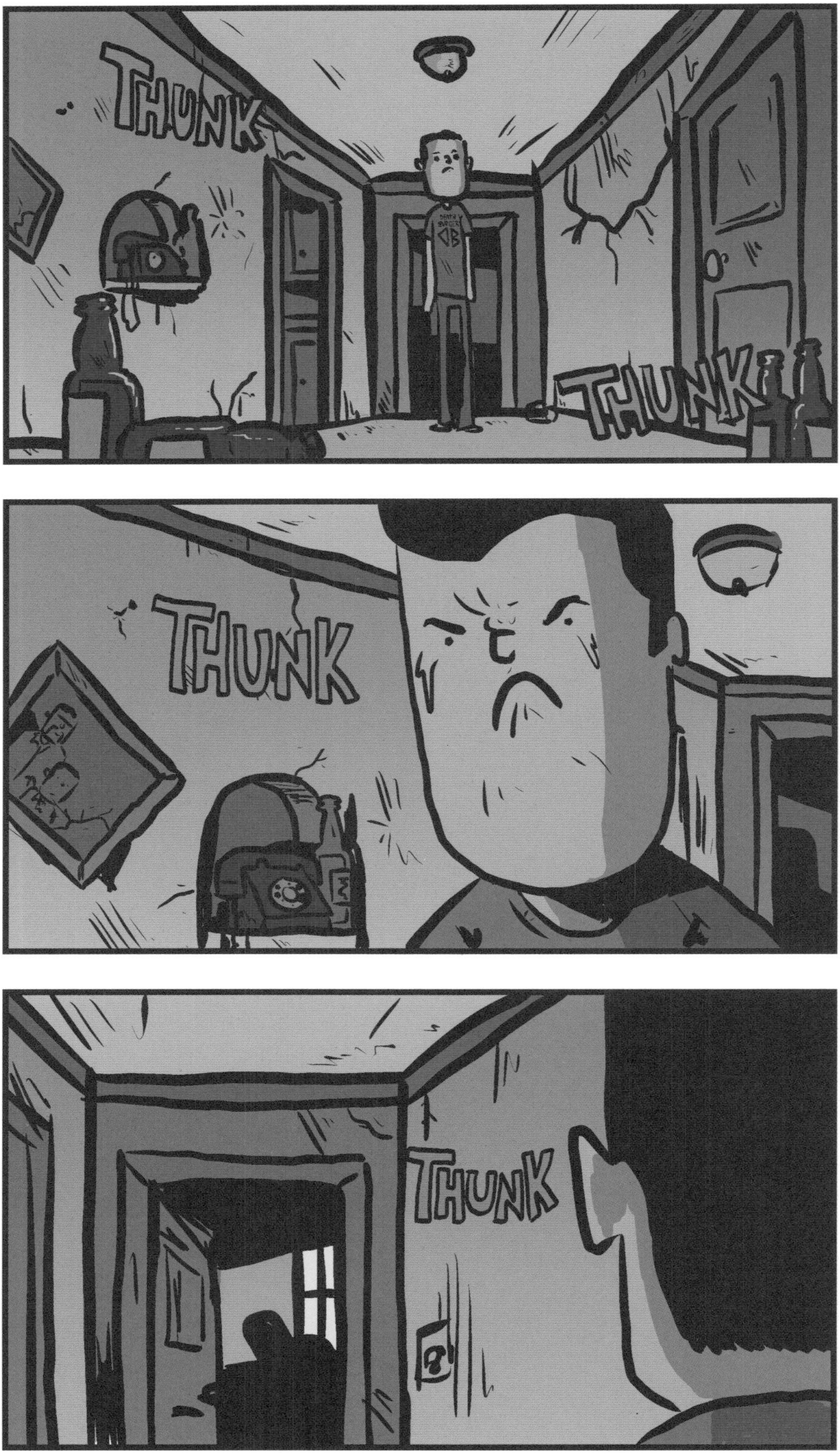
THUNK
THUNK
THUNK
THUNK

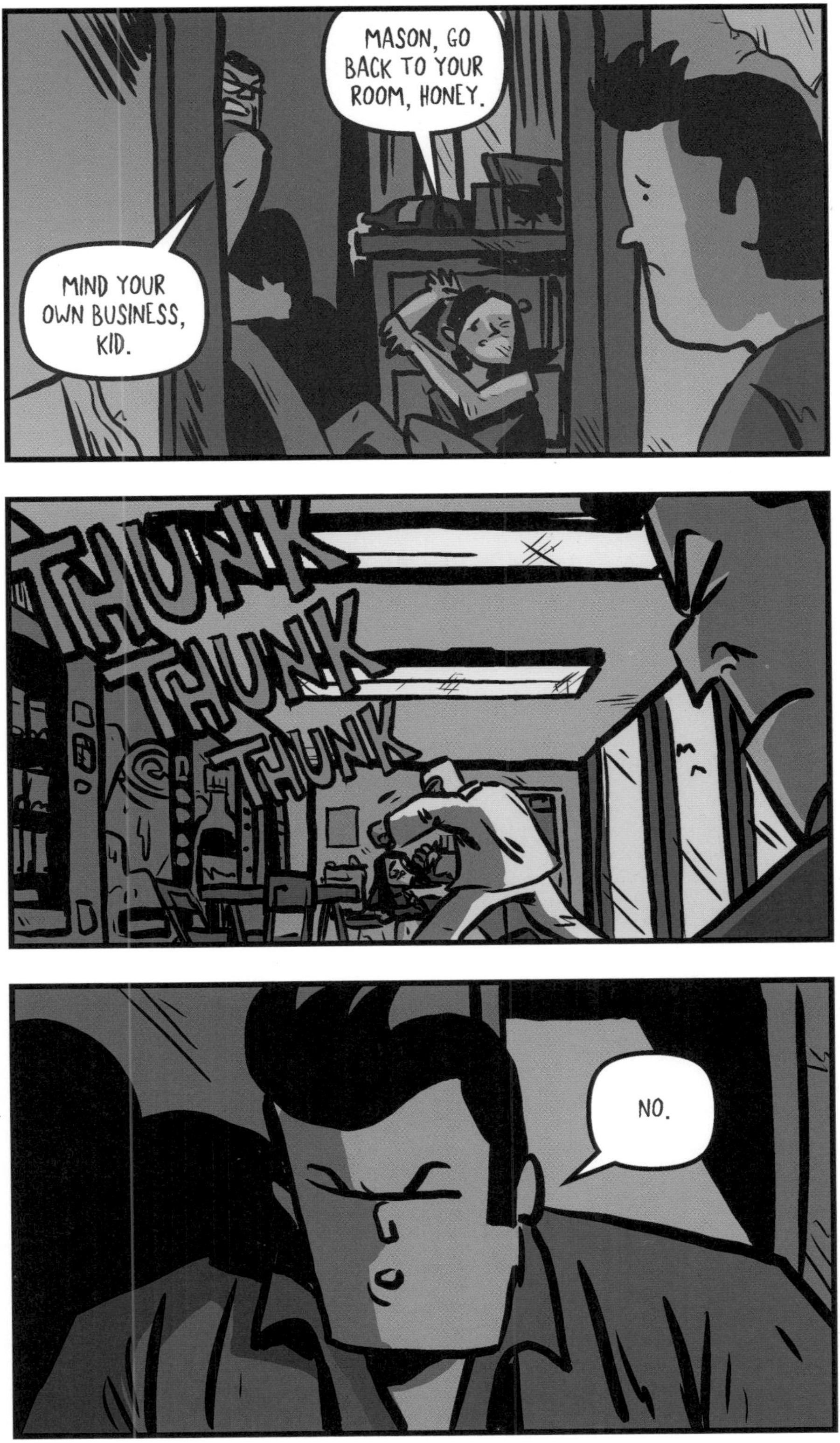
MASON, GO BACK TO YOUR ROOM, HONEY.
MIND YOUR OWN BUSINESS, KID.
THUNK
THUNK
THUNK
NO.

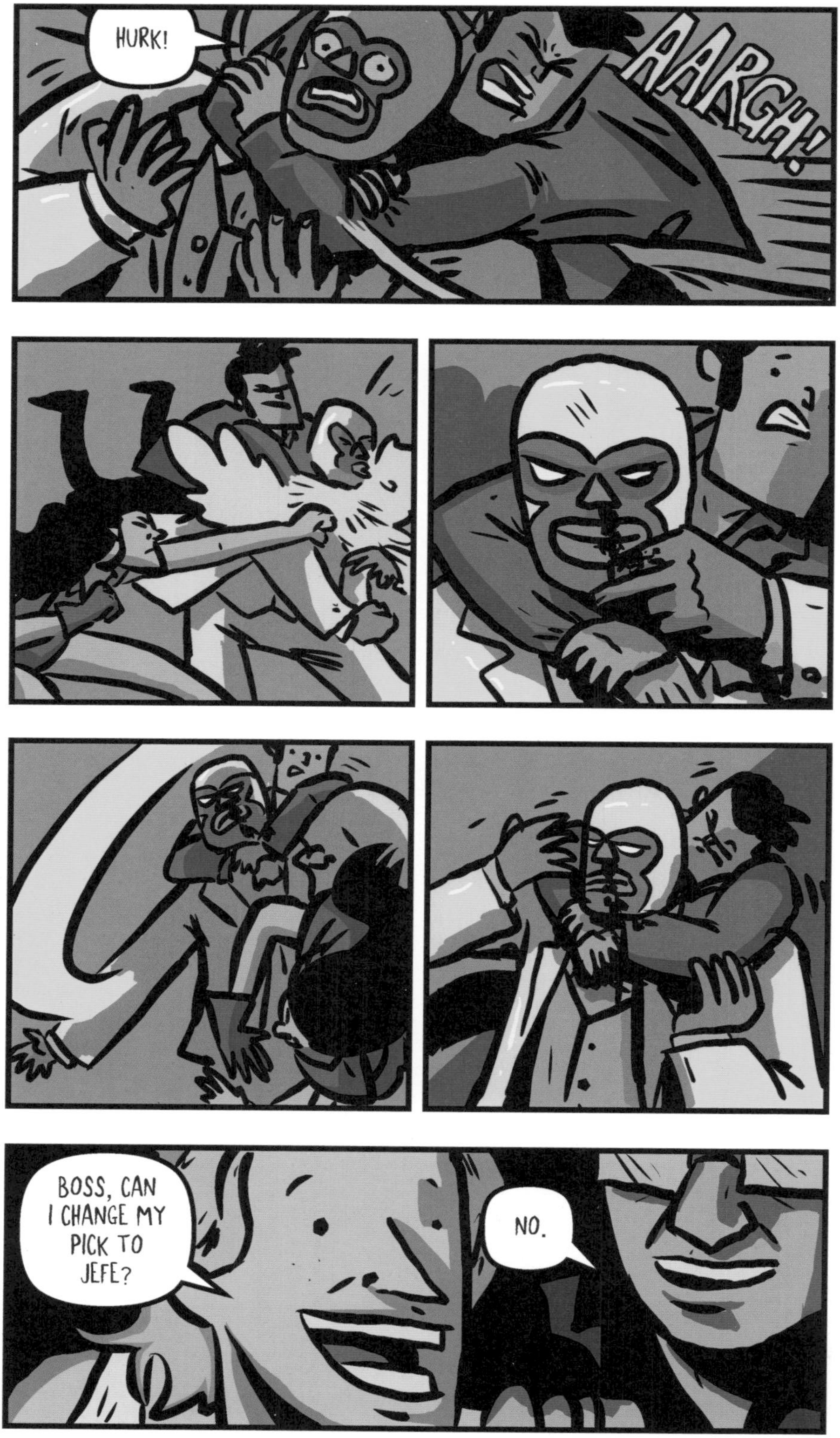
HURK!
AARGH!
BOSS, CAN I CHANGE MY PICK TO JEFE?
NO.

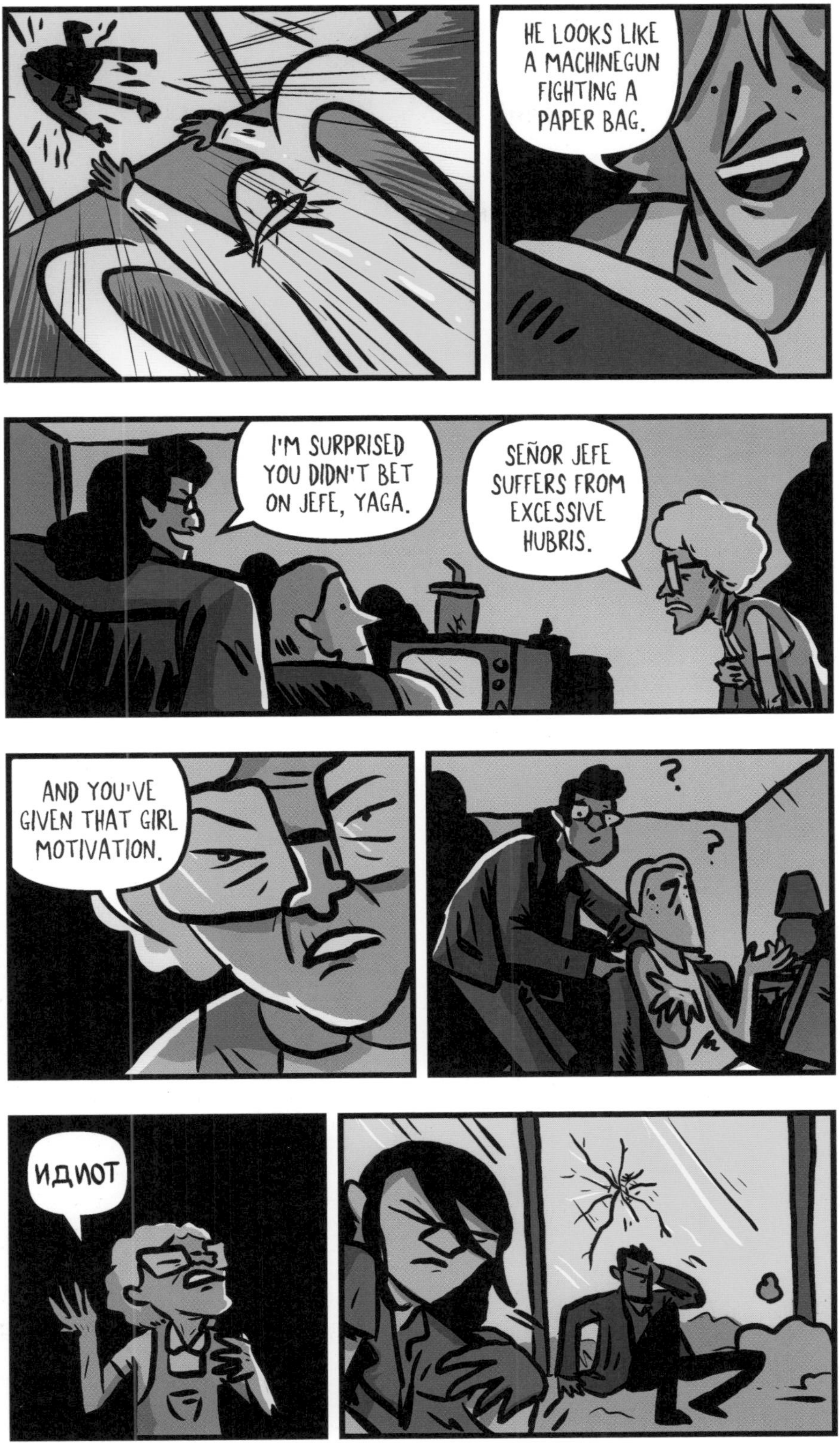
HE LOOKS LIKE A MACHINEGUN FIGHTING A PAPER BAG.
I'M SURPRISED YOU DIDN'T BET ON JEFE, YAGA.
SEÑOR JEFE SUFFERS FROM EXCESSIVE HUBRIS.
AND YOU'VE GIVEN THAT GIRL MOTIVATION.
?
?
ИДИОТ

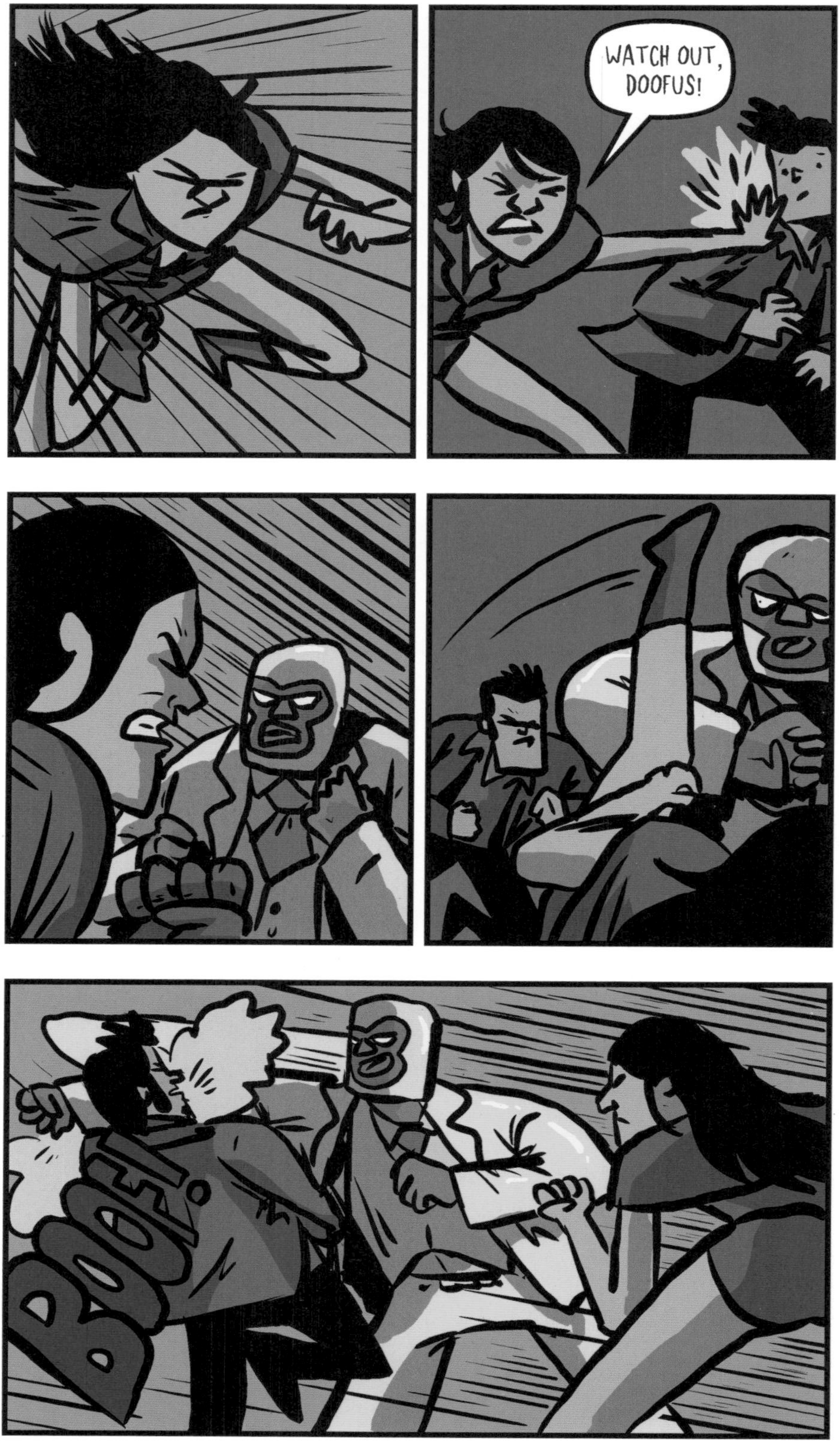
WATCH OUT, DOOFUS!
BOOF!

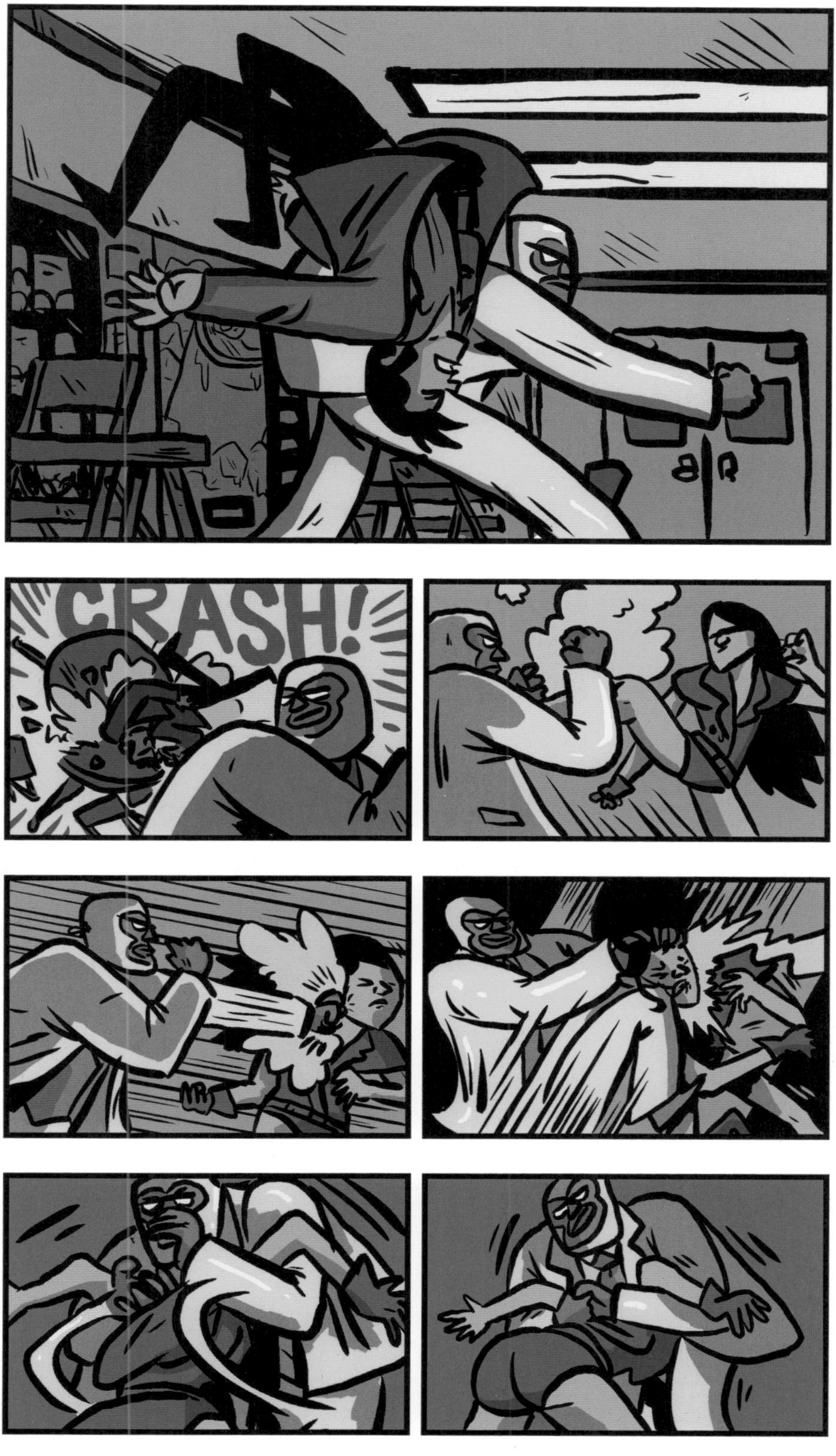
CRASH!

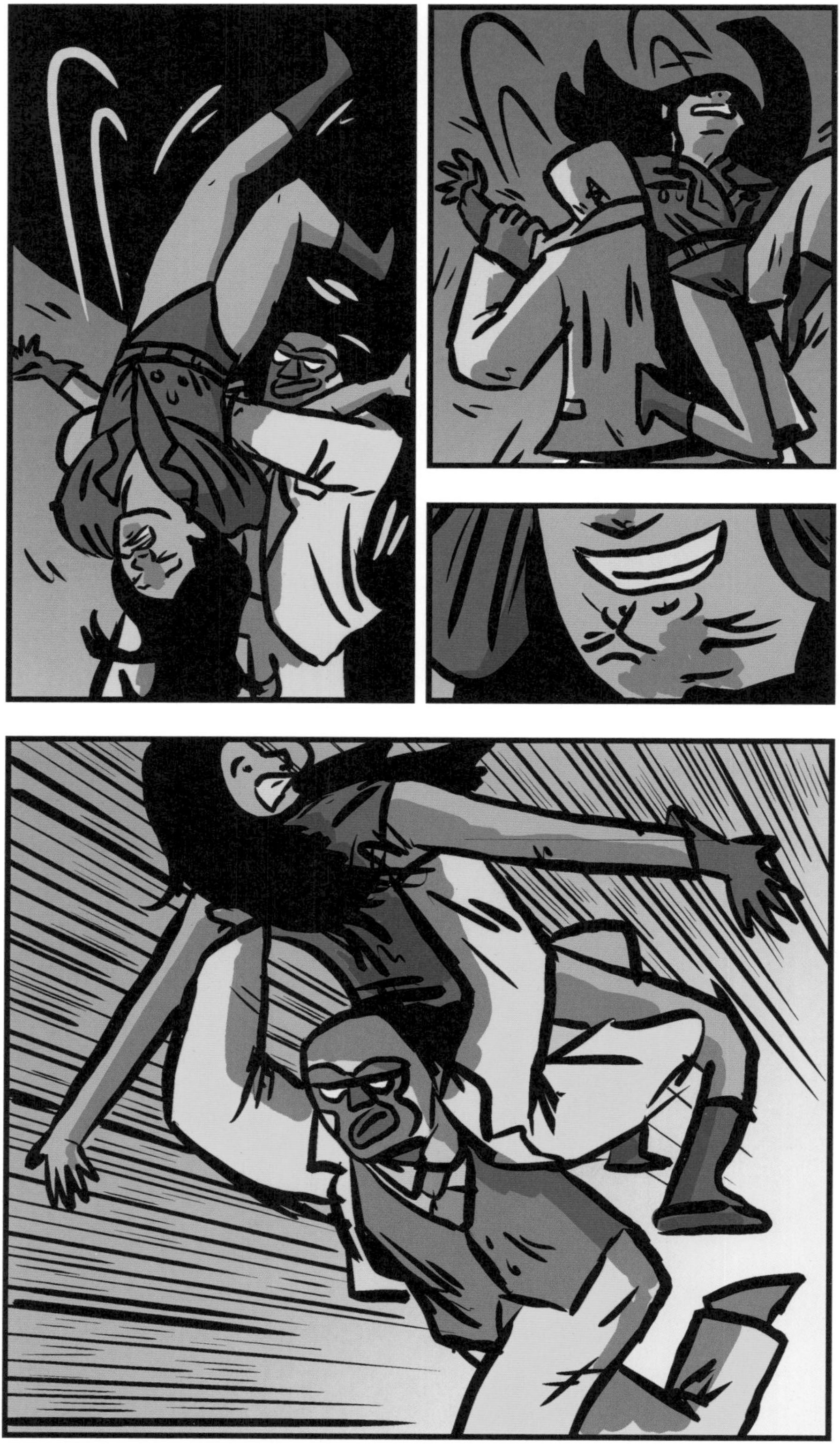

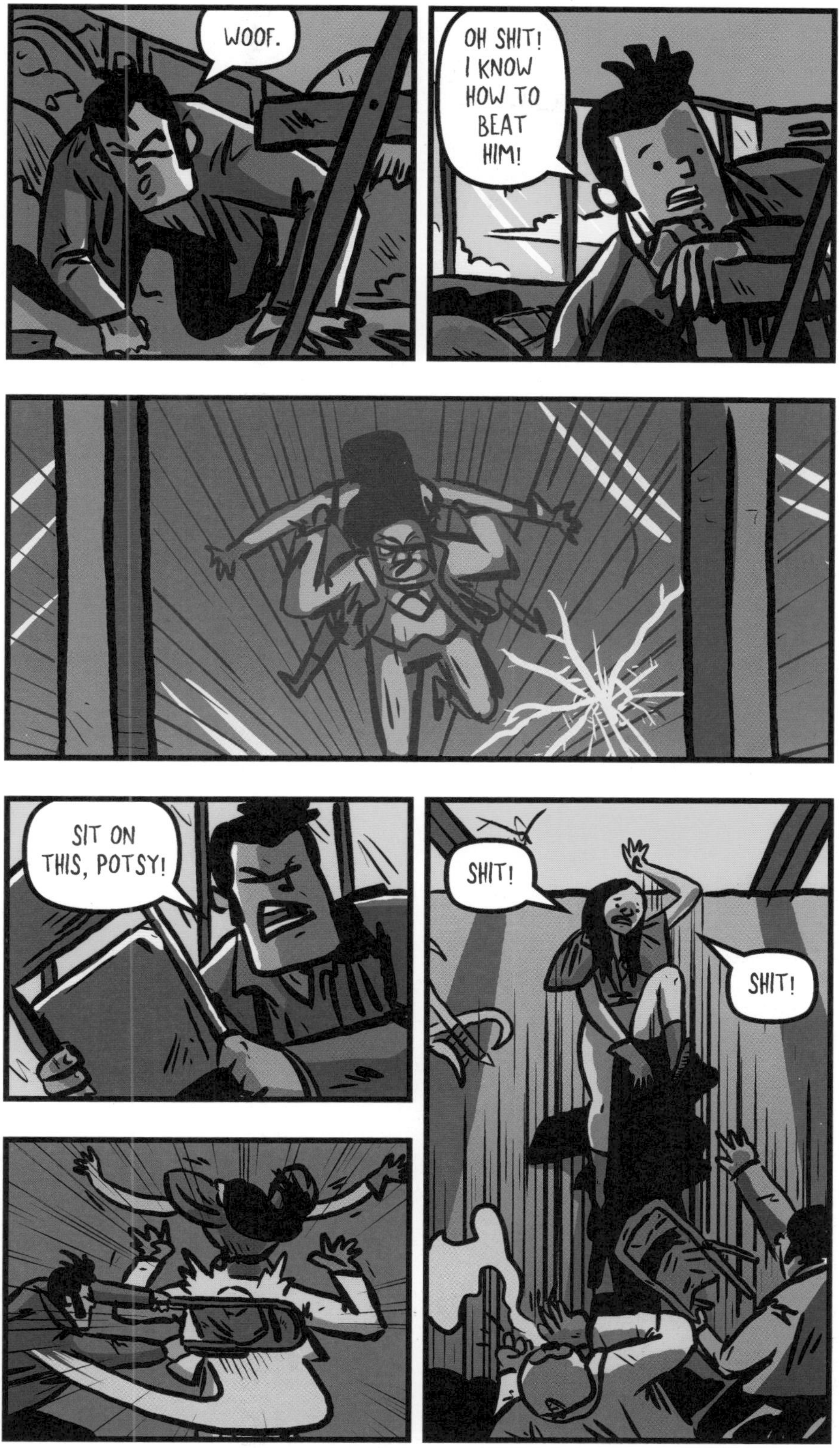
WOOF.
OH SHIT! I KNOW HOW TO BEAT HIM!
SIT ON THIS, POTSY!
SHIT!
SHIT!

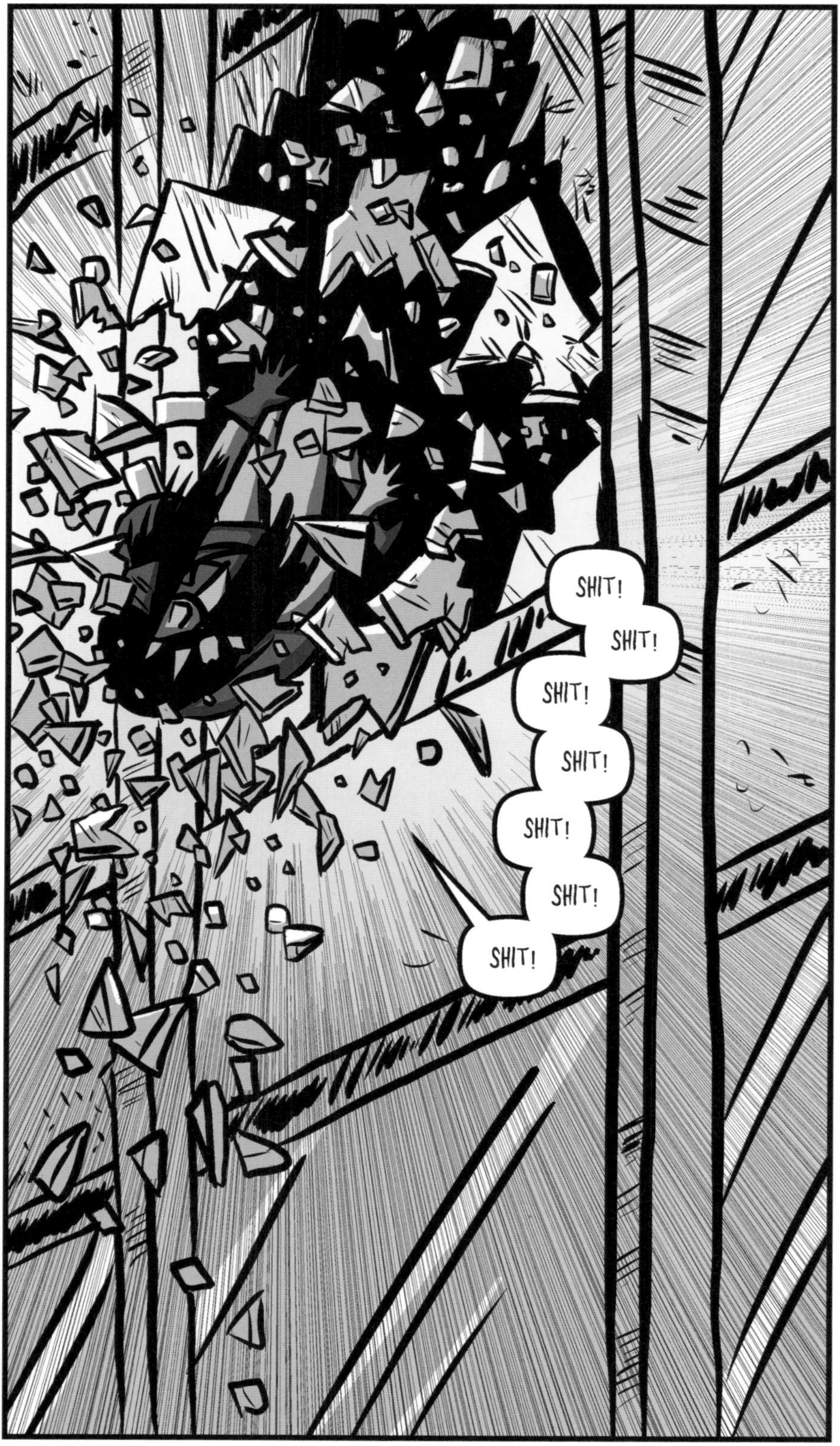
SHIT!
SHIT!
SHIT!
SHIT!
SHIT!
SHIT!
SHIT!

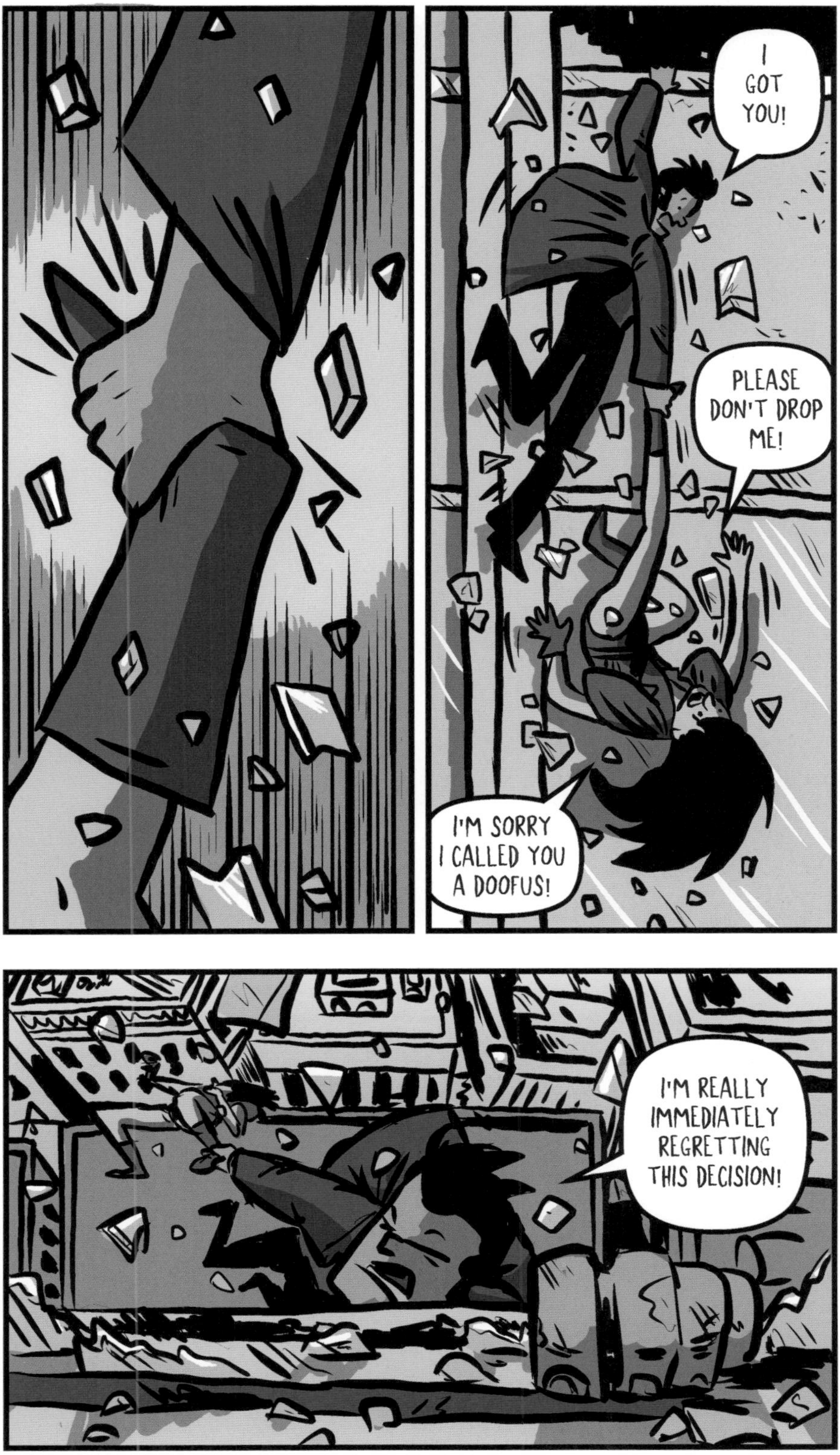
I GOT YOU!
PLEASE DON'T DROP ME!
I'M SORRY I CALLED YOU A DOOFUS!
I'M REALLY IMMEDIATELY REGRETTING THIS DECISION!

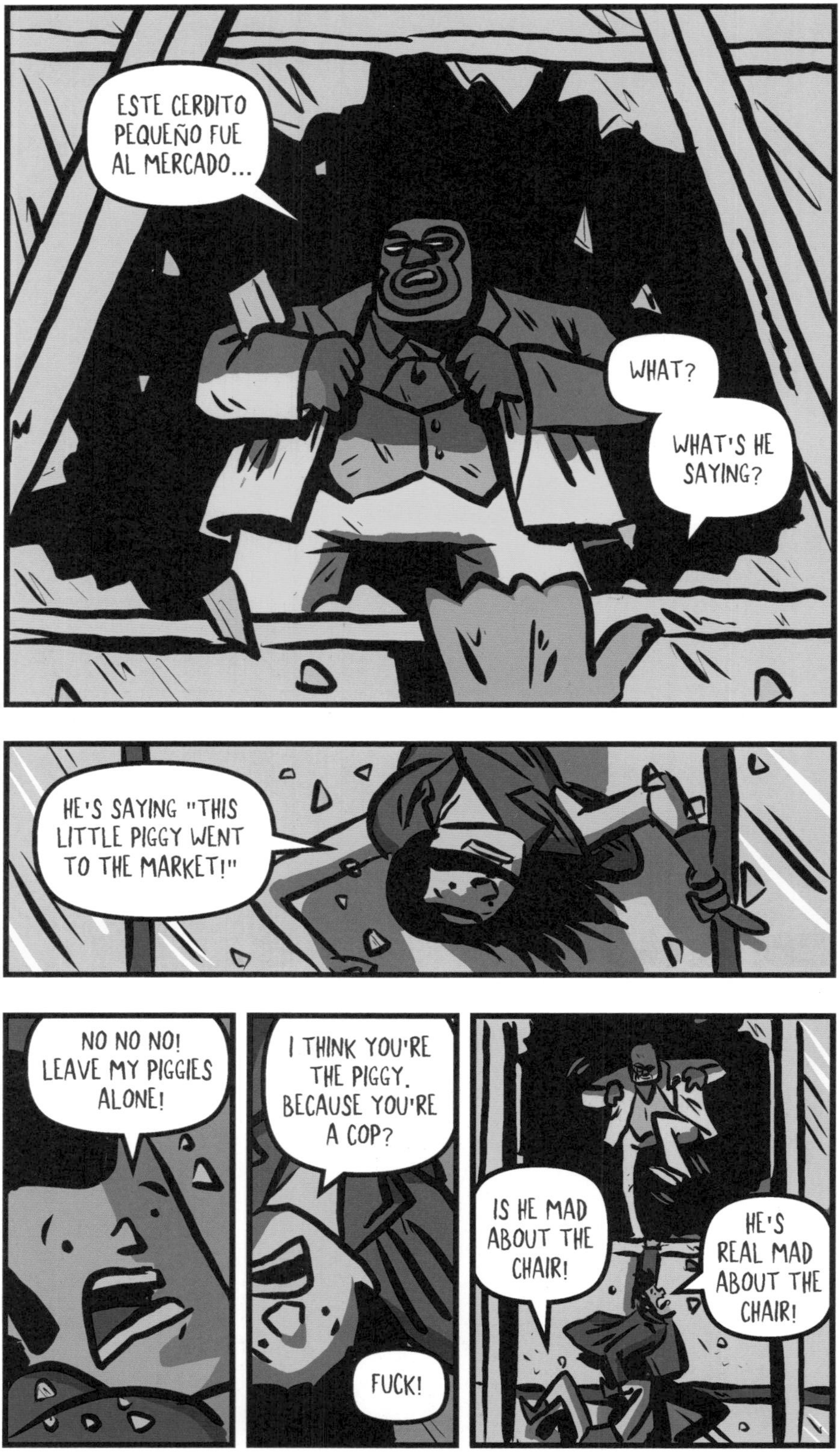
ESTE CERDITO PEQUEÑO FUE AL MERCADO...
WHAT?
WHAT'S HE SAYING?
HE'S SAYING "THIS LITTLE PIGGY WENT TO THE MARKET!"
NO NO NO! LEAVE MY PIGGIES ALONE!
I THINK YOU'RE THE PIGGY. BECAUSE YOU'RE A COP?
FUCK!
IS HE MAD ABOUT THE CHAIR!
HE'S REAL MAD ABOUT THE CHAIR!

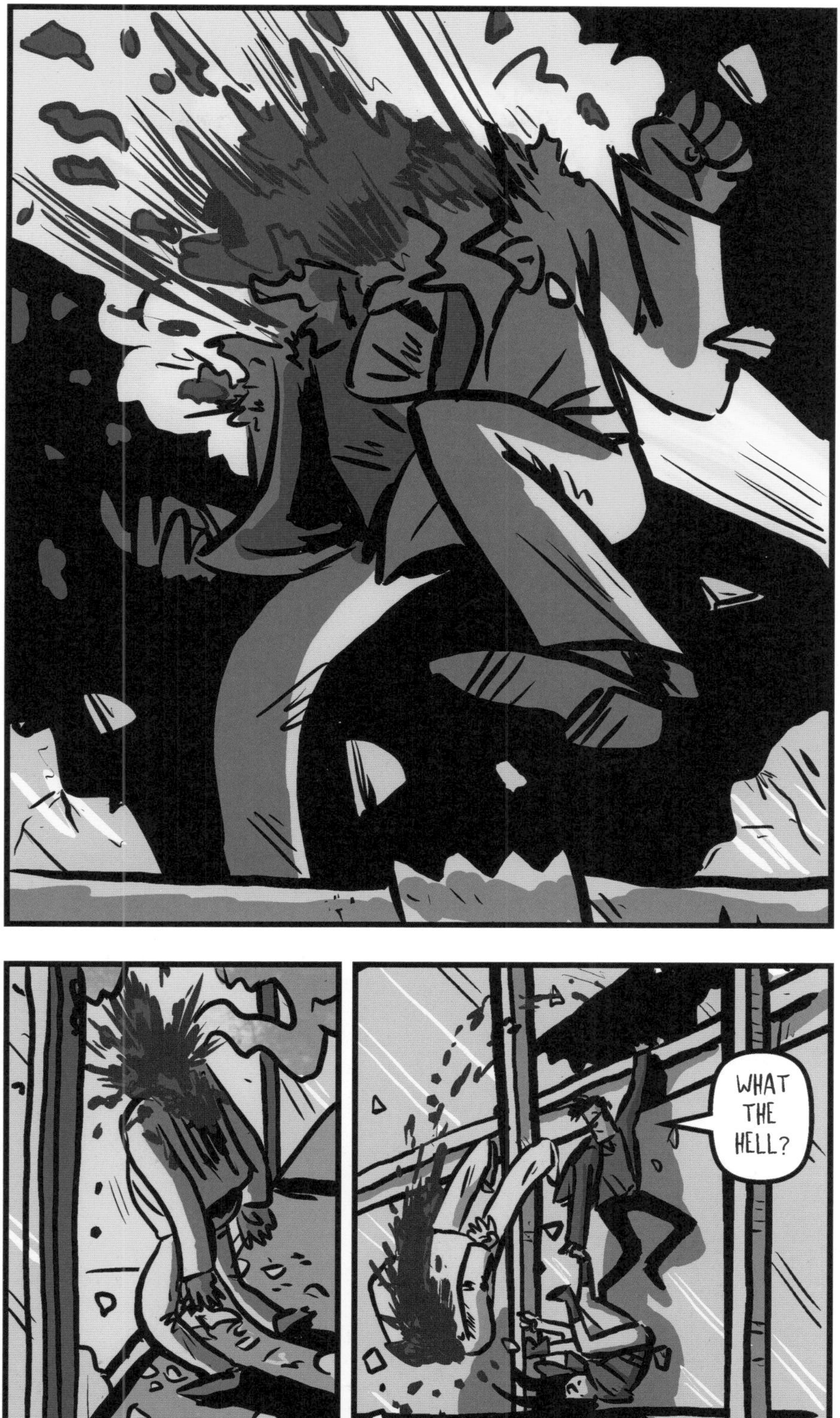
WHAT THE HELL?

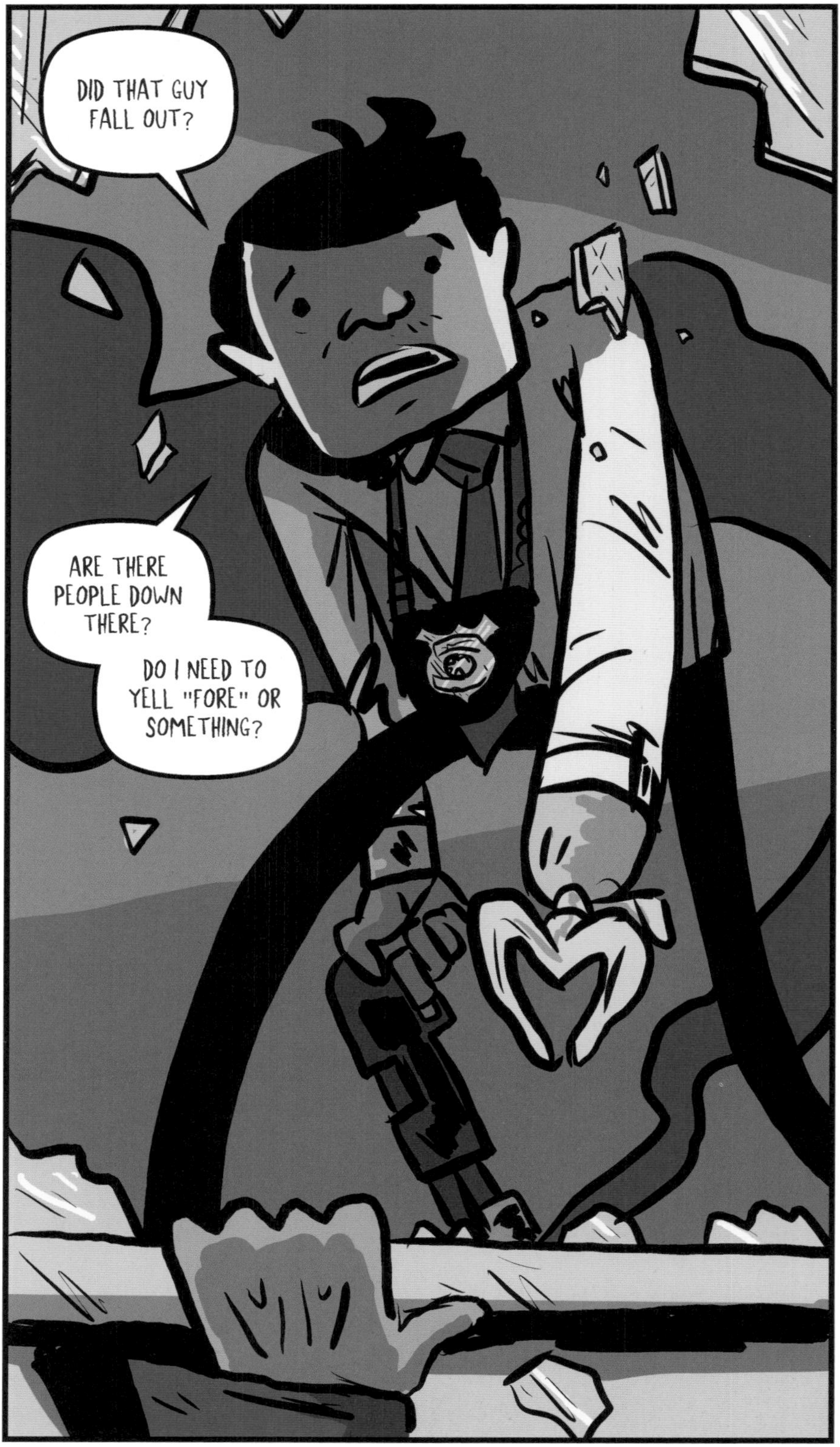
DID THAT GUY FALL OUT?
ARE THERE PEOPLE DOWN THERE?
DO I NEED TO YELL "FORE" OR SOMETHING?

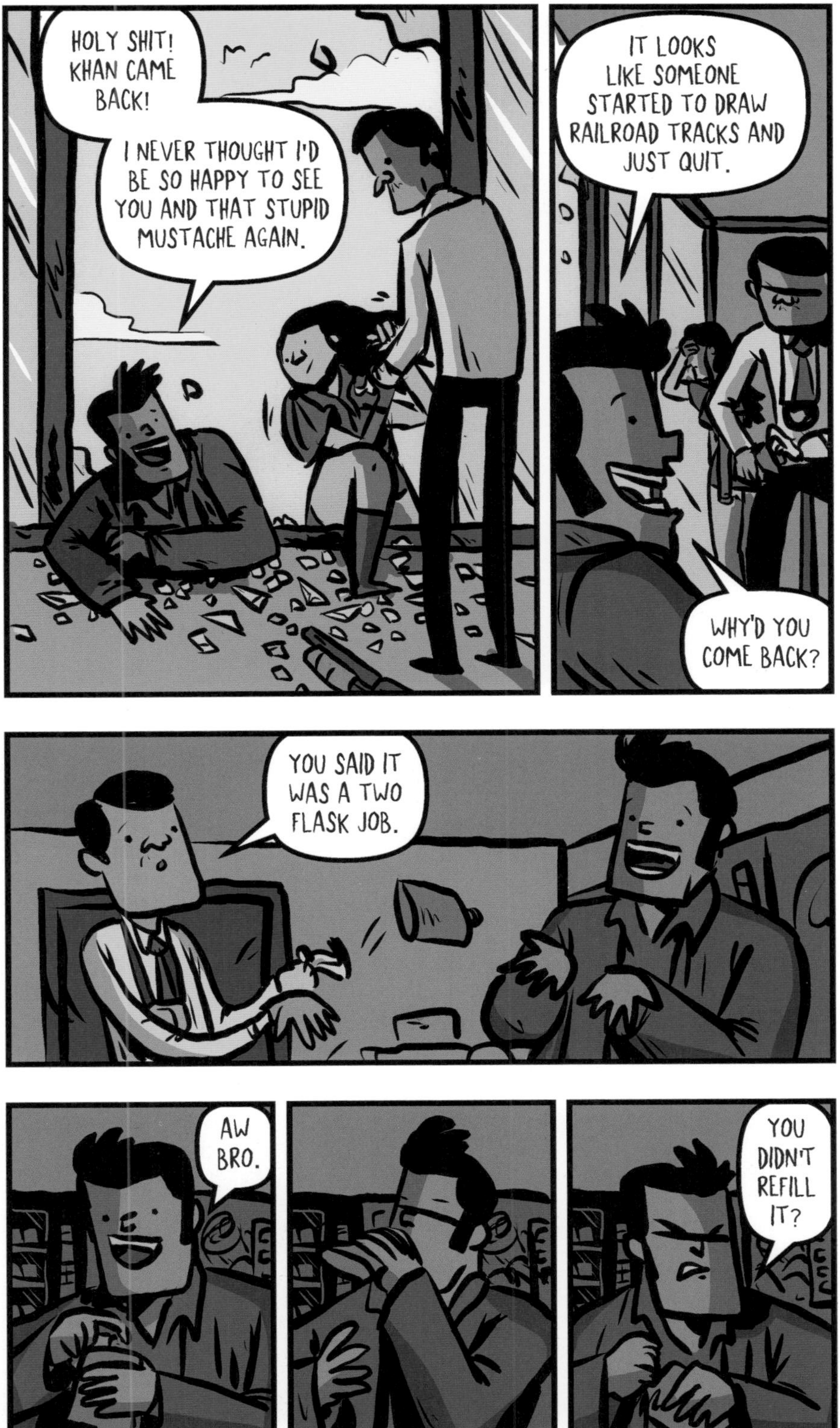
HOLY SHIT! KHAN CAME BACK!
I NEVER THOUGHT I'D BE SO HAPPY TO SEE YOU AND THAT STUPID MUSTACHE AGAIN.
IT LOOKS LIKE SOMEONE STARTED TO DRAW RAILROAD TRACKS AND JUST QUIT.
WHY'D YOU COME BACK?
YOU SAID IT WAS A TWO FLASK JOB.
AW BRO.
YOU DIDN'T REFILL IT?

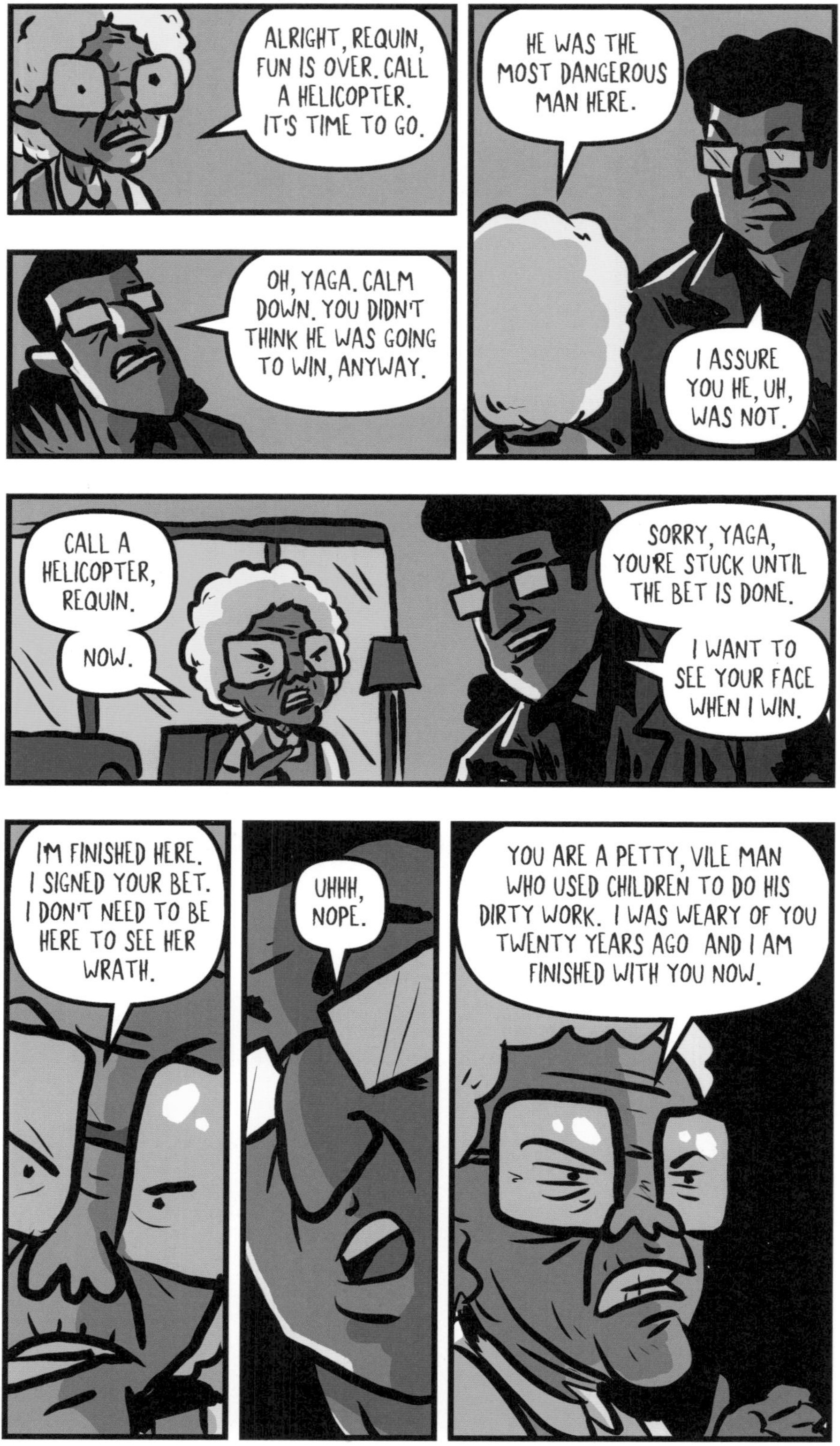
ALRIGHT, REQUIN, FUN IS OVER. CALL A HELICOPTER. IT'S TIME TO GO.
HE WAS THE MOST DANGEROUS MAN HERE.
OH, YAGA. CALM DOWN. YOU DIDN'T THINK HE WAS GOING TO WIN, ANYWAY.
I ASSURE YOU HE, UH, WAS NOT.
CALL A HELICOPTER, REQUIN.
NOW.
SORRY, YAGA, YOU'RE STUCK UNTIL THE BET IS DONE.
I WANT TO SEE YOUR FACE WHEN I WIN.
I'M FINISHED HERE. I SIGNED YOUR BET. I DON'T NEED TO BE HERE TO SEE HER WRATH.
UHHH, NOPE.
YOU ARE A PETTY, VILE MAN WHO USED CHILDREN TO DO HIS DIRTY WORK. I WAS WEARY OF YOU TWENTY YEARS AGO AND I AM FINISHED WITH YOU NOW.

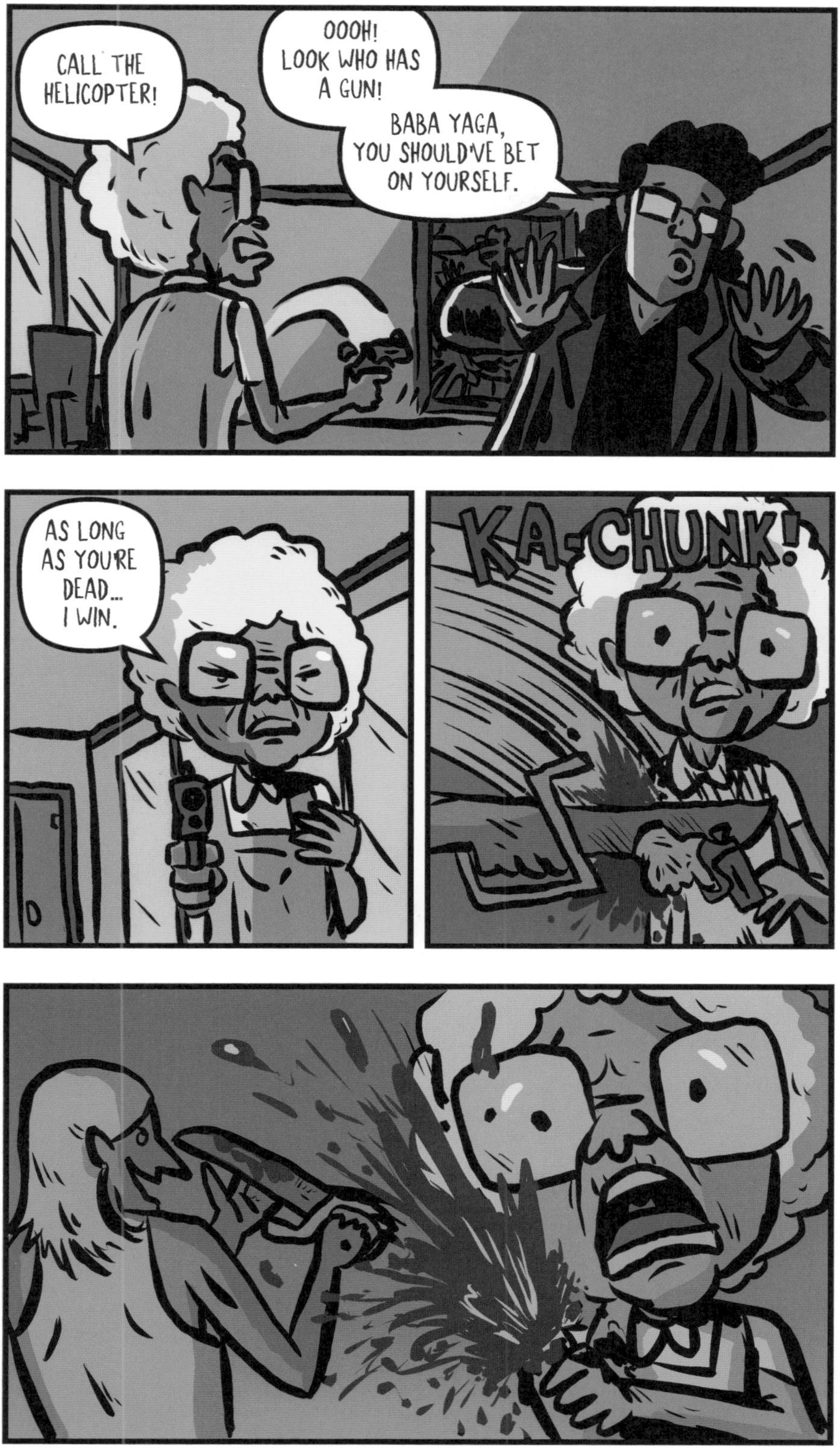
CALL THE HELICOPTER!
OOOH! LOOK WHO HAS A GUN!
BABA YAGA, YOU SHOULD'VE BET ON YOURSELF.
AS LONG AS YOU'RE DEAD... I WIN.
KA-CHUNK!

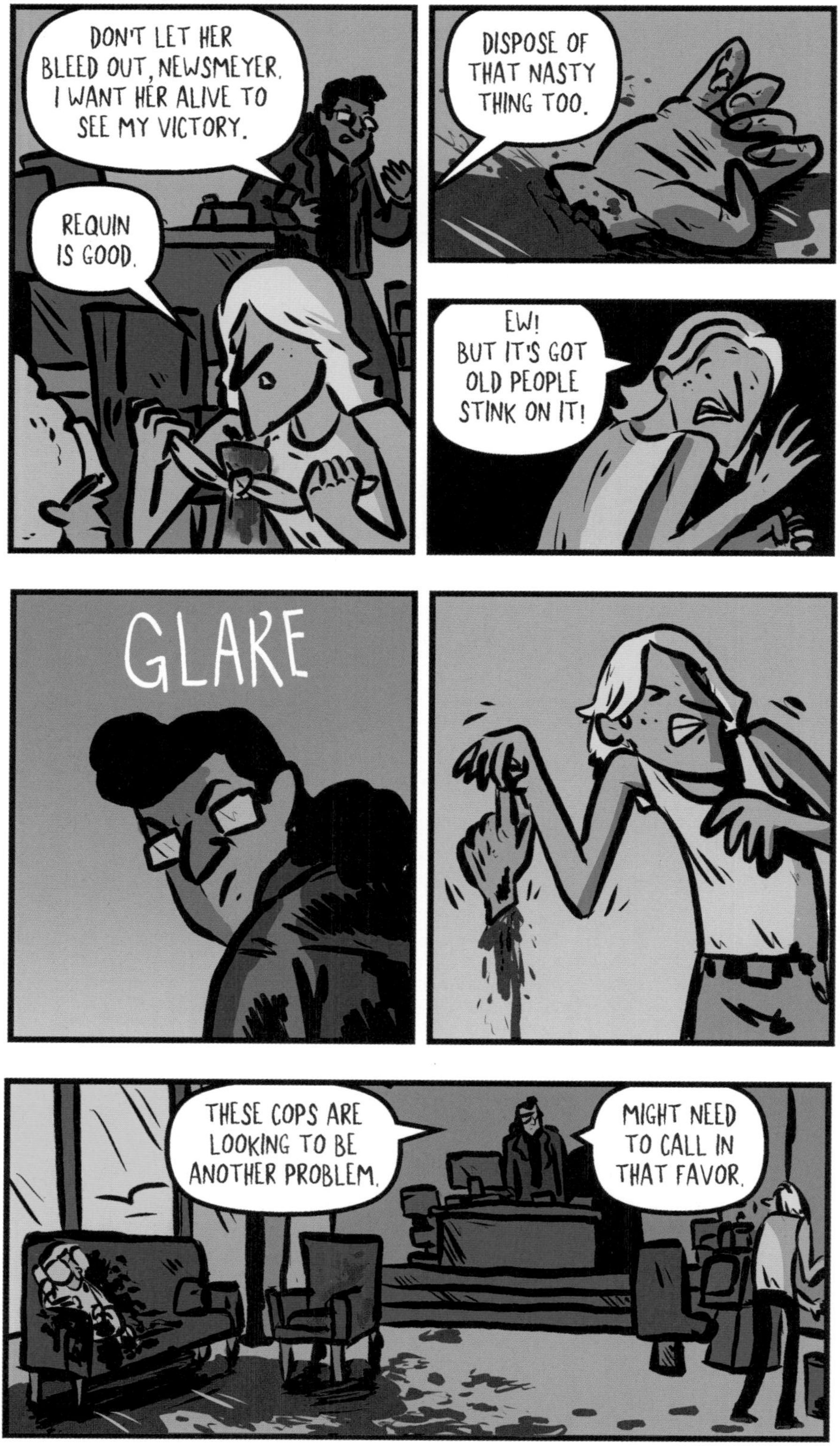
DON'T LET HER BLEED OUT, NEWSMEYER. I WANT HER ALIVE TO SEE MY VICTORY.
REQUIN IS GOOD.
DISPOSE OF THAT NASTY THING TOO.
EW! BUT IT'S GOT OLD PEOPLE STINK ON IT!
GLARE
THESE COPS ARE LOOKING TO BE ANOTHER PROBLEM.
MIGHT NEED TO CALL IN THAT FAVOR.

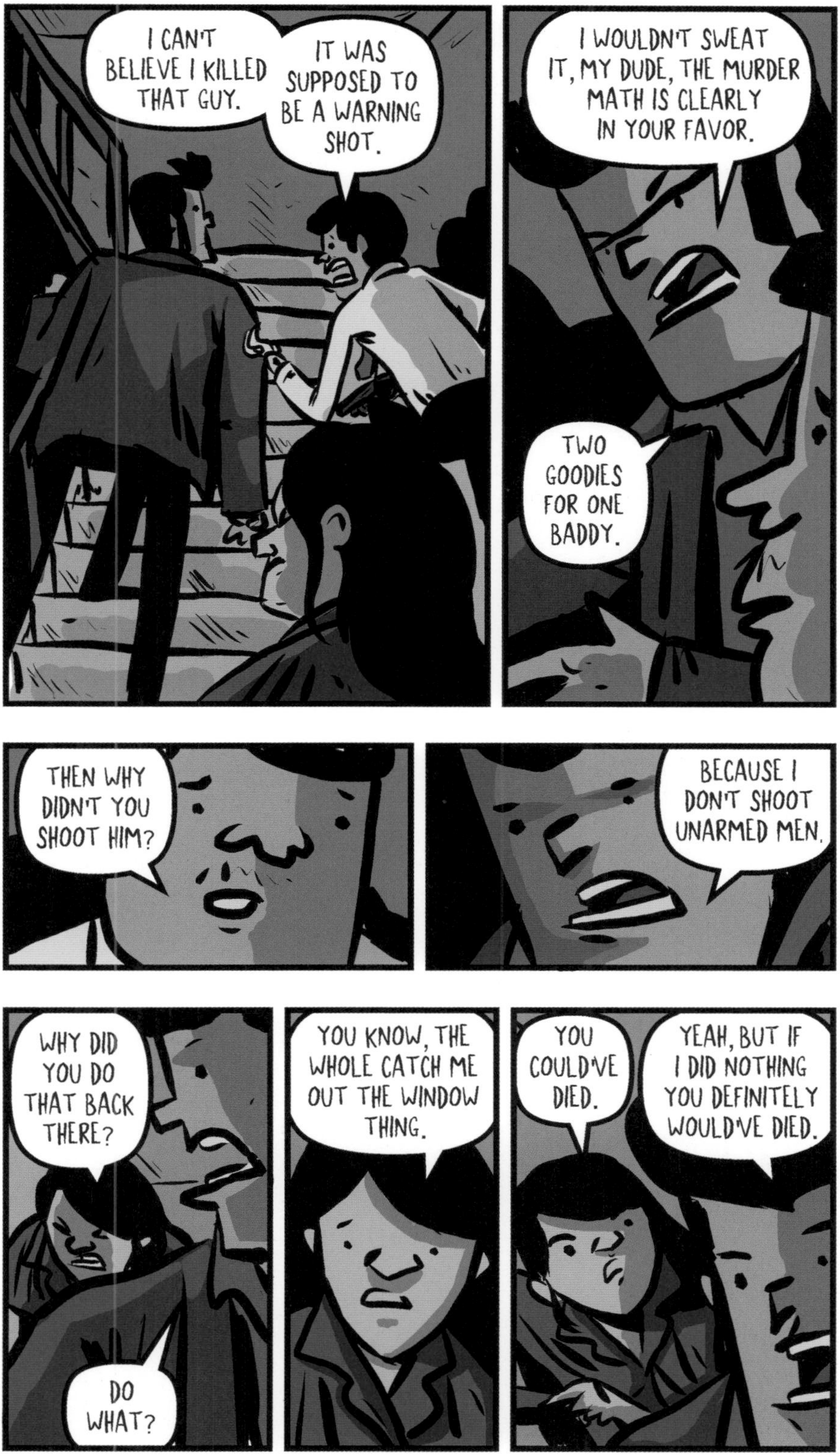
I CAN'T BELIEVE I KILLED THAT GUY.
IT WAS SUPPOSED TO BE A WARNING SHOT.
I WOULDN'T SWEAT IT, MY DUDE, THE MURDER MATH IS CLEARLY IN YOUR FAVOR.
TWO GOODIES FOR ONE BADDY.
THEN WHY DIDN'T YOU SHOOT HIM?
BECAUSE I DON'T SHOOT UNARMED MEN.
WHY DID YOU DO THAT BACK THERE?
DO WHAT?
YOU KNOW, THE WHOLE CATCH ME OUT THE WINDOW THING.
YOU COULD'VE DIED.
YEAH, BUT IF I DID NOTHING YOU DEFINITELY WOULD'VE DIED.

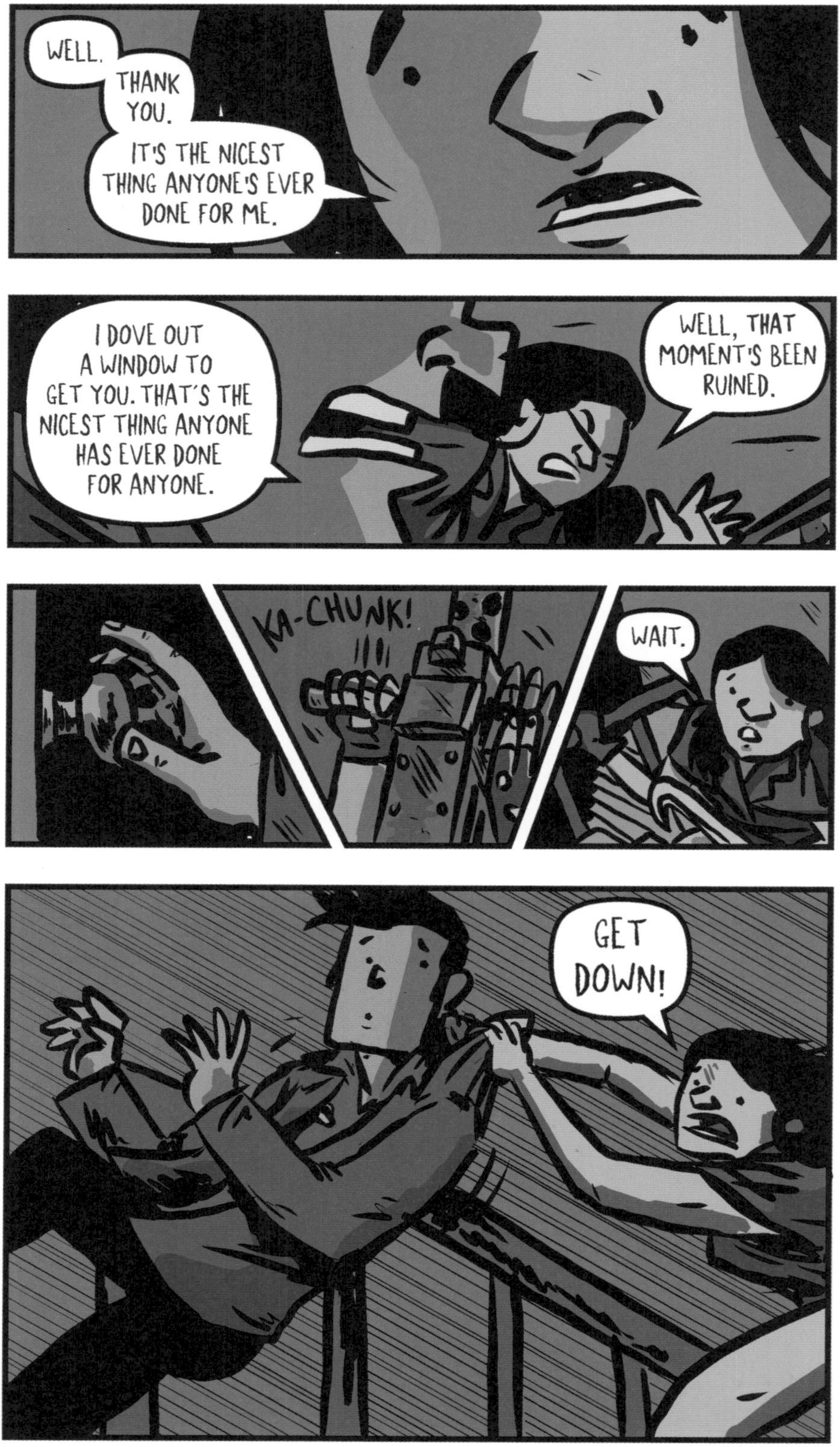
WELL.
THANK YOU.
IT'S THE NICEST THING ANYONE'S EVER DONE FOR ME.
I DOVE OUT A WINDOW TO GET YOU. THAT'S THE NICEST THING ANYONE HAS EVER DONE FOR ANYONE.
WELL, THAT MOMENT'S BEEN RUINED.
KA-CHUNK!
WAIT.
GET DOWN!

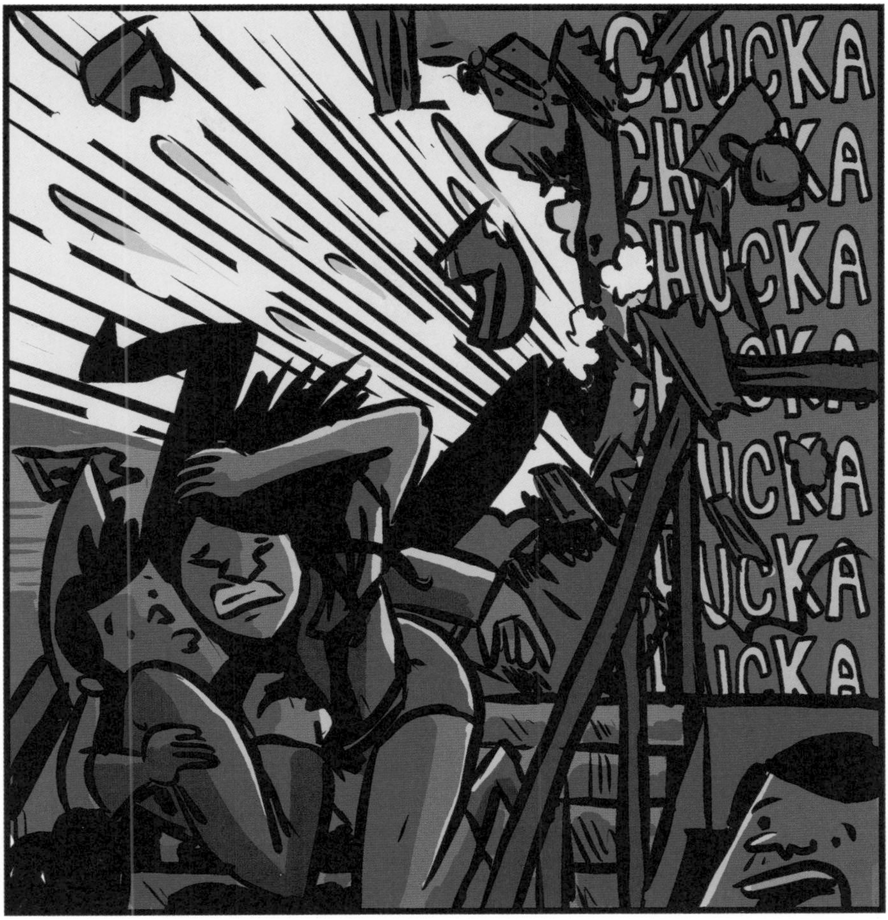
CHUCKA
CHUCKA
CHUCKA
CHUCKA
CHUCKA

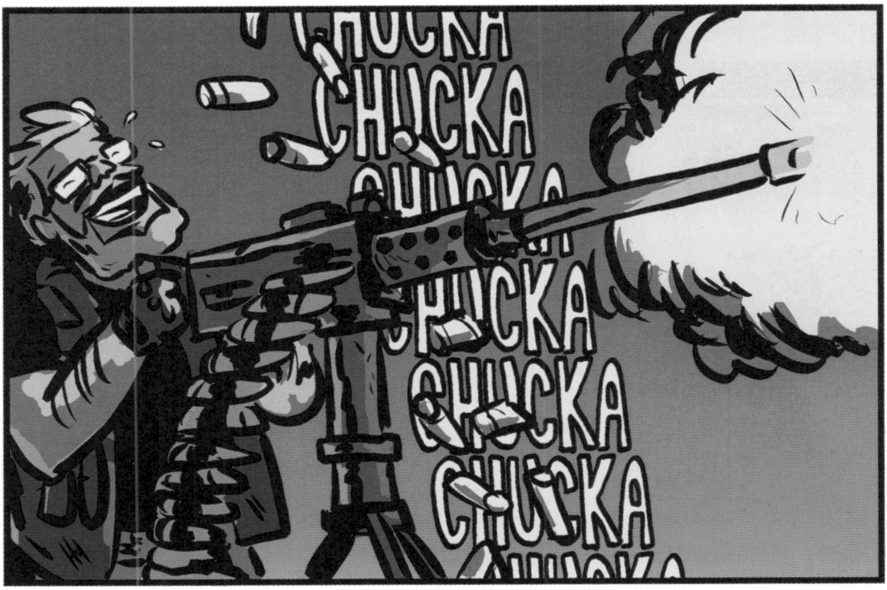
CHUCKA
CHUCKA
CHUCKA
CHUCKA

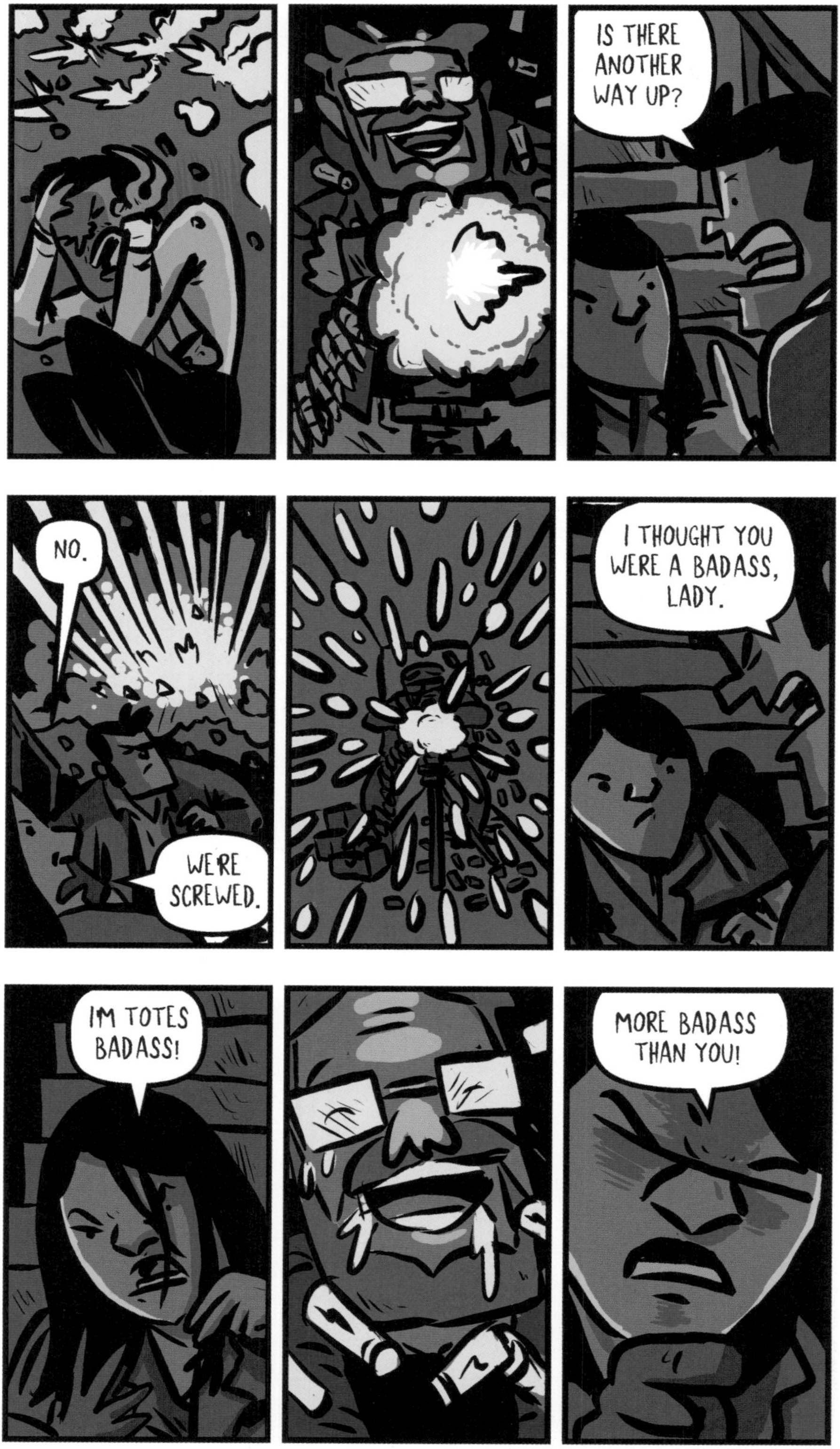
IS THERE ANOTHER WAY UP?
NO.
WE'RE SCREWED.
I THOUGHT YOU WERE A BADASS, LADY.
I'M TOTES BADASS!
MORE BADASS THAN YOU!

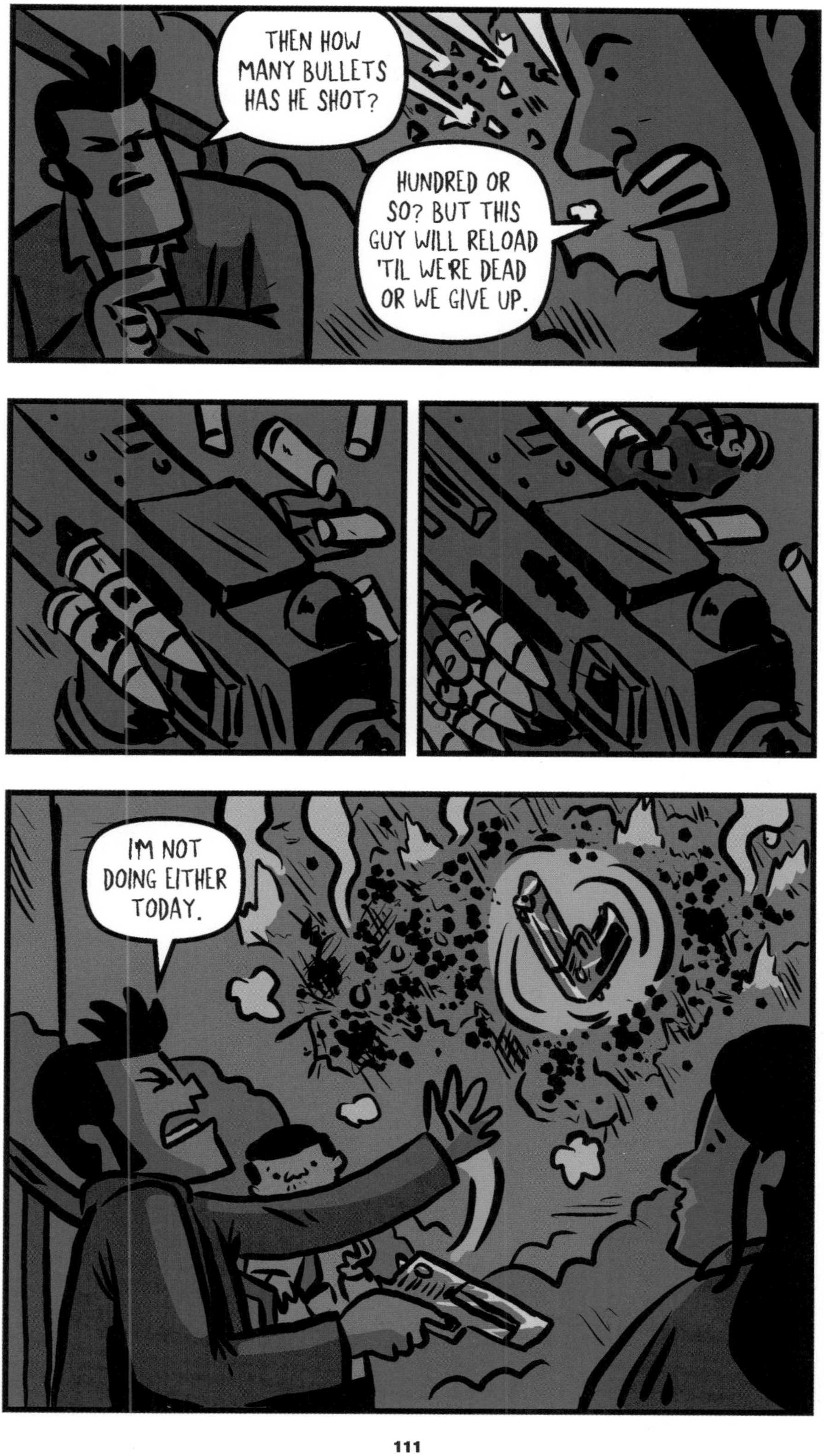
THEN HOW MANY BULLETS HAS HE SHOT?
HUNDRED OR SO? BUT THIS GUY WILL RELOAD 'TIL WE'RE DEAD OR WE GIVE UP.
I'M NOT DOING EITHER TODAY.

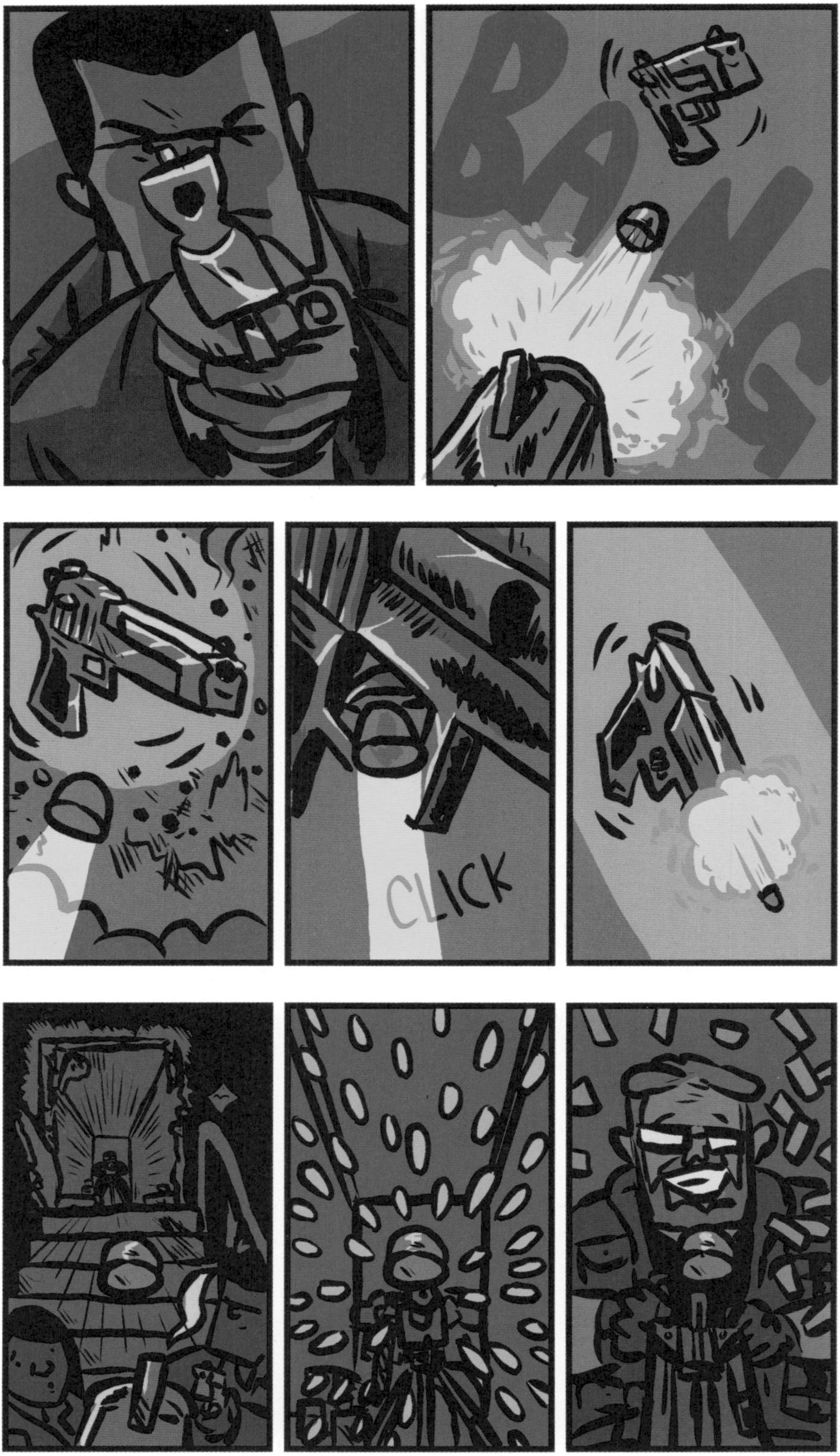
BANG
CLICK

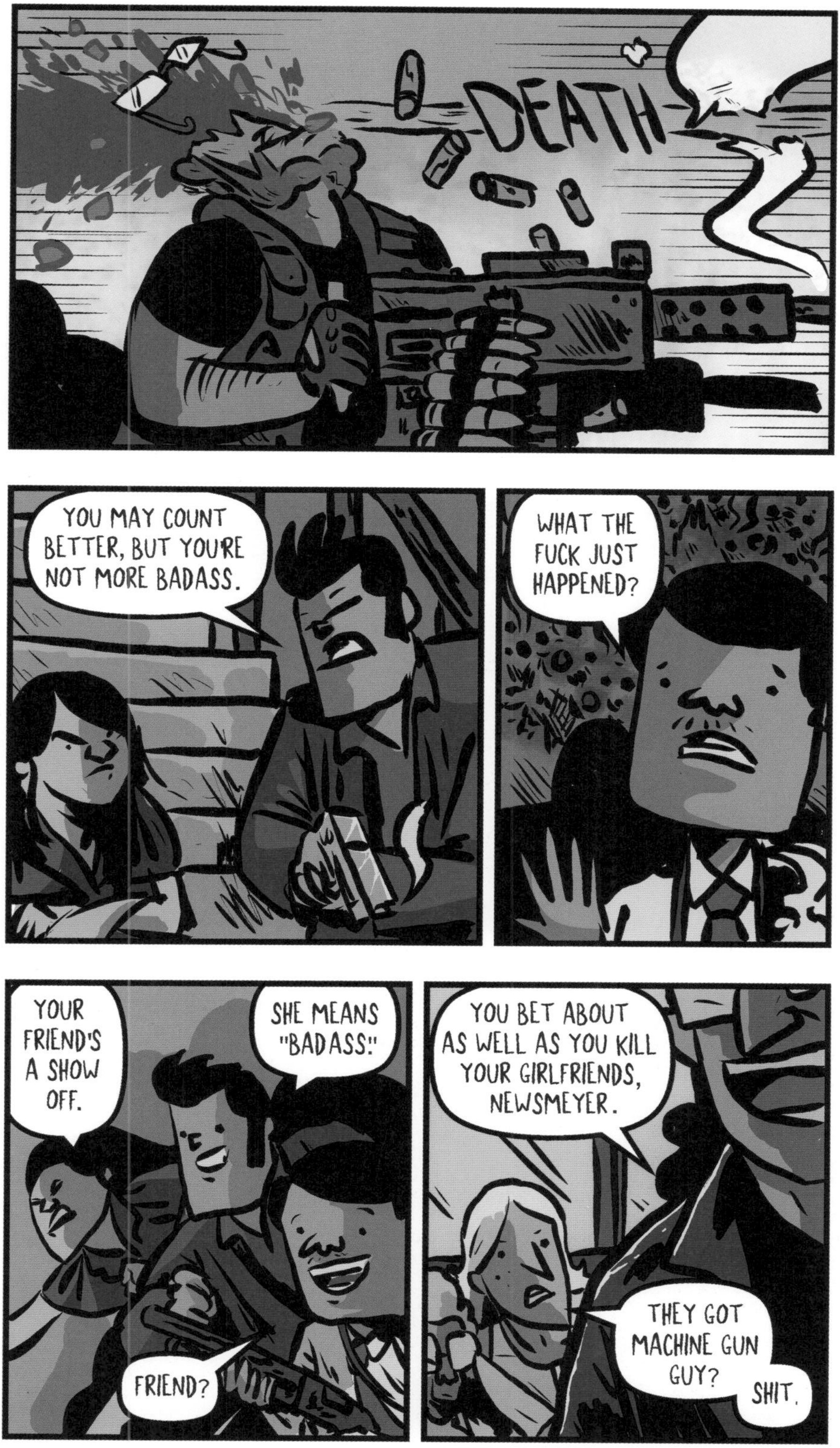
DEATH
YOU MAY COUNT BETTER, BUT YOU'RE NOT MORE BADASS.
WHAT THE FUCK JUST HAPPENED?
YOUR FRIEND'S A SHOW OFF.
SHE MEANS "BADASS."
FRIEND?
YOU BET ABOUT AS WELL AS YOU KILL YOUR GIRLFRIENDS, NEWSMEYER.
THEY GOT MACHINE GUN GUY?
SHIT.

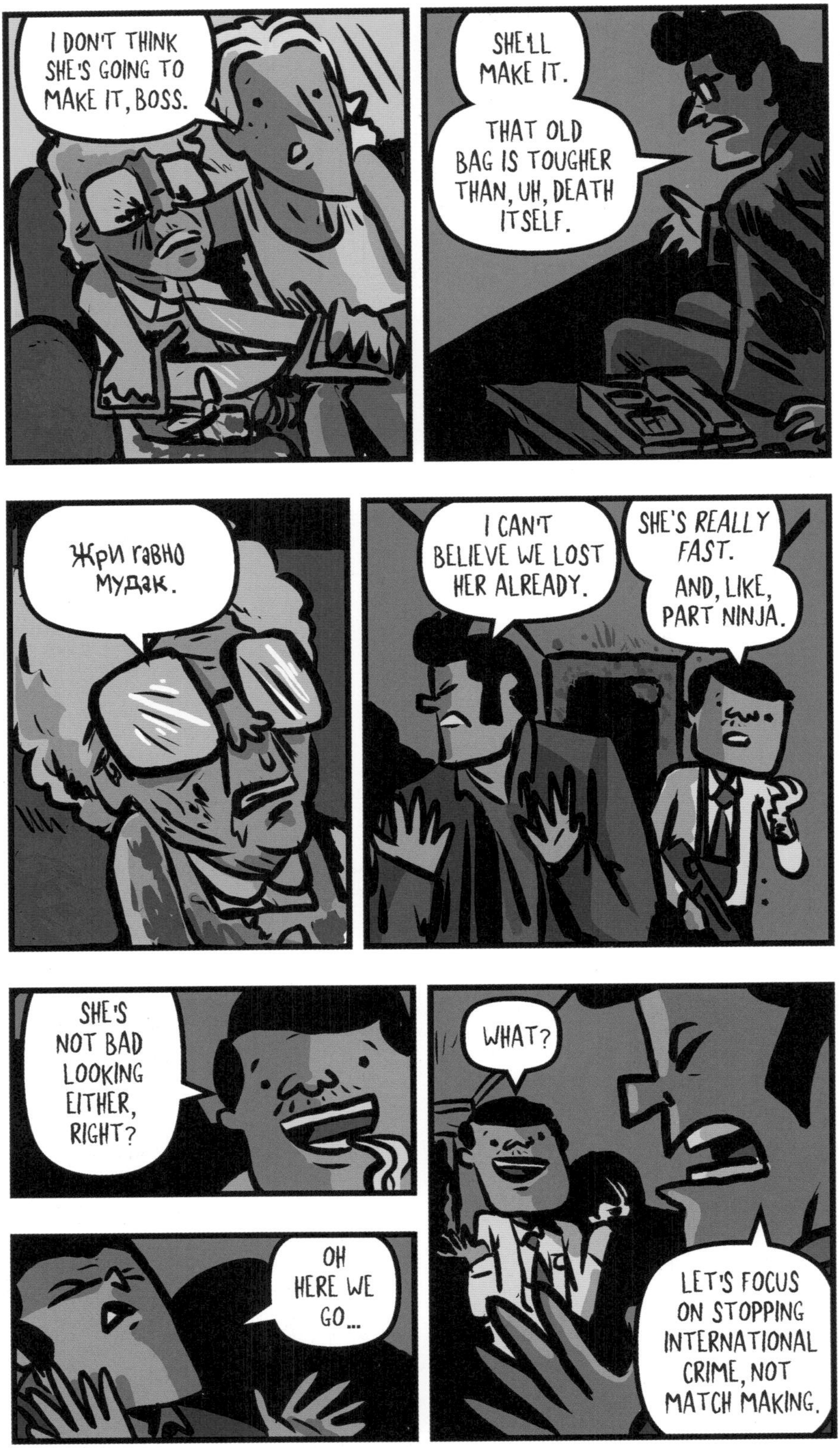
I DON'T THINK SHE'S GOING TO MAKE IT, BOSS.
SHE'LL MAKE IT.
THAT OLD BAG IS TOUGHER THAN, UH, DEATH ITSELF.
Жри гавно мудак.
I CAN'T BELIEVE WE LOST HER ALREADY.
SHE'S *REALLY FAST*.
AND, LIKE, PART NINJA.
SHE'S NOT BAD LOOKING EITHER, RIGHT?
OH HERE WE GO...
WHAT?
LET'S FOCUS ON STOPPING INTERNATIONAL CRIME, NOT MATCH MAKING.

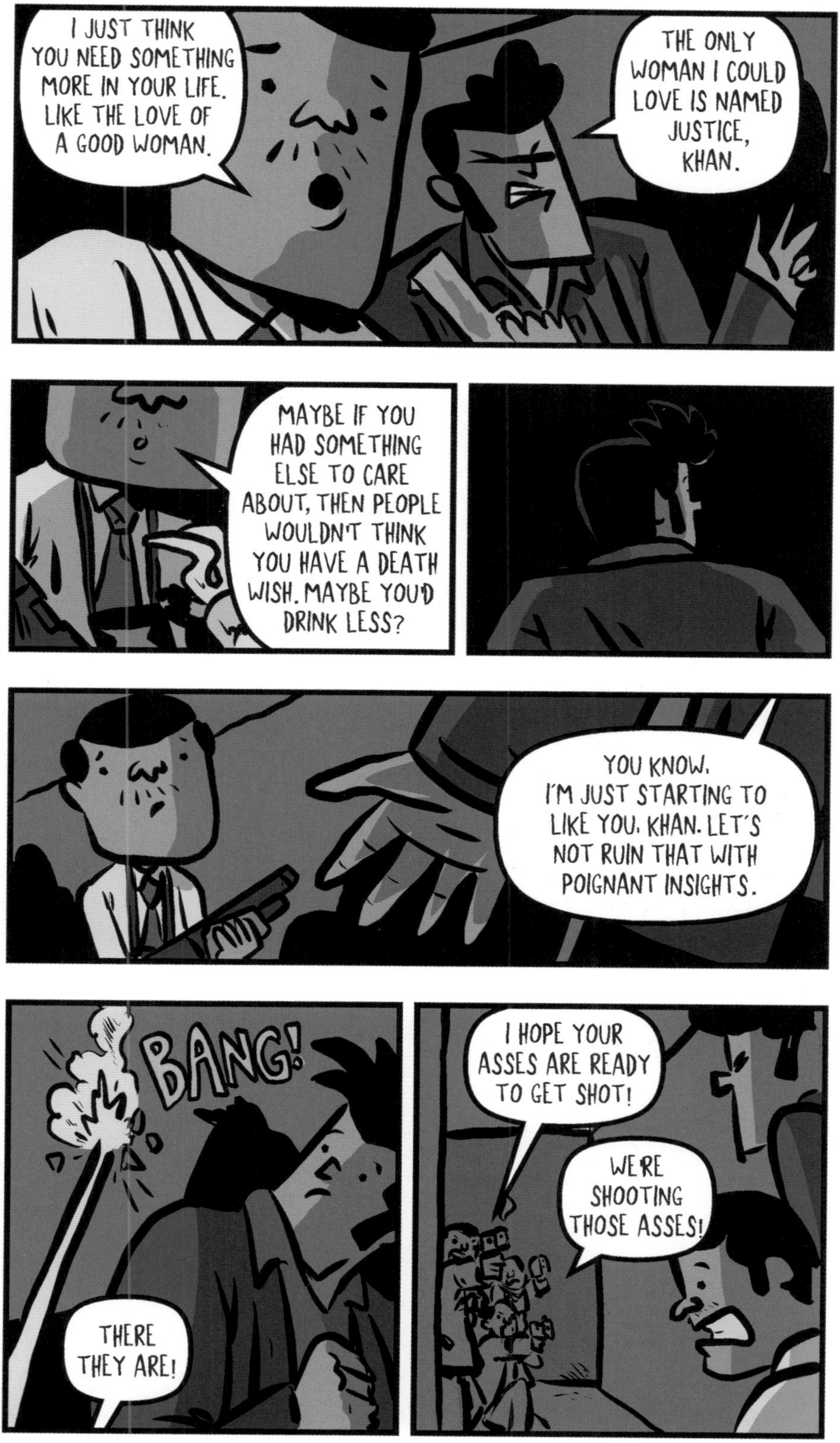
I JUST THINK YOU NEED SOMETHING MORE IN YOUR LIFE. LIKE THE LOVE OF A GOOD WOMAN.
THE ONLY WOMAN I COULD LOVE IS NAMED JUSTICE, KHAN.
MAYBE IF YOU HAD SOMETHING ELSE TO CARE ABOUT, THEN PEOPLE WOULDN'T THINK YOU HAVE A DEATH WISH. MAYBE YOU'D DRINK LESS?
YOU KNOW. I'M JUST STARTING TO LIKE YOU. KHAN. LET'S NOT RUIN THAT WITH POIGNANT INSIGHTS.
BANG!
THERE THEY ARE!
I HOPE YOUR ASSES ARE READY TO GET SHOT!
WE'RE SHOOTING THOSE ASSES!

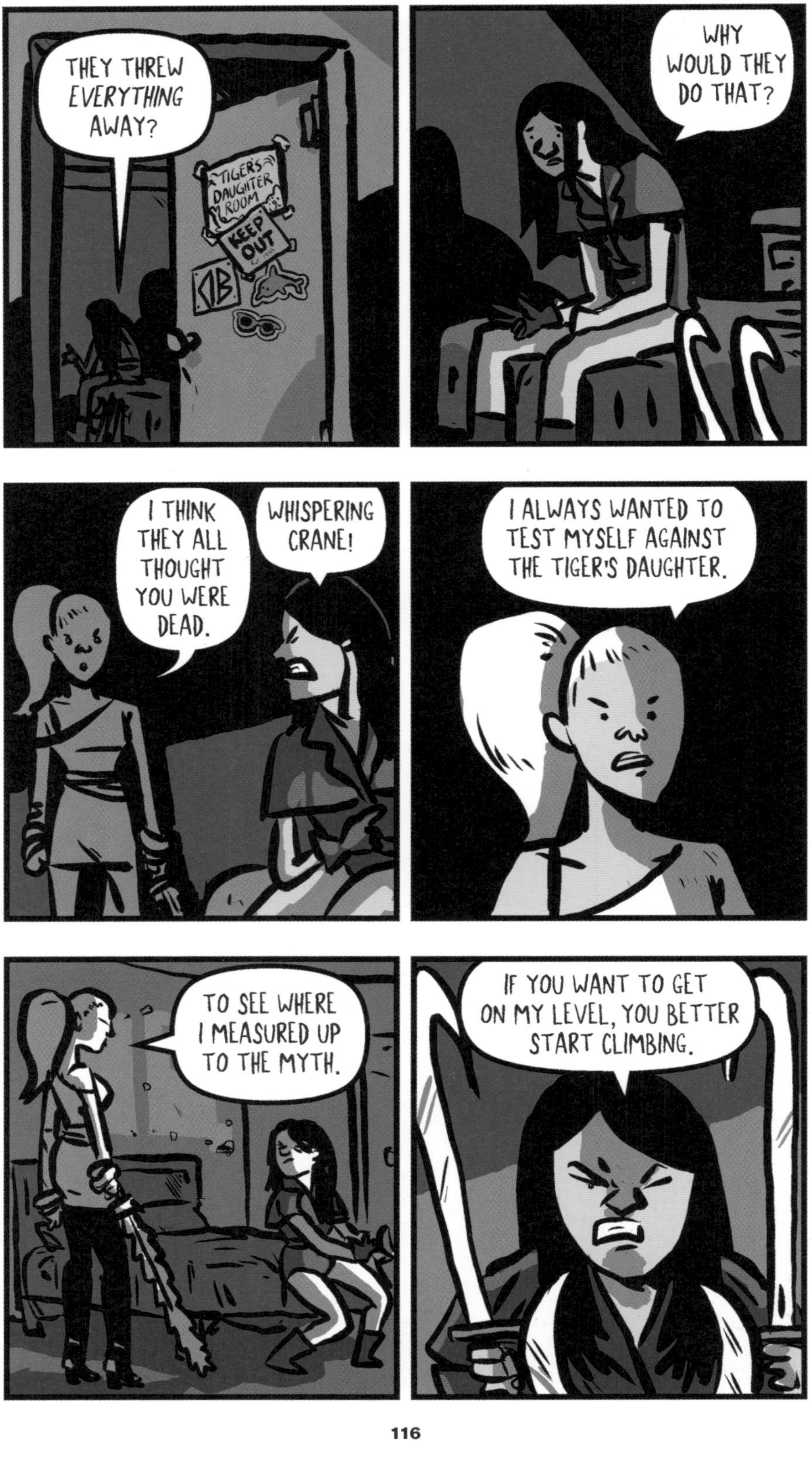
THEY THREW EVERYTHING AWAY?
TIGER'S DAUGHTER ROOM
KEEP OUT
WHY WOULD THEY DO THAT?
I THINK THEY ALL THOUGHT YOU WERE DEAD.
WHISPERING CRANE!
I ALWAYS WANTED TO TEST MYSELF AGAINST THE TIGER'S DAUGHTER.
TO SEE WHERE I MEASURED UP TO THE MYTH.
IF YOU WANT TO GET ON MY LEVEL, YOU BETTER START CLIMBING.

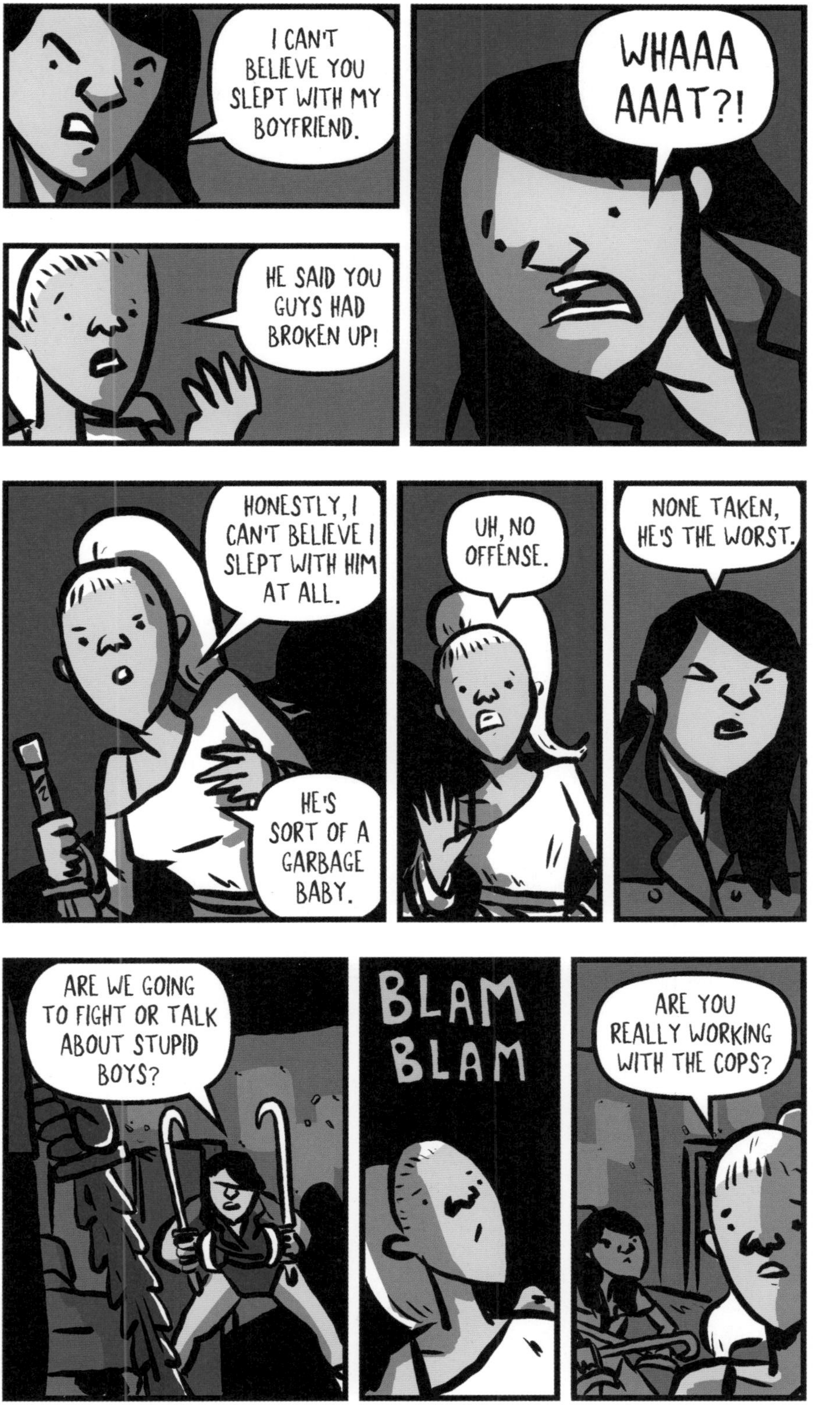
I CAN'T BELIEVE YOU SLEPT WITH MY BOYFRIEND.
WHAAA AAAT?!
HE SAID YOU GUYS HAD BROKEN UP!
HONESTLY, I CAN'T BELIEVE I SLEPT WITH HIM AT ALL.
HE'S SORT OF A GARBAGE BABY.
UH, NO OFFENSE.
NONE TAKEN, HE'S THE WORST.
ARE WE GOING TO FIGHT OR TALK ABOUT STUPID BOYS?
BLAM BLAM
ARE YOU REALLY WORKING WITH THE COPS?

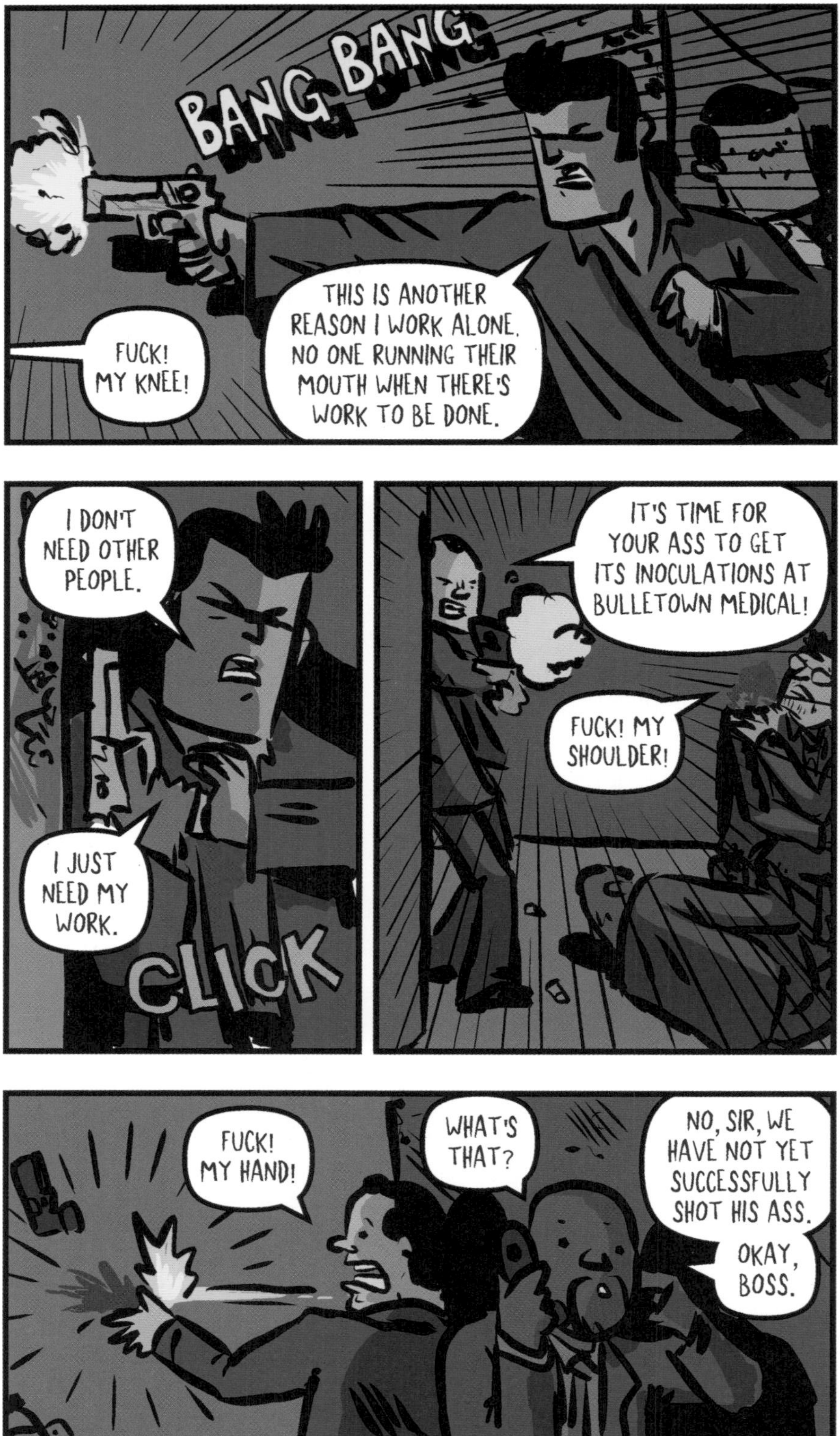
BANG BANG
THIS IS ANOTHER REASON I WORK ALONE. NO ONE RUNNING THEIR MOUTH WHEN THERE'S WORK TO BE DONE.
FUCK! MY KNEE!
I DON'T NEED OTHER PEOPLE.
I JUST NEED MY WORK.
CLICK
IT'S TIME FOR YOUR ASS TO GET ITS INOCULATIONS AT BULLETOWN MEDICAL!
FUCK! MY SHOULDER!
FUCK! MY HAND!
WHAT'S THAT?
NO, SIR, WE HAVE NOT YET SUCCESSFULLY SHOT HIS ASS.
OKAY, BOSS.

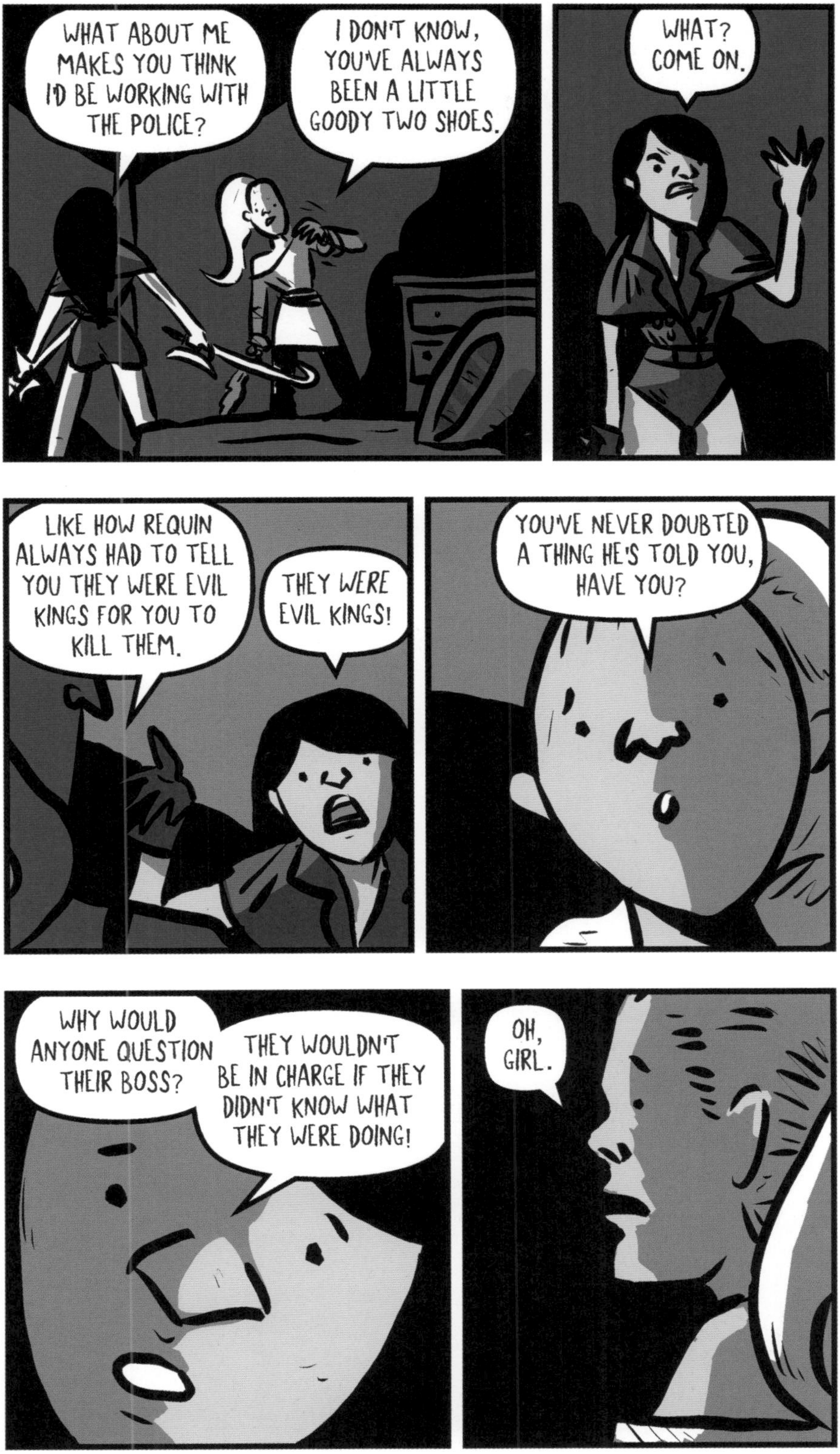
WHAT ABOUT ME MAKES YOU THINK I'D BE WORKING WITH THE POLICE?
I DON'T KNOW, YOU'VE ALWAYS BEEN A LITTLE GOODY TWO SHOES.
WHAT? COME ON.
LIKE HOW REQUIN ALWAYS HAD TO TELL YOU THEY WERE EVIL KINGS FOR YOU TO KILL THEM.
THEY *WERE* EVIL KINGS!
YOU'VE NEVER DOUBTED A THING HE'S TOLD YOU, HAVE YOU?
WHY WOULD ANYONE QUESTION THEIR BOSS?
THEY WOULDN'T BE IN CHARGE IF THEY DIDN'T KNOW WHAT THEY WERE DOING!
OH, GIRL.

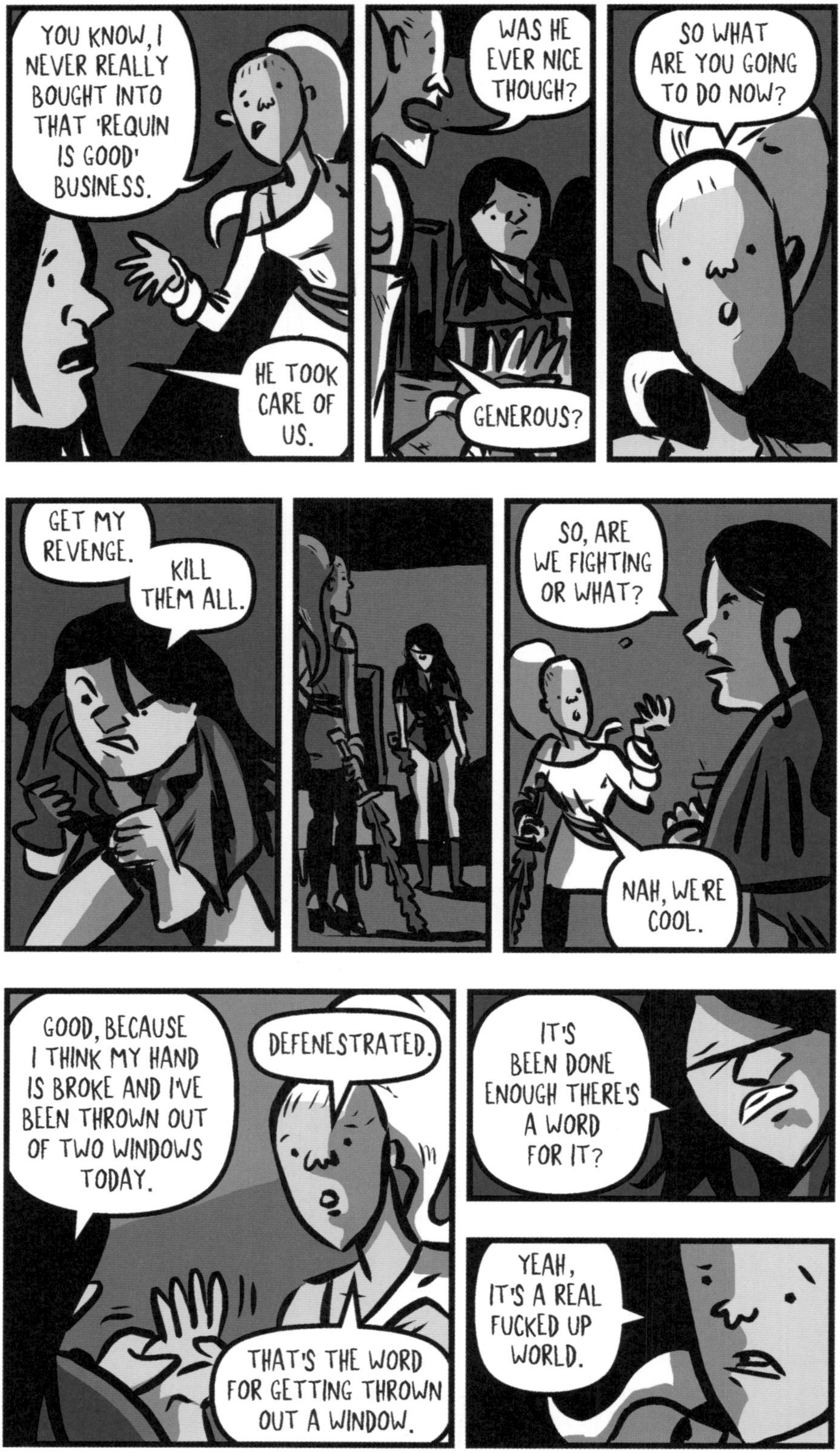
YOU KNOW, I NEVER REALLY BOUGHT INTO THAT 'REQUIN IS GOOD' BUSINESS.
HE TOOK CARE OF US.
WAS HE EVER NICE THOUGH?
GENEROUS?
SO WHAT ARE YOU GOING TO DO NOW?
GET MY REVENGE.
KILL THEM ALL.
SO, ARE WE FIGHTING OR WHAT?
NAH, WE'RE COOL.
GOOD, BECAUSE I THINK MY HAND IS BROKE AND I'VE BEEN THROWN OUT OF TWO WINDOWS TODAY.
DEFENESTRATED.
THAT'S THE WORD FOR GETTING THROWN OUT A WINDOW.
IT'S BEEN DONE ENOUGH THERE'S A WORD FOR IT?
YEAH, IT'S A REAL FUCKED UP WORLD.

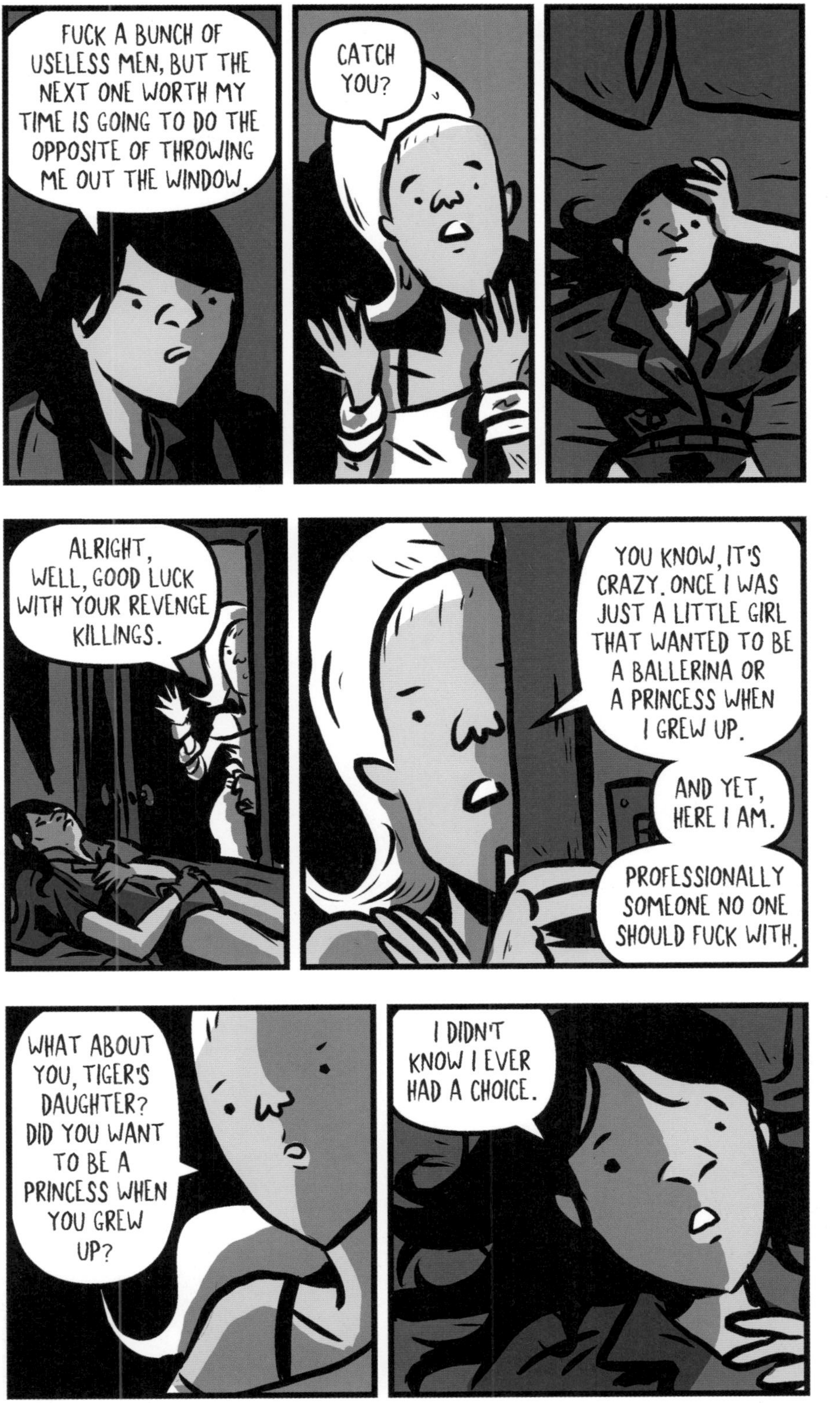
FUCK A BUNCH OF USELESS MEN, BUT THE NEXT ONE WORTH MY TIME IS GOING TO DO THE OPPOSITE OF THROWING ME OUT THE WINDOW.
CATCH YOU?
ALRIGHT, WELL, GOOD LUCK WITH YOUR REVENGE KILLINGS.
YOU KNOW, IT'S CRAZY. ONCE I WAS JUST A LITTLE GIRL THAT WANTED TO BE A BALLERINA OR A PRINCESS WHEN I GREW UP.
AND YET, HERE I AM.
PROFESSIONALLY SOMEONE NO ONE SHOULD FUCK WITH.
WHAT ABOUT YOU, TIGER'S DAUGHTER? DID YOU WANT TO BE A PRINCESS WHEN YOU GREW UP?
I DIDN'T KNOW I EVER HAD A CHOICE.

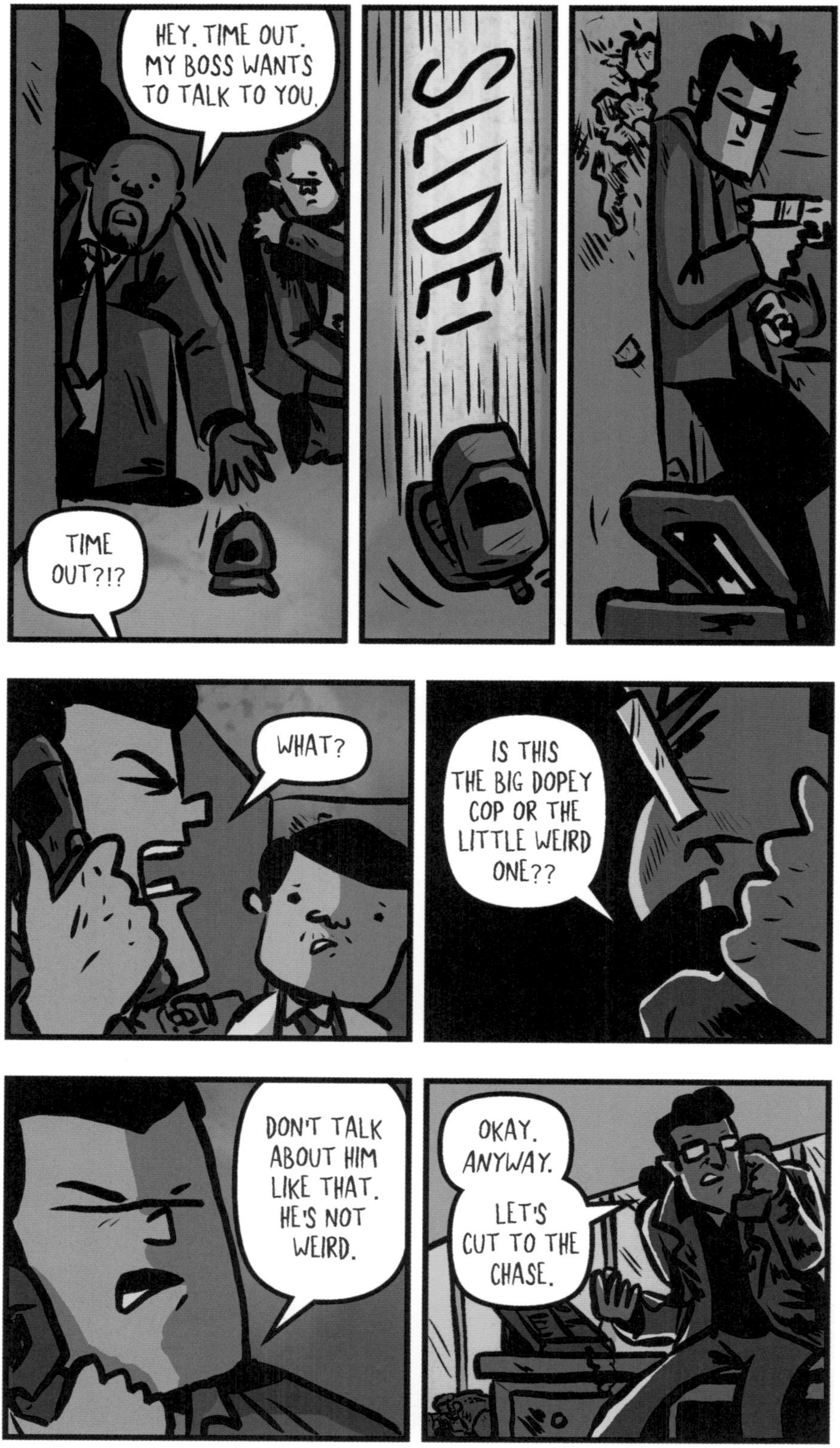
HEY. TIME OUT. MY BOSS WANTS TO TALK TO YOU.
TIME OUT?!?
SLIDE!
WHAT?
IS THIS THE BIG DOPEY COP OR THE LITTLE WEIRD ONE??
DON'T TALK ABOUT HIM LIKE THAT. HE'S NOT WEIRD.
OKAY. ANYWAY.
LET'S CUT TO THE CHASE.

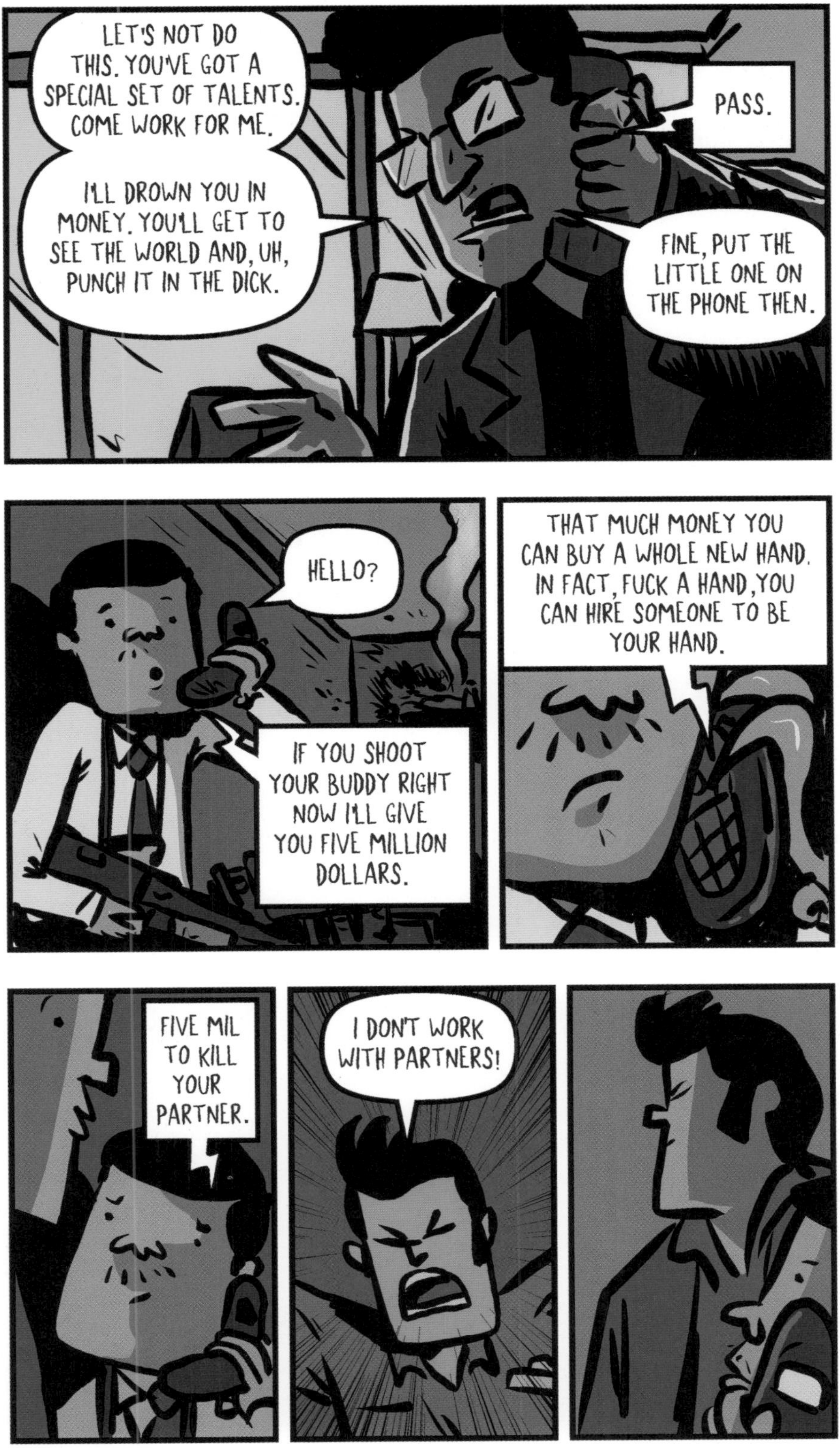
LET'S NOT DO THIS. YOU'VE GOT A SPECIAL SET OF TALENTS. COME WORK FOR ME.
I'LL DROWN YOU IN MONEY. YOU'LL GET TO SEE THE WORLD AND, UH, PUNCH IT IN THE DICK.
PASS.
FINE, PUT THE LITTLE ONE ON THE PHONE THEN.
HELLO?
IF YOU SHOOT YOUR BUDDY RIGHT NOW I'LL GIVE YOU FIVE MILLION DOLLARS.
THAT MUCH MONEY YOU CAN BUY A WHOLE NEW HAND. IN FACT, FUCK A HAND, YOU CAN HIRE SOMEONE TO BE YOUR HAND.
FIVE MIL TO KILL YOUR PARTNER.
I DON'T WORK WITH PARTNERS!

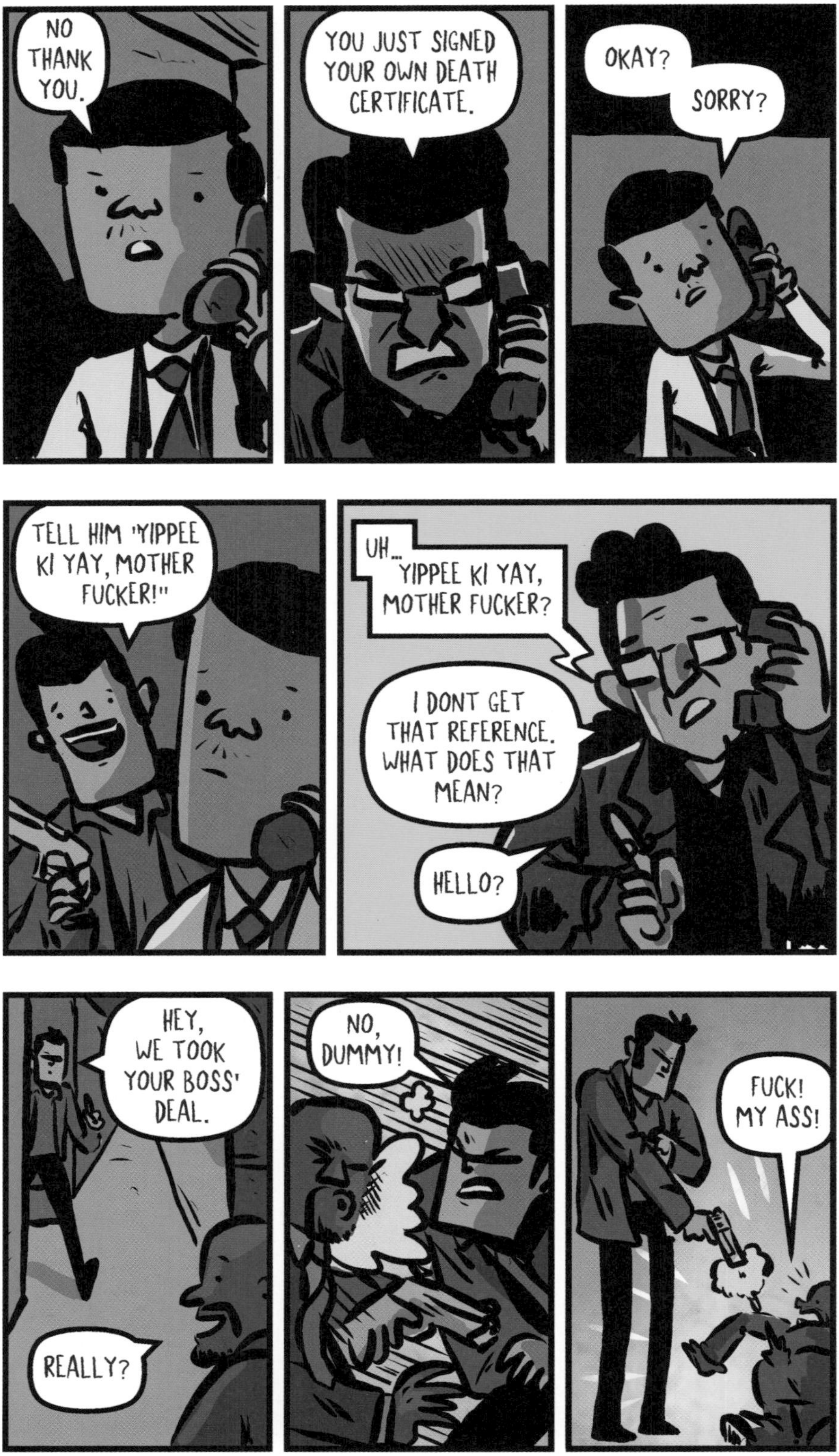
NO THANK YOU.
YOU JUST SIGNED YOUR OWN DEATH CERTIFICATE.
OKAY?
SORRY?
TELL HIM "YIPPEE KI YAY, MOTHER FUCKER!"
UH... "YIPPEE KI YAY, MOTHER FUCKER?
I DONT GET THAT REFERENCE. WHAT DOES THAT MEAN?
HELLO?
HEY, WE TOOK YOUR BOSS' DEAL.
REALLY?
NO, DUMMY!
FUCK! MY ASS!

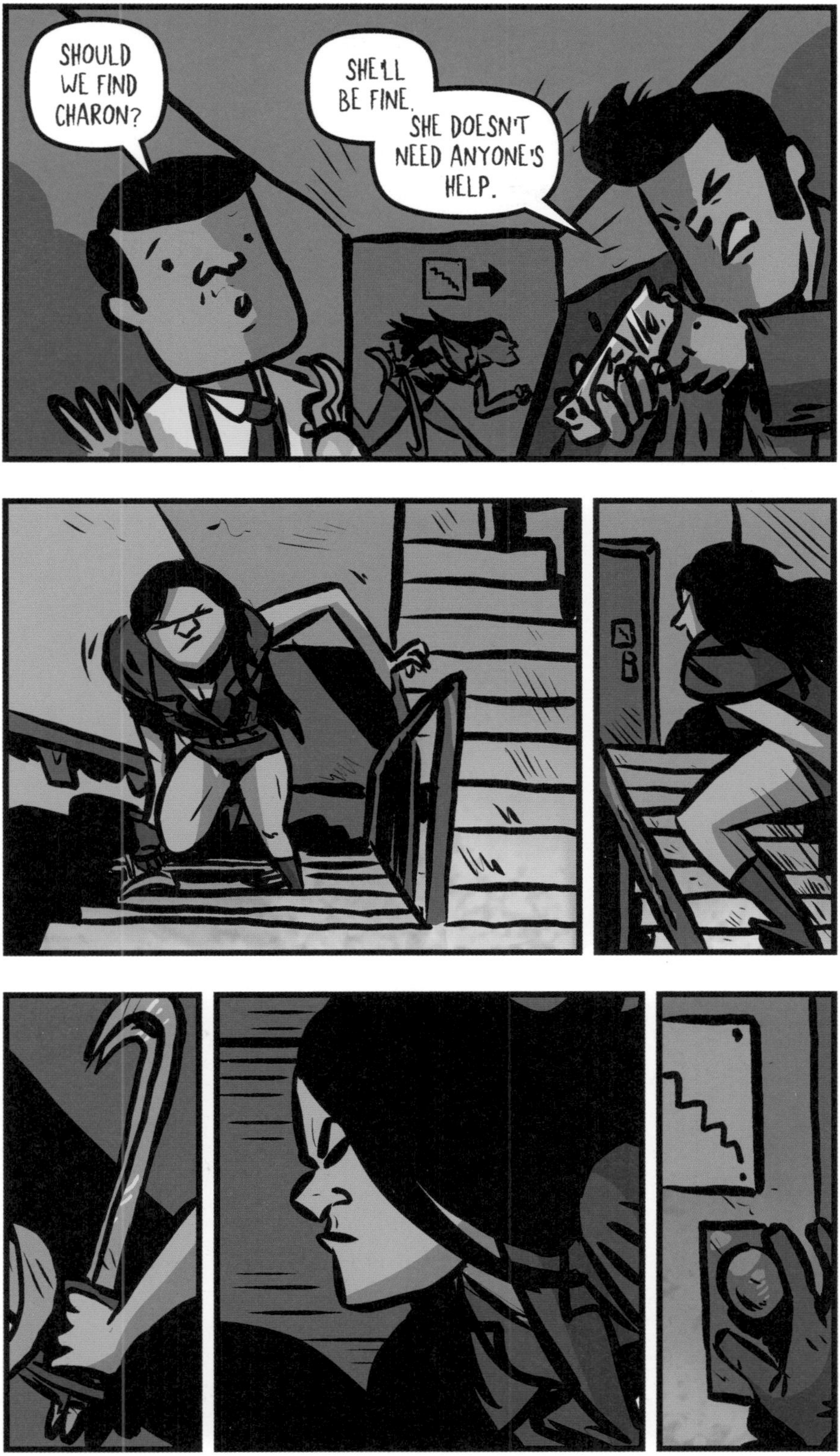
SHOULD WE FIND CHARON?
SHE'LL BE FINE.
SHE DOESN'T NEED ANYONE'S HELP.

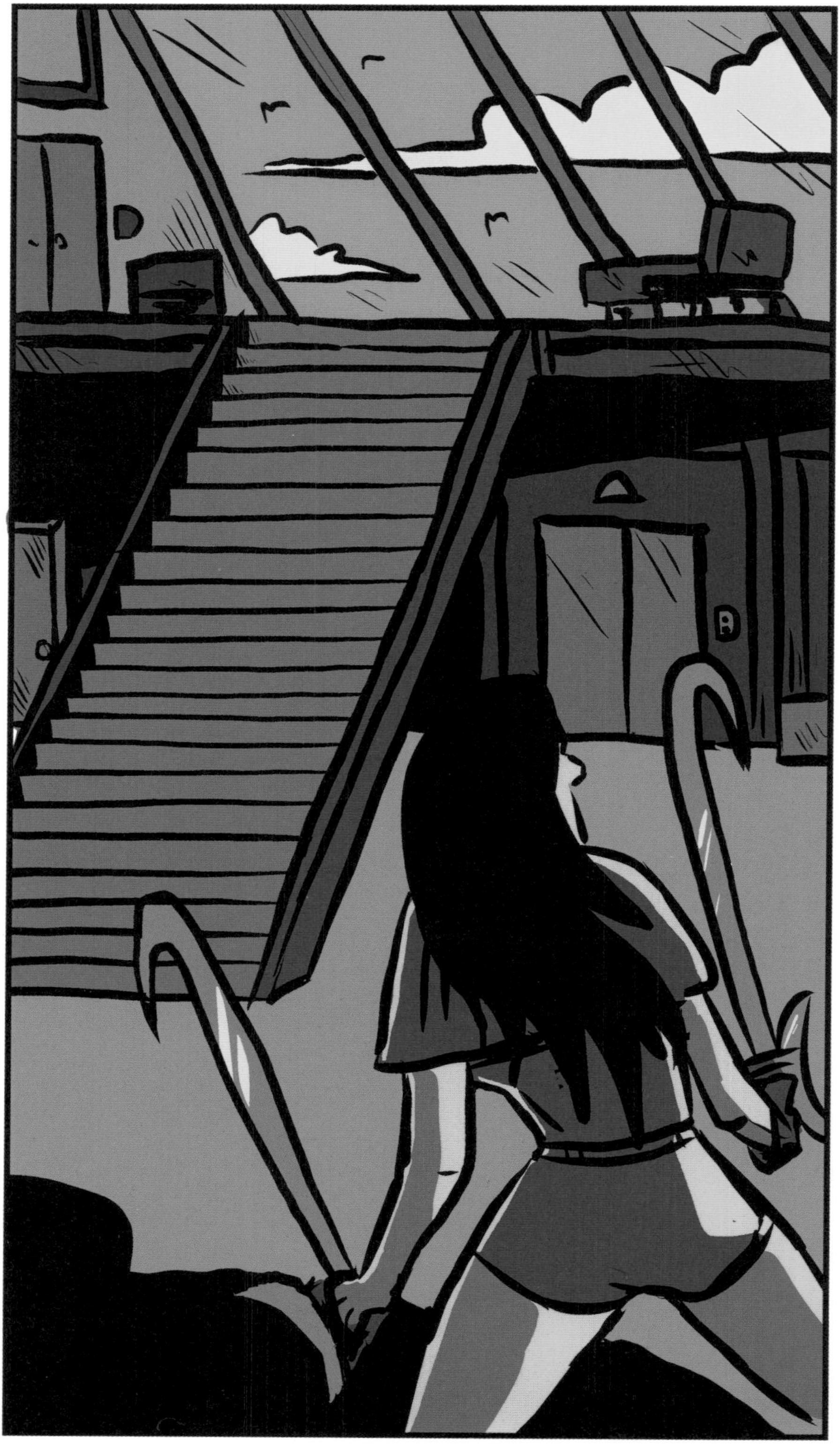

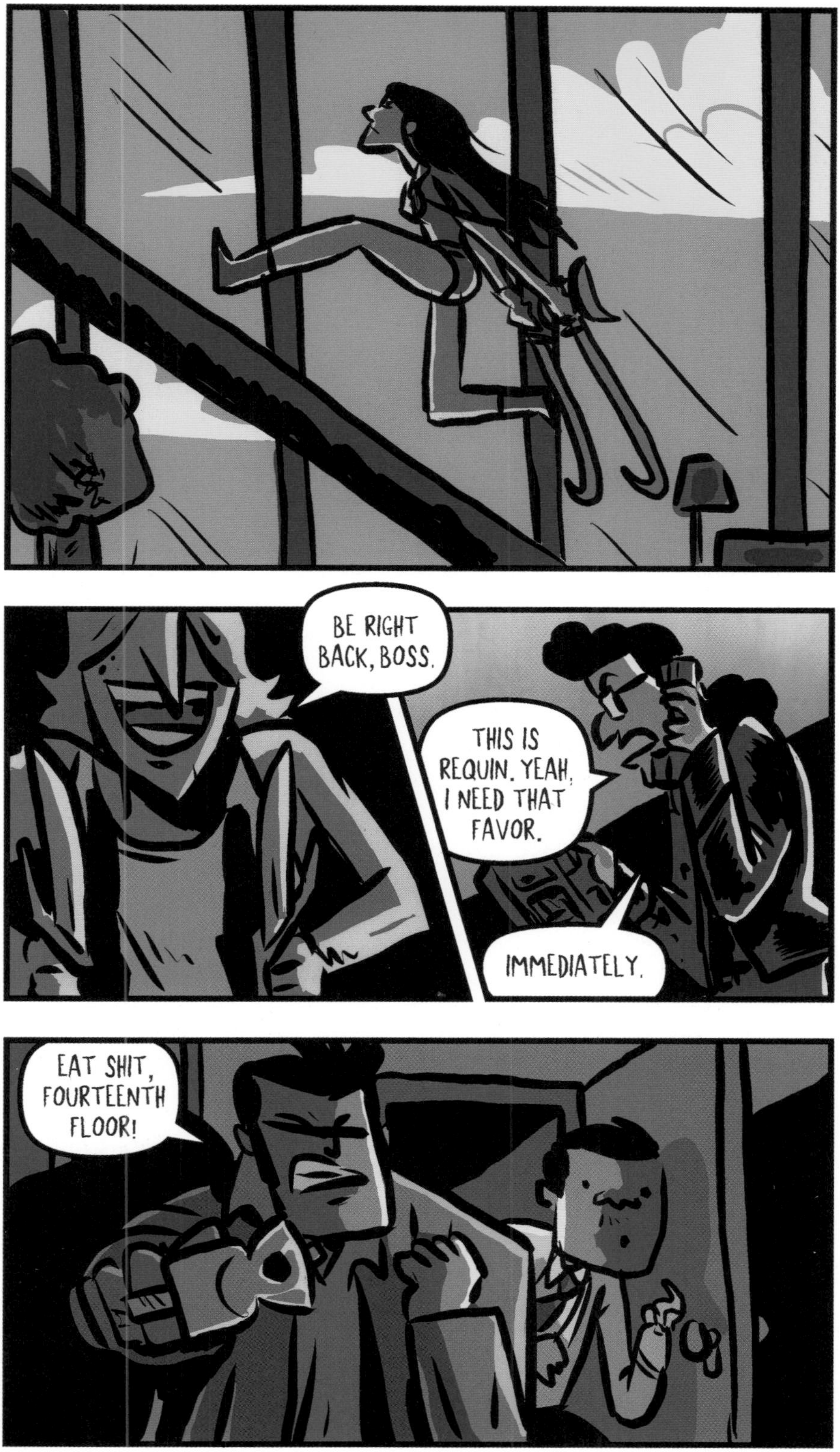
BE RIGHT BACK, BOSS.
THIS IS REQUIN. YEAH, I NEED THAT FAVOR.
IMMEDIATELY.
EAT SHIT, FOURTEENTH FLOOR!

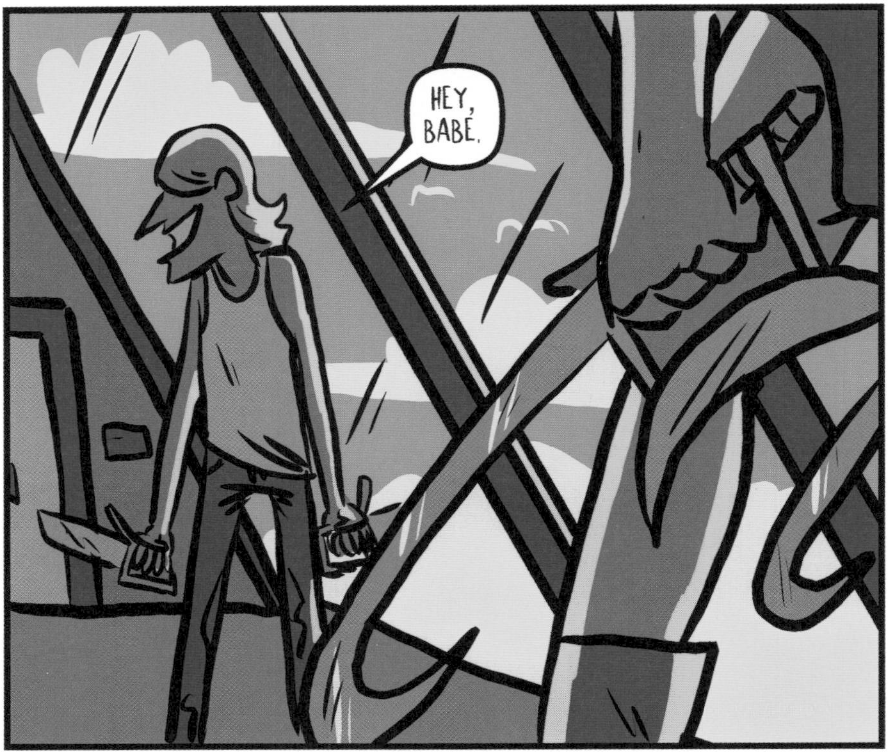
HEY, BABE.

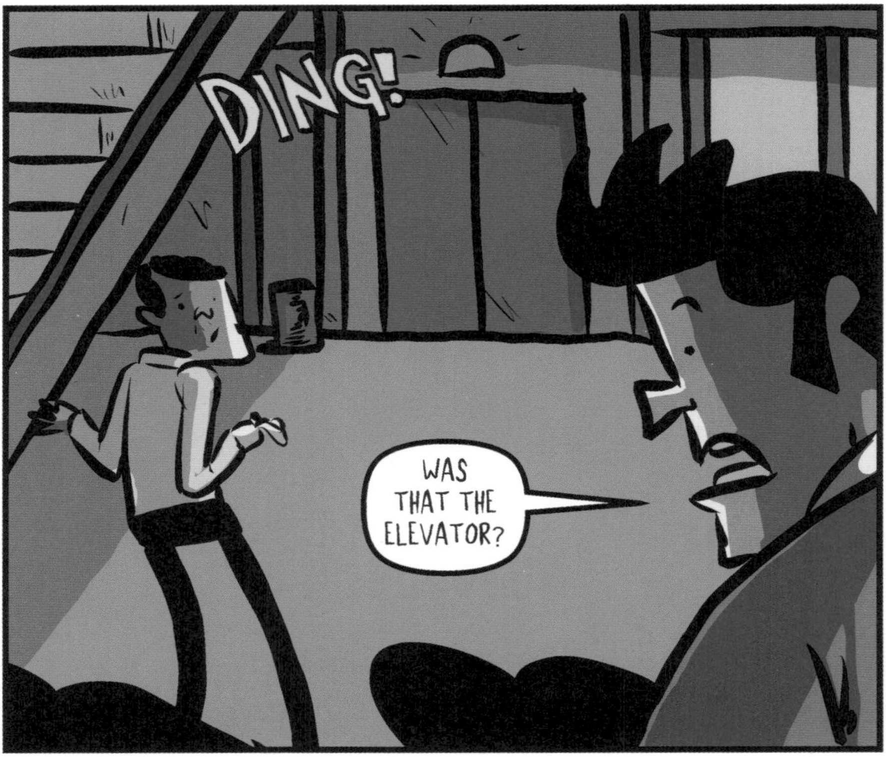
DING!
WAS THAT THE ELEVATOR?

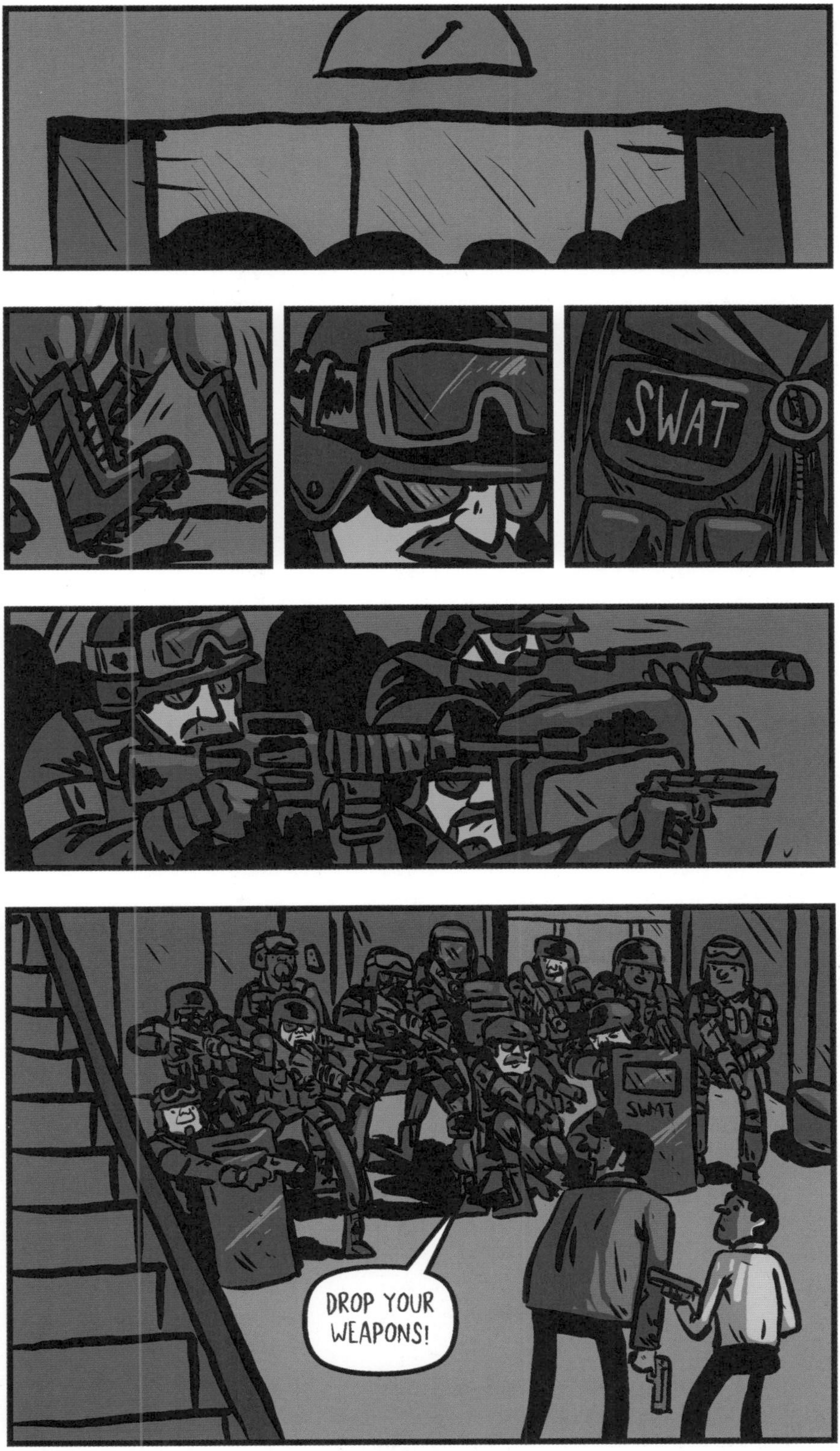
SWAT
SWAT
DROP YOUR WEAPONS!

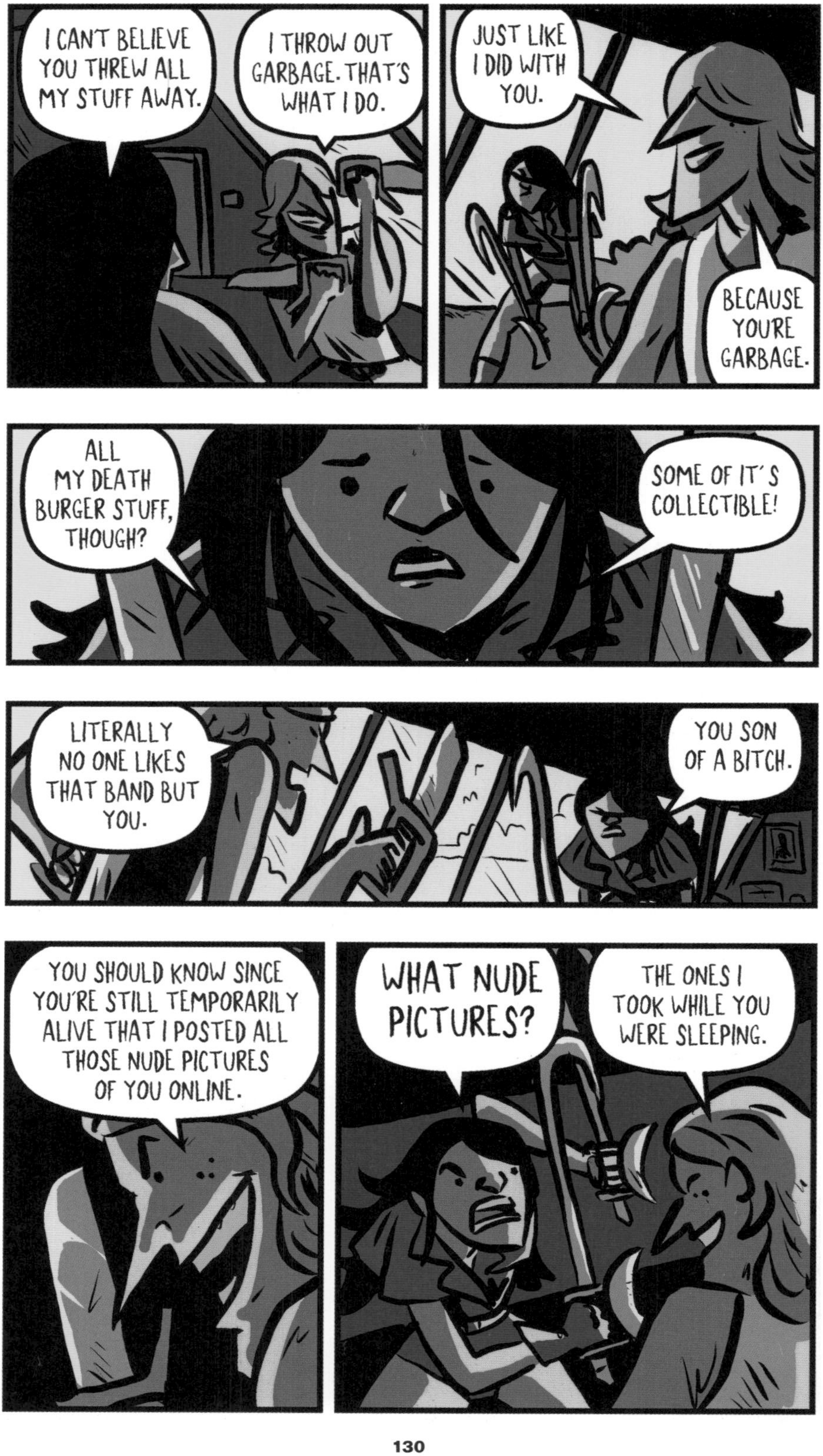
I CAN'T BELIEVE YOU THREW ALL MY STUFF AWAY.
I THROW OUT GARBAGE. THAT'S WHAT I DO.
JUST LIKE I DID WITH YOU.
BECAUSE YOU'RE GARBAGE.
ALL MY DEATH BURGER STUFF, THOUGH?
SOME OF IT'S COLLECTIBLE!
LITERALLY NO ONE LIKES THAT BAND BUT YOU.
YOU SON OF A BITCH.
YOU SHOULD KNOW SINCE YOU'RE STILL TEMPORARILY ALIVE THAT I POSTED ALL THOSE NUDE PICTURES OF YOU ONLINE.
WHAT NUDE PICTURES?
THE ONES I TOOK WHILE YOU WERE SLEEPING.

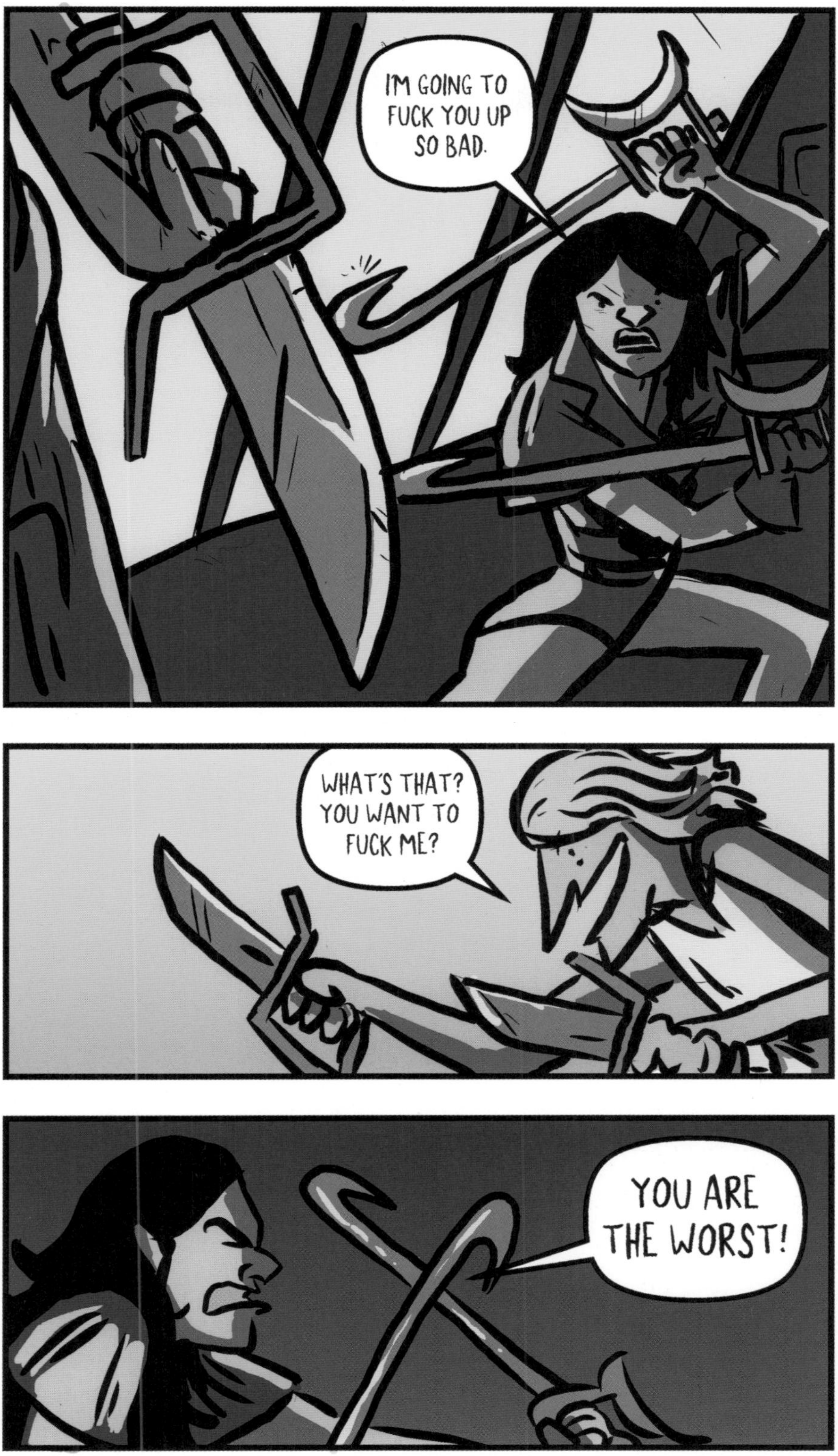
I'M GOING TO FUCK YOU UP SO BAD.
WHAT'S THAT? YOU WANT TO FUCK ME?
YOU ARE THE WORST!

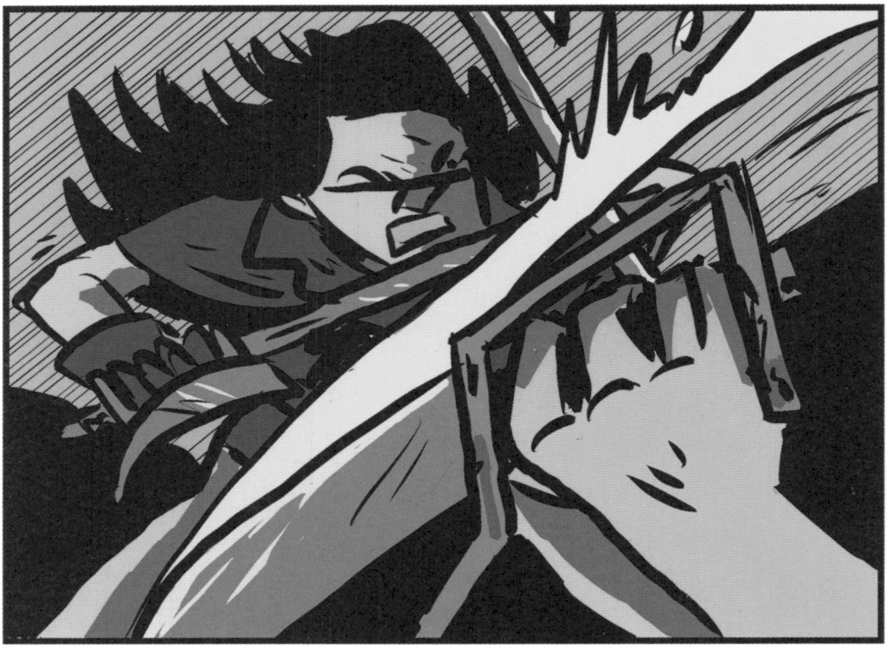

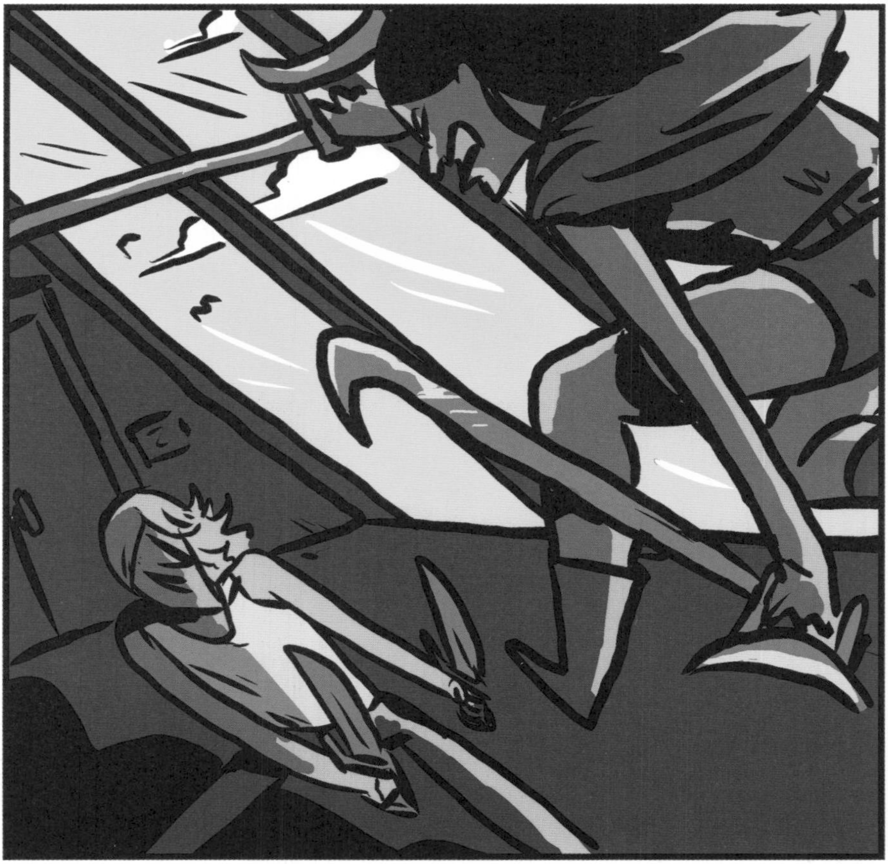

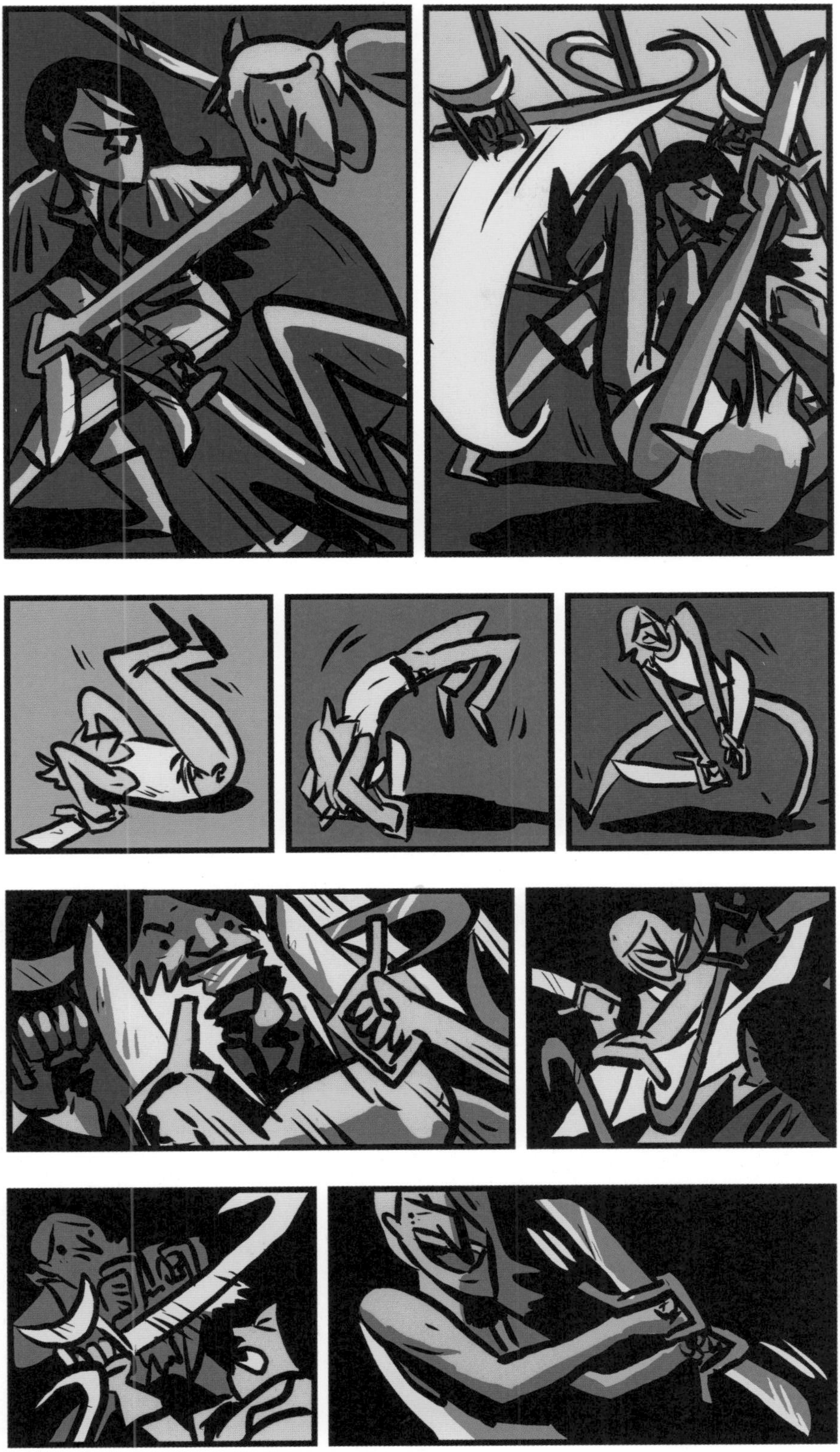

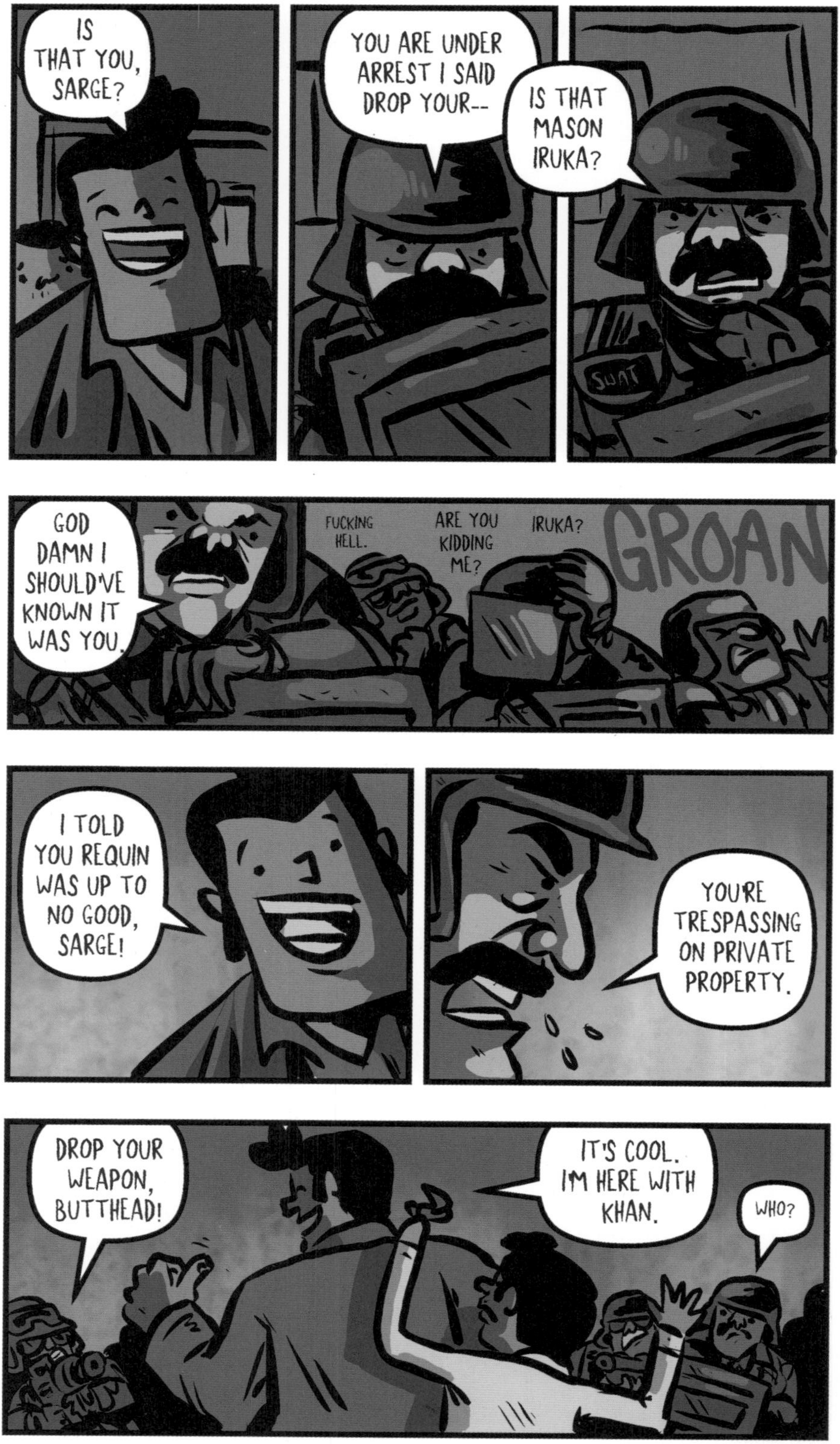
IS THAT YOU, SARGE?
YOU ARE UNDER ARREST I SAID DROP YOUR--
IS THAT MASON IRUKA?
SWAT
GOD DAMN I SHOULD'VE KNOWN IT WAS YOU.
FUCKING HELL.
ARE YOU KIDDING ME?
IRUKA?
GROAN
I TOLD YOU REQUIN WAS UP TO NO GOOD, SARGE!
YOU'RE TRESPASSING ON PRIVATE PROPERTY.
DROP YOUR WEAPON, BUTTHEAD!
IT'S COOL. I'M HERE WITH KHAN.
WHO?

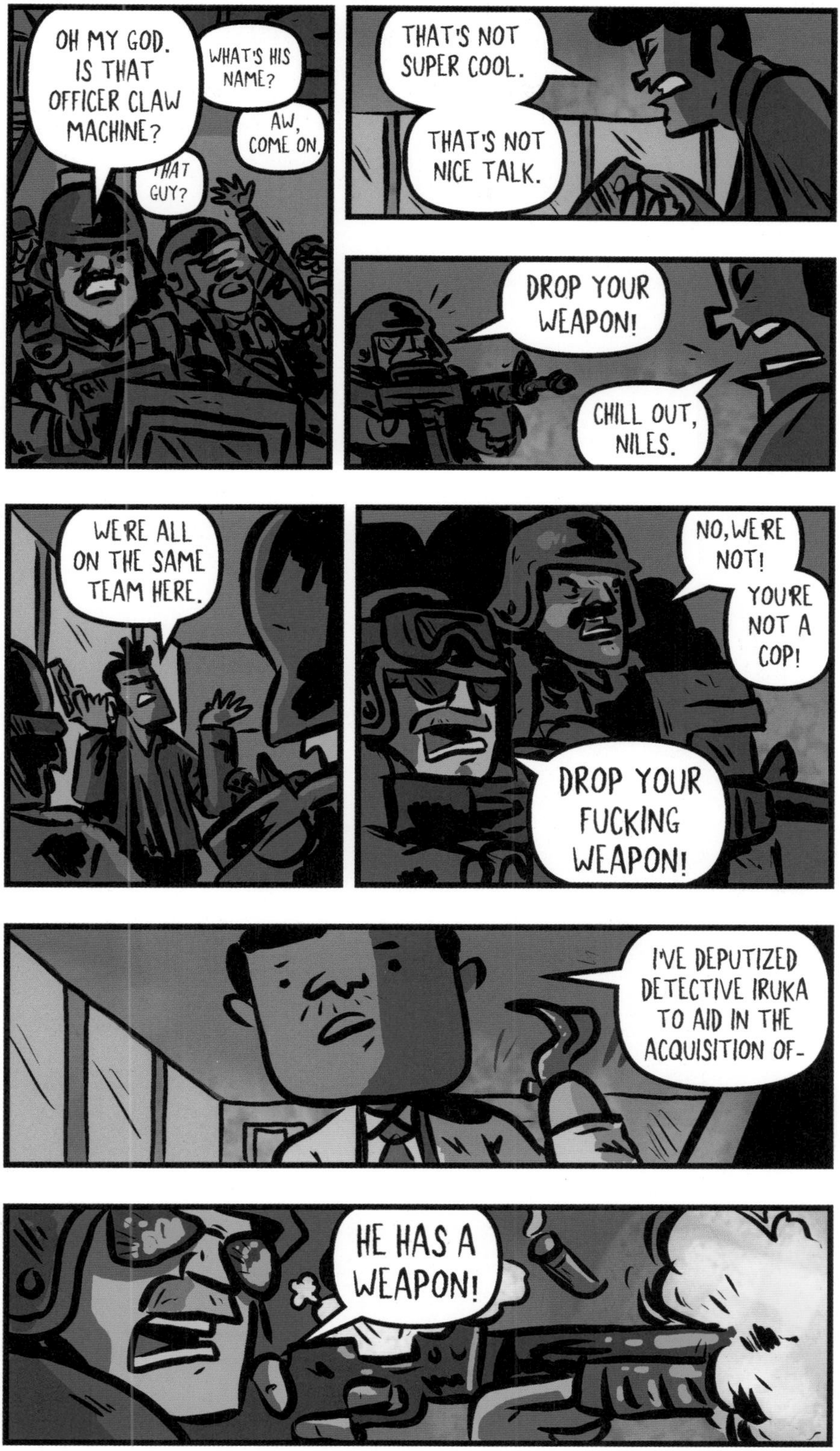
OH MY GOD. IS THAT OFFICER CLAW MACHINE?
WHAT'S HIS NAME?
THAT GUY?
AW, COME ON.
THAT'S NOT SUPER COOL.
THAT'S NOT NICE TALK.
DROP YOUR WEAPON!
CHILL OUT, NILES.
WE'RE ALL ON THE SAME TEAM HERE.
NO, WE'RE NOT!
YOU'RE NOT A COP!
DROP YOUR FUCKING WEAPON!
I'VE DEPUTIZED DETECTIVE IRUKA TO AID IN THE ACQUISITION OF-
HE HAS A WEAPON!

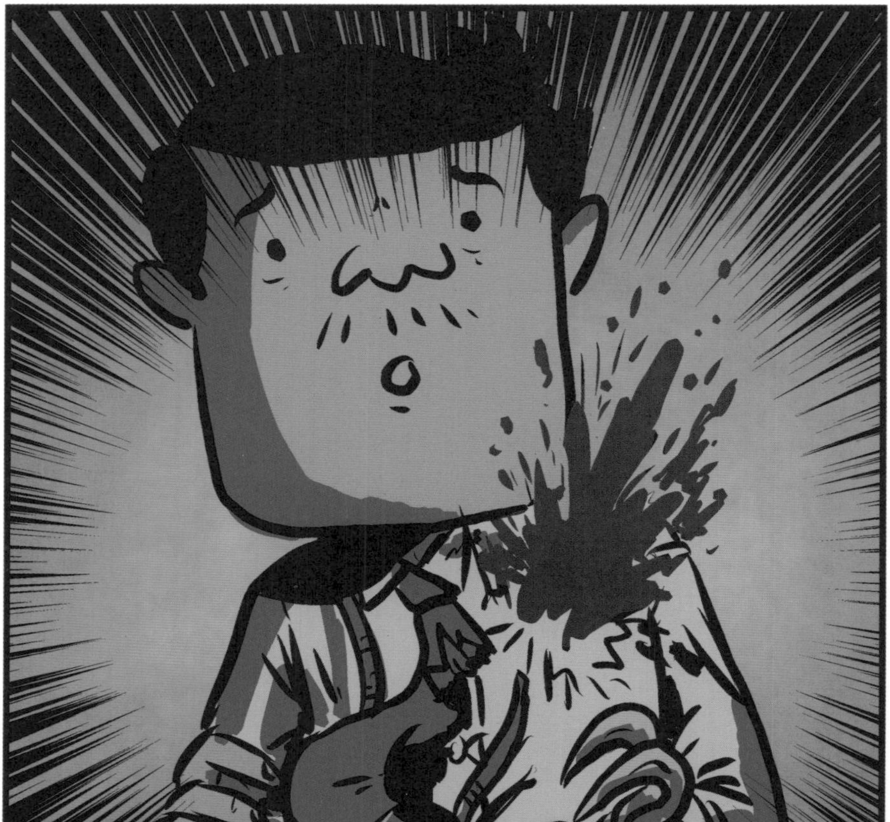

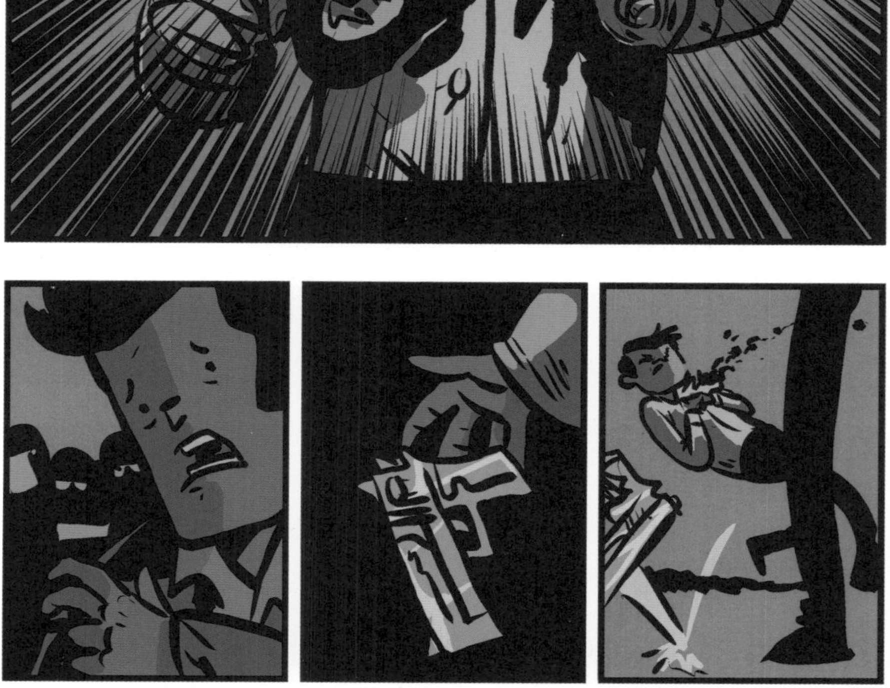

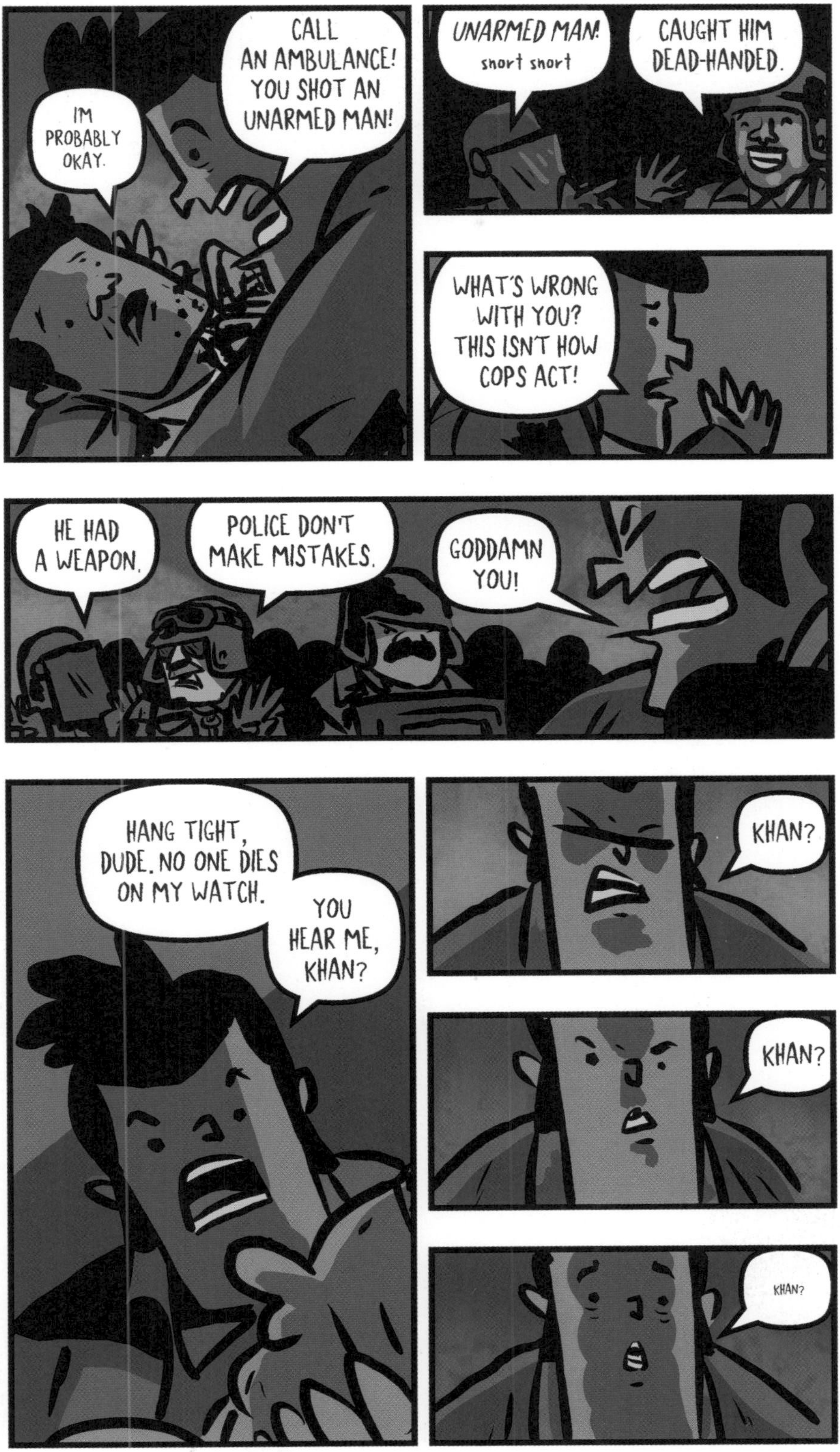
I'M PROBABLY OKAY.
CALL AN AMBULANCE! YOU SHOT AN UNARMED MAN!
UNARMED MAN! snort snort
CAUGHT HIM DEAD-HANDED.
WHAT'S WRONG WITH YOU? THIS ISN'T HOW COPS ACT!
HE HAD A WEAPON.
POLICE DON'T MAKE MISTAKES.
GODDAMN YOU!
HANG TIGHT, DUDE. NO ONE DIES ON MY WATCH.
YOU HEAR ME, KHAN?
KHAN?
KHAN?
KHAN?

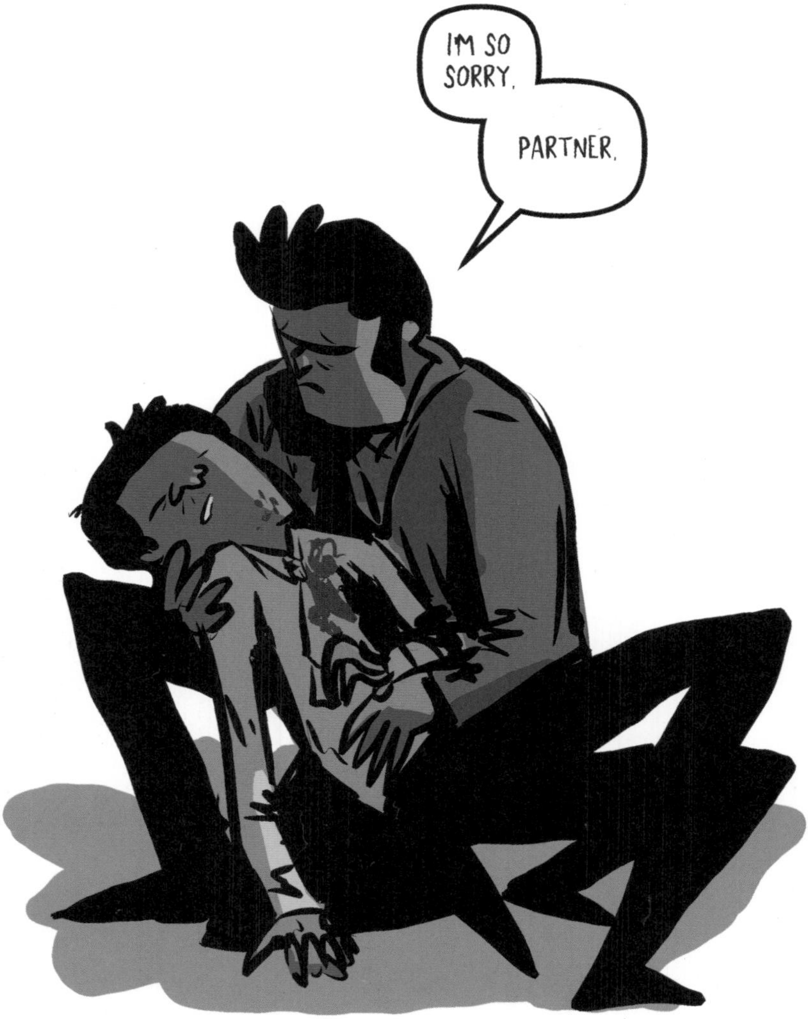
I'M SO SORRY.
PARTNER.

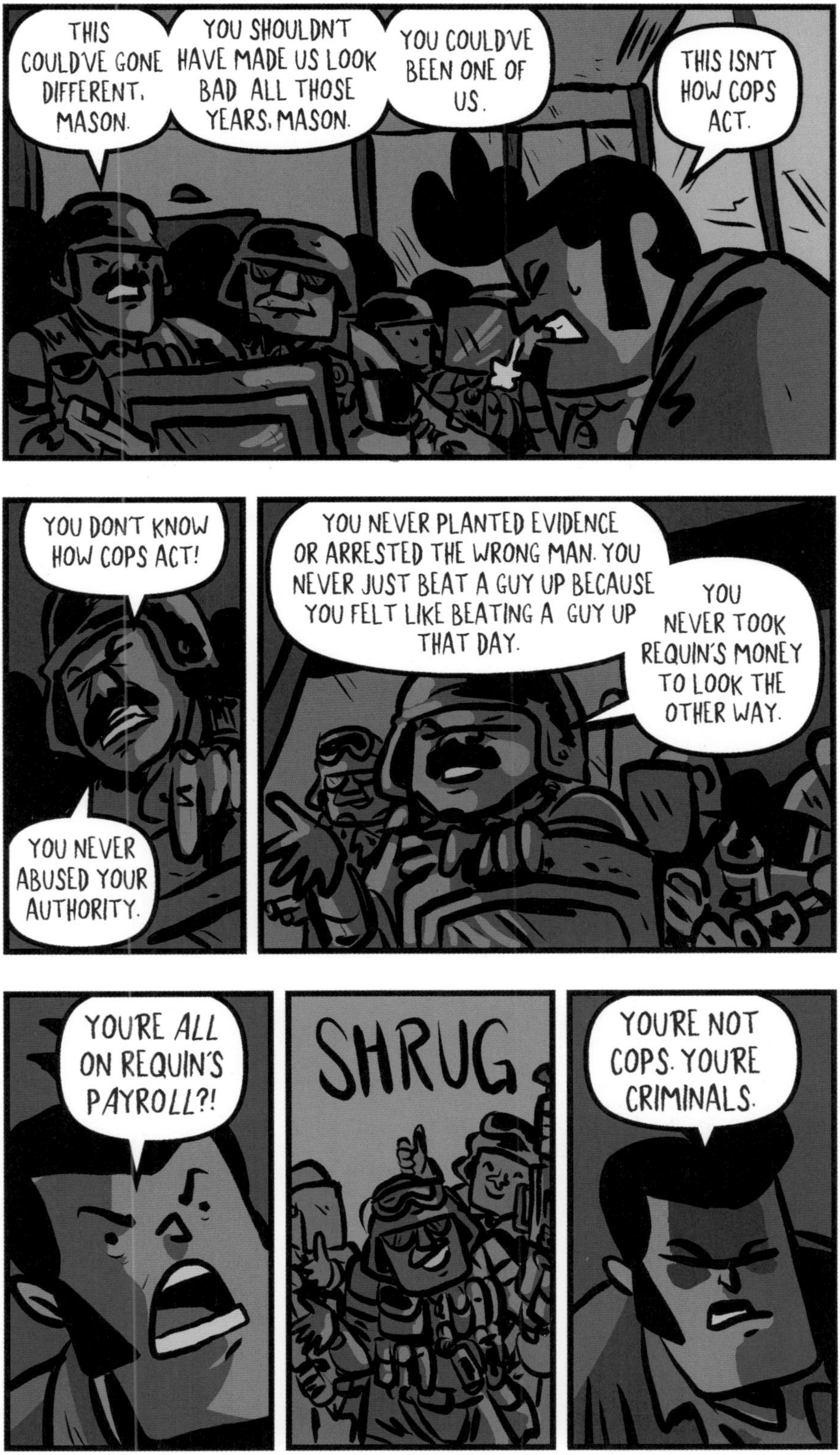
THIS COULD'VE GONE DIFFERENT, MASON.
YOU SHOULDN'T HAVE MADE US LOOK BAD ALL THOSE YEARS, MASON.
YOU COULD'VE BEEN ONE OF US.
THIS ISN'T HOW COPS ACT.
YOU DON'T KNOW HOW COPS ACT!
YOU NEVER ABUSED YOUR AUTHORITY.
YOU NEVER PLANTED EVIDENCE OR ARRESTED THE WRONG MAN. YOU NEVER JUST BEAT A GUY UP BECAUSE YOU FELT LIKE BEATING A GUY UP THAT DAY.
YOU NEVER TOOK REQUIN'S MONEY TO LOOK THE OTHER WAY.
YOU'RE *ALL* ON REQUIN'S *PAYROLL*?!
SHRUG
YOU'RE NOT COPS. YOU'RE CRIMINALS.

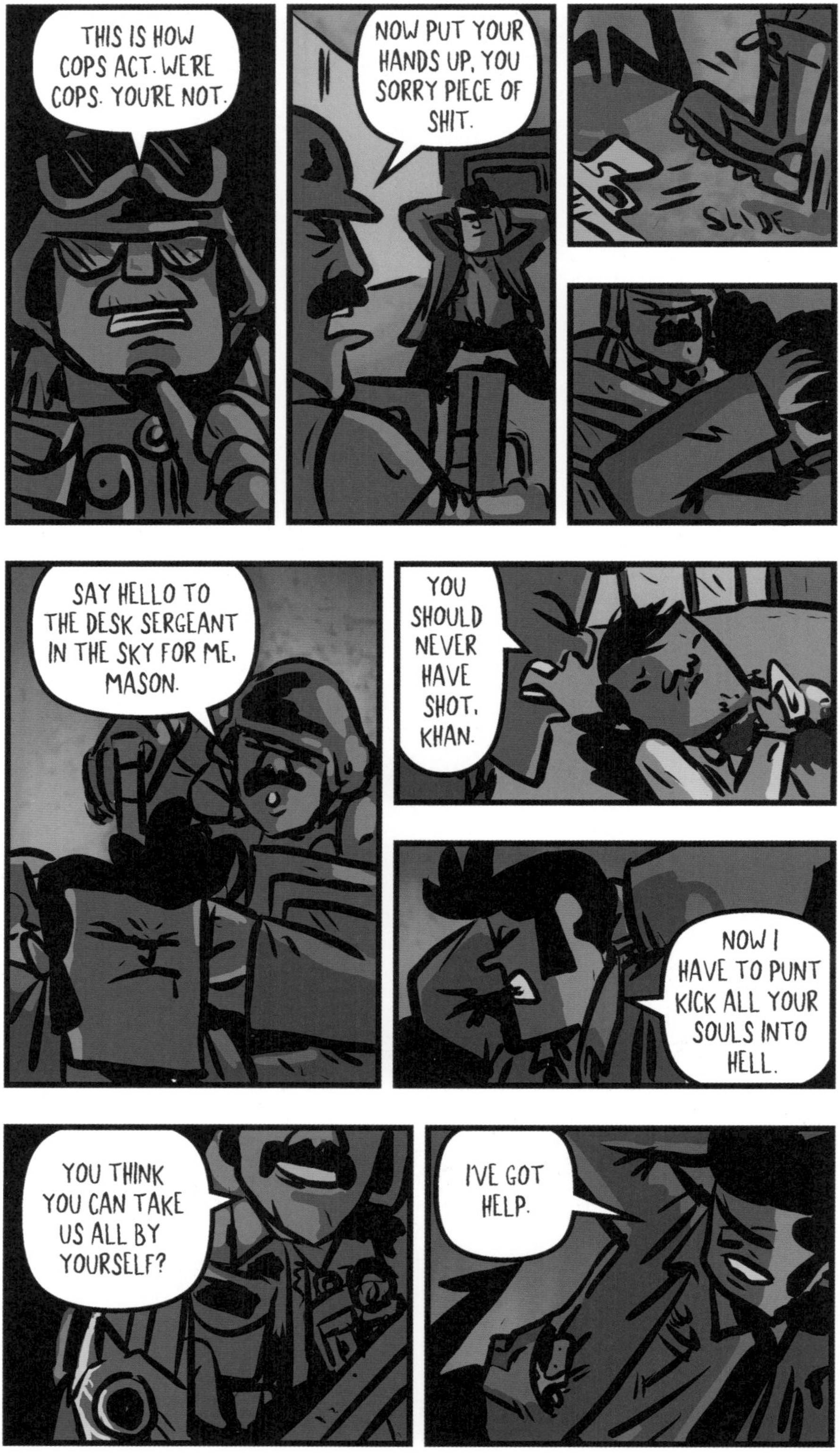
THIS IS HOW COPS ACT. WE'RE COPS. YOU'RE NOT.
NOW PUT YOUR HANDS UP, YOU SORRY PIECE OF SHIT.
SLIDE
SAY HELLO TO THE DESK SERGEANT IN THE SKY FOR ME, MASON.
YOU SHOULD NEVER HAVE SHOT, KHAN.
NOW I HAVE TO PUNT KICK ALL YOUR SOULS INTO HELL.
YOU THINK YOU CAN TAKE US ALL BY YOURSELF?
I'VE GOT HELP.

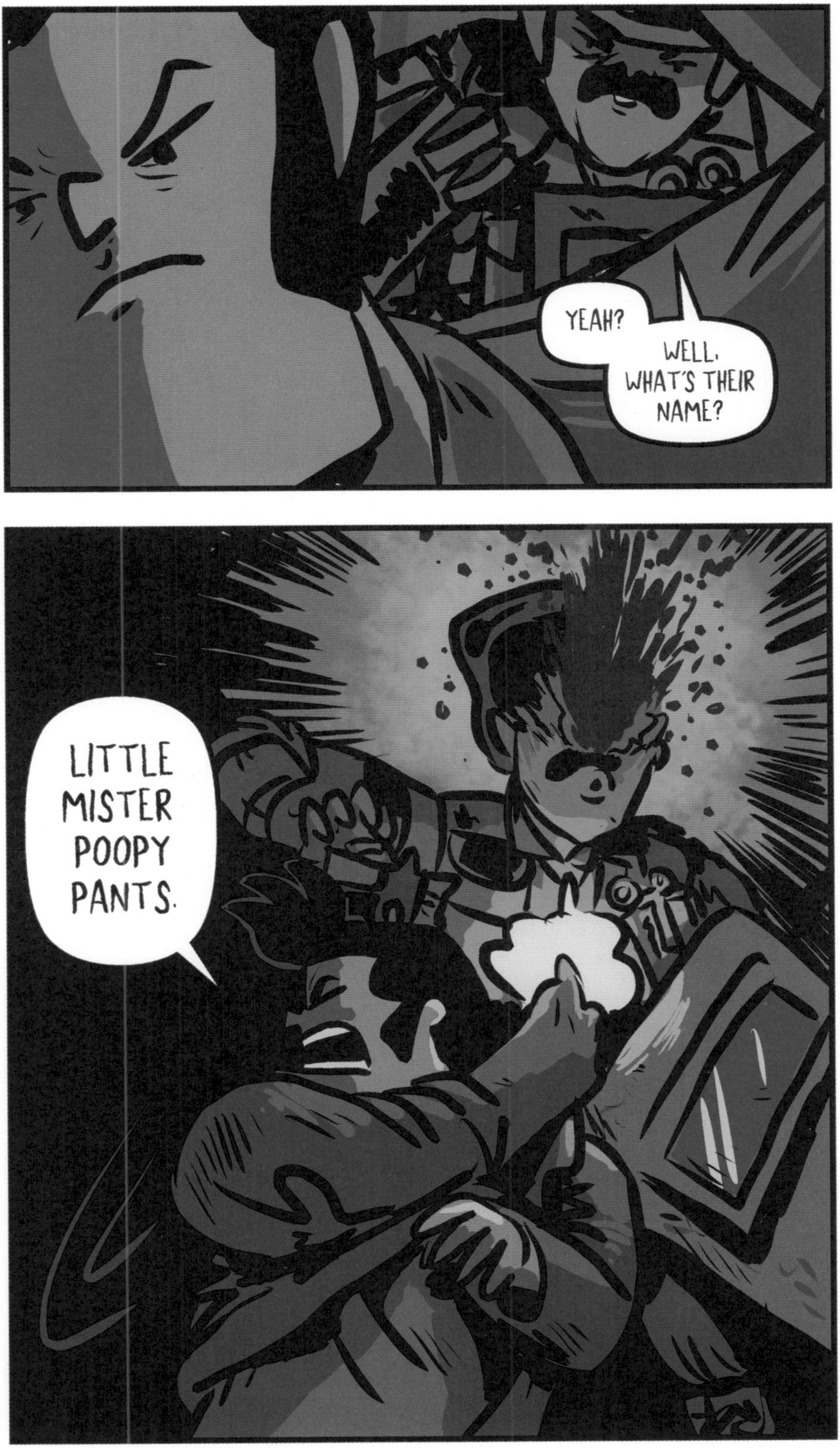
YEAH?
WELL, WHAT'S THEIR NAME?
LITTLE MISTER POOPY PANTS.

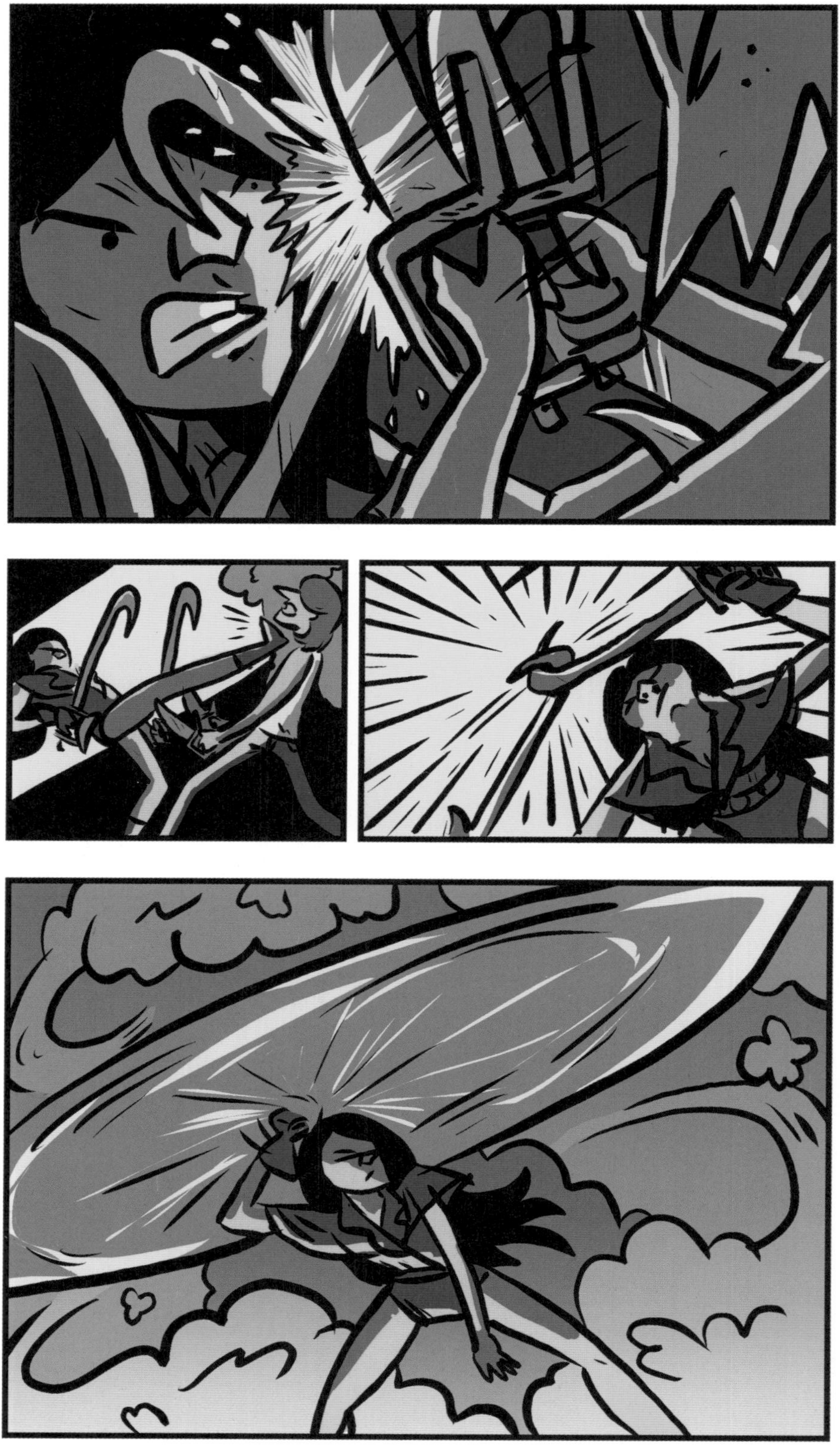

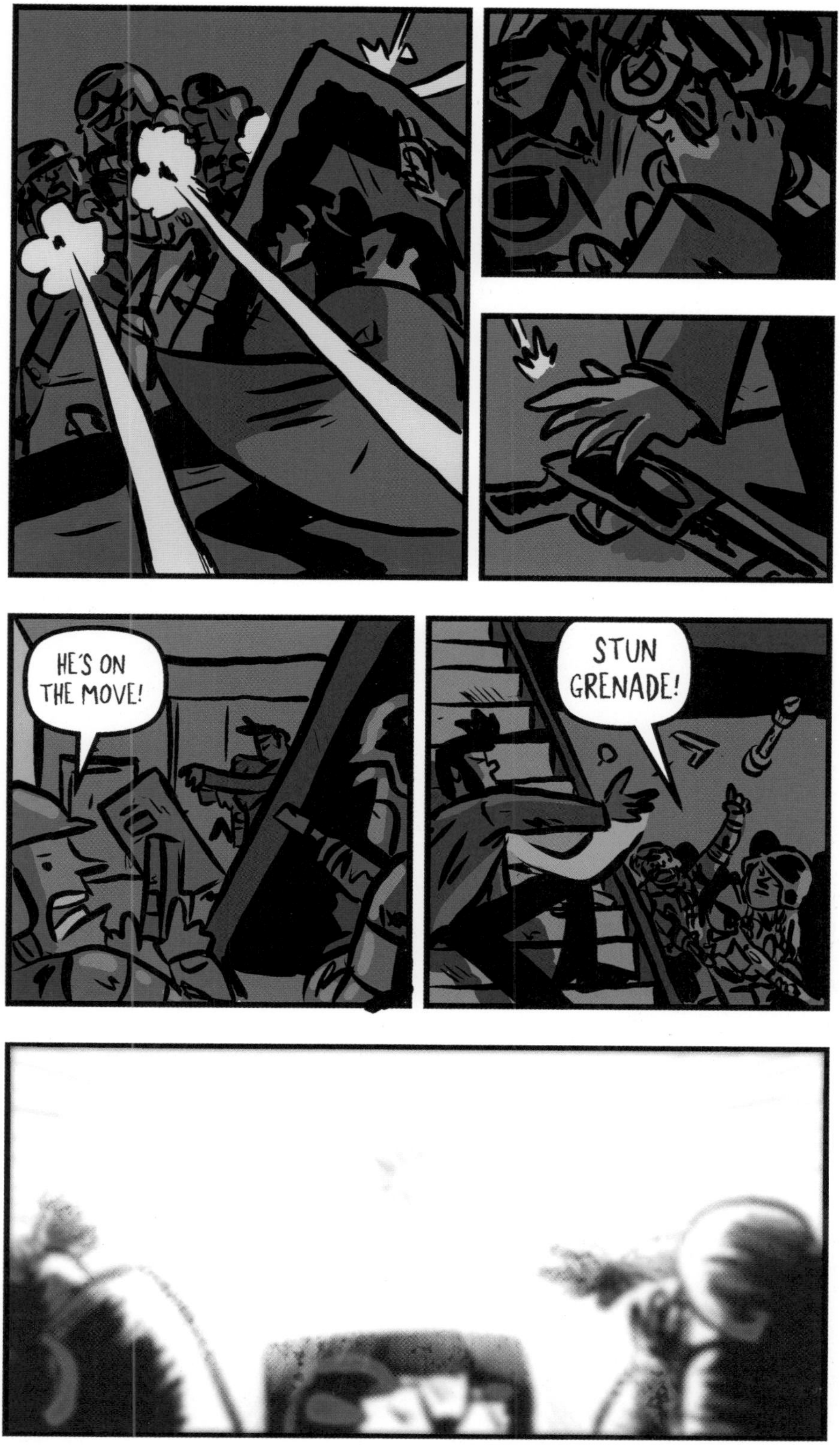
HE'S ON THE MOVE!
STUN GRENADE!

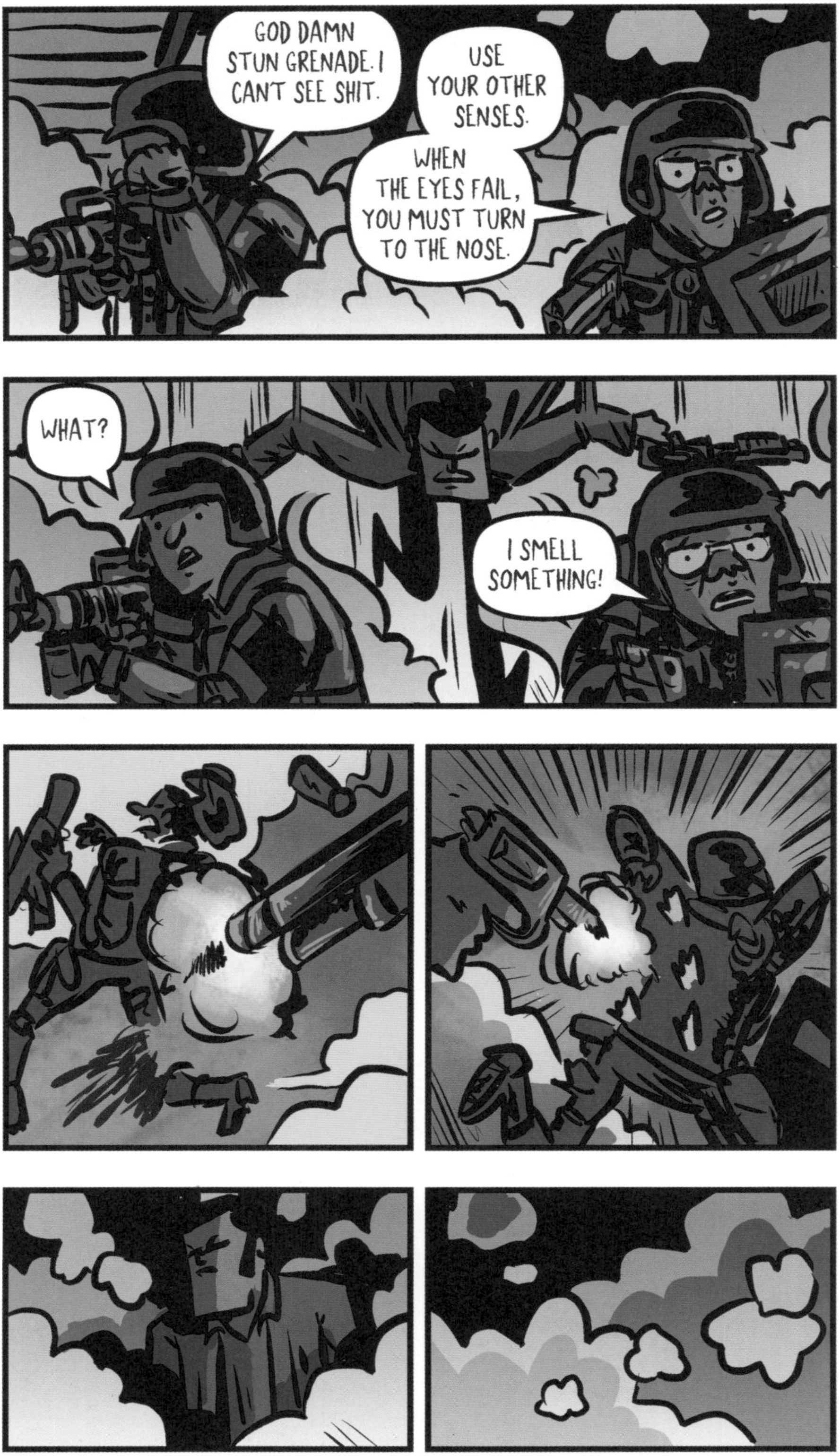
GOD DAMN STUN GRENADE. I CAN'T SEE SHIT.
USE YOUR OTHER SENSES.
WHEN THE EYES FAIL, YOU MUST TURN TO THE NOSE.
WHAT?
I SMELL SOMETHING!

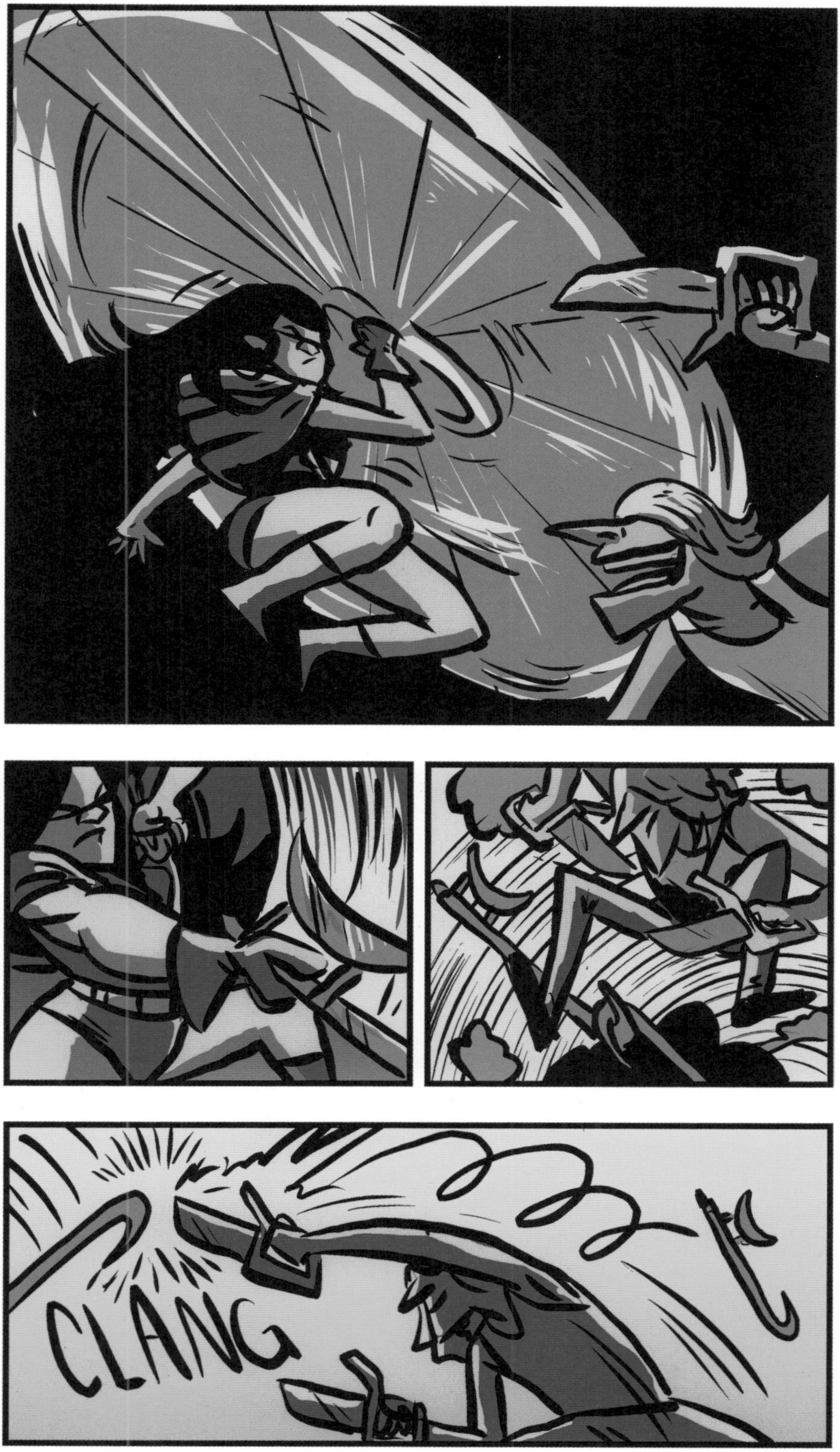
CLANG

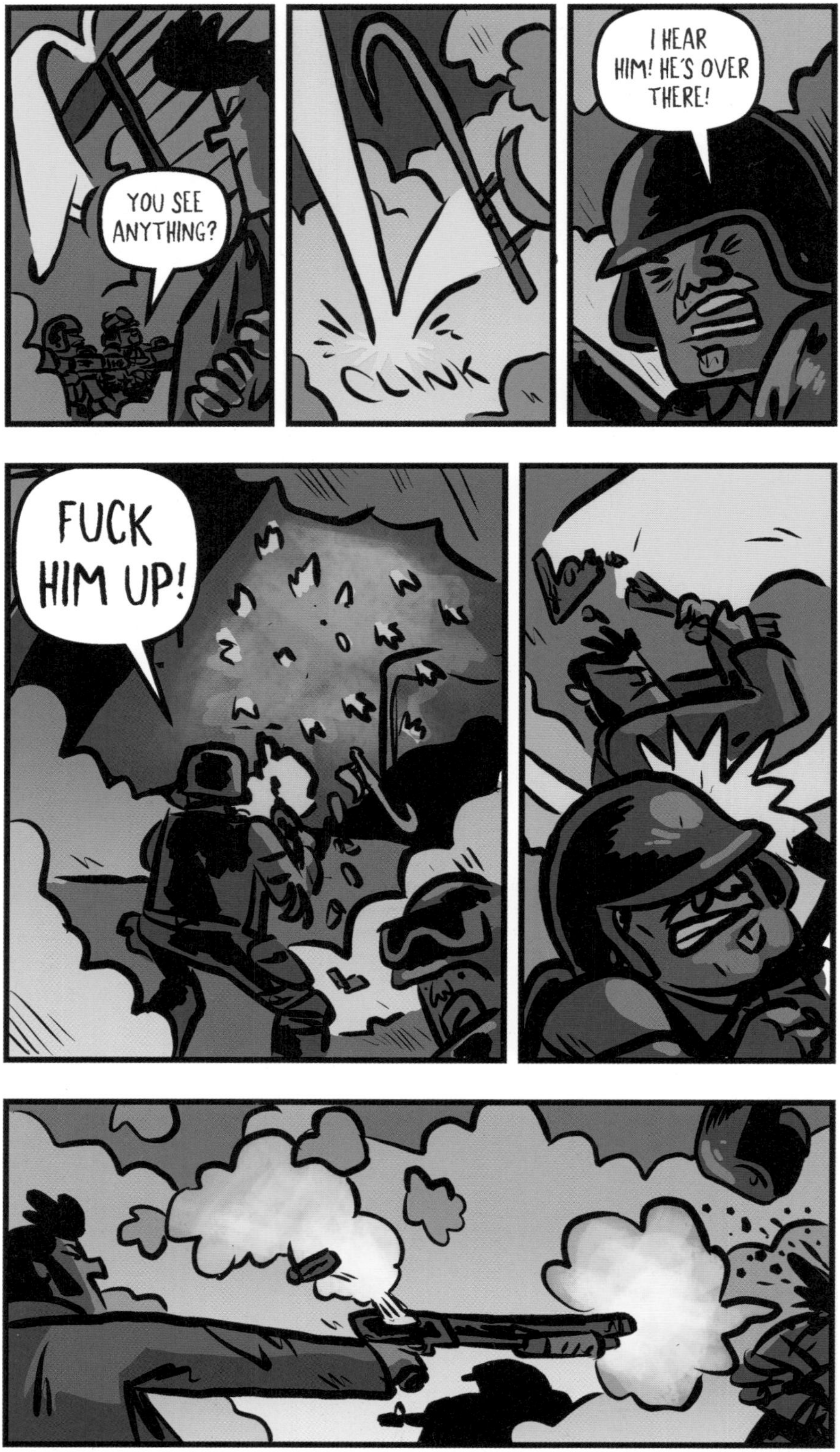
YOU SEE ANYTHING?
CLINK
I HEAR HIM! HE'S OVER THERE!
FUCK HIM UP!

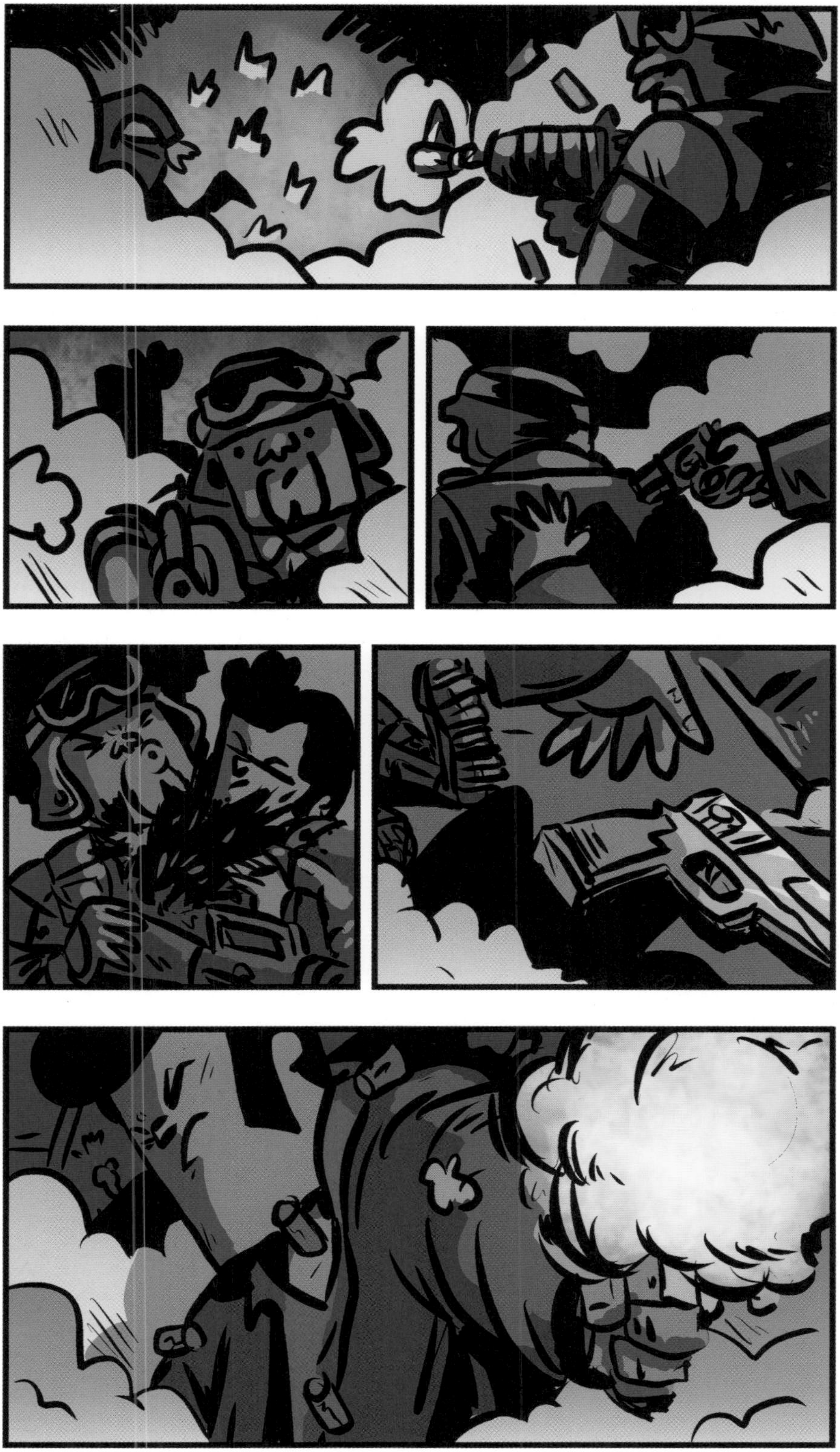

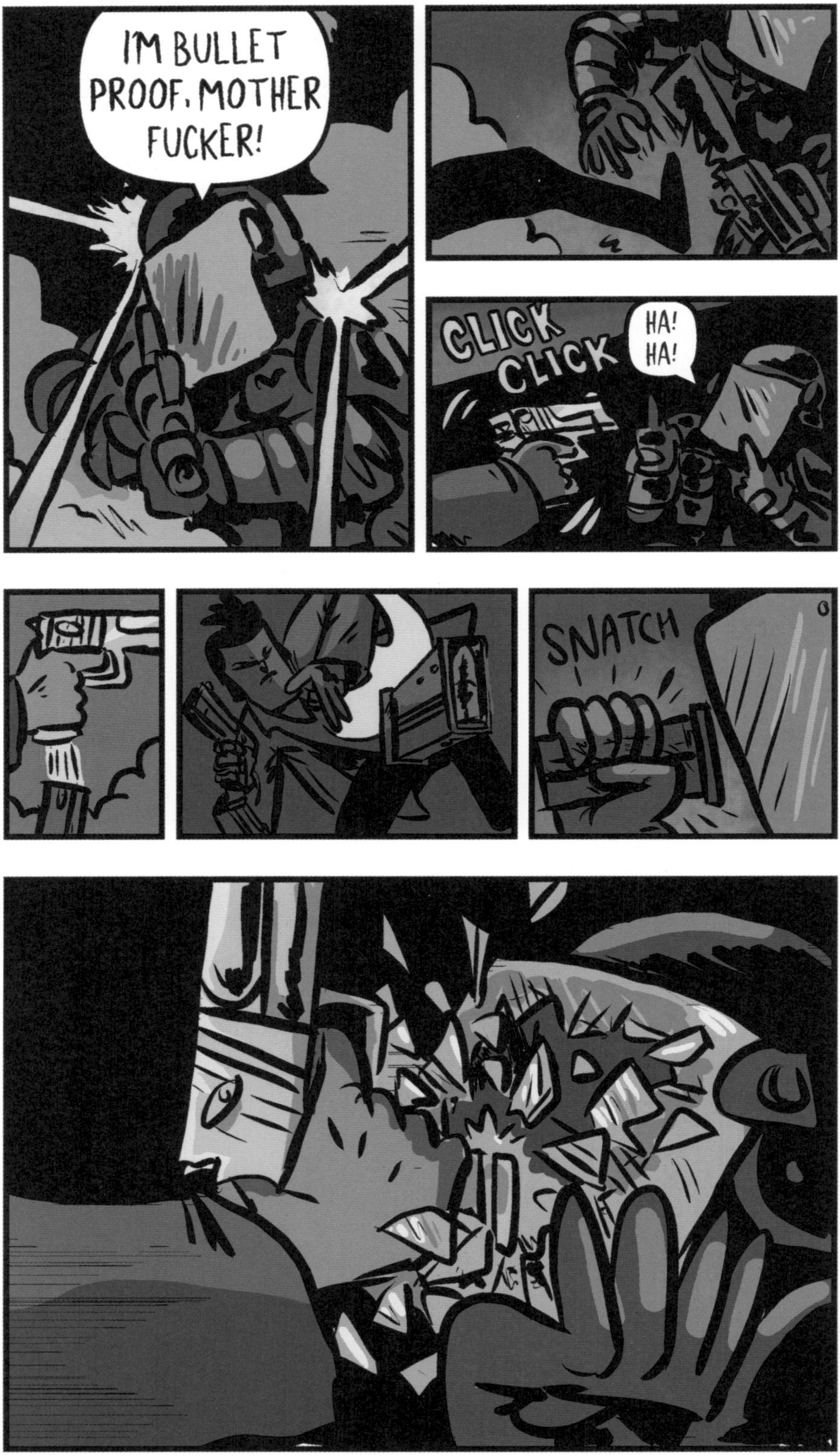
I'M BULLET PROOF, MOTHER FUCKER!
CLICK
CLICK
HA! HA!
SNATCH

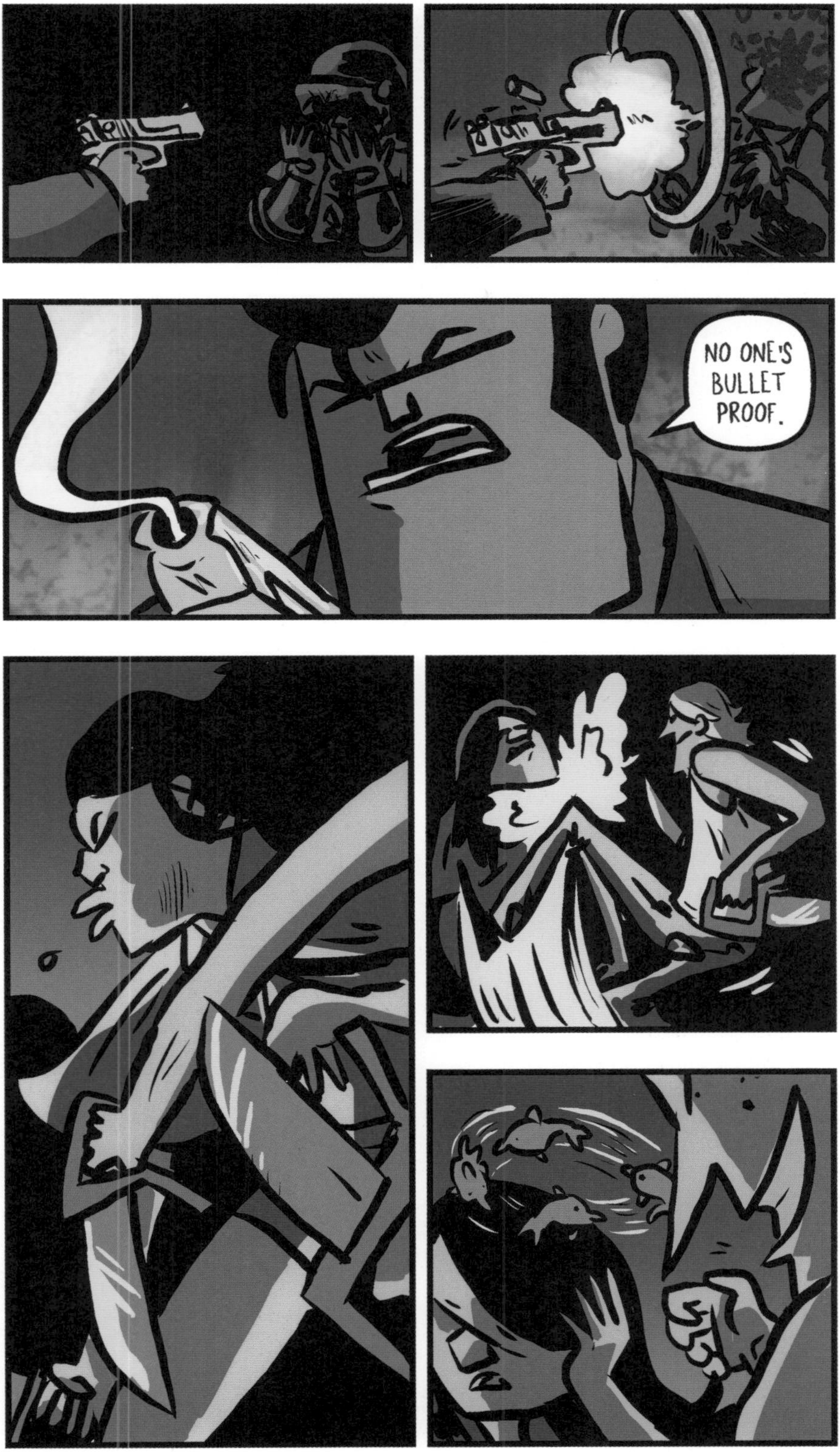
NO ONE'S BULLET PROOF.

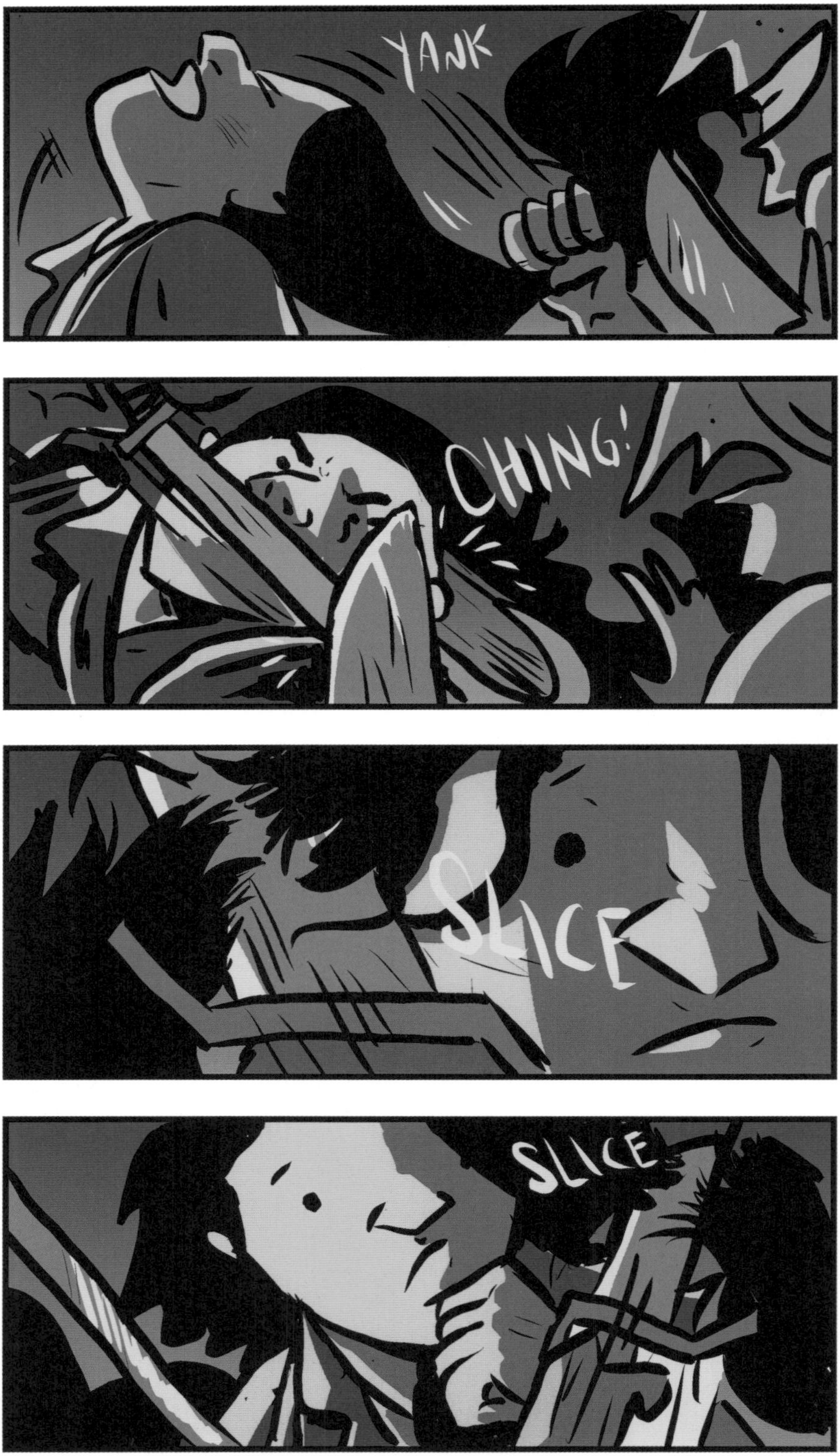
YANK
CHING!
SLICE
SLICE

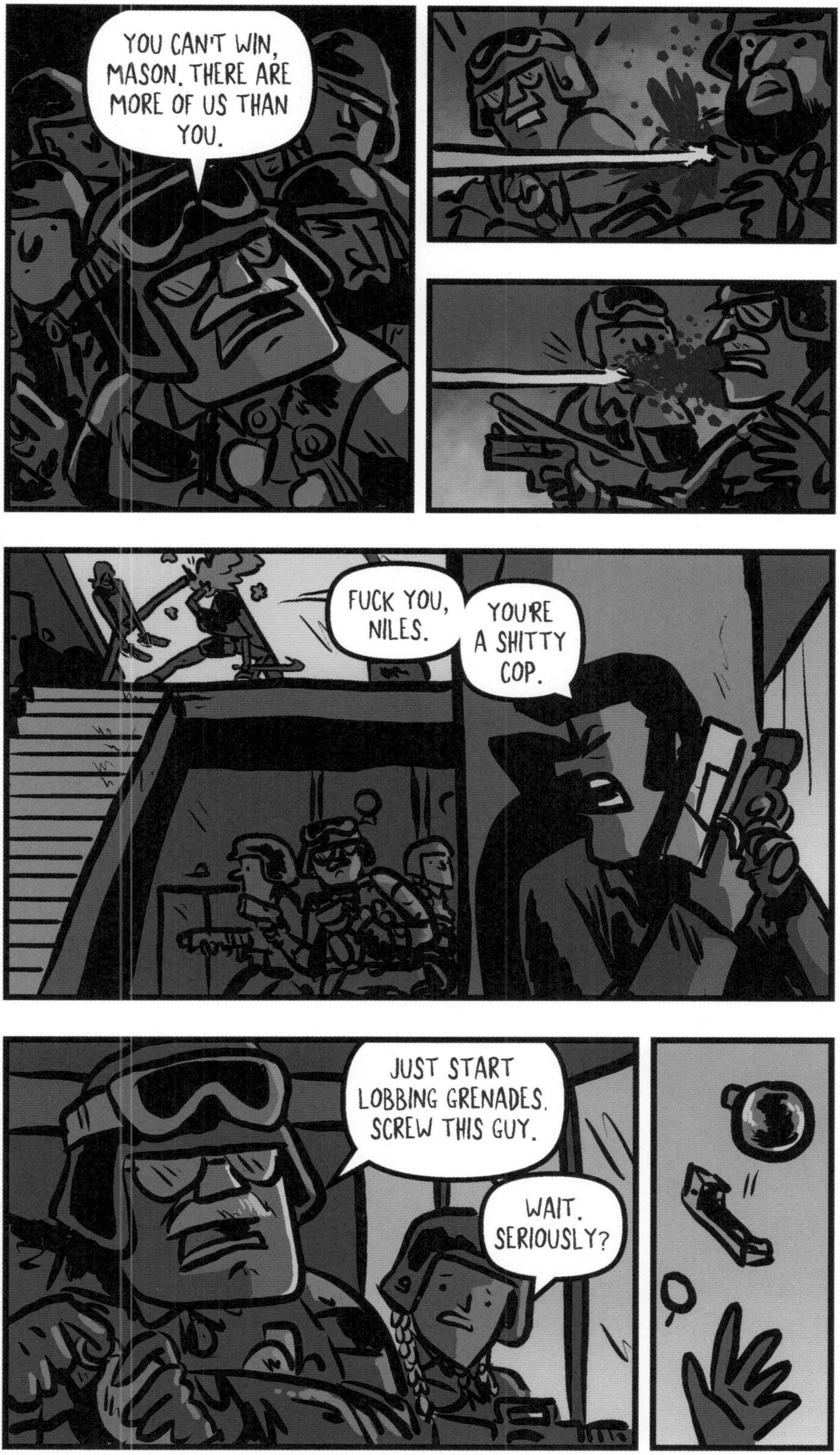

YOU CAN'T WIN, MASON. THERE ARE MORE OF US THAN YOU.
FUCK YOU, NILES.
YOU'RE A SHITTY COP.
JUST START LOBBING GRENADES. SCREW THIS GUY.
WAIT. SERIOUSLY?

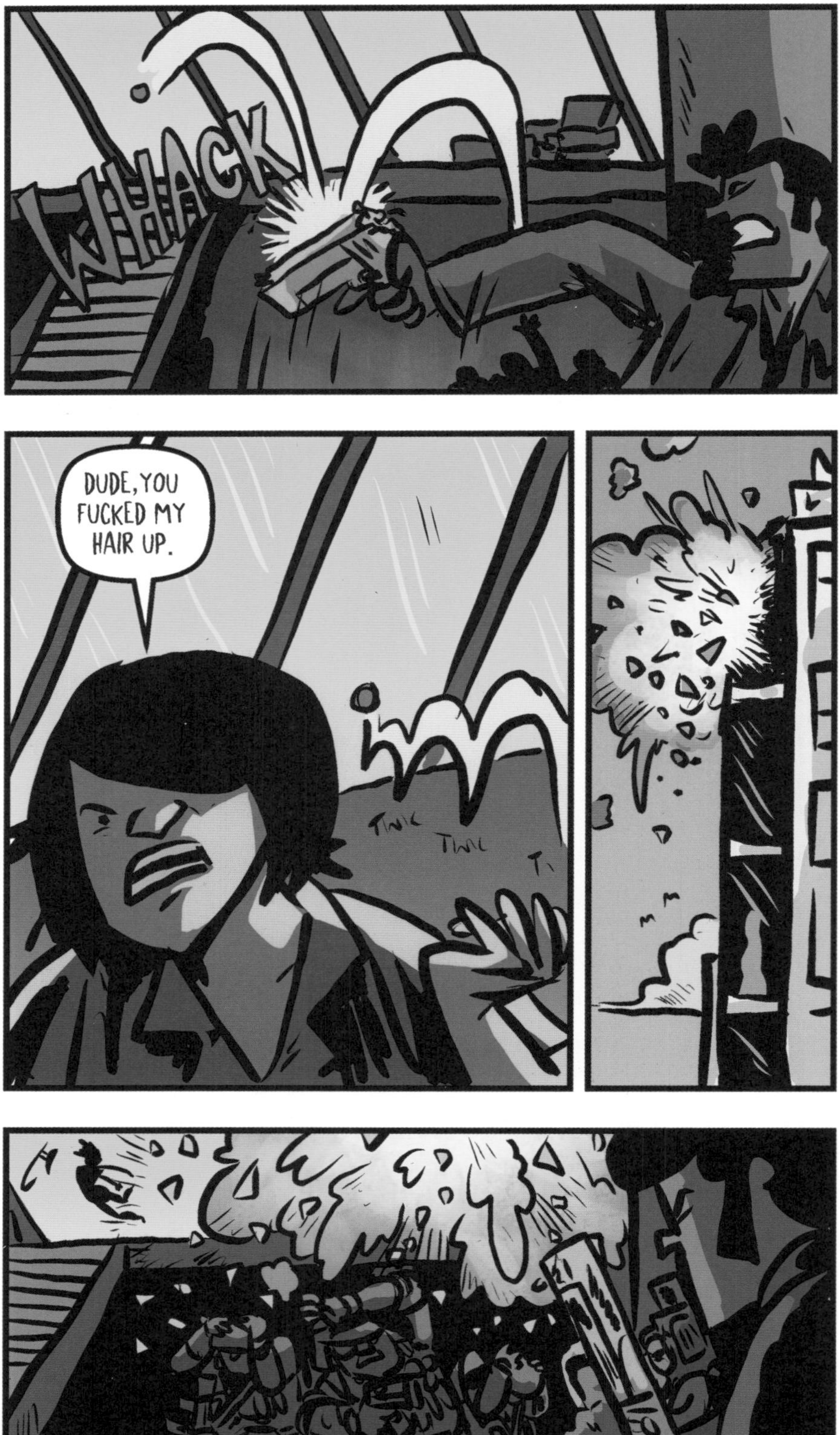
WHACK
DUDE, YOU FUCKED MY HAIR UP.
TINK
TINK
T

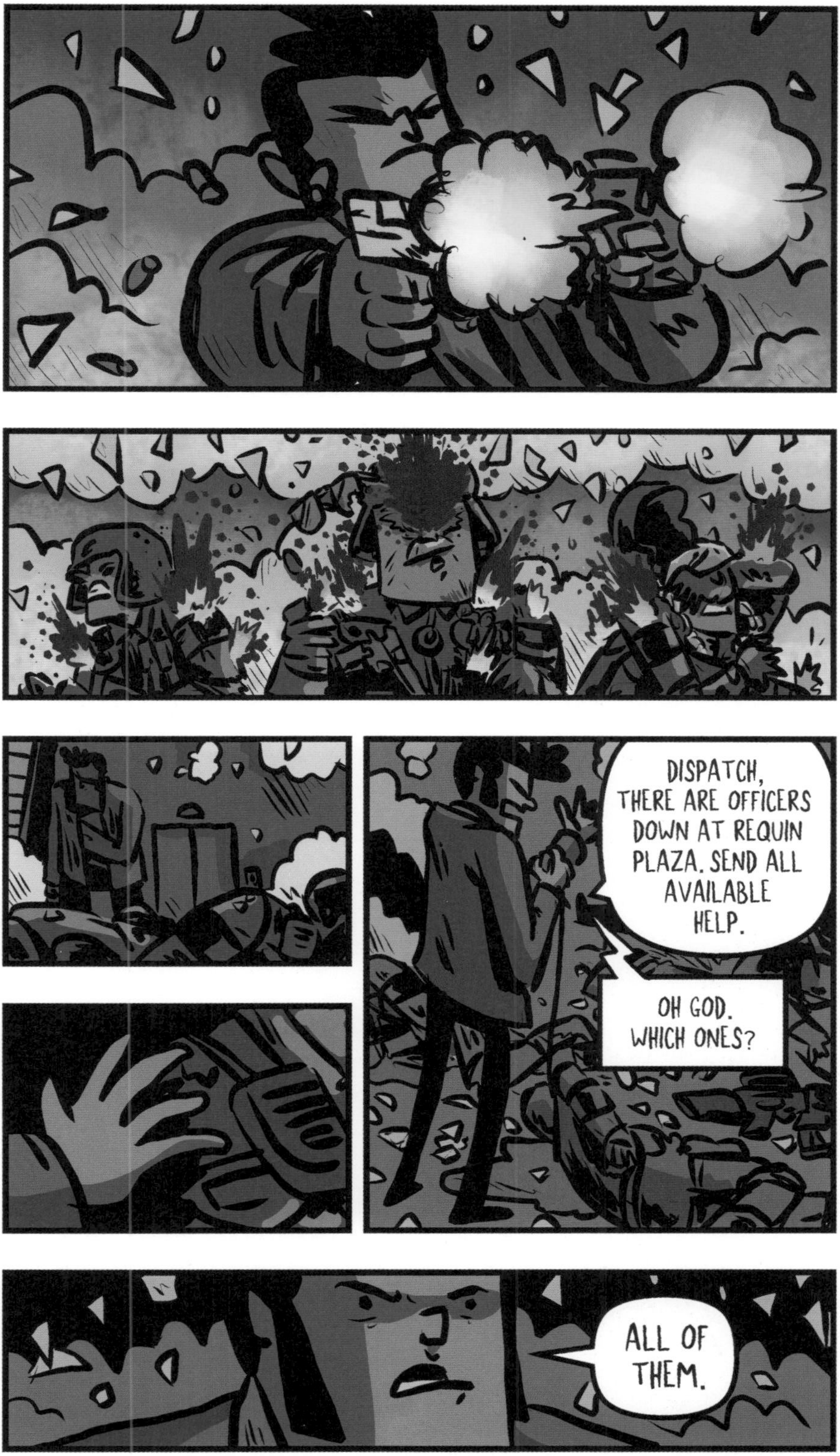
DISPATCH, THERE ARE OFFICERS DOWN AT REQUIN PLAZA. SEND ALL AVAILABLE HELP.
OH GOD. WHICH ONES?
ALL OF THEM.

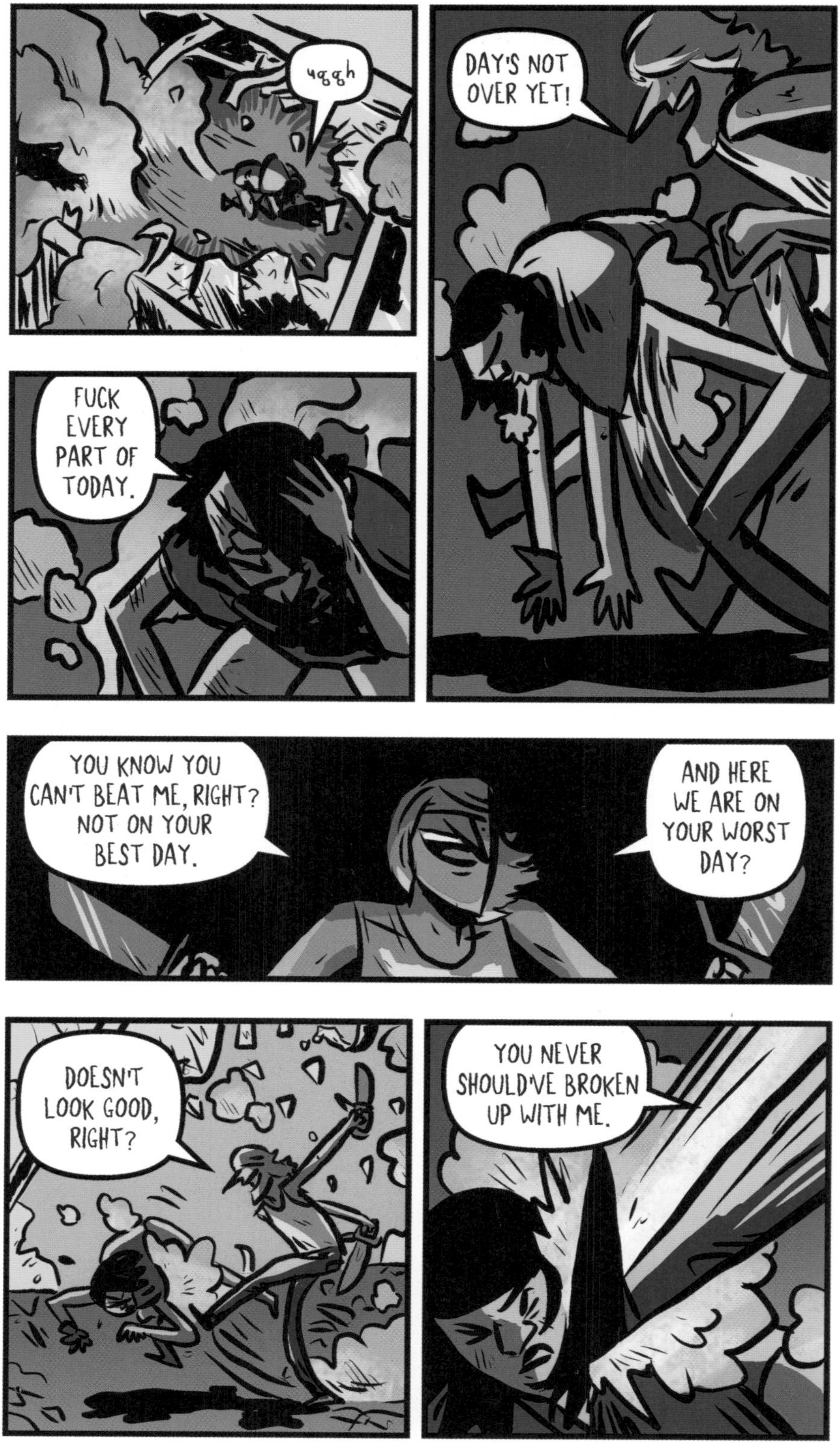
uggh
DAY'S NOT OVER YET!
FUCK EVERY PART OF TODAY.
YOU KNOW YOU CAN'T BEAT ME, RIGHT? NOT ON YOUR BEST DAY.
AND HERE WE ARE ON YOUR WORST DAY?
DOESN'T LOOK GOOD, RIGHT?
YOU NEVER SHOULD'VE BROKEN UP WITH ME.

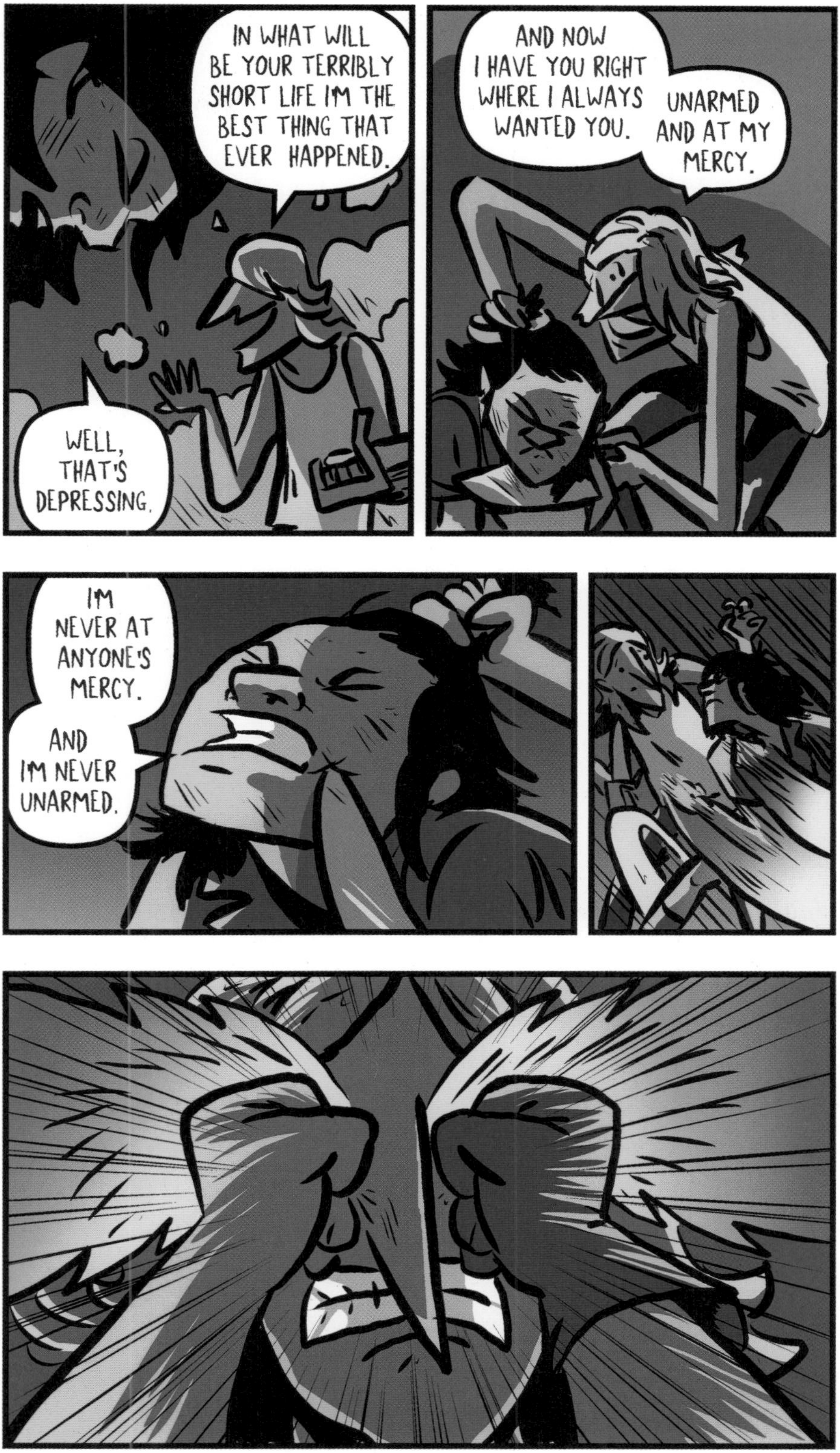
IN WHAT WILL BE YOUR TERRIBLY SHORT LIFE I'M THE BEST THING THAT EVER HAPPENED.
WELL, THAT'S DEPRESSING.
AND NOW I HAVE YOU RIGHT WHERE I ALWAYS WANTED YOU.
UNARMED AND AT MY MERCY.
I'M NEVER AT ANYONE'S MERCY.
AND I'M NEVER UNARMED.

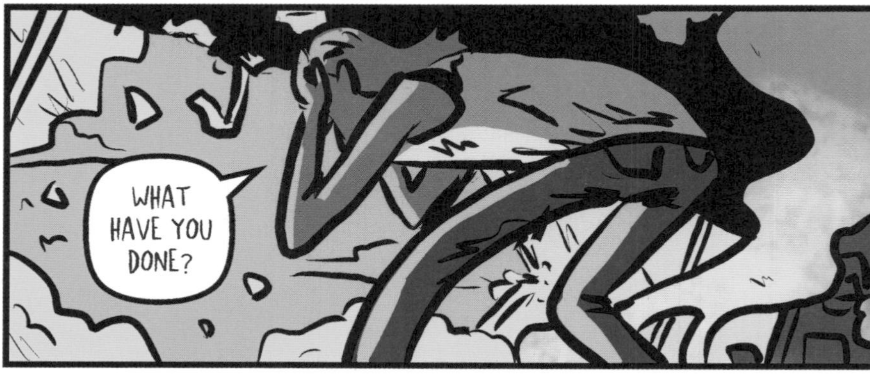
WHAT HAVE YOU DONE?

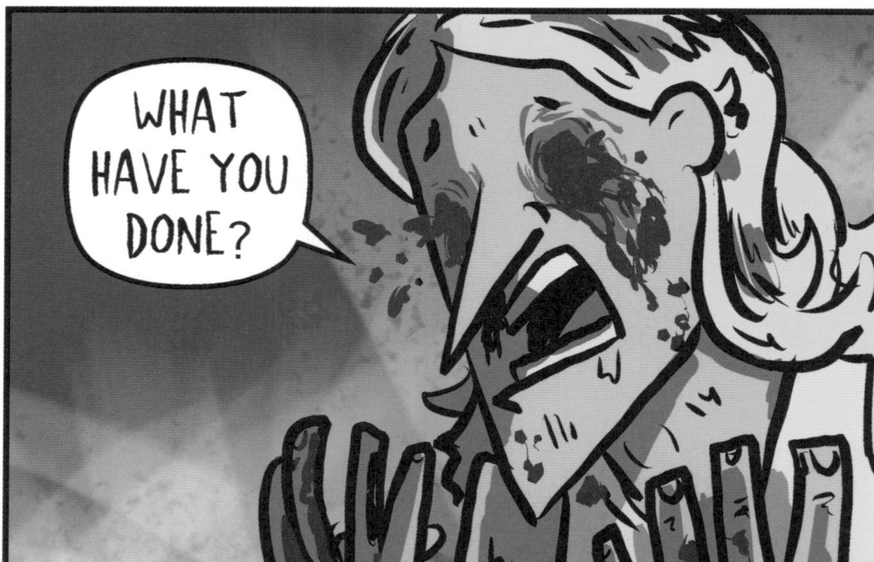
WHAT HAVE YOU DONE?

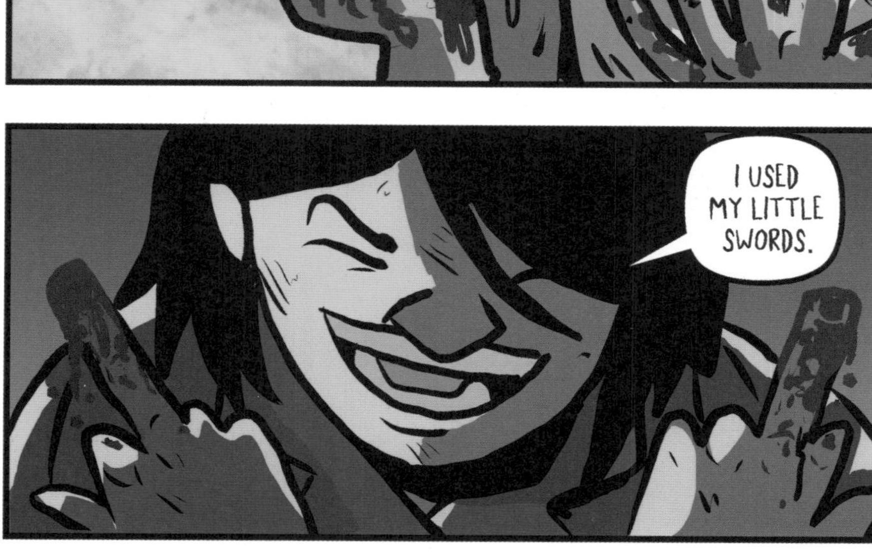
I USED MY LITTLE SWORDS.

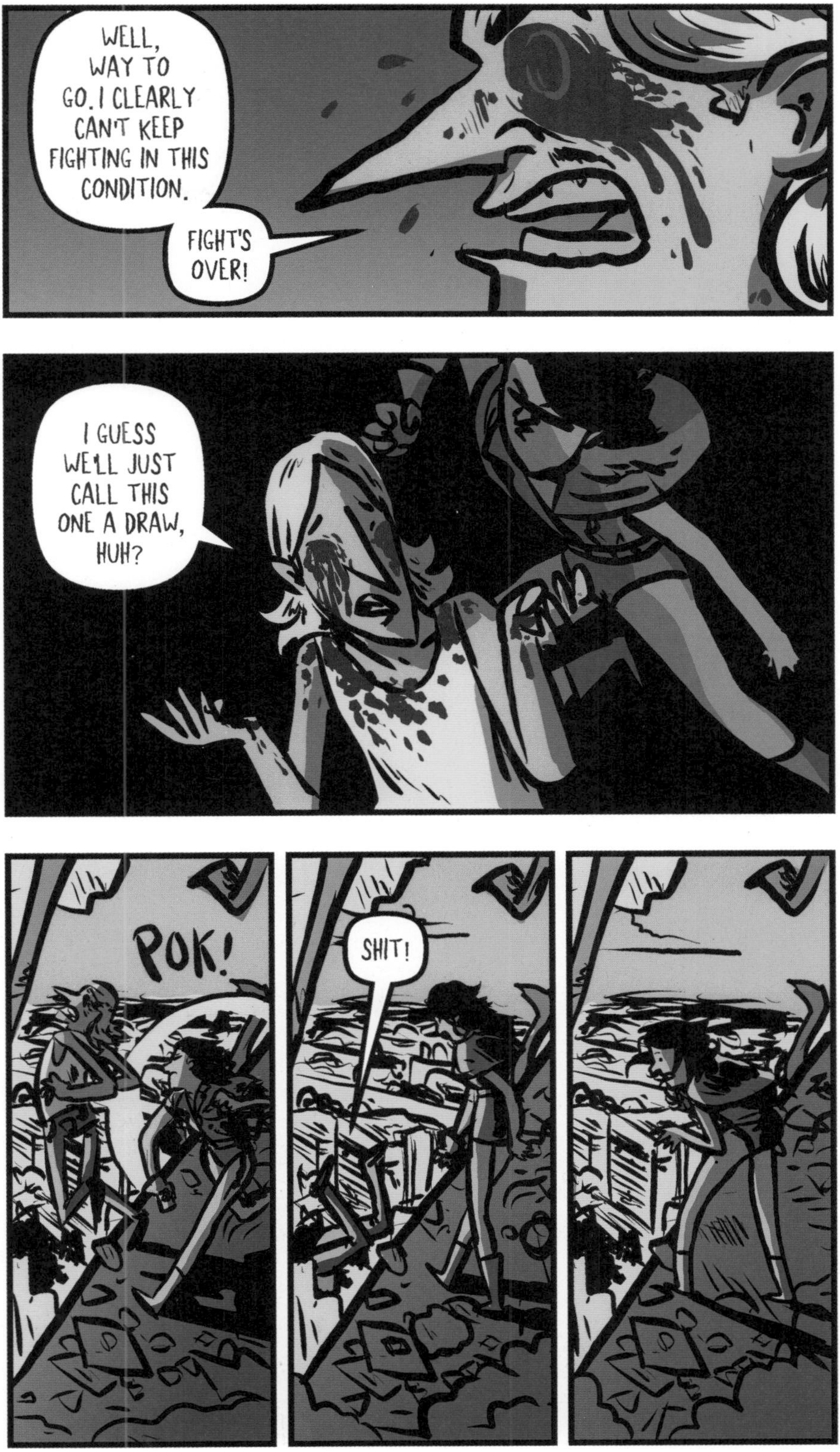
WELL, WAY TO GO. I CLEARLY CAN'T KEEP FIGHTING IN THIS CONDITION.
FIGHT'S OVER!
I GUESS WE'LL JUST CALL THIS ONE A DRAW, HUH?
POK!
SHIT!

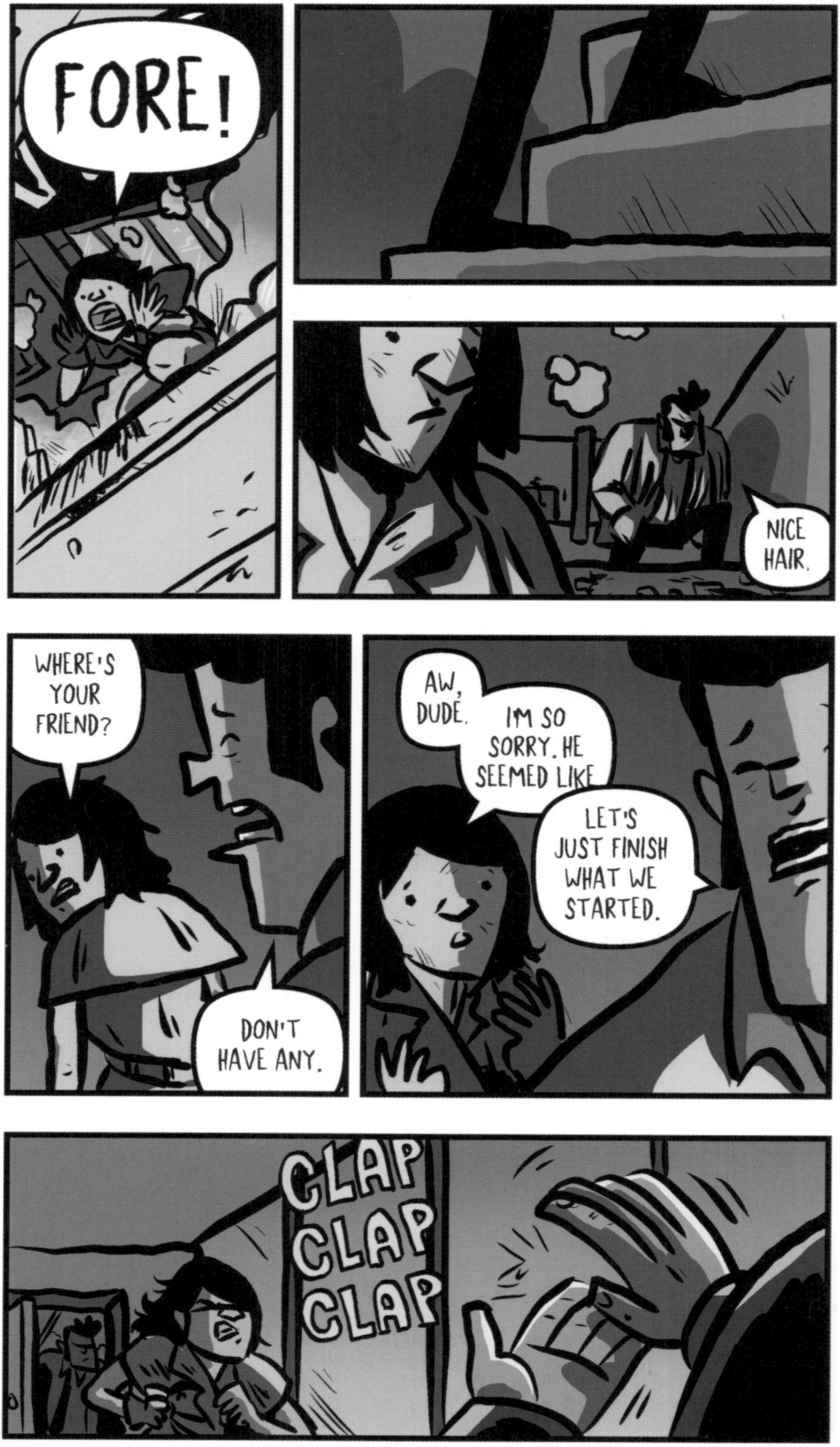
FORE!
NICE HAIR.
WHERE'S YOUR FRIEND?
DON'T HAVE ANY.
AW, DUDE.
I'M SO SORRY. HE SEEMED LIKE
LET'S JUST FINISH WHAT WE STARTED.
CLAP
CLAP
CLAP

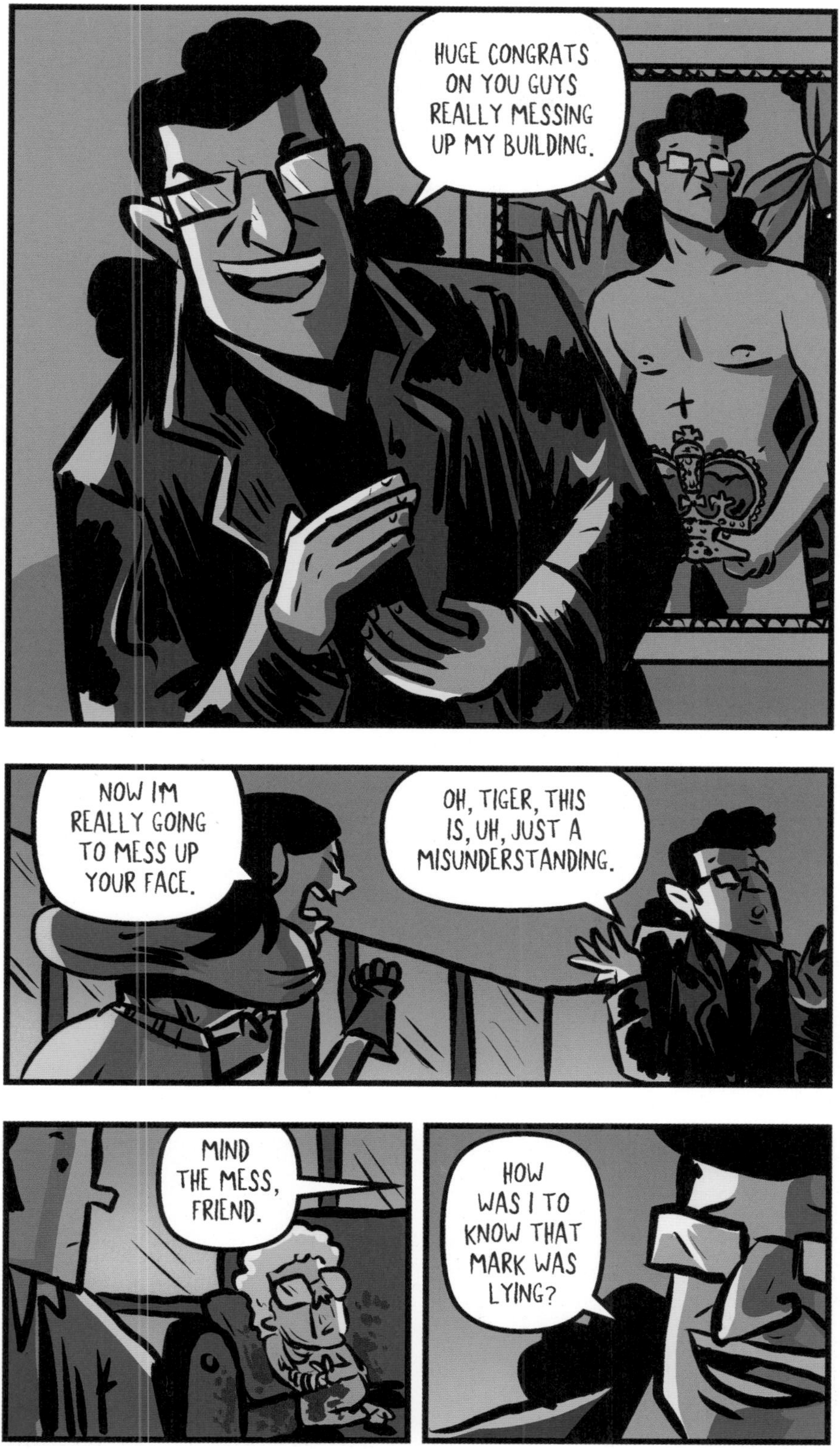
HUGE CONGRATS ON YOU GUYS REALLY MESSING UP MY BUILDING.
NOW I'M REALLY GOING TO MESS UP YOUR FACE.
OH, TIGER, THIS IS, UH, JUST A MISUNDERSTANDING.
MIND THE MESS, FRIEND.
HOW WAS I TO KNOW THAT MARK WAS LYING?

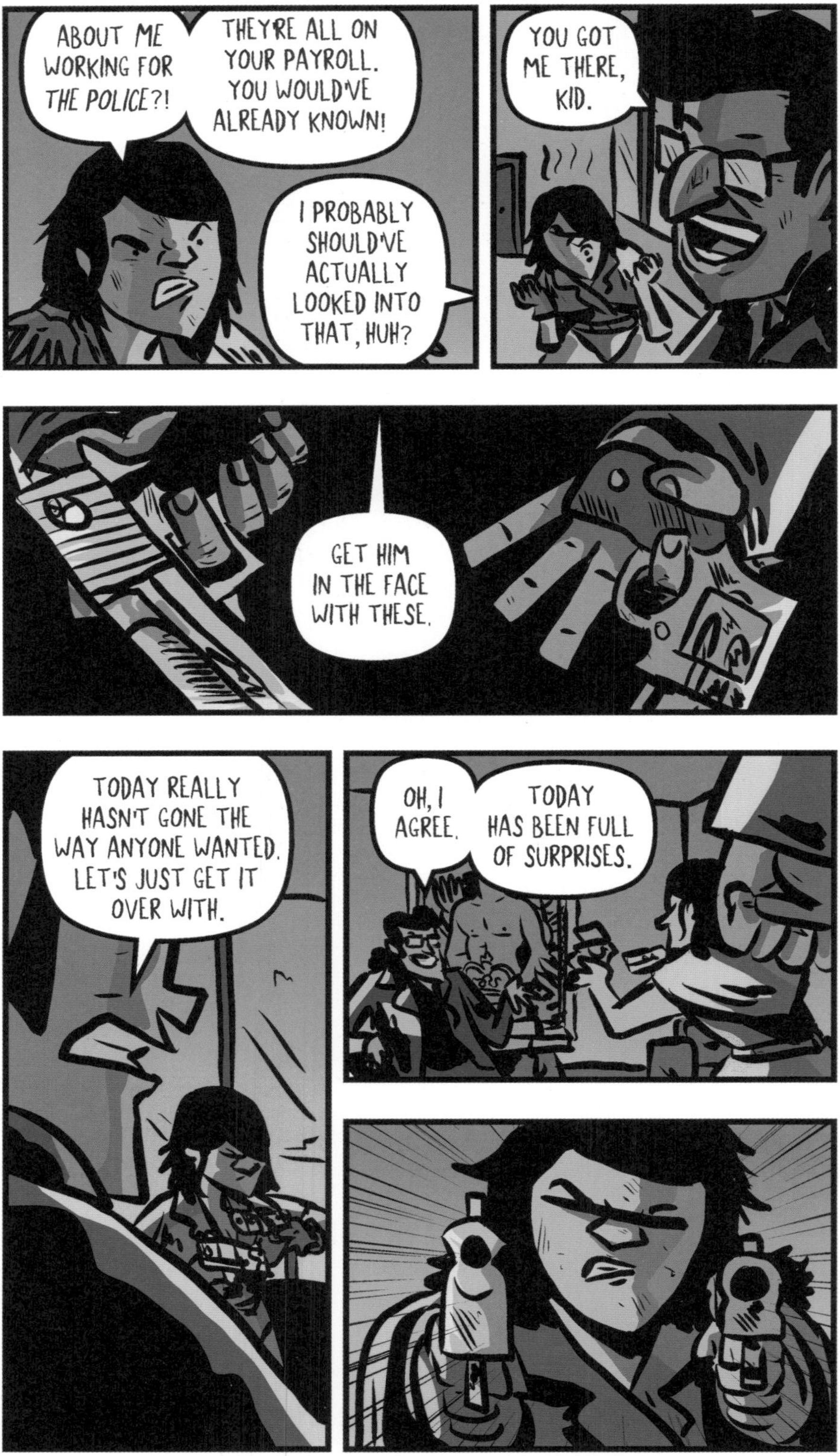
ABOUT ME WORKING FOR THE POLICE?!
THEY'RE ALL ON YOUR PAYROLL. YOU WOULD'VE ALREADY KNOWN!
I PROBABLY SHOULD'VE ACTUALLY LOOKED INTO THAT, HUH?
YOU GOT ME THERE, KID.
GET HIM IN THE FACE WITH THESE.
TODAY REALLY HASN'T GONE THE WAY ANYONE WANTED. LET'S JUST GET IT OVER WITH.
OH, I AGREE.
TODAY HAS BEEN FULL OF SURPRISES.

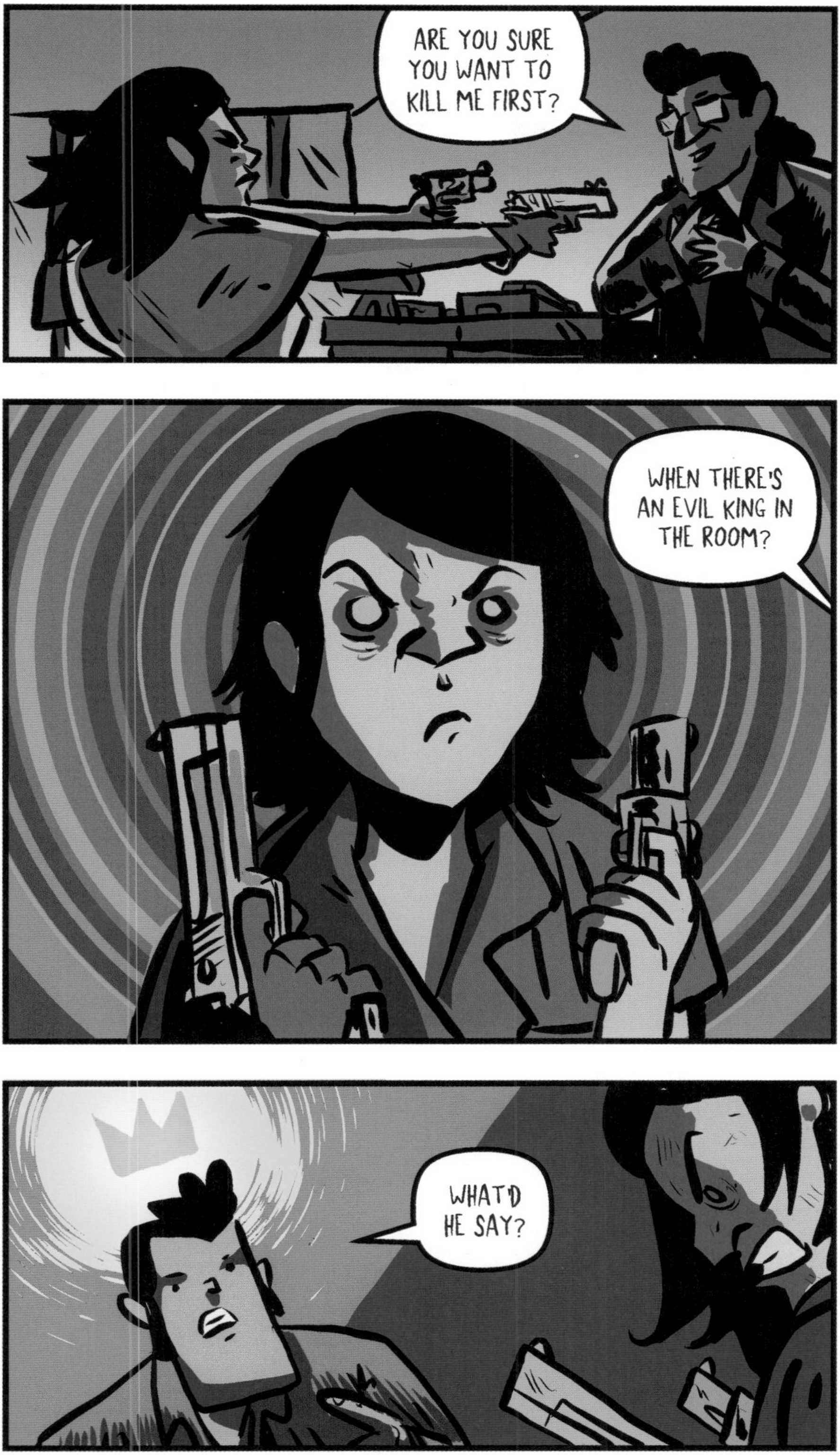
ARE YOU SURE YOU WANT TO KILL ME FIRST?
WHEN THERE'S AN EVIL KING IN THE ROOM?
WHAT'D HE SAY?

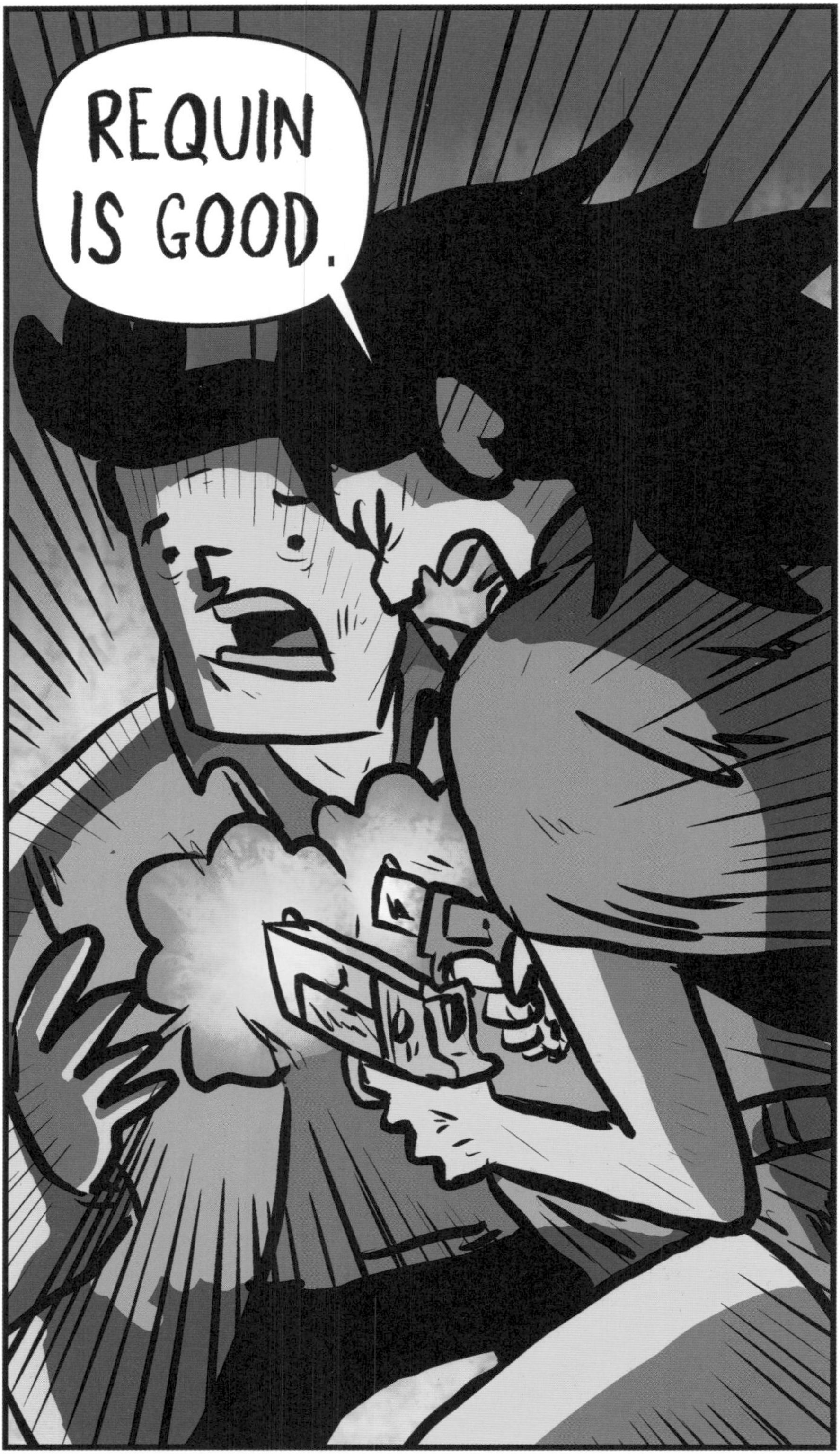
REQUIN IS GOOD.

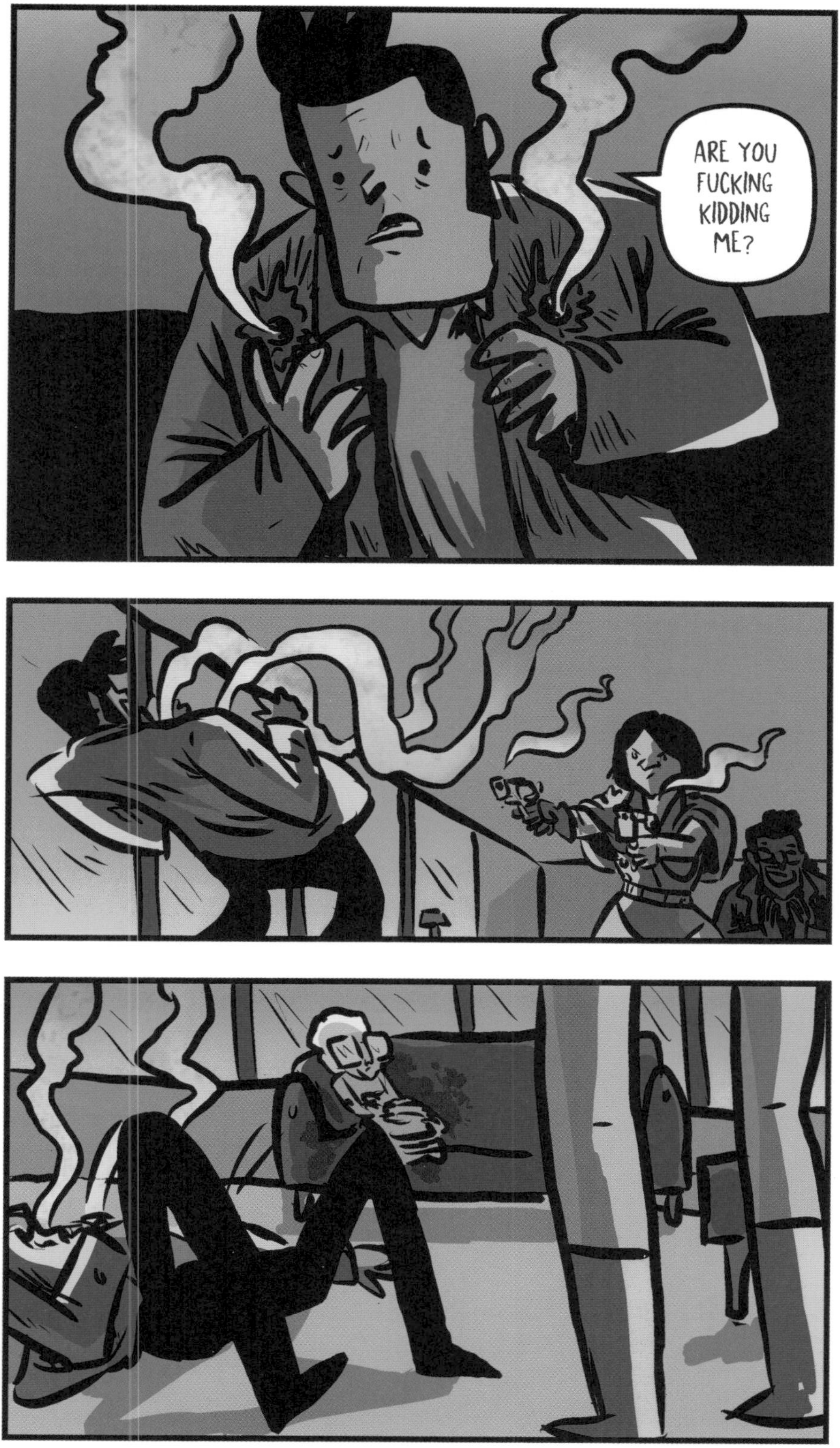
ARE YOU FUCKING KIDDING ME?

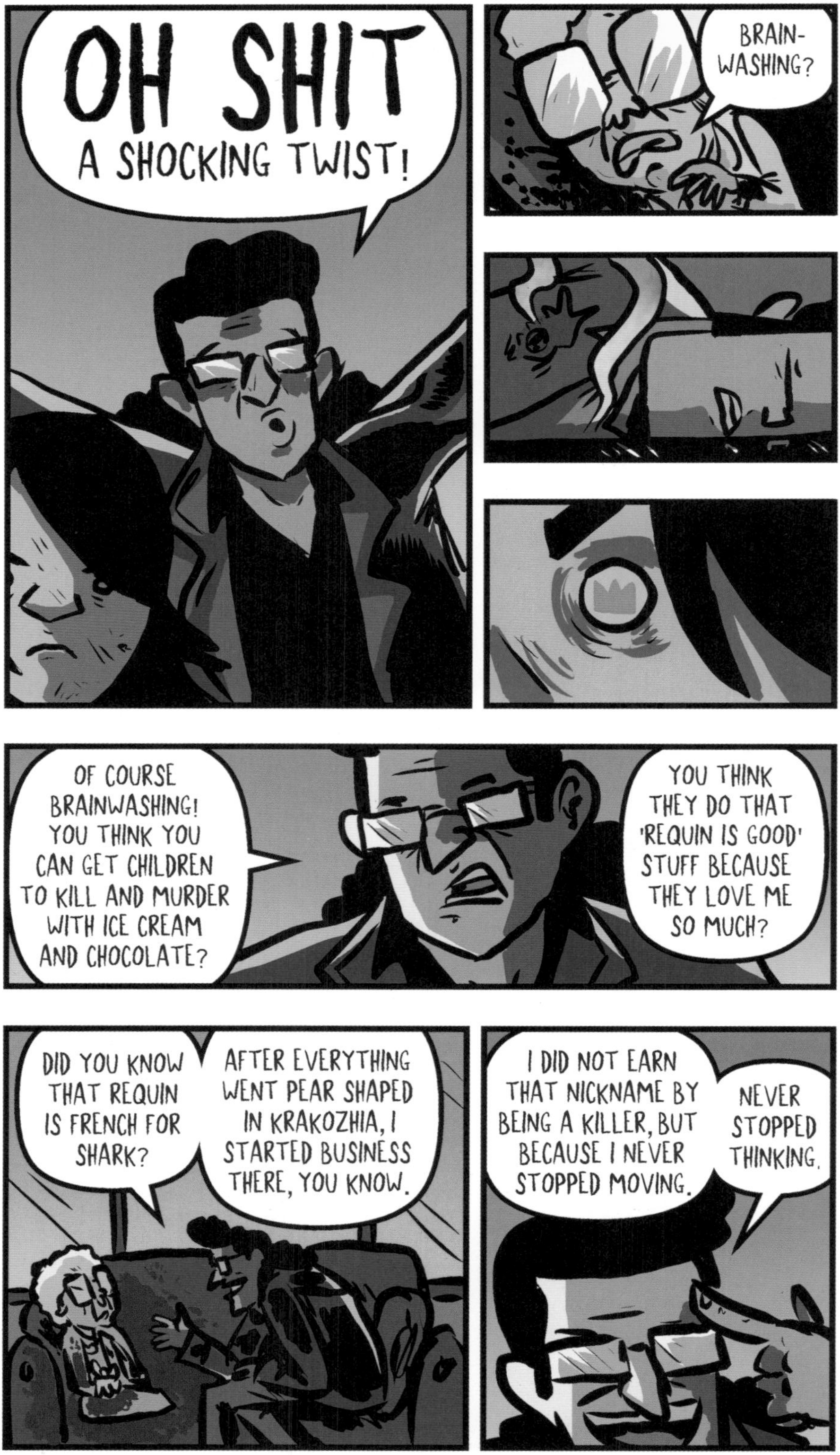
OH SHIT
A SHOCKING TWIST!
BRAIN-WASHING?
OF COURSE BRAINWASHING! YOU THINK YOU CAN GET CHILDREN TO KILL AND MURDER WITH ICE CREAM AND CHOCOLATE?
YOU THINK THEY DO THAT 'REQUIN IS GOOD' STUFF BECAUSE THEY LOVE ME SO MUCH?
DID YOU KNOW THAT REQUIN IS FRENCH FOR SHARK?
AFTER EVERYTHING WENT PEAR SHAPED IN KRAKOZHIA, I STARTED BUSINESS THERE, YOU KNOW.
I DID NOT EARN THAT NICKNAME BY BEING A KILLER, BUT BECAUSE I NEVER STOPPED MOVING.
NEVER STOPPED THINKING.

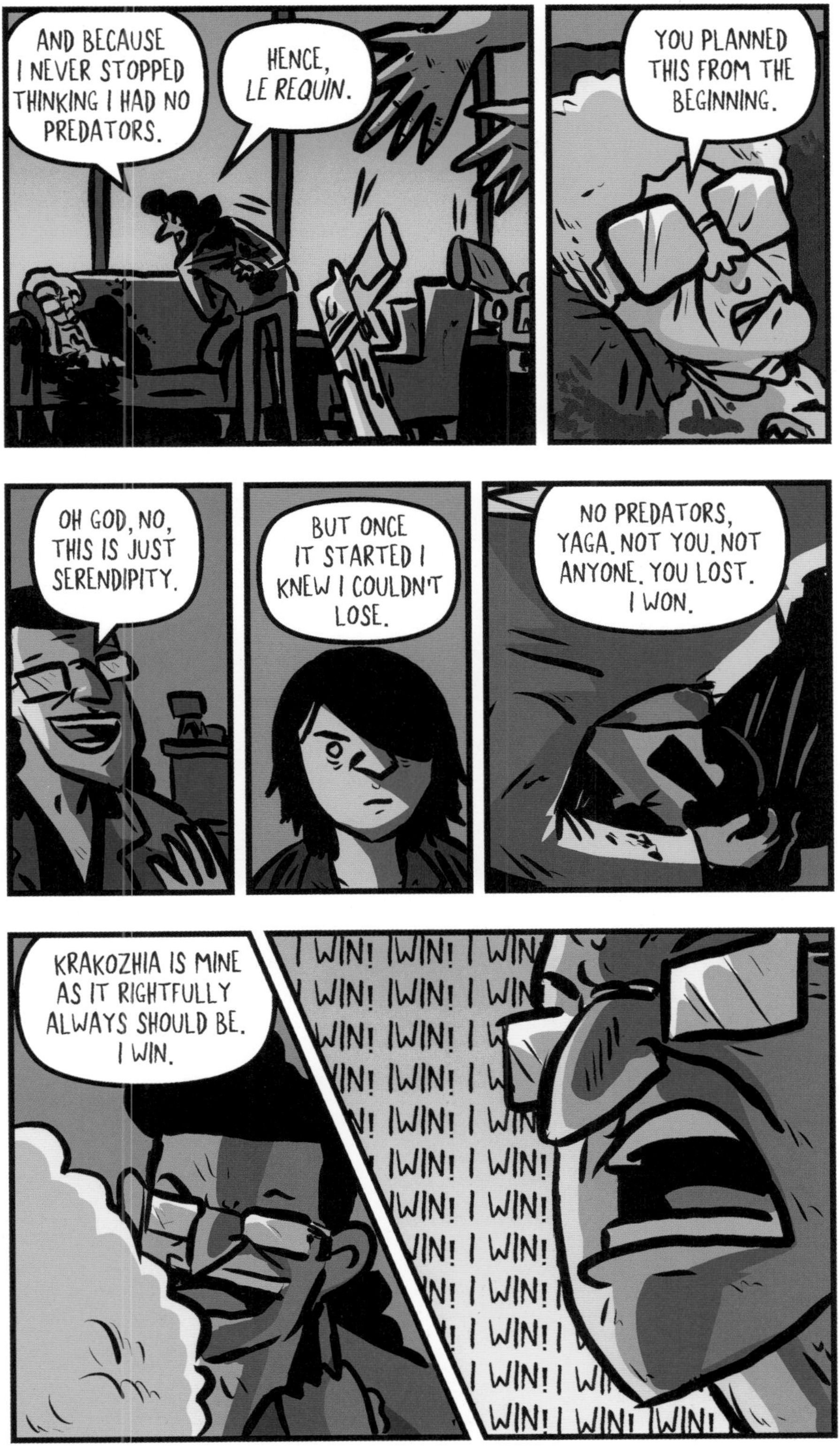
AND BECAUSE I NEVER STOPPED THINKING I HAD NO PREDATORS.
HENCE, LE REQUIN.
YOU PLANNED THIS FROM THE BEGINNING.
OH GOD, NO, THIS IS JUST SERENDIPITY.
BUT ONCE IT STARTED I KNEW I COULDN'T LOSE.
NO PREDATORS, YAGA. NOT YOU. NOT ANYONE. YOU LOST. I WON.
KRAKOZHIA IS MINE AS IT RIGHTFULLY ALWAYS SHOULD BE. I WIN.
I WIN! I WIN! I WIN! I WIN! I WIN!

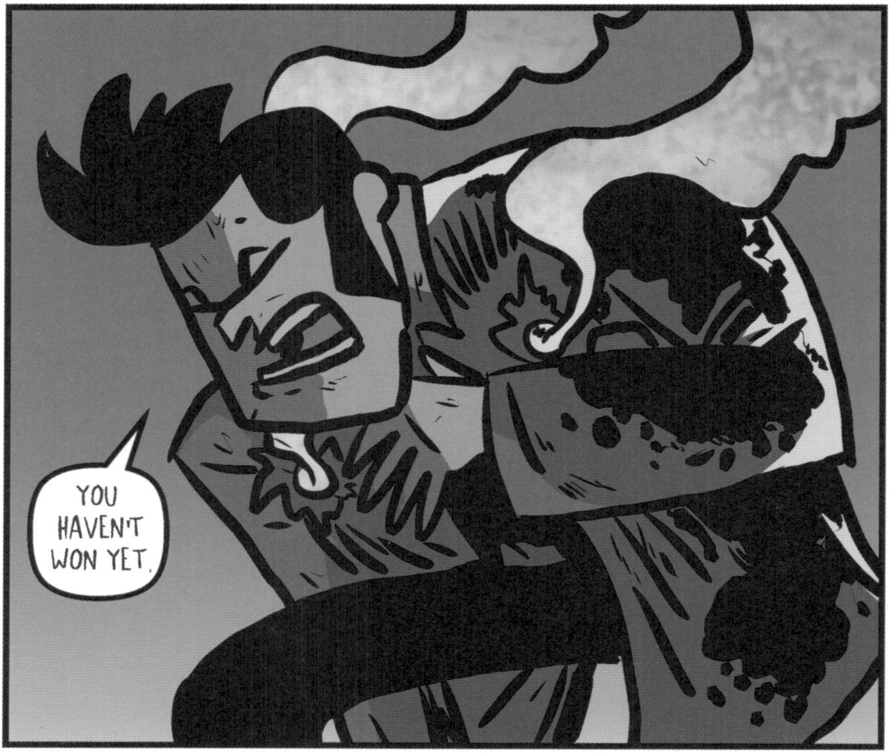
YOU HAVEN'T WON YET.

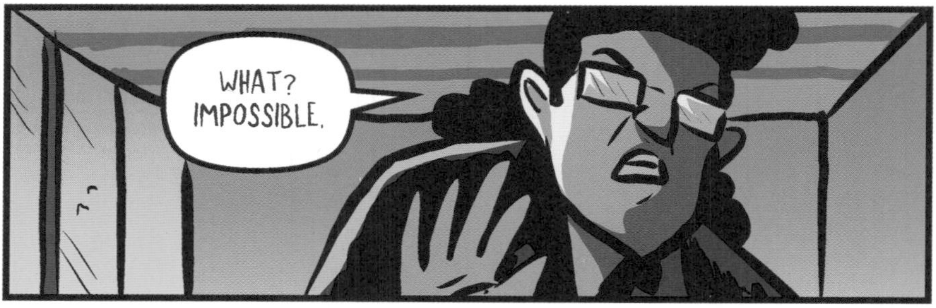
WHAT? IMPOSSIBLE.

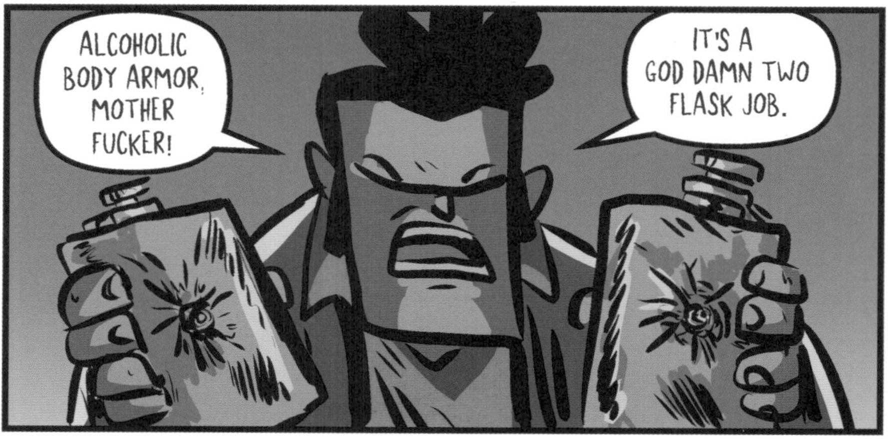
ALCOHOLIC BODY ARMOR, MOTHER FUCKER!
IT'S A GOD DAMN TWO FLASK JOB.

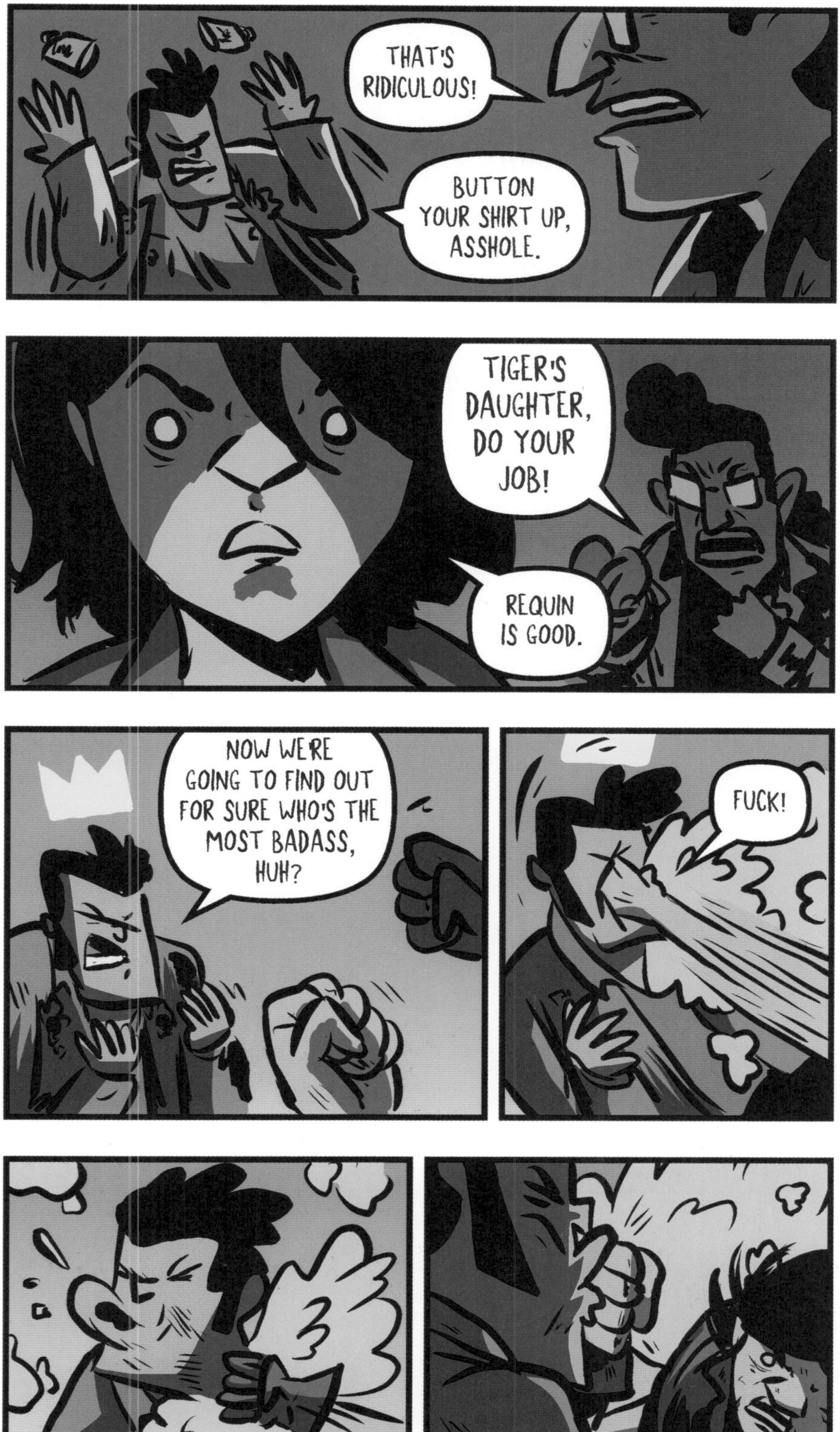
THAT'S RIDICULOUS!
BUTTON YOUR SHIRT UP, ASSHOLE.
TIGER'S DAUGHTER, DO YOUR JOB!
REQUIN IS GOOD.
NOW WE'RE GOING TO FIND OUT FOR SURE WHO'S THE MOST BADASS, HUH?
FUCK!

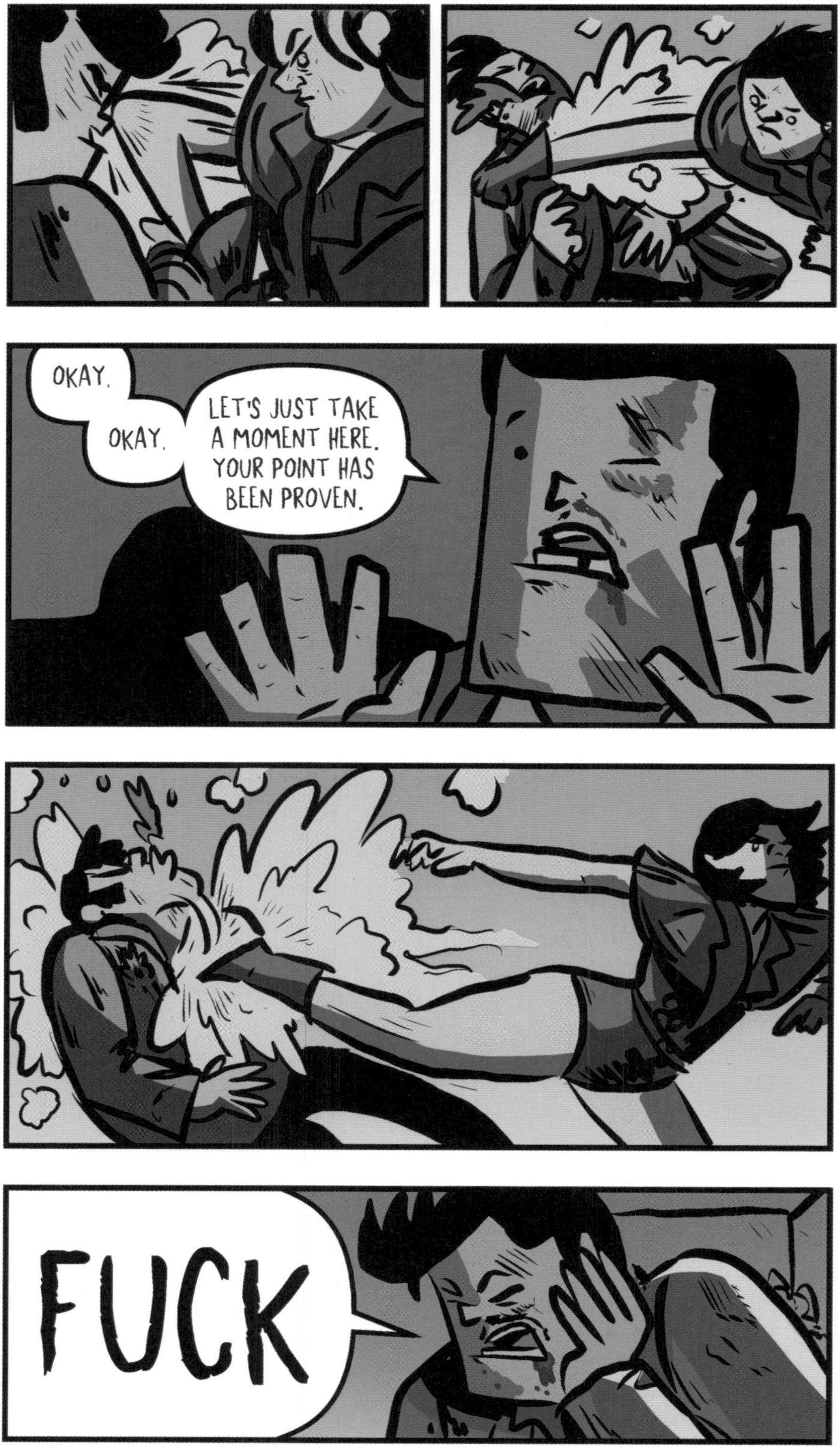
OKAY.
OKAY.
LET'S JUST TAKE A MOMENT HERE. YOUR POINT HAS BEEN PROVEN.
FUCK

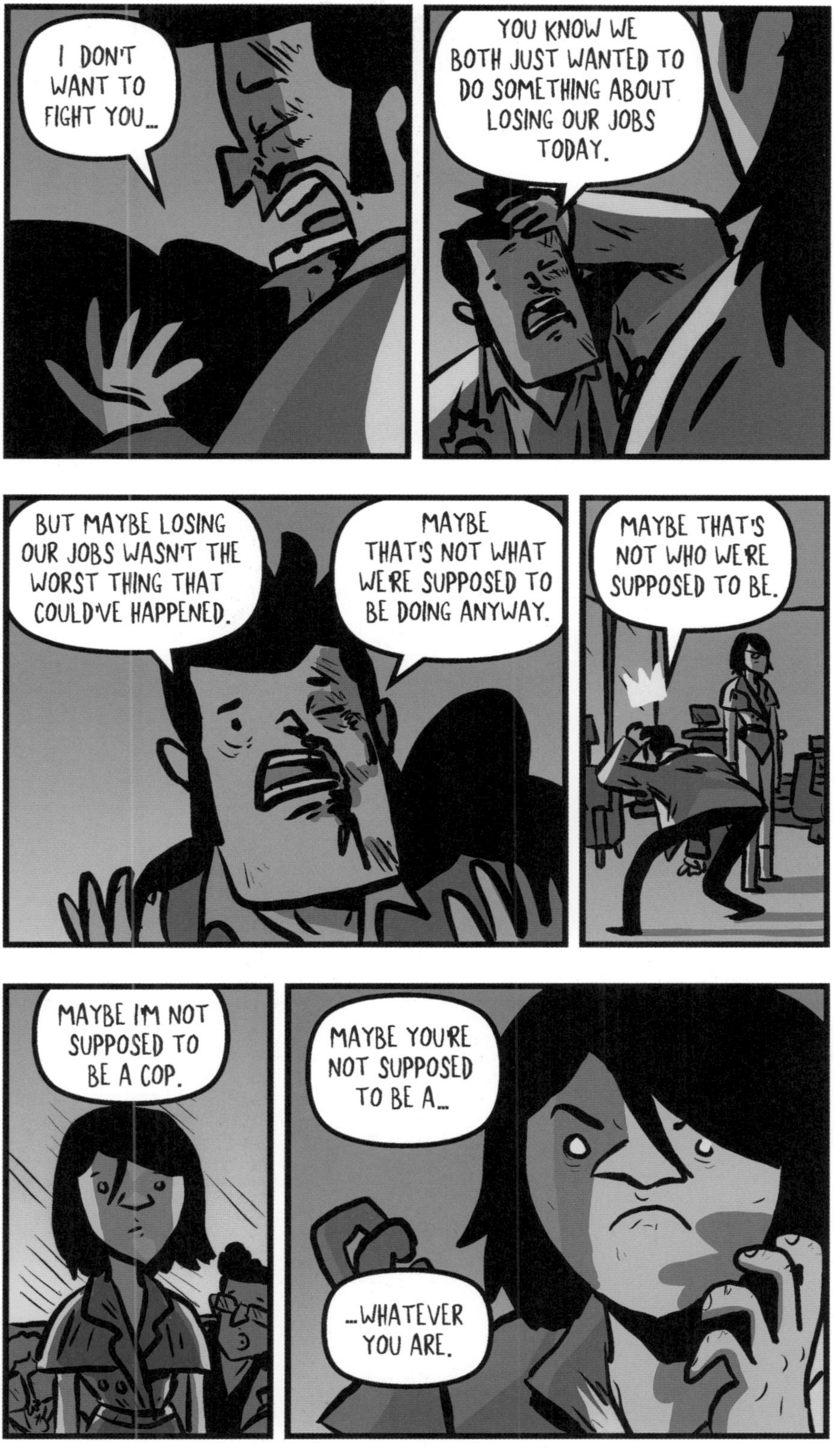
I DON'T WANT TO FIGHT YOU...
YOU KNOW WE BOTH JUST WANTED TO DO SOMETHING ABOUT LOSING OUR JOBS TODAY.
BUT MAYBE LOSING OUR JOBS WASN'T THE WORST THING THAT COULD'VE HAPPENED.
MAYBE THAT'S NOT WHAT WE'RE SUPPOSED TO BE DOING ANYWAY.
MAYBE THAT'S NOT WHO WE'RE SUPPOSED TO BE.
MAYBE I'M NOT SUPPOSED TO BE A COP.
MAYBE YOU'RE NOT SUPPOSED TO BE A...
...WHATEVER YOU ARE.

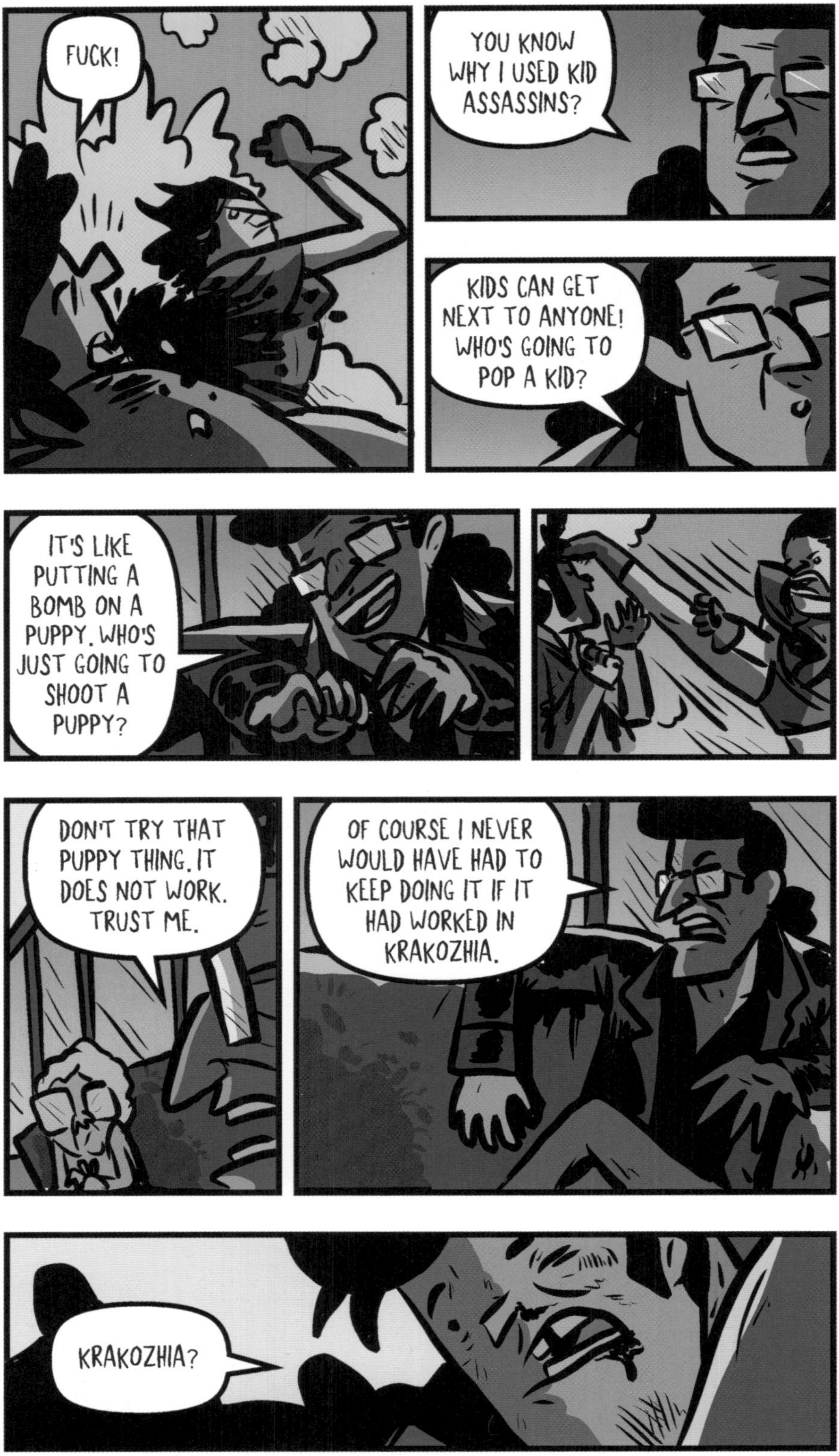
FUCK!
YOU KNOW WHY I USED KID ASSASSINS?
KIDS CAN GET NEXT TO ANYONE! WHO'S GOING TO POP A KID?
IT'S LIKE PUTTING A BOMB ON A PUPPY. WHO'S JUST GOING TO SHOOT A PUPPY?
DON'T TRY THAT PUPPY THING. IT DOES NOT WORK. TRUST ME.
OF COURSE I NEVER WOULD HAVE HAD TO KEEP DOING IT IF IT HAD WORKED IN KRAKOZHIA.
KRAKOZHIA?

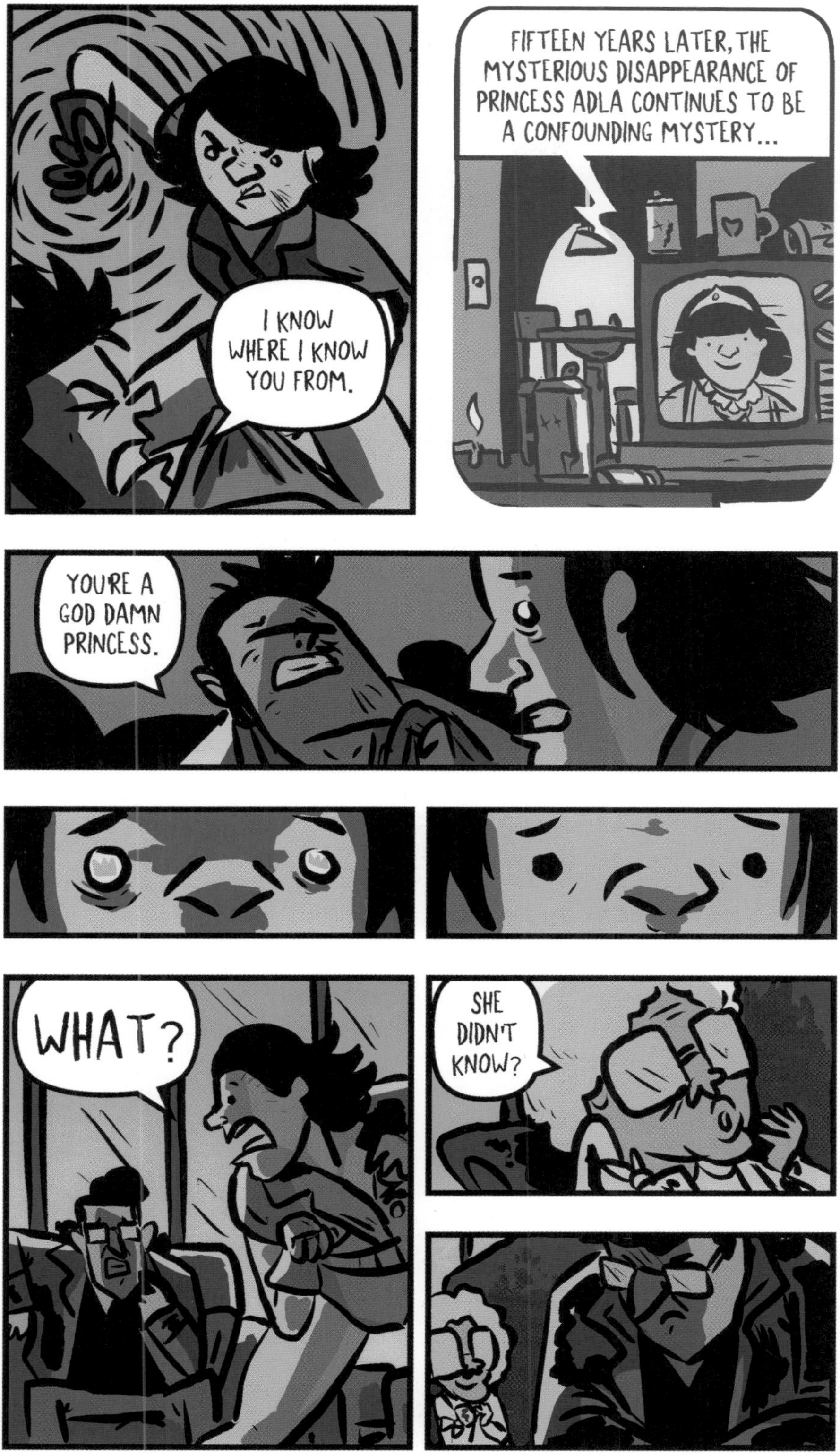
I KNOW WHERE I KNOW YOU FROM.
FIFTEEN YEARS LATER, THE MYSTERIOUS DISAPPEARANCE OF PRINCESS ADLA CONTINUES TO BE A CONFOUNDING MYSTERY...
YOU'RE A GOD DAMN PRINCESS.
WHAT?
SHE DIDN'T KNOW?

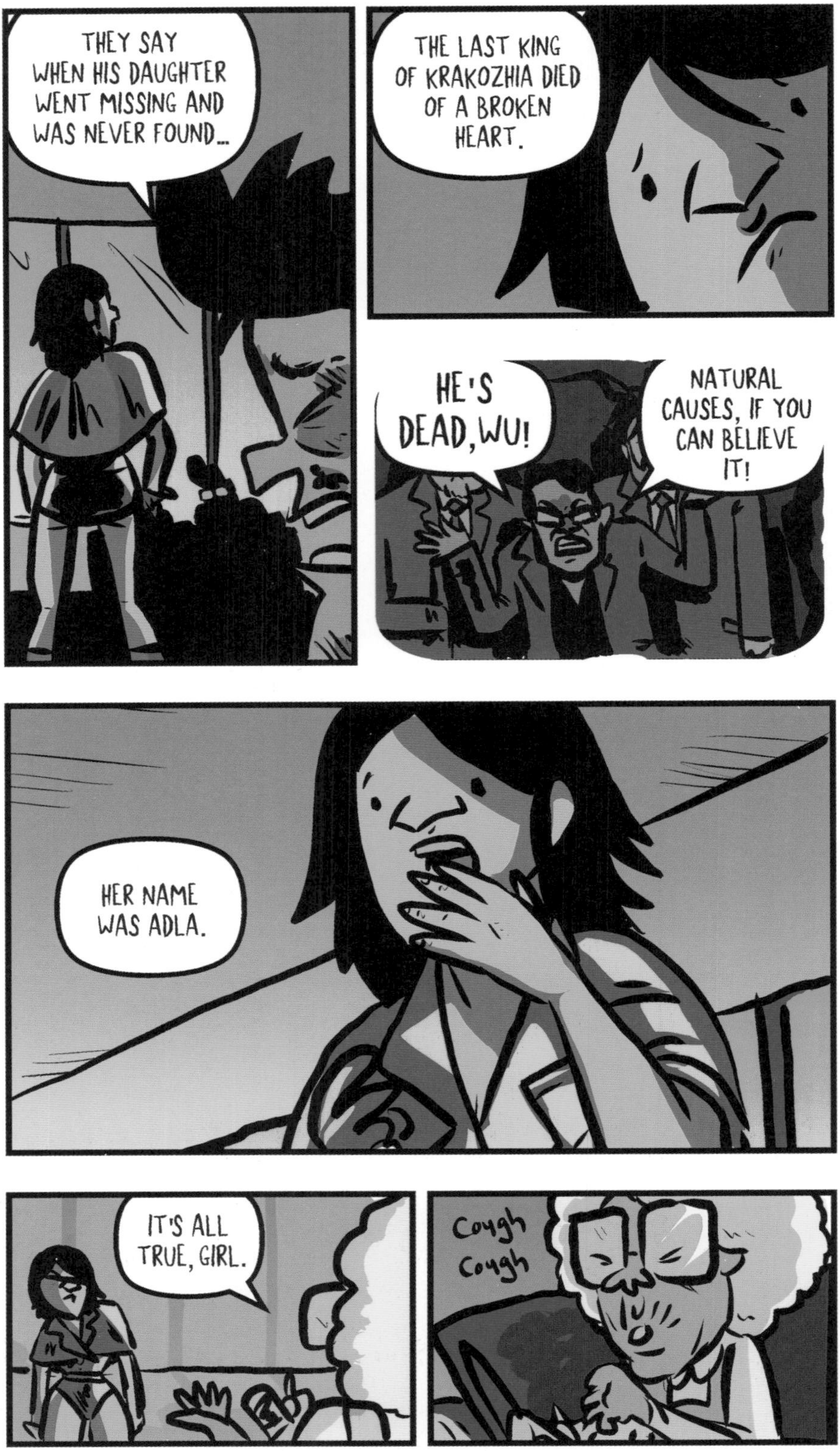
THEY SAY WHEN HIS DAUGHTER WENT MISSING AND WAS NEVER FOUND...
THE LAST KING OF KRAKOZHIA DIED OF A BROKEN HEART.
HE'S DEAD, WU!
NATURAL CAUSES, IF YOU CAN BELIEVE IT!
HER NAME WAS ADLA.
IT'S ALL TRUE, GIRL.
Cough Cough

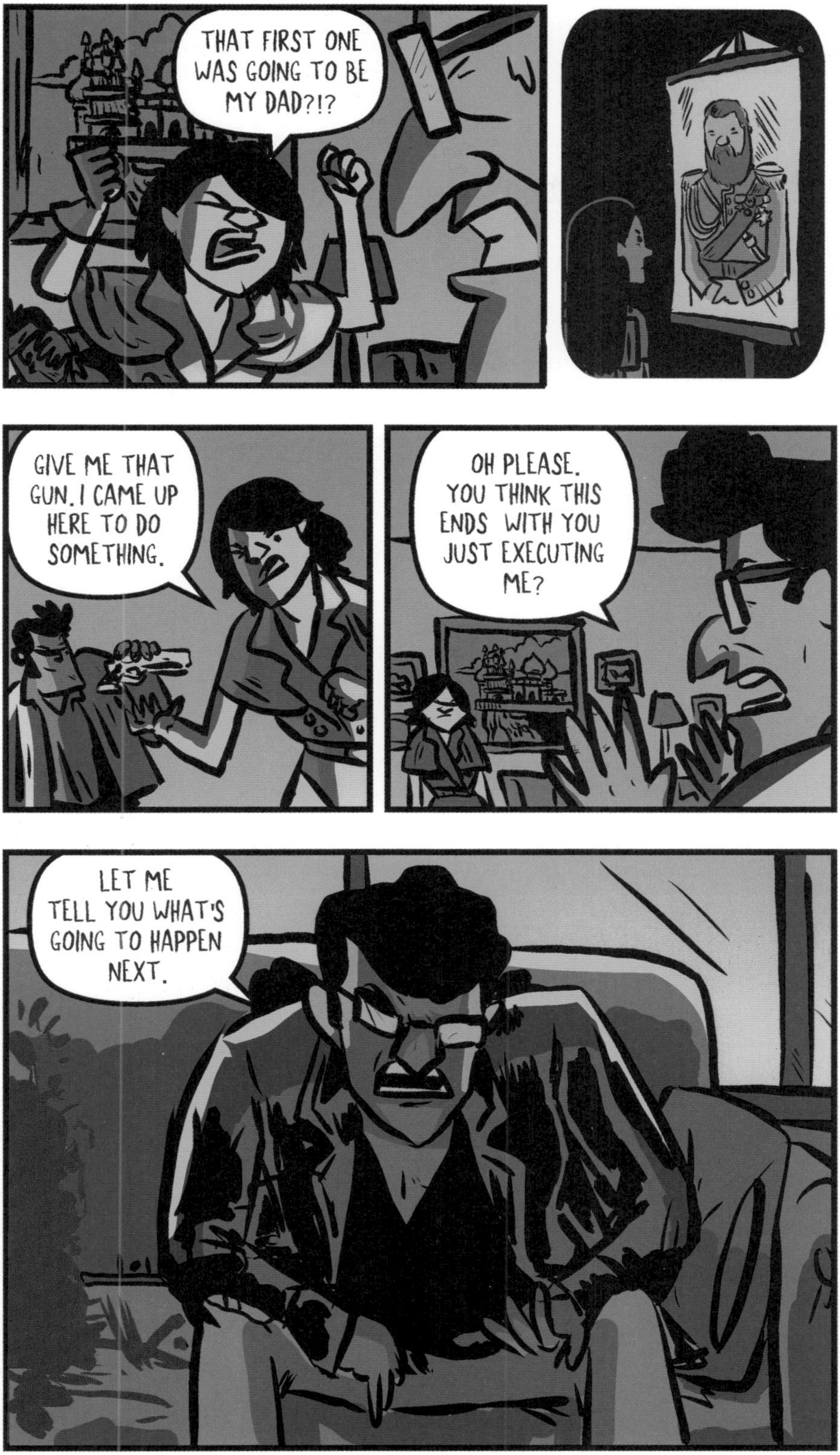
THAT FIRST ONE WAS GOING TO BE MY DAD?!?
GIVE ME THAT GUN. I CAME UP HERE TO DO SOMETHING.
OH PLEASE. YOU THINK THIS ENDS WITH YOU JUST EXECUTING ME?
LET ME TELL YOU WHAT'S GOING TO HAPPEN NEXT.

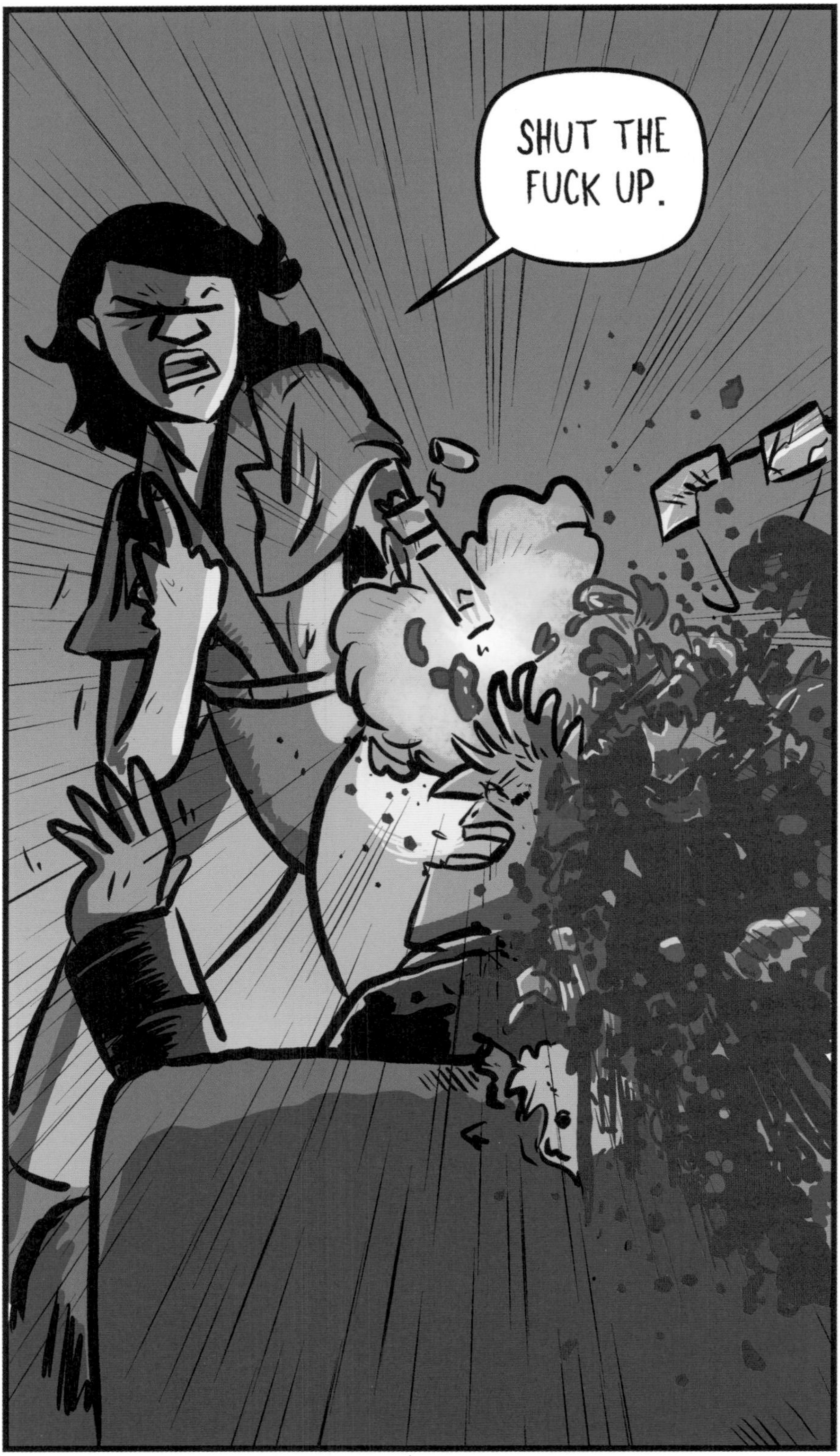
SHUT THE FUCK UP.

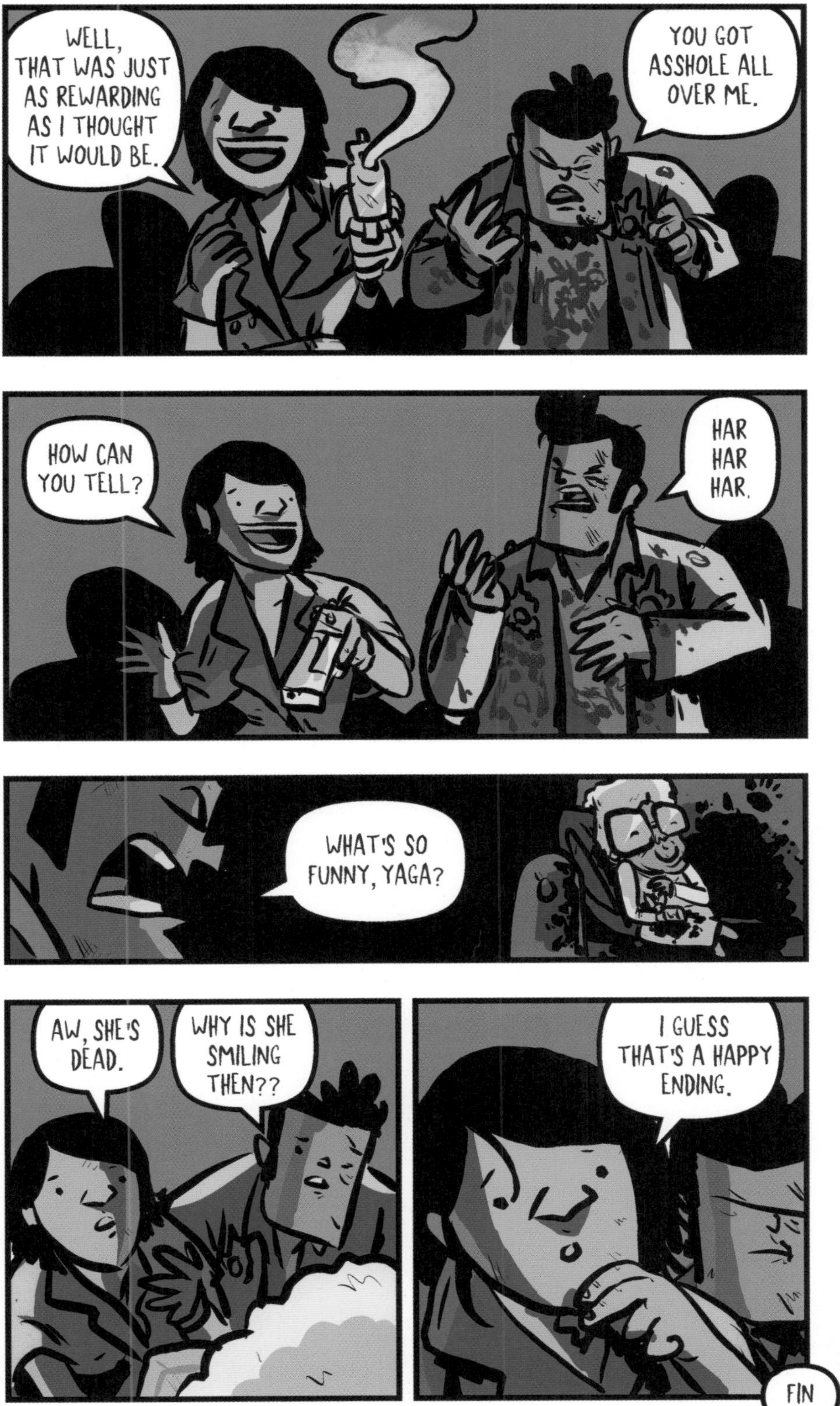
WELL, THAT WAS JUST AS REWARDING AS I THOUGHT IT WOULD BE.
YOU GOT ASSHOLE ALL OVER ME.
HOW CAN YOU TELL?
HAR HAR HAR.
WHAT'S SO FUNNY, YAGA?
AW, SHE'S DEAD.
WHY IS SHE SMILING THEN??
I GUESS THAT'S A HAPPY ENDING.
FIN

THANKS TO

ANDY HIRSCH, TIM LOCKRIDGE, ADAM P. KNAVE,
JORDAN WITT, LUKE MCCLUNG, CHRIS WALSH,
PETER WINSKY, CHRIS SIMS, JESSE FARRELL,
KIERAN SHIACH, TIM STARKS, ERICA HENDERSON,
CHRIS SCHWEIZER, DAVE ROBBINS, ERIC REID,
CAITLIN DIMOTTA, MY KICKSTARTER BACKERS
AND ALL MY PATREON SUPPORTERS.

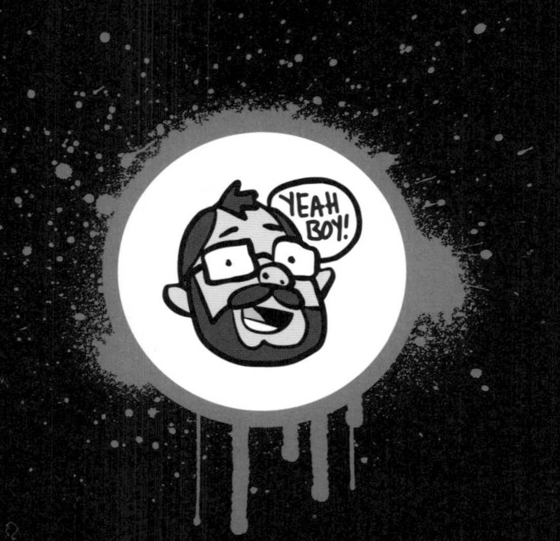
YEAH BOY!

KYLE STARKS
is an Eisner-nominated comic creator from southern Indiana. He is married to the most amazing wife and has two beautiful daughters.

He is best known as the writer and occasional artist of Oni Press's *RICK AND MORTY* and his Image books *SEXCASTLE* and *ROCK CANDY MOUNTAIN*.

His hobbies consist of reading, long walks, and running wild through the back alleys of his hometown, butt naked, with a pack of frenzied City Wolves. He became the Alpha just last year in an embarrassing but necessary ceremony. It was his proudest moment since the birth of his eldest daughter.

On Thursdays, the pack of City Wolves take a break from knocking over trashcans and antagonizing night joggers to do karaoke at a bowling alley called Spare Balls.

Thursdays are great.

DAVID 'LUIGI' ANDERSON

is a Texas-born, Atlanta-based artist who has been drawing ever since he could hold a pencil. It wasn't until he was almost out of college that he managed to put to good use all the hours spent with crayon in hand, filling page after page in his favorite coloring books when Oni Press gave him his first coloring job. The rest has been history; a great new career working with incredible talent on awesome books.

People have said he's really good at this whole coloring business, but people say a lot of things that aren't true, so you may not want to believe them just yet.

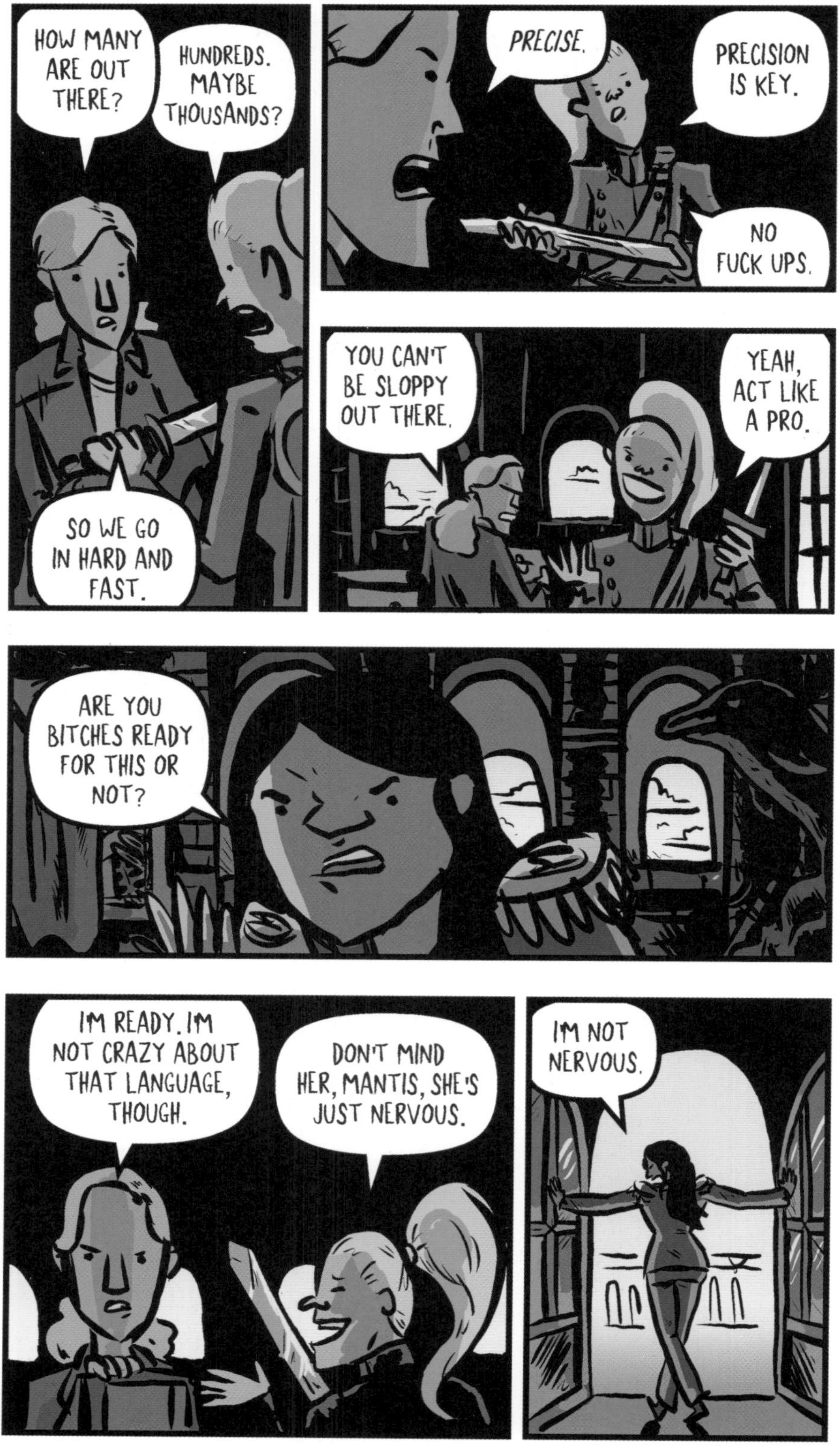
HOW MANY ARE OUT THERE?
HUNDREDS. MAYBE THOUSANDS?
SO WE GO IN HARD AND FAST.
PRECISE.
PRECISION IS KEY.
NO FUCK UPS.
YOU CAN'T BE SLOPPY OUT THERE.
YEAH, ACT LIKE A PRO.
ARE YOU BITCHES READY FOR THIS OR NOT?
I'M READY. I'M NOT CRAZY ABOUT THAT LANGUAGE, THOUGH.
DON'T MIND HER, MANTIS, SHE'S JUST NERVOUS.
I'M NOT NERVOUS.

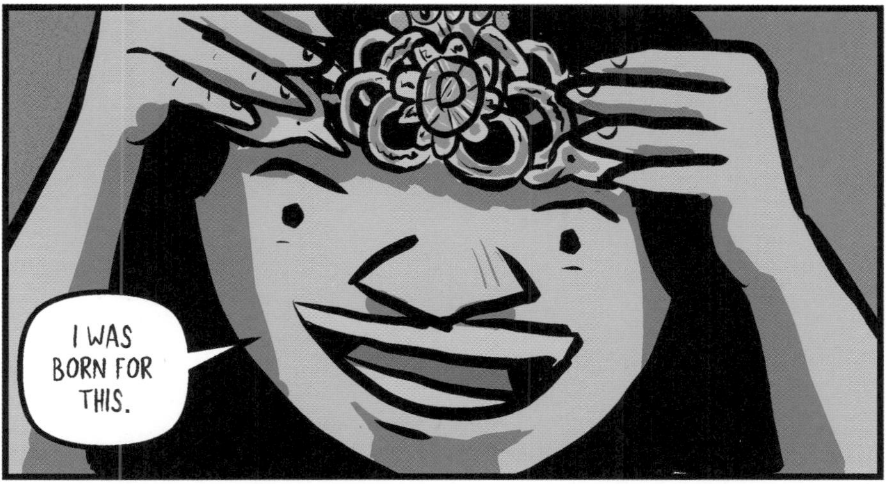
I WAS BORN FOR THIS.

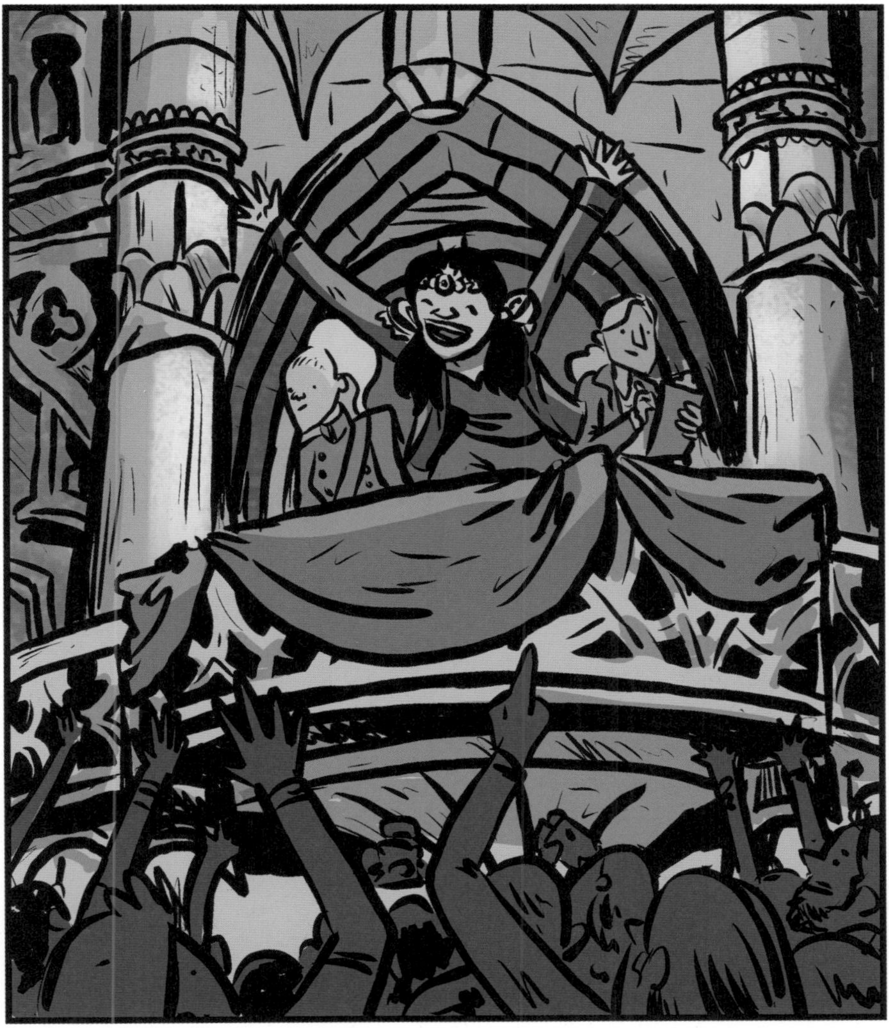

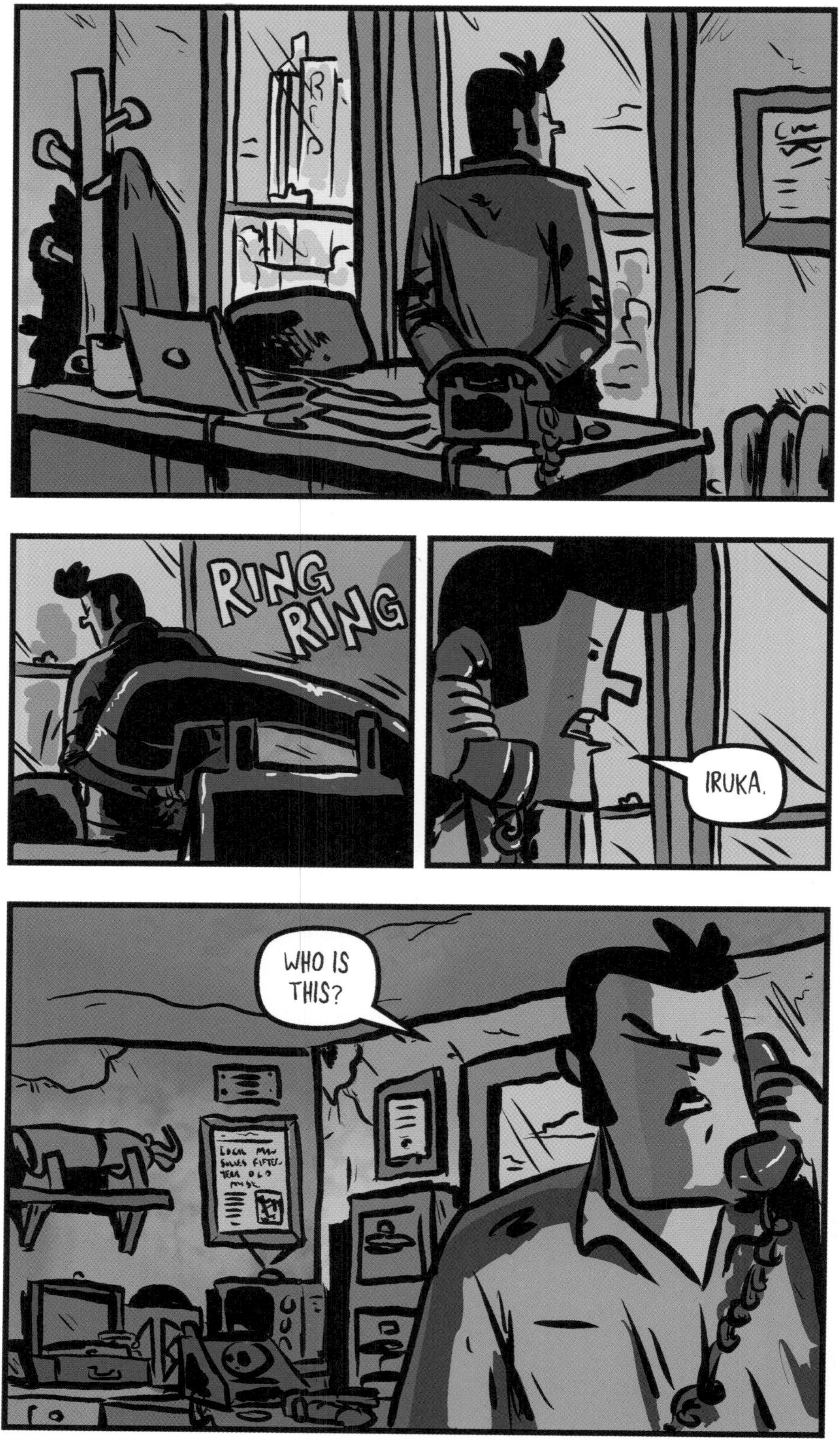
RING RING
IRUKA.
WHO IS THIS?

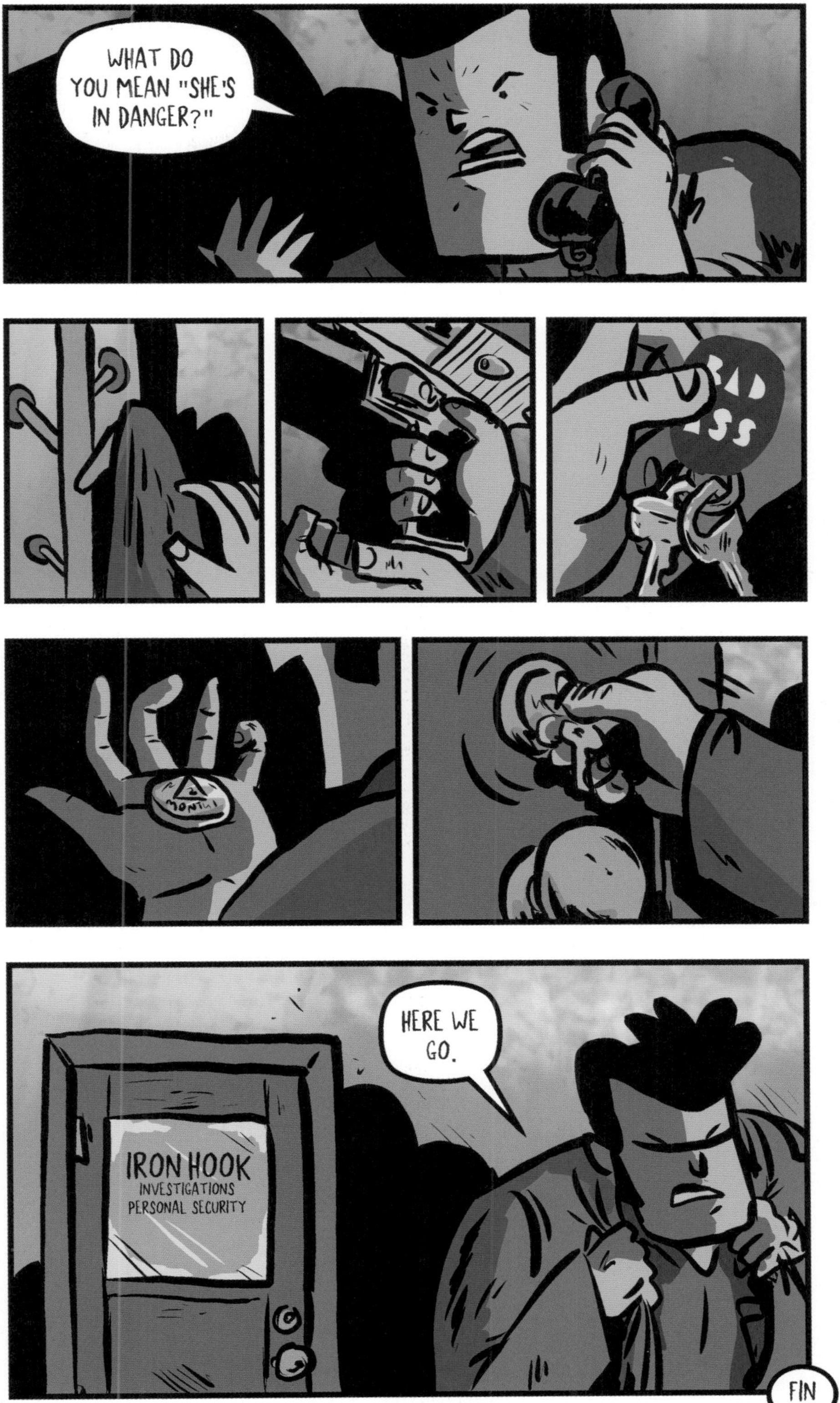
WHAT DO YOU MEAN "SHE'S IN DANGER?"
IRON HOOK
INVESTIGATIONS
PERSONAL SECURITY
HERE WE GO.
FIN

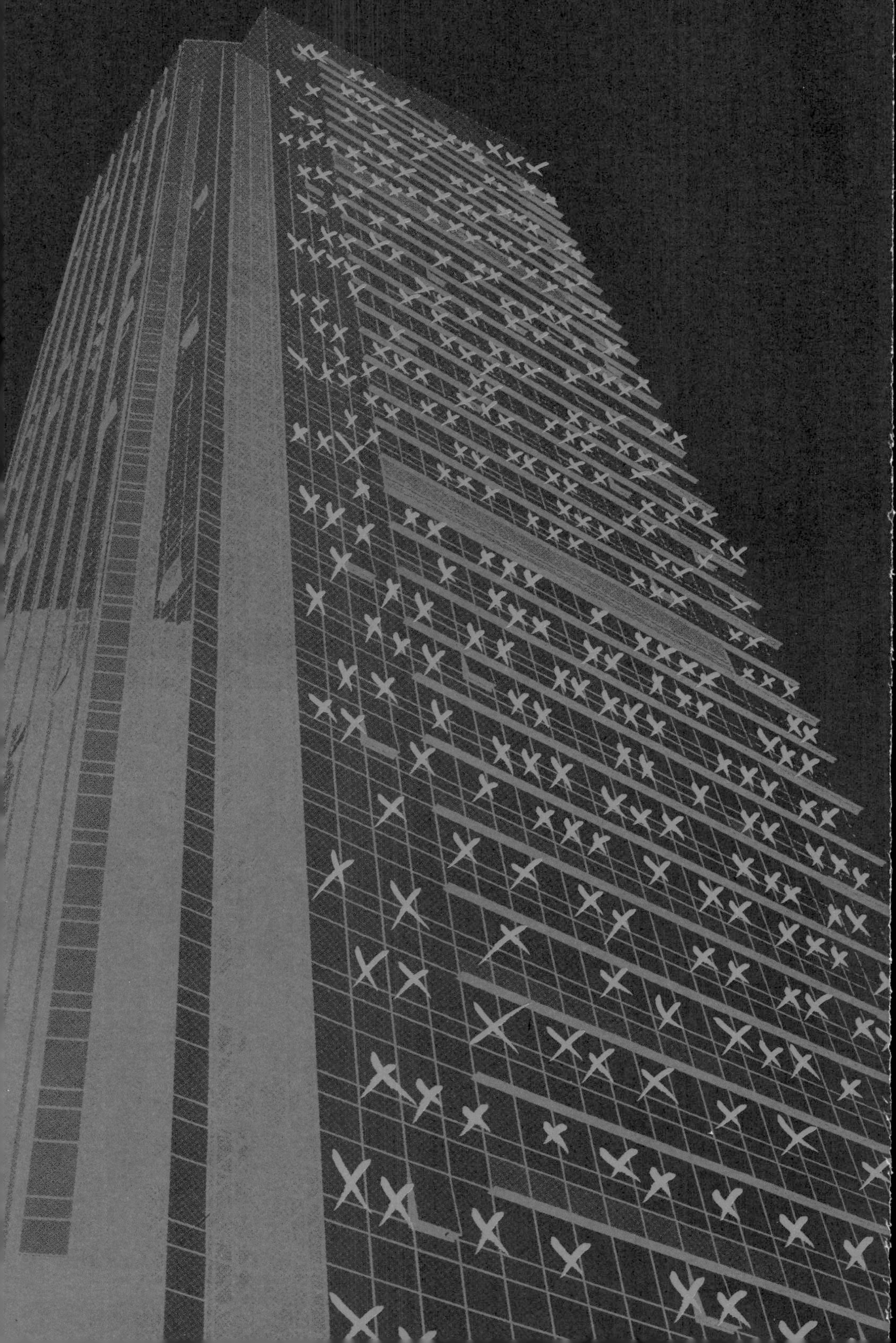